The Eyes of Malta

The Crucial Role of Aerial Reconnaissance
and ULTRA Intelligence, 1940-1943

Salvo Fagone

Helion & Company

Helion & Company Limited
Unit 8 Amherst Business Centre
Budbrooke Road
Warwick
CV34 5WE
England
Tel. 01926 499 619
Email: info@helion.co.uk
Website: www.helion.co.uk
Twitter: @helionbooks
Visit our blog at blog.helion.co.uk

Published by Helion & Company 2023
Designed and typeset by Mary Woolley (www.battlefield-design.co.uk)
Cover designed by Paul Hewitt, Battlefield Design (www.battlefield-design.co.uk)

Text © Salvo Fagone 2023
Images © as individually credited
Maps drawn © Salvo Fagone 2023

ISBN 978-1-804512-41-8

British Library Cataloguing-in-Publication Data.
A catalogue record for this book is available from the British Library.

For details of other military history titles published by Helion & Company Limited contact the
above address or visit our website: http://www.helion.co.uk.

We always welcome receiving book proposals from prospective authors.

The earth is empty.

Look down on the earth from thirty-three thousand feet, and man ceases to exist.
Man's traces are not to be read at this distance.
Our telescopic lenses serve here as microscopes. It wants this microscope – not to
photograph man, since he escapes even the telescopic lens – to perceive the signs of his
presence. Highways, canals, convoys, barges. Man fructifies the microscope slide.

I am a glacial scientist, and their war has become for me a laboratory experiment.

Flight to Arras (*Pilote de guerre*)
Antoine de Saint-Exupéry

Contents

Acknowledgements

When I started this book, I had no idea of the large amount of data I would find in archives around the world. As I went into their veritable mazes, especially in US and British archives, I was amazed. The French and British air forces first, followed a few years later by the American ones, produced and stored an enormous number of reports on Sicily and beyond. It was therefore not easy to choose what to publish in this volume, or which mission to give more importance to over others. All of this, together with the hundreds of pages of data coming from the secret Ultra intelligence service; the tens of thousands of documents from RAF, RAAF and SAAF squadrons preserved in The National Archives of London; or the kilometres of microfilms of the AFHRA at Maxwell or NARA in Washington, D.C., which contain thousands of reports from USAAF missions; meant I was spoiled for choice.

I owe the realisation of this work to the encouragement of some friends, without whom this book would not have been possible. My passion for the events of the air war over Sicily has been combined over the past few years with that of many other people around the globe. The search for some American aviators, missing in action over Sicily, took me inside another world. My life crossed paths with American writer Robert Richardson. I owe the beginning of this long adventure to him. Without his encouragement to take the idea seriously, I would certainly never have started a work of this magnitude.

A dutiful thanks also goes to my South African friend Brian Spurr for the photos of his father, a laboratory photographer of the RAF's No. 2 Photographic Reconnaissance Unit during the Second World War; and to Italian writer Alessandro Ragatzu for his precious support and his exceptional knowledge of the American and English archives.

I also thank my New Zealand friend Geoff Sheehan, son of an RAF Spitfire pilot shot down over Sicily, for providing me with some documents from the Auckland archives; British researcher Frank McMeiken for his exceptional data on Ultra; Cranfield University professor David Brown; and English writer and former Cold War airman Ken Delve, for the precious exchange of information and documents on Sicily and Operation *Husky*.

Returning down under, thank you to New Zealand military history author, the late Richard Stowers, for the night-time photos taken by his father, a crew member of one of the Vickers Wellington bombers that flew raids over Sicily; and Australian Andy Wright for his patience, for helping direct me through the vast wartime RAF and Commonwealth aircrew aeronautical bibliographies, and for the translation and correction of my manuscript from Italian to English. Also in Australia, I would like to thank RAAF Group Captain David Fredericks, Director History and Heritage Branch, and Ms Imogen Telfer, Air Force Imagery Archive Curator, for their valuable contribution and service. To the Italian Archivio Centrale dello Stato (ACS) for having granted me the publication of the photographic collection of the Second World

War. I wish to thank you my friend Keith Bastard, son of Frank, Adrian Warburton's right-hand man, for his contribution. My thanks also go to Canadian Chris Philpotts, nephew of veteran pilot Laurie Philpotts, Adrian Warburton's teammate, for the photos of his grandfather and his logbook. Thanks also go to Angelo Plumari for the realisation of the graphics in this volume, Alessandro Emanuele, Andrea Di Bernardo, Antonio Bonanno, Bruno Fochesato, Claudio Gioia, Dr. Giulio Grilletta, Daniele Gatti, Darren Prior, Dick Boulais, Pier Ferrari, Robert Penoyer, Tammy Horton, Tascha Morrison, Thanos Antonelos, Tinus Le Roux and Umberto Lugan. To those I have not mentioned out of pure forgetfulness, and who in some way contributed to the realisation of my first essay, even though simple clarifications or information, thank you.

My greatest thanks goes to my family, my wife Annalisa and our children Antonio, Eleonora and Alberto, to whom I dedicate this long work. It is my duty to apologise to them for the time I took from them in these long years spent consulting documents and writing this text. To them, who supported me even in the most difficult moments, when I thought I would never be able to complete this complicated and unprecedented study, I owe more than I can ever repay.

Salvo Fagone
Catania, Sicily, 2022

1

Development of Photo-Reconnaissance

In the 1920s, aerial photography, both civilian and military, mainly dealt with the creation of maps, especially in those areas of the world where cartography had so far been very lacking; for example, the Philippines, where the Americans performed topographical surveys, the Middle East and India, where the British were most active, and Africa, where the French had several colonies. Proponents of civil aerial photography, then, were very enthusiastic about the production and large-scale diffusion of the images taken from above major cities. Those images that achieved the greatest success were the angled photos because they were more suggestive and more easily interpretable.

The aircraft engaged in early aerial imagery carried bulky, heavy equipment. Ongoing improvements led to lighter and more efficient tools, which led to the development and realisation of photographic equipment, installed both vertically and obliquely in the aircraft (from which the Trimetrogon[1] system of WWII would evolve), free from vibrations and distortions and equipped with wide-angle lenses, and multiple lens machines capable of covering larger areas of terrain. Photographic film was also improving; an increasingly fine grain made it possible to obtain more and more detailed images, even if taken at high altitudes. In England, the greatest impulse to aerial reconnaissance was provided by Wing Commander Sidney Cotton, an Australian by birth, who is considered a pioneer of aerial photography. Cotton had been a pilot in the Royal Naval Air Service during WWI and, on behalf of British Intelligence, made some risky flights to Germany, the Middle East and Italy in 1939.

Cotton's experiences culminated in the modification of a civilian aircraft, a Lockheed 12A, in which he hid photographic equipment. He mounted three small series cameras in a vertical/oblique configuration, positioning the lenses behind sliding panels to make them invisible on the ground. The Lockheed was painted light green, which made it perfectly camouflaged even at low altitudes.[2] Warm air was piped throughout the photographic system to prevent it from freezing. Fitted with extra fuel tanks, the Lockheed had an operating range of approximately

---

1   Trimetrogon is an aerial photographic detection method that involves the use of three cameras in a single set. One of the cameras is pointed directly downwards and the other two are oriented from both sides at an angle of 30 degrees.

2   In the same period, Cotton was recruited to head up the RAF's fledgling No. 1 Photographic Development Unit (PDU) at Heston Aerodrome.

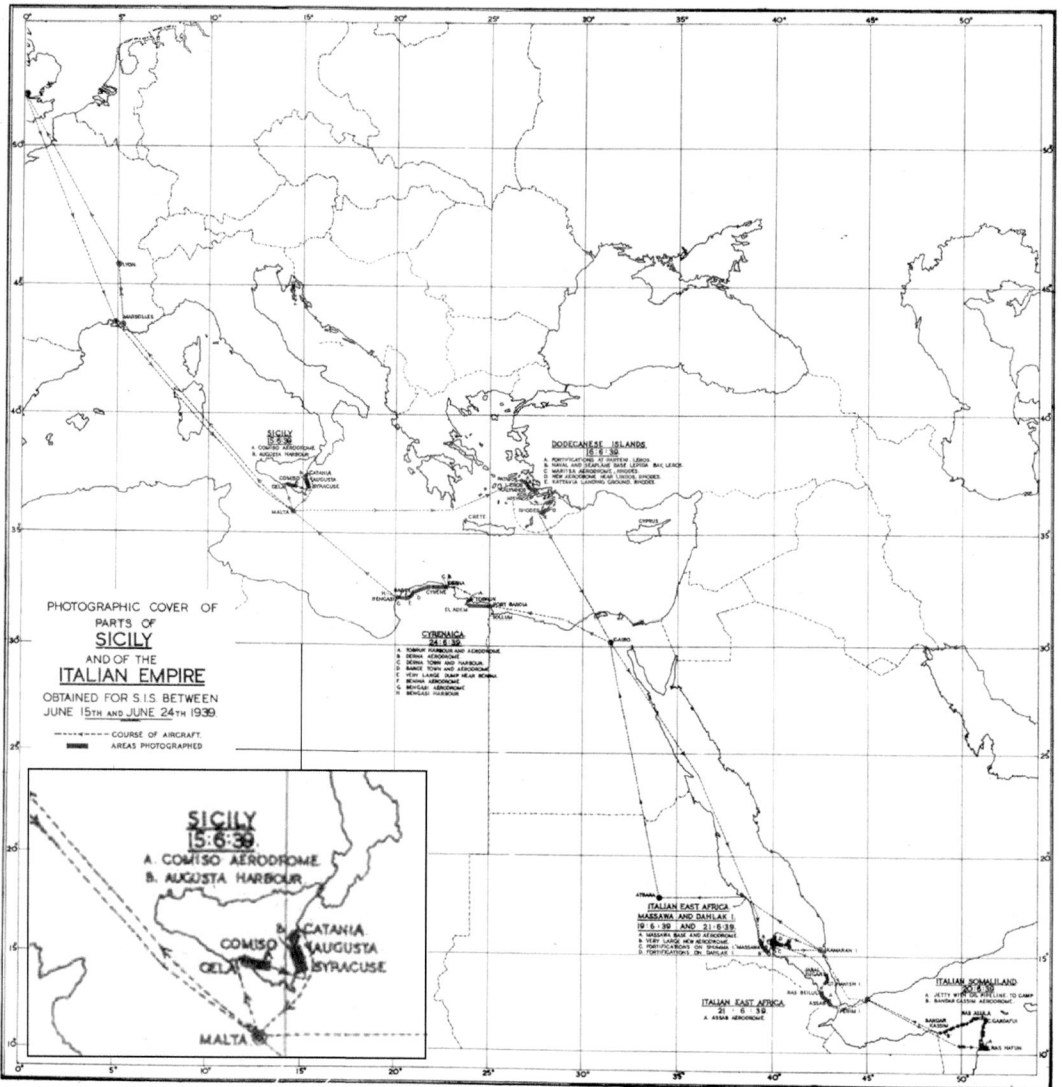

Preliminary survey of the Italian Empire carried out by Wing Commander Sidney Cotton. (MEIU)

1,600 miles and, above 20,000 feet, Cotton could photograph an 11.5-mile-wide swath dozens of miles long. This gave a photo scale of roughly 1:48,000 on the 5-inch-wide film.

On 14 June 1939, Cotton and Bob Niven (his Canadian co-pilot) flew from Heston airport, in England, to Malta, where they met Flying Officer Maurice V. 'Shorty' Longbottom, an aviator with much experience in the field of reconnaissance. During the following days, the three flew to Sicily and took excellent photos of Comiso, Augusta, Catania and Syracuse. Subsequently, also in June, Cotton and Niven photographed the islands of Kos and Leros, in the Dodecanese, and the city of Cairo.

In the meantime, the *Luftwaffe* had certainly not been idle. Towards the second half of 1937, Theodore Rowehl, an aerial reconnaissance veteran, carried out some secret missions with a Heinkel He 111 C-03 (a pre-production example of the famous He 111 bomber) together with a unit called *Kommando Rowehl*. The reconnaissance, cleverly concealed under the guise of flights for the transport of civilians, was carried out over Great Britain, France and the Soviet Union.[3] Rowehl's organisation was able to have free access to all of Europe. The air routes between 1938 and 1939 covered England, the English Channel and the North Sea, the Baltic coast to Leningrad and even the Black Sea. The Heinkel carried two cameras, placed vertically, and they provided exceptionally detailed photos. The problems for the *Luftwaffe* came with the outbreak of war, however, as the cameras were very large and heavy, and the aircraft therefore had to fly at relatively low altitudes. This left them particularly vulnerable to being intercepted and shot down and, in fact, resulted in significant losses, especially during the early stages of the conflict. The problems were eventually solved by using lighter cameras and aircraft such as the Messerschmitt Bf 109, Junkers Ju 88 and the Messerschmitt Me 110, 210 and 410, all capable of reaching substantially higher altitudes.

---

3   Chris Goss, *Heinkel He 111: The Early Years – Fall of France, Battle of Britain and the Blitz* (Barnsley: Frontline Books, 2016), p.3.

Distant photography of Italian territories between 1935–1939[4]					
Date	Squadron	A/C	Crew	Areas photographed	Remarks
18.6.36				East coast of Sicily: Catania to Cape Passero	Photographs taken at the end of the Abyssinian crisis of 1935/6 and forwarded to A.M. by H.Q.Med in September 1937 for comparison with those of July and Augusta 1937
22.6.36				South coast of Sicily: Licata to Cape Scaramia	
25.5.37	202 F.B.	Scapa K4196	P/O Farrar and Sgt Otter with W/C Grenfell (H.Q. Med.)	Pantelleria	A.M. request. To check intelligence reports of aerodrome construction. Poor photography and negative results.
	202 F.B.	Scapa K7304	F/L Bower and F/L Atkinson with F/L P. Broad (H.Q. Med)		
15.7.37	202 F.B.	Scapa K4195	F/O Crosbie and Mason	Pantelleria	To check sortie of 25.7.37. Excellent photo confirmed airfield construction.
9.8.37	202 F.B.	Scapa K7304	F/L Bower and P/O Burges	Sicily: Augusta and Syracuse	Request of Naval C.-in-C. Med. To cover any concentrations of Naval shipping prior to maneuvers in Sicily
16.11.37	202 F.B.	Scapa K6932	F/L Bower and P/O Burges with A.O.C. Med. A/Cdre P.C. Maltby	Pantelleria	Taken on outward and return flights
7.4.38	202 F.B.		Pantelleria		To check progress.
21.6.38	202 F.B.		Pantelleria, Lampedusa and Linosa		To check progress.
9.12.38	202 F.B.		F/O Harger, MacCallum and Logbottom	Pantelleria and coast of SW. Sicily from Marsala to Terranova	

4   Air Historical Branch (AHB) RAF, Narrative, Photographic Reconnaissance Vol. 1, Appendix III.

Types of photographs

Vertical and Oblique Photos

Between the late 1930s and early 1941, American War Department scholars provided an overview of the basics of aerial photography, including terminology and photographic products, all collected in the comprehensive Air Corps Field Manual FM 1-35. According to these studies, photographs can be divided into three basic types: vertical, oblique and composite. The vertical photos maintain an almost horizontal focal plane with respect to the surface of the earth, as they look straight down on the target, and thus manage to provide a wealth of details of otherwise inaccessible areas, as well as a uniform scale within the same frame, with minimal distortion limited to the edges. However, compared to maps or oblique photos, it becomes difficult to distinguish the depth of the objects photographed. Oblique photos are created using an intentionally inclined focal plane. While the size of the physical photographic print remains the same as the vertical one, usually 9 x 9 inches, the area covered by the oblique image is typically trapezoidal. It is possible to classify oblique photos into two different types: low oblique, which does not include the horizon in the photo, and high oblique. For both high and low, the technique still provides a different perspective, as terrain reliefs are better highlighted than a vertical photo, even if the image does not offer a uniform scale. This type of photo is usually used to investigate details that would have been impossible to observe in vertical photos.

Composite Photos

Composites, as the name suggests, combine a number of images for analysis. Stereo images are generated by capturing two photos in the same place, with a 60 percent overlap between the two images for viewing through a stereoscope. Using this method, interpreters manage to see details that are difficult to see in a standard vertical photo. The effect is three-dimensional and allows interpreters to measure the height of the object and better identify any camouflage. Another fundamental type of imagery is that of night photography, which allows the identification of enemies in the dark thanks to the use of special devices called flash bombs, which, exploding in mid-air, produce an intense beam of light over the target. Strip photos, or photographic strips, derive from a series of images of the same scale superimposed vertically or obliquely and arranged side by side. The pilots achieve this by taking a sequence of photos along the flight path of the aircraft. Mosaics are obtained simply by combining two or more overlapping strips of multiple flightpaths. By combining strips and mosaics, using glue, tape or paper clips, composite photos can be obtained covering hundreds of square miles.

Mosaics proved to be valuable resources when borders, coasts, or other very large areas required examination. The production of mosaics and strips, however, was a complex process as it was necessary for all photos to be in scale and it was also essential to reduce the effects of inclination between images taken at different angles, match the variations in black and white tones, and eliminate any distortions. Once the photographic staff had addressed these issues, they could build the mosaic.

Photographic intelligence and its interpretation steps

Photographic intelligence is a military study derived from the analysis of photos, usually of the same object or target taken at different times, however, so any significant changes can be observed. This investigation is carried out by a group of photographic interpreters – highly qualified specialists – who in turn pass the information to the parties that have requested the analysis. Depending on the tactical urgency of the intelligence produced, the information thus acquired can be disclosed verbally or through written reports. Prints, target charts or special maps can also accompany these reports. Below is a brief description of the various types of Air Force reports.

First phase reports

These can be communicated verbally, by radio or by telegraph. They come from a quick analysis of the photographs. Speed is of the essence. First phase reports often have to answer questions such as: What is the enemy battle order of a certain group at some airfields? Are there cargo ships about to leave a certain port? Is there an unusual concentration of wagons or locomotives in a certain railway yard? Is there an exceptional movement along a certain stretch of road or railway?

Second phase reports

These are more detailed and deal with the perspectives of the target that do not require a meticulous study. Often, they concern the conditions of a railway yard, the presence and alternation of ships in ports, or the arrival of some ships from other ports, or analyse the details of an airfield, such as the quantity and type of aircraft present and the areas in which they are parked. Or, again, they examine the maintenance of bridges and railway lines and repair or consolidation works compared to the previous aerial coverage.

Third phase reports

These go into detail, probing every objective data. They thoroughly study all military and industrial installations, often pointing out the nerve centres of enemy industry or transportation. From these reports it is established which bomb load is necessary to break down a certain target and make it unusable and, in the case of bridges or road links, the time required and the material engineers will have to use in reconstruction. In the event of a planned landing operation, all of the frames of the beaches are studied for months by experts to identify the strengths and weaknesses, the minefields both on land and in the water, and any change in coastal defences.

Fourth phase reports

Also known as BDA (Bomb Damage Assessment). This consists of photographing and interpreting the objectives immediately after a bombing attack. A first, second or third phase report can be requested in advance. It is different from the other work of the photographic units because it has the highest priority both in flight and in processing. It must be delivered immediately to the Air Force Bombardment Wing, or equivalent, so the decision can be made as to whether the mission needs to be repeated or not. Usually, the objective is photographed between half an hour and three quarters of an hour after the raid to allow smoke and dust to dissipate. This time element, however, depends entirely on the nature of the bombed target and, of course, weather conditions.

2

10 June 1940
The Beginning of Hostilities

For Italy, the war began on 10 June 1940, but, from the beginning of the month, in anticipation of combat operations, the *Regia Aeronautica* relocated the *Seconda Squadra Aerea*, which had at least 140 Savoia-Marchetti SM.79 Sparviero (Sparrowhawk) bombers on strength, to Sicily, dispersed between the airfields at Catania Fontanarossa, Comiso, Gela Ponte Olivo, Sciacca and Castelvetrano. Forty Fiat CR.42 Falco (Falcon) biplanes and 26 of the new Macchi MC.200 Saetta (Lightning) fighters were sent to Catania Fontanarossa, Palermo Boccadifalco and Trapani. To these were added approximately 50 CANT Z.501 Gabbiano (Gull) and CANT Z.506 Airone (Heron) seaplanes, for maritime reconnaissance and rescue, at the seaports of Augusta, Siracusa and Marsala. On 8 June, two pairs of Z.501s took off from Augusta to carry out a preventative reconnaissance mission over Malta, Tripoli and Lampedusa. At the same time, also from Augusta, two *Regia Marina* cruisers left their moorings for the open sea. However, a counterorder, the first of many, as described by Tullio Marcon in his work *Augusta 1940-1943 Cronache della piazzaforte (Chronicles of the Stronghold),[1]* called them back to port. The cruisers *Alberico da Barbiano* and *Luigi Cadorna*, escorted by the destroyers *Lanciere* and *Corazziere*, sailed the following day to carry out a mine-laying mission between the islands of Lampedusa and Kerkennah with the torpedo boats *Polluce* and *Calipso*.

At the beginning of the conflict, the Italian battle fleet of the *Regia Marina* comprised five battleships, of which at least three were modern, and a large number of submarines, but, unlike the Mediterranean Fleet of Britain's Royal Navy, it had no aircraft carriers, a significant factor that played a decisive role in the outcome of the naval war in the Mediterranean. Another decisive element during the entire Second World War was the decryption of the German secret code (encrypted, in turn, by the electro-mechanical 'Enigma' machine), initially thanks to the work of some Polish mathematicians well before the outbreak of the war. This Ultra Secret intelligence (or just 'Ultra') allowed British intelligence organisations the possibility of anticipating a good part of Axis operations in Sicily.

---

1   Cfr. Tullio Marcon, *Augusta 1940-1943 Cronache della piazzaforte* [Chronicles of the Stronghold] (Augusta: Mendola, 1976).

Trapani Milo airfield. Some Fiat CR.42s and Macchi MC.200s near the hangar in 1940. On the right can be seen the tail of a Reggiane Re.2000. (Alessandro Ragatzu)

Dawn of Italian air reconnaissance

On 11 June 1940, the day after Italy's declaration of war on Great Britain and France, at first light of the day, 15 SM.79 bombers were already warming their powerful 750hp Alfa Romeo 126 engines. At 4:50 a.m., they took off from Comiso, under the orders of Colonnello Arnaldo Lubelli, to bomb the military arsenal at Cospicua (Burmola), one of the Three Cities within the Grand Harbour of Malta. Before leaving the coast of Sicily, the bombers passed other SM.79s from Catania Fontanarossa, escorted by nine Macchi MC.200s of the *6° Gruppo CT* (*Caccia Terrestre* – land-based fighters), the latter landing at Comiso for refuelling. The attack was carried out from a height of 17,000 feet; the prompt reaction of the anti-aircraft defences was intense, especially in the final stages of the approach. The presence of clouds at 10,000 feet did not permit any photographic survey.

The following day, at 5:20 a.m., an SM.79 took off from Comiso with photographic equipment on board. Tenenti Nito Guarino and Antonio Anzano were in command of the aircraft. From an altitude of a little over 20,000 feet, they surveyed the naval presence in the port of Valletta but, due to a bank of clouds, were unable to ascertain the damage caused by the recent bombing of Cospicua. The mission was repeated on 14 June when, with phonogram n. 7 (an official order), *3ª Divisione Aerea* command directed an SM.79 of the *68ª Squadriglia* to carry out a visual, photographic and offensive reconnaissance.

On the night of 20/21 June, the Italians carried out their first nocturnal raid against Malta, when six SM.79s of *34° Stormo BT* (*Bombardamento Terrestre* – land-based bombers) and one

Benito Mussolini and Adolf Hitler, during a meeting held near an Axis airfield, discuss plans for attacks on enemy territory. (Archivio Centrale dello Stato 26696, 26706)

from the *Reparto Volo* (Flying Detachment) of the *3° Divisione* took off singly at regular intervals. Forty-two 100kg bombs were dropped on the island during a four-hour period. Among the causalities was the floating dock – a 40,000-ton structure – which was sunk in the Grand Harbour.

Formations of Savoia Marchetti SM.79s of the *254ª Squadriglia, 105° Gruppo, 46° Stormo BT* were directed to bomb Malta. Fighter cover was soon discovered to be essential as the SM.79 was vulnerable to enemy fighters, even the few Gloster Gladiator biplanes based on the island. (ACS 04097, 24389)

Eleven days after Italy's entry into the war, the *Regia Aeronautica* sent an SM.79 from the *214ª Squadriglia, 52° Gruppo, 34° Stormo BT,* to Malta to carry out a photographic exploration of Mikabba (Luqa) and the Grand Harbour. The Italian trimotor was damaged by anti-aircraft fire but managed to return to Gela Ponte Olivo with its precious photographic exposures intact. The following morning, SM.79s from Castelvetrano airport flew photographic missions to the port of Bizerte, a major French naval base in Tunisia.

On 4 October 1940, nine MC.200s of the *6° Gruppo CT* departed Catania Fontanarossa airport for a raid on Malta. Among the *Gruppo's* aircraft was an MC.200, equipped with an on-board camera, tasked with carrying out a photo-reconnaissance of the islands. It was MM4585, of the *72ª Squadriglia,* flown by Tenente Pilota Mario Nasoni, who was shot down over Malta at 10:15 a.m. by Sergeant Reginald Hyde of No. 261 Squadron RAF, flying a Hawker Hurricane Mk.I (N2715). At the beginning of the conflict, small cameras of the AC 81 type were installed in Italian aircraft, especially in fighter aircraft like the CR.42 and MC.200.

On 26 November, the *Regia Aeronautica* sent three CR.42s from Comiso on a reconnaissance of Valletta and Marsa Scirocco (Marsaxlokk). Sadly, Tenente Giuseppe Beccaria, flying MM4340 of the *70ª Squadriglia CT, 23° Gruppo Autonomo CT,* was killed when he was shot down.

Two days later, two SM.79s of the *34° Stormo BT,* which took off at 8:20 a.m. from Catania Fontanarossa for an aerial photography sortie, scoured the Sicilian channel far and wide in search of English ships. Operation *Collar* was underway as the British pushed through supplies to the Maltese stronghold now exhausted by the siege.

On 15 April 1941 the *Regia Aeronautica* formed the *173ª Squadriglia Autonoma RST* (*Ricongnizione Strategica Terrestre* – land-based strategic reconnaissance). This unit was the only one to use the twin-engine Fiat CR.25. Their first operation was on 24 July 1941, searching for a submarine off Palermo. On 5 August, six aircraft were detached to Sciacca airfield as anti-submarine escort for a convoy returning from Libya. The following day, they flew to Trapani to escort merchant shipping over the next few weeks, sometimes using Pantelleria as a staging base. On 6 September, they flew a reconnaissance sortie over Malta and, from 11 to 13 September, two sections of CR.25s were detached to Pantelleria and Castelbenito to counter torpedo bomber attacks. Four aircraft were detached to Catania on 17 October 1941. The following month, ten were at Catania carrying out shipping reconnaissance and protecting III Naval Division against torpedo bombers.

In May 1941, due to the scarcity of photo-reconnaissance aircraft available to Italian units in Sicily, the *Regia Aeronautica,* with the *1° Stormo CT,* tried to create a specialist photographic version of the widely used MC.200 in the hangars of Catania Fontanarossa airport. The engineer from Macchi seconded to the project, Vittorio Lana, cut open the left side of the fuselage of one of the most robust fighter aircraft ever built to make room for the camera. Macchi subsequently installed cameras just behind the pilot's seat.

The following month, the *97ª Squadriglia, 9° Gruppo CT,* received its first Macchi MC.202 photographic Folgore (Thunderbolt, MM7711, individual code '97-1'). In September, the new MC.202 was tested in the skies over Malta, then moved to the *76ª Squadriglia,* of the same

Gruppo, in November, and thus operated from Comiso, while the *96ª* and *97ª Squadriglie* moved to Martuba, Libya.[2]

On 22 June 1941, the *Regia Aeronautica* sent a CANT Z.1007bis, MM23309 of *Sezione RST* (*Ricongnizione Strategica Terrestre* – land-based strategic reconnaissance), from Comiso to the skies over Malta for a photographic mission. Under the command of Tenente Renato Limiti and Sottotenente Renato Tobia, it was escorted by MC.200s of the *10° Gruppo CT*. The scout, due to the sudden failure of a valve, and consequent damage to a cylinder of the right engine, was forced to return to base. The mission was repeated on the 25th when an SM.79 of the *58ª Squadriglia, 32° Gruppo, 10° Stormo BT*, with Colonello Pilota Ranieri Cupini, the *Gruppo* commander, at the controls, took off from Trapani Chinisia airport (Trapani Bo Rizzo) early in the morning with a large escort (50 MC.200s of the *10° Gruppo CT*, *4° Stormo* and the *16° Gruppo CT, 54° Stormo*) led by Tenente Colonello Pilota Carlo Romagnoli.

The Macchi MC.200 testing programme continued until the final days of July 1941 when Tenente Franco Lucchini, of the *90ª Squadriglia, 4° Stormo CT*, test flew a camera-equipped MC.200 of the *10° Gruppo CT* from Catania Fontanarossa. The *Regia Aeronautica* was hoping to obtain results at least equivalent to those obtained using the CANT Z.1007bis and SM.79 which were proving too vulnerable to enemy fighters. On the 27th, however, the Macchi was lost during a disastrous landing at Catania Fontanarossa when, due to a sudden loss of altitude, possibly caused by an irregular oxygen supply, a struggling Lucchini was forced to make an emergency landing. While the aircraft was badly damaged, the pilot only suffered a few minor injuries to his face. It was thus necessary to convert to another MC.200 and it was not long before it was test flown by Tenente Stefano Soprana.

After completing the experimental phase, on 3 August an attempt was made to use the photographic Macchi over Malta, a mission entrusted to Soprana. During the flight, he noticed a technical problem with his fuel gauge. Forced to return, Soprana managed to take some test shots of the coast of Sicily. This time the photos were clear and were delivered directly to Tenente Colonnello Pilota Mario Piccini, at Comiso, who approved the operation, ordering a new mission to Malta for the next day.[3] On 23 September 1941, the photographic reconnaissance carried out by two MC.200s of the *54° Stormo CT* on Malta almost met a tragic fate when the Italian fighters, flown by Tenente Pilota Adriano Visconti and Sottotenente Pilota Gabriele Ferretti, risked being intercepted by two Hurricanes of No. 249 Squadron. In the end, however, the interception was foiled thanks to the skill of the Italian pilots.

2   Giorgio Apostolo, *C.202 Aer. Macchi* (Torino: La Bancarella Aeronautica, 1996), p.27.
3   Antonio Duma, *Quelli del cavallino rampante* [*Those of the prancing horse*] (Roma: Aeronautica Militare, 2007), p.203.

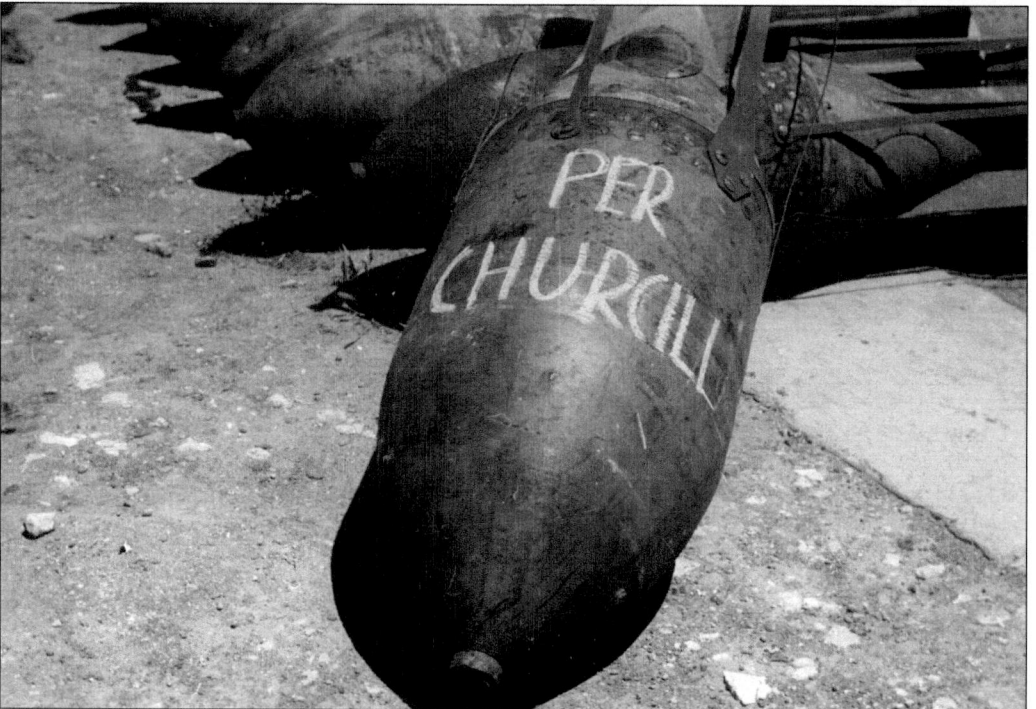

Irreverent messages addressed to the British by some cheeky armourer, a custom of the early phases of the war. (ACS 02196, 02755)

The *Regia Aeronautica* used several photographic cameras during the war, many of which were operated manually. This image shows the manual use of an APR-87 type camera. (ACS 05425)

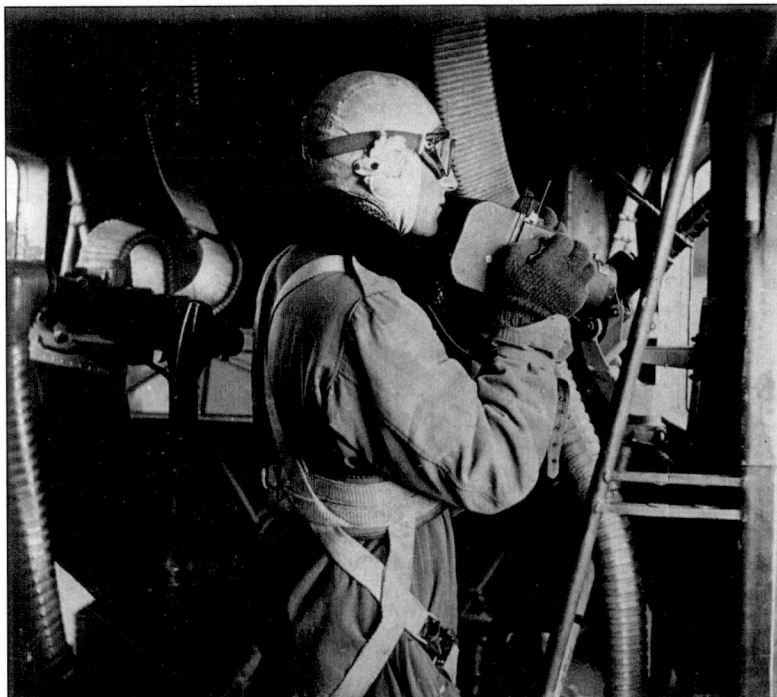

A crew member holding an APR-3 type camera in a CANT Z.1007bis. (ACS 14617)

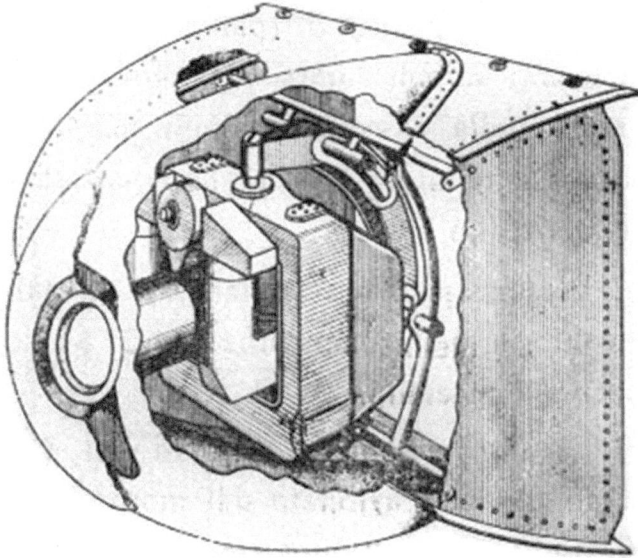

Position of the AC 81 camera
in the right wing of the
Macchi MC.200.

English and French air reconnaissance at the beginning of the war

When Italy declared war on Britain and France, the RAF did not have any photographic units in Egypt comparable to what it had in the United Kingdom. The only aircraft capable of being used for such activities was Lockheed Hudson N7364, masquerading as a civilian machine ('G-AGAR') nicknamed 'Cloudy Joe', which had carried out espionage flights over the Soviet centres of Baku and Batum in March and April 1940.[4] Repainted with RAF insignia, it arrived at Heliopolis (Egypt), after leaving Heston in England on 4 June 1940, with Flying Officer R.G.M. 'Johnny' Walker as first pilot and Squadron Leader Hugh Macphail as second pilot. The two pilots and some specialists formed a new unit called the Intelligence Photographic Flight (IPF). After its inauguration, the Heliopolis section also took charge of the photographic material produced by No. 228 Squadron posted to Kalafrana, Malta, in September 1940. That unit flew maritime reconnaissance with the large Short Sunderland Mk.I flying boats.

The first to perform offensive photographic reconnaissance of the Sicilian islands, however, were the French from *Forces Aériennes d'Afrique du Nord* whose aircraft, flying from Algerian bases, photographed air-naval movements in the western Mediterranean. On 2 May 1940, therefore, before Italy entered the war, the French issued a directive, 'Instruction particuliere n° 24', within which express reference was made to Italy possibly entering the war and the strategies to be adopted should this occur. French reconnaissance of North Africa was entrusted

---

4   The Lockheed was to be used on 12 sorties between 14 June 1940 and 20 February 1941. It was eventually written off in March 1941 after it was damage during a ground strafing by Italian Fighters on Heraklion airfield. Cfr. Edward Leaf, *Above All Unseen: The Royal Air Force's Photographic Reconnaissance Unit 1939-1945* (Sparkford: Patrick Stephens Limited, 1997), p.121.

to the GR I/61 (*Groupe de Reconnaissance*), which operated from Youks-les-Bains in Algeria with the Glenn Martin 167F Maryland, an American-made, twin engine, long-range bomber.

Maritime reconnaissance by No. 228 Squadron. (MEIU)

During the 13 June 1940 mission to photograph the air and naval bases on Sicily, the French detected a substantial strengthening of the enemy forces. Analysis of the Sicilian airfields showed 45 aircraft at Catania Fontanarossa, 35 at Comiso, 7 seaplanes moored to buoys at Augusta, and a significant presence of ships at anchor off Trapani (including 20 warships). Among the other places covered by the French reconnaissance sorties were Syracuse, Noto and Pantelleria. All surveys were carried out at altitudes ranging from 13,000 to 27,500 feet. A directive issued by Général Vuillemin to the French *Groupe de Reconnaissance* observed:

> The GR I/61 group as well as the bombing groups will participate in the survey operation, for the benefit of the navy, on the Italian ports on the Tyrrhenian Sea, Sardinia, Sicily, Gulf of Taranto, the Otranto Channel and Tripolitania.

> Joseph Vuillemin (Le Général Commandant Chef des Forces Aériennes)

Subsequent French reconnaissance flights confirmed the Italians' intent to massively deploy air and naval forces on the island. On 21 June 1940, the *Groupe de Reconnaissance* observed 12 seaplanes on the buoys and 20 large boats moored north of the Marsala seaplane base. The frenzied naval activity in the ports of Sicily worried the French enough for them to carry out a preventative bombing raid. On 22 June 1940, at 10:40 a.m., 27 bombers of GBM I/62 (*Groupe*

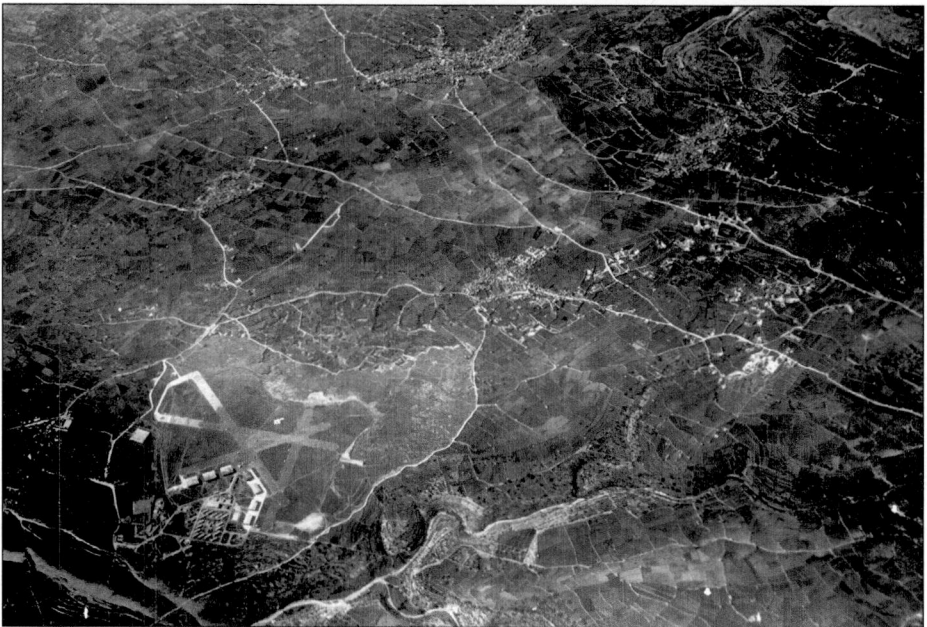

The port of Valletta and Luqa airfield photographed from an altitude of about 20,000 feet by an SM.79 from the *59ª Squadriglia*. The *Regia Aeronautica* reconnaissance machine took off at 5:20 a.m. on 12 June 1940 from Comiso, under the command of Sottotenente Nino Guarino and Antonio Anzano. An APR-3 camera was used. (Mario Molari)

de Bombardement Moyen) dropped 164 fifty-kilogram bombs and 490 ten-kilogram incendiary bombs on the port of Trapani. Two boats sank in the raid, a hangar was set on fire and a fuel depot hit. Although the bombing was completely unexpected, the DICAT (*Difesa Contraerea Territoriale* – Territorial Anti-Aircraft Defence) batteries placed west of the city responded. Also, two CR.42s of the *Regia Aeronautica* approached the French formation but were unable to engage.

On 23 June 1940, Palermo also suffered its first French raid. The attack occurred in two different waves; the first consisted of seven Maryland bombers, four from GBM I/62 and three from GBM II/62 of the *Aviation de Bombardement du Sud-Est (et Tunisie)* of the *Armée de l'Air*, from Bizerte (Tunisia); with the second consisting of five twin engine LeO 451 bombers of GB II/11 from Youks-les-Bains and led by Colonel Chopin (only three arrived over Palermo). The Marylands arrived over their target, from the sea in an east-north-east direction and at an altitude of 11,500–13,000 feet, at 6:20 p.m., attacking the port, city and shipyards but causing little damage. Subsequently, at 7:25 p.m., the three LeO 451s, approaching from the same direction but at very low altitude, attempted to attack the port but were repelled by the 76/40mm guns of the Italian anti-aircraft defences.

On the morning of 24 June, the French returned to Sicily. This time they used American-made Douglas DB-7 aircraft to ascertain the extent of the damage to Palermo. On the return flight, they also photographed military installations in the territories of Vizzini, Syracuse, Augusta, Catania and Gela.

A captain of the *Regia Aeronautica* uses a stereoscope to analyse the photos taken during an aerial reconnaissance sortie. (ACS 11264)

Macchi MC.200s of the *4° Stormo CT*, based at Catania Fontanarossa. The symbol of the 'Cavallino Rampante' on the fuselage of the aircraft can be clearly seen. (ACS 27506)

An aircraft of the *98ª Squadriglia, 7° Gruppo, 5° Stormo CT*. The codes '98-4' suggest the pilot is probably Capitano Sergio Maurer, seen here at Catania Fontanarossa in June 1941. The installation of an APR-3 photographic camera is visible on the right wing. In the background is a Junkers Ju52/3m. (ACS 31024)

The CANT Z.506 was a three-engine, low-wing, multi-role floatplane, produced by Cantieri Riuniti dell'Adriatico, Cantiere Navale Triestino (C.R.D.A., CANT) from the mid-thirties. This is the maritime rescue version. Note the large red cross. (ACS 13731)

The CANT Z.501 from 141ª Squadriglia in a seaplane base. (ACS 20019)

3

No. 431 General Reconnaissance Flight and the Maryland

The main photographic section for the Royal Air Force in Malta, for which Flight Sergeant Geoffrey J. Buxton was responsible, was located at the Kalafrana seaplane base. Even before the start of the conflict, the negatives taken in June 1939 during Sidney Cotton's clandestine Lockheed 12A flights were kept in Kalafrana.

Less than 60 miles from the Sicilian coast, Malta immediately became the primary target for the enemy air forces in Sicily. From the beginning of hostilities, the air defence of the small archipelago was initially entrusted to a handful of Gloster Sea Gladiator biplanes, under the command of the Fighter Flight at Hal Far, which were delivered to Malta in early 1940 by HMS *Glorious*.[1] Despite the Sea Gladiators being regarded as obsolete before the outbreak of the war, outclassed in terms of speed and firepower, and hamstrung by a spares source largely limited to delivered aircraft not yet assembled, they were flown aggressively and held the line until more modern aircraft arrived (Hurricanes arrived in initially small numbers from June onwards and, as seen in the previous chapter, made their presence felt). There were only three operating airfields: to the south, Hal Far, headquarters of the Fleet Air Arm, the air component of the Royal Navy; to the north, Takali; and centrally located Luqa, the largest of the three. To them could be added an emergency strip called Safi, located halfway between Takali and Luqa.

With conflict imminent, the RAF, in the spring of 1940, also carried out photographic reconnaissance over Italy, mainly concentrating on Milan, Genoa, Livorno and other places that would be targets in the event war was declared between the two nations. In the Middle East, the RAF was especially involved in preventative surveys of German activity in Iran and Iraq; preventative reconnaissance was also planned for the Italian Dodecanese.

On 6 August 1940, the RAF sent Sergeant Harry Ayre and Captain K.L. Ford from Malta, in Blackburn Skua L2911, on a reconnaissance sortie of the ports of Catania, Syracuse and Augusta; the latter was of crucial importance because it hosted the cruisers *Alberico da Barbiano* and *Alberto da Giussano*, and the destroyers *Zeno* and *Pigafetta*, that were engaged the day before in laying the 7AN anti-ship mine barrier between the island of Pantelleria and Tunisia. The sortie was in anticipation of a torpedo strike on Augusta planned for the late evening of 13

---

1   Brian Cull, Frederick Galea, *Hurricanes Over Malta June 1940-April 1942* (London: Grub Street Publishing, 2001), p.6.

August by Fairey Swordfish biplanes of 830 Naval Air Squadron (NAS) of the Fleet Air Arm.[2] The delicate and dangerous reconnaissance lasted two hours and 20 minutes. Neither *Regia Aeronautica* fighters nor anti-aircraft fire was encountered, as Harry Ayre wrote in his logbook:

> Did recce in Skua with Capt Ford RM [Royal Marines] over Sicily, looking for enemy convoy forming up. No sign of convoy but much shipping in Catania, Augusta and Syracuse harbours. Few naval ships. Flew right [over] one Italian cruiser. No AA fire. Was sorry we had no bombs.[3]

In all likelihood, the Anglo–French reconnaissance activity on the island did not go unnoticed. In the meantime, in Sicily, the General Staff of the *Regia Aeronautica*, on 31 August 1940, issued a directive that ordered the dispersal and camouflaging of aircraft:

> Please note that the aircraft must be kept as far away from the hangars as possible, because these are an attractive target, and normally targeted by the enemy. For the masking of aircraft, in the absence of appropriate camouflage nets, appropriate materials are to be used, such as branches and suitably coloured end-of-use tarpaulins.

The directive also stated that, in order to deceive enemy bombers, 'it is useful to place on the landing field, or on the periphery of it, in a suitable position, simulated targets using aircraft and parts that are no longer in use.'[4] Moreover, as a precaution, large ships were removed from Augusta, especially given the destroyer *Leone Pancaldo*, on the evening of 10 July, was sunk by three 813 NAS Swordfish torpedo bombers from the aircraft carrier HMS *Eagle*. On this matter, Admiral Sir Andrew Cunningham observed sometime later:

> I shall always remember the *Eagle*, Captain A.R.M. Bridge. She played a great part during the approach and subsequent action, and never have there been more skillful or gallant fliers than those young men who manned her seventeen Swordfish; never has better work been done than by those who kept them in the air. Although they did not succeed in hitting a battleship, they hit a cruiser, and carried out a prodigious amount of work between 4:00 a.m. and sunset. Constant reconnaissance and search, with the launching of two striking forces with that small number of air-crews and aircraft was an astonishing performance. The next day a third striking force was flown off to attack shipping in Augusta and succeeded in sinking a destroyer. The action was most unsatisfactory to us. I suppose it was too much to expect the Italians to stake

---

2   On that occasion, one of the aircraft of 830 NAS was shot down and crashed off Augusta and the pilot, David Watkin Waters, and his telegraphist/air gunner, S.D. Harris, were taken prisoners. The episode is mentioned in Bulletin n. 66 of August 14 1940.
3   Cull, Galea, *Hurricanes Over Malta*, p.23.
4   Ufficio Difesa Aerea, protocollo n. C/15013. Oggetto: Provvedimenti per la protezione A.A. sugli aeroporti. (Air Defence Office, protocol no. C/15013. Subject: Provisions for the protection of AA on airfields).

everything on a stand-up fight. Yet, if they had timed their attacks better with all the types of arms employed they might have given us much trouble.[5]

At 1:45 a.m. on 6 September 1940, following preparation by No. 22 Squadron at North Coates, three Marylands left Thorney Island, overlooking the English Channel near Portsmouth, to fly over occupied France under the cover of darkness, finally touching down at Luqa after six hours and 45 minutes. During the flight over Sardinia, they took advantage of the first light of the day to take photos of the island. The three Martin 167F Marylands ('F' for 'France' as these aircraft were ordered by that country before the war) were responsible for forming No. 431 General Reconnaissance Flight at Luqa on 19 September under the command of soon to be Squadron Leader Ernest Alfred 'Tich' Whiteley, an Australian in the RAF. The three aircraft were AR705, AR707, AR712; these new American machines had Curtiss-Wright engines and many more electrical components than British aircraft.[6] The now well-known Skua L2911 was also added to the newly formed reconnaissance flight.[7]

The flight was formed following Movement Order No. 7/1940 of No. 22 Squadron, Coastal Command, North Coates, from which the crews of the first three aircraft were derived. The crews of the Marylands were:

AR705	F/L	E.A. Whiteley	37588	Pilot
	P/O	P.S. Devine	40808	Observer
	Corpl	J.S. Shephard	569200	W/E/M/AG
AR707	Sgt	J.W.T. Bibby	566007	Pilot
	Sgt	F. Bastard	745136	Air Observer
	Sgt	P.D.J. Moren	755069	WOp/AG
AR709*	P/O	Buckbarrow	42557	Pilot
	Sgt	J.M. Alexander	745637	Observer
	Sgt	P.H.D. McConnell	755712	WOp/AG
AR712	P/O	J. Foxton	41575	Pilot
	P/O	A. Warburton	41635	Observer
	Sgt	R.V. Gridley	640154	WOp/AG

(*AR709 was held in reserve)

5   Andrew Browne Cunningham, *A sailor's odyssey: The autobiography of Admiral of the Fleet Viscount Cunningham of Hyndhope* (London: Hutchinson, 1951), p.263.
6   The Maryland was a well-armed light bomber with a streamlined and riveted aluminum fuselage in which photographic equipment could be easily mounted. Produced by the American Glenn L. Martin Company, the aircraft was capable of a maximum speed of just over 300mph and could fly at least 1,300 miles without the need for additional fuel tanks. Only 450 were built.
7   The National Archives London, Royal Air Force, Operations Record Books, 431 Flight AIR 27/610/1.

On arrival at Luqa, 431 Flight came under the administration of Mediterranean Command, and absorbed the personnel of No. 3 Anti-Aircraft Co-operation Unit, Hal Far, which was disbanded with effect from 19 September 1940. Command of the flight was initially assumed by Captain K.L. Ford, Royal Marines.

Pilot Officer Paddy Devine and Corporal John Shephard, an excellent radio operator and machine gunner who, due to his experience in the mechanical and electrical field, was personally chosen by Whiteley and subsequently became a key member of the unit, arrived in the first Maryland with Whiteley. The crew of the second Maryland was made up of Sergeants J.W. Bibby (pilot), Frank Bastard and Pax 'Paddy' Moren. Pilot Officers James Foxton and Adrian Warburton arrived in the third Maryland[8] with Sergeant Robert Victor Gridley. The station commander, Wing Commander R. Carter Jonas, met them at Luqa. The Royal Navy had been eagerly awaiting the arrival of these aircraft in the Mediterranean as there were concerns the modern Italian naval fleet, undoubtedly greater on paper in terms of size, firepower and speed, could successfully challenge for naval supremacy of the Mediterranean. Consequently, one of the first operational uses of the new unit was to constantly monitor and photograph every naval movement, especially at the ports of Taranto and Messina, and, in general, central and southern Italy. This work was supported by two excellent photographers, Corporals Harry Kirk and Jim McNeil.

Personnel of the new No. 431 General Reconnaissance Flight. Left to right, Flying Officer Boys-Stones, Pilot Officer Adrian Warburton and Sergeant Jack Levy. (Keith Bastard)

8   A very young Pilot Officer Adrian Warburton was, at that time, filling the role of observer (navigator). Joining an Army territorial unit in 1937, Warburton moved to the RAF in the autumn of 1938. His superiors were so unimpressed by his daring take-offs and landings that he was not allowed to fly a Maryland to Malta. He was also an eccentric officer, dismissive in many aspects, but would become one of the most famous photo-reconnaissance pilots of the Second World War.

Sergeant Jack Levy. (Keith Bastard)

Sergeant Frank Bastard in front of a Glenn Martin 167F Maryland from No. 431 General Reconnaissance Flight, Malta. (Keith Bastard)

The Marylands, thanks to their impressive range, managed to ensure coverage from Libya to Naples, to Corfu and the coasts of Albania. On 8 September 1940, their vertical photographic equipment immortalised the African sky, obtaining the first negatives of Tripoli harbour. After covering Benghazi, the photo-reconnaissance sorties all followed an almost identical route: first, the overflight of the Sicilian coasts, then the Ionian islands and, finally, east to the heel of Italy.

At 8:00 a.m. on 14 September, Maryland I AR712, under the command of Pilot Officer Foxton, Flying Officer Warburton and Sergeant Gridley reported:

Reconnaissance of Tripoli, Sicily, Pantelleria. Naval Units seen 1 Cruiser, 3 Destroyers. Photograph taken. Moderate inaccurate A.A. Fire.[9]

After a few days of operations, a debilitating illness ('Malta Dog', similar to dysentery) forced Foxton and Bibby to be grounded, meaning the flight had to resort to the two reserve pilots, Devine and Warburton, previously employed as observers.

---

9   The National Archives London, Royal Air Force, 431 General Reconnaissance Flight Appendices AIR 27/610/1.

At 12:00 p.m. on 22 September, Blackburn Skua L2911, under the command of Captain K.L. Ford and Sub-lieutenant W.R. Nowell, took off from Luqa. They flew over the east coast of Sicily to monitor naval traffic, especially *Regia Marina* vessels engaged in the laying of minefields in Maltese waters. The Skua crew, however, as reported in the Operations Record Book (ORB) of 431 General Reconnaissance Flight, returned with little to report; only a few small boats were sighted.[10] However, at 2:25 p.m., off Taormina, the silhouettes of five Fiat CR.42 biplane fighters, clearly intent on making an interception, were seen. It was at this point the Skua turned for Malta. At 4:00 p.m. the following day, the Skua, with Nowell and Pilot Officer Pinkerton on board, returned to the east coast of Sicily. This time a small formation of Macchi MC.200s forced an early return.

On 26 September, 431 General Reconnaissance Flight performed, with Pilot Officer Adrian Warburton flying Maryland I AR712, a sortie to Corfu. Unfortunately, Warburton's take-off was so poor it tore a wheel off, leading to an 'immediate emergency landing'. The unit's records kindly referred to the incident as a 'hydraulic failure'. The two non-commissioned officers who made up Warburton's crew, Sergeants Bastard and Moren, later commented: 'The anti-aircraft and the enemy fighters of Messina and Taranto were a piece of cake, compared to take-offs and landings with Warburton in command.'[11]

In any case, the battered Maryland was destroyed the next day during a heavy Italian bombing raid on Malta by nine SM.79s of the *34° Stormo BT* (*Bombardamento Terrestre* – land-based bombers) that left Catania Fontanarossa heavily escorted by CR.42s of the *23° Gruppo Autonomo CT* (*Caccia Terrestre* – land-based fighters) from Comiso.[12]

To meet the needs of 431 General Reconnaissance Flight, its commanding officer, Ernest Whiteley, 'acquired' two Blenheim Mk.IVs (T2115 and T2164) and their crews (led by Flight Lieutenant T.M. Horgan and Flying Officer V.R. Ferguson) in October; they had been destined for Egypt and had landed at Malta for fuel. The main routes followed by the Maltese scouts, during daily operations lasting at least four hours, can be found in the unit's October records: 'Reco. Malta-Sicily-Corfu-Malta, Reco. Malta-Greece-Malta, Reco. Taranto-Brindisi-Corfu, Reco. Sicily-Corfu-Taranto Harbor.'[13]

On 30 October, at 7:30 a.m., Whiteley sent Maryland I AR705 on a photographic survey of Brindisi and Taranto with Warburton as pilot and Sergeants J.W. Strong and D.S. Moren as crew. Forced to descend due to dense cloud cover over the Apulian cities, they spotted and shot down a Cant Z.506 seaplane which plunged into the sea. Lunchtime on 9 November had just passed when Maryland I AR705, with Pilot Officer Jones and Sergeants J.H. Spires and P.H. McConnell on board, was on a sortie over the Tyrrhenian coast of Sicily. Near Messina they saw what they believed to be the silhouettes of three submarines. Proceeding towards the

---

10 Unlike the sortie carried out on 14 September when some merchant ships and warships were sighted in the ports of Messina, Catania, Syracuse and Augusta.

11 Tony Spooner, *Warburton's War: The Life of Maverick Ace Adrian Warburton* (Manchester: Crécy Publishing, 2003), p.46, and Paul McDonald, *Malta's Greater Siege and Adrian Warburton* (Barnsley: Pen & Sword Aviation, 2015), p.97.

12 That September, Malta suffered 25 air raids. By 1943, the total was 3,340. Cfr. Tony Spooner, *Warburton's War: The Life of Maverick Ace Adrian Warburton*, p.44.

13 The National Archives London, Royal Air Force, 431 General Reconnaissance Flight Appendices AIR 27/610/2.

Ionian coast, and then flying over Augusta, they observed two large warships.[14] They returned to Malta at 3:20 p.m.

In November, Admiral Sir Andrew Cunningham, commander of the British naval fleet in the Mediterranean, decided to launch a torpedo attack against the Italian naval fleet in Taranto, using the obsolete, but effective, Fairey Swordfish. Embarked on HMS *Illustrious*, the naval flyers requested 431 General Reconnaissance Flight carry out some preliminary photo-reconnaissance of the Italian naval base. Six Vickers Wellington bombers from No. 37 Squadron, which left Feltwell, England, at 11:00 p.m. on 8 November, would also contribute, even though only five of them made it to Luqa as one was forced to return to base with mechanical problems.[15] One aircraft, however, was damaged in the vicinity of Pantelleria and two members of the crew wounded.[16]

The port of Taranto as captured on 14 November 1940 by No. 431 General Reconnaissance Flight in a series of strip photos. In the centre are numerous naval units moored in the Mare Piccolo (including two cruisers). Top centre, the battleship *Duilio*, having been hit by a torpedo, is protected by torpedo nets.
(Frank Bastard)

14   The two large warships sighted were the cruisers *Armando Diaz* and *Alberto da Giussano*; on 12 November, they left their moorings off Augusta in a hurry, escorted by the destroyers of the *14ᵃ Squadriglia*, (Regia Marina) with the order to retreat to Palermo. Marcon, *Augusta 1940-1943*, p.29.
15   AIR 27/388/25 During the crossing, the Wellington crews took the opportunity to bomb the nearby island of Pantelleria. Another seven bombers arrived on the 13th and another three on the 19th, to which would be added those of No. 148 Squadron in December. On the night of the 13th, four Wellingtons bombed Taranto naval base.
16   Captains of the five Wellingtons were: Flight Lieutenant Baird-Smith, and Sergeants Thomas, Gillanders, Noden and Spiller. The National Archives London, Royal Air Force, Operations Record Books, 37 Squadron AIR 27/388/25.

At 12:10 p.m. on 10 November 1940, Warburton, flying Maryland I AR705 with Sergeants Moren and Bastard–the latter in the role of observer–made one of the final flights over Taranto before the torpedo attack scheduled for the night of 11/12 November. They flew around the port twice at extremely low level for preliminary photographic reconnaissance, then returned for a third pass despite heavy anti-aircraft fire and an approaching CR.42. Their photographs revealed the presence of five warships, 14 cruisers and 27 destroyers within the port area.

On 17 November, 14 aircraft were launched by the aircraft carrier HMS *Argus* to bolster the defences on Malta; these 12 Hurricanes and two Skuas were part of Operation *White*. The threat of the Italian fleet in the Sicilian channel, however, forced them to launch from maximum range; only four Hurricanes (and a Skua) managed to land; the other Hurricanes ran out of fuel and ditched in sea. Only one pilot was rescued.

At 5:45 a.m. the same day, Maryland AR705 took off from Luqa with Ernest Whiteley and Sergeants Strong and Gridley on board. They tried to establish radio contact with the incoming fighters to help guide them to Malta. This, however, was in vain as one of the two Skuas (L2987, Petty Officer Eric J. Stockwell and Sub-lieutenant R.C. Neil), which was to lead a formation, flew off course due to a malfunctioning radio and, having remained airborne until almost out of fuel, landed on the beach of Isola delle Correnti, near Portopalo. The Maryland finally landed at 10:45 a.m., after locating the Skua in Sicily; there was no trace of the Hurricanes or their occupants.

Some days later, at exactly 12:00 p.m. on 20 November, a special sortie was entrusted to the crew of Blenheim T2115. Flight Lieutenant Horgan and Sergeants Bastard and Moren were sent to Sicily to search for a Wellington, transporting high-ranking officers from Stradishall, England, to Egypt, that was expected to refuel at Malta. The No. 214 Squadron Wellington (T2873), with Air Marshal Owen Tudor Boyd, the newly appointed Air Officer Commanding-in-Chief Middle East, on board, encountered bad weather and made an emergency landing near Comiso.[17]

In Malta, as well as in Sicily, the arrival of vehicles and personnel continued, the latter largely voluntarily enlisted. Among these was Sergeant G. Berrett,[18] a wireless operator and air gunner (WOp/AG), who joined 431 General Reconnaissance Flight:

That day – September 15, 1940 – later to be known as the last day of the Battle of Britain – was a fateful day for me. The flight commander summoned the gunners on that morning and asked for volunteers to join a reconnaissance flight which was to be based in Malta. He couldn't elucidate any more, it may be dangerous. The aircraft concerned, the Glenn Martin Type 167F, was a relatively unknown quantity that had been destined for fallen France but diverted to the UK before the Germans could capture them.

Unknown to us, three Marylands (as the RAF called them) had already departed for Malta on September 6 and successfully completed the journey. Sqn Ldr 'Tich' Whiteley commanded the newly-formed 431 (General reconnaissance) Flight and he, very successfully, established the unit at Luqa, the main drome in Malta, and photographic

17   Other sources claim the Wellington was forced down by Italian fighters.
18   According to the 431 General Reconnaissance Flight ORB, Berrett flew his first reconnaissance sortie on 23 December 1940.

reconnaissance was already being carried out … Shortly after volunteering for the job, I and a rather tall young man, Jimmy 'Alex' Alexander, a navigator, were introduced to Plt Off Julian 'Willie' Williams who was to be our pilot. The other two crew members, as I vaguely remember, were: Flg Off Boyes Stones [sic, Boys-Stones], Sgt Batchelor, Sgt Levy; and Sgt Gimson DFM (Pilot, navigator and WOP/AG respectively). Of those nine only Sgt Alexander (prisoner of war) and I survived. … With little notice were told that we would leave in the early hours from Thorney Island, Hampshire, for Malta on December 19, 1940. … Meanwhile our duties consisted of photographing enemy ports and airfields and finding enemy convoys. We flew to Naples, to the north, and all points south to Tripoli in Western Desert … The only serious occasion I have recorded was that on one trip to Catania and Messina we flew back 100 miles (160 km) on one engine. This was the only time I had trepidation about the Maryland itself. My position as wireless operator was not very comfortable. I sat on a fold-down seat in the cupola facing aft with a single Vickers Gas-Operated (VGO) machine-gun at hand. … I left the squadron in December 1941 … I had been fortunate to have flown with excellent pilots (74 operations were with my original skipper Flt Lt Williams DFC). I flew two sorties with the renowned Sqn Ldr 'Warby' Warburton DFC, mad as a hatter, but with several 'kills' to his credit.[19]

In the late morning of 15 December, this time in Maryland I AR707, Warburton, and Sergeants J.H. Spires and J. Levy, was returning from a sortie covering the ports of Crotone, Taranto and Messina. As they were about to leave the coast of Sicily to return to Malta, about 10 miles from Syracuse, although the weather conditions were not the best, they spotted an Italian submarine right below them; they machine-gunned it from very low altitude.

On 24 December, Maryland AR713, which left Luqa at 8:05 a.m., was over Naples for a typical photographic survey. On board were Adrian Warburton and Sergeants Alexander and Moren. They had just photographed two cruisers and dropped some propaganda leaflets from 2,000 feet when, 10 miles from the city, they attacked an SM.79, causing it to crash and catch fire. Bollettino n. 201 of 25 December reported: 'At around 12:20 a.m. yesterday, the 24th, an enemy plane flew over Naples and its surroundings, dropping some incendiary bombs and the usual leaflets.'

On the 31st, 431 General Reconnaissance Flight was engaged in two different sorties over Taranto, Brindisi and Pantelleria. The first commenced at 7:45 a.m. when Flying Officer Boys-Stones and Sergeants Bastard and Moren took Maryland I AR707 aloft. They first flew to Taranto before photographing Brindisi. It was an eventful trip:

Intercepted by 2 CR.42's and 1 Macchi off Taranto. Never got in. Attacked SM.75 on way back. Damage port engine. Weather fine. Cloud over Taranto and Brindisi.[20]

19   Jim Berrett, 'Malta's Marylands', *FlyPast*, January 2003, pp.26–32.
20   The National Archives London, Royal Air Force, Operations Record Books, 69 Squadron AIR 27/606/8.

Cruisers of the *Regia Marina*: *Trento, Trieste and Bolzano* of the III Naval Division at anchor at the port of Messina. Above them is a balloon barrage. (Antonio Bonanno)

A Savoia Marchetti SM.79 and a CANT Z.1007bis hidden under olive trees in the dispersal areas of a Sicilian airfield. (ACS 00119, 04810)

Ground crew in Belgium cover a Fiat BR.20 bomber with a camouflage net, likely during the final phase of the Battle of Britain. (ACS 06007, 06724)

The other Maryland, AR713, left about three hours after AR707 with Flying Officer Devine at the controls and Sergeants A.W. Spires and McConnell on board. The visibility was excellent and allowed airfields at Pantelleria to be photographed.

In December, the flight performed 32 sorties, reaching, despite the few aircraft available, an important milestone: completing a set of photographs for all sensitive objectives in Sicily. The Maryland proved to be an excellent photographic reconnaissance aircraft thanks to the F24 photographic equipment supplied (equipped with 8-inch focal lenses mounted vertically) and, of course, the overall performance of the aircraft and its valiant crews. During the winter, and especially in bad weather conditions, Ernest Whiteley used a Leica camera, made for personal use but adapted by technicians on Malta, to take some oblique photos from the aircraft; the experiment produced very satisfactory results.

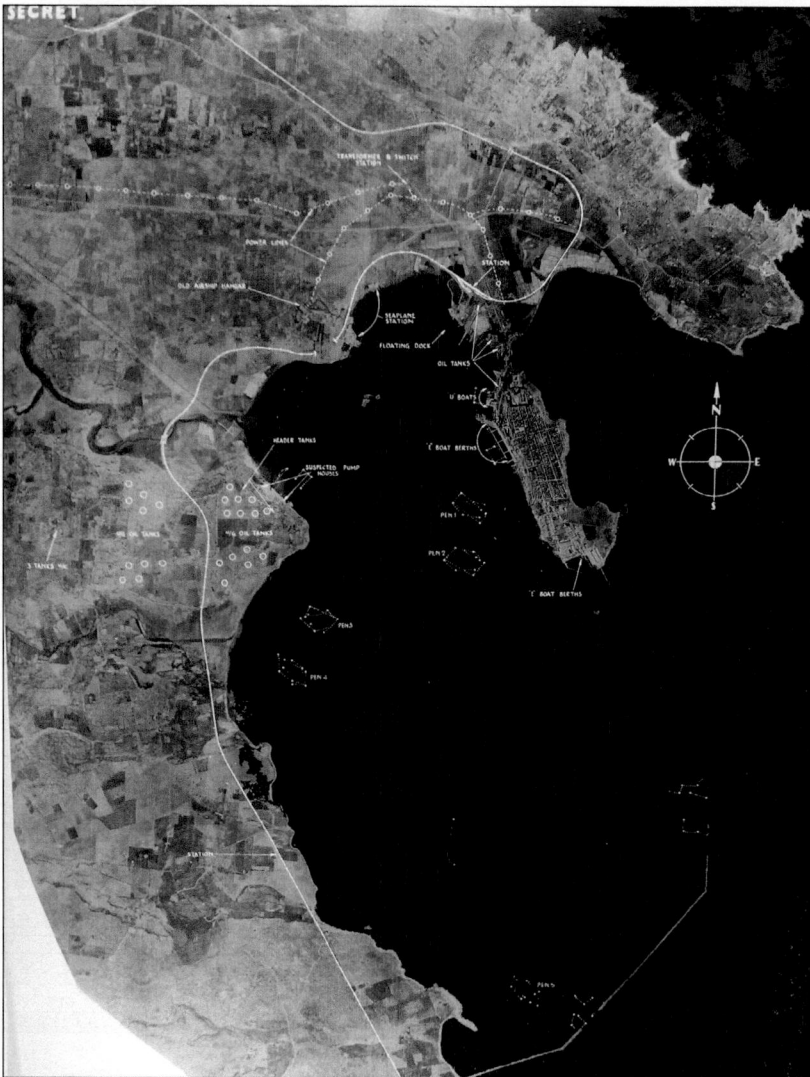

The analysis of this aerial photo of Augusta highlights the fuel tanks, hangars, and anti-aircraft and marine defences. (MEIU)

Air Marshal Owen Tudor Boyd on the right. Boyd became a prisoner of war in Sicily. He spent much of the war in the Castle Vincigliata (Castello di Vincigliata) camp near Florence, Italy. (ACS 07384)

On 13 February 1942, Maryland AR733 of No. 69 Squadron, on a sortie to Cape Bon and Pantelleria, was attacked by two German Bf 109 fighters whose fire killed Sergeant Arthur Charles Moore. Sergeant Watson, from his gunnery position, managed to shoot down one of the attackers. Pilot Officer T.M. Channon was able to make an emergency landing on Malta. (Paul Lazell)

4

1941
Birth of No. 69 Squadron RAF

Arrival of *X CAT* (January–February 1941)

Führer Adolf Hitler's failed attempt to sweep the RAF from the skies of Britain led the Reich to focus on new horizons. Shortly before the end of 1940, Germany had considerable military aviation capability available for use in other theatres. It was therefore decided to deploy these air forces to the Mediterranean. Hermann Göring, the head of the *Luftwaffe*, after several negotiations with the high command of the *Regia Aeronautica*,[1] decided to send *X CAT* (10° *Corpo Aereo Tedesco* – German Air Corps) to Sicily. This unit, known to the Germans as *X Fliegerkorps* (10th Air Corps), was under the command of General der Flieger Hans F. Geisler, with Generalleutnant Martin Harlinghausen, a fellow anti-shipping expert, as his chief-of-staff. The headquarters were established in Taormina in the province of Messina.

By 12 January 1941, *X CAT* already had 247 aircraft on Sicily, including 92 Junkers Ju 88s, 41 Heinkel He 111s, 80 Junkers Ju 87 Stukas and 34 Messerschmitt Bf 110s, spread across the airfields at Catania, Comiso, Trapani and Palermo. The total force deployed to the Sicilian air bases would reach 307 aircraft, with 14,798 men, to which must be added the command echelons of the various flying units with 310 more personnel, a *Gruppe* with 30 Ju 52/3m transports (KG zbV9) and a courier *Staffel* flying six Ju 52/3m aircraft (which would have operated from Reggio Calabria).[2]

Geisler, commander-in-chief of the *Luftwaffe* in Sicily, also brought with him a strategic reconnaissance staff, 1.(F)/121 with 12 Ju 88s of several variants (D-5, A-5 and A-1), and some Bf 110E-3s and Bf 109F-4/Rs.[3] More of these would soon arrive.

---

1 On 6 December 1940, the Inspector-General of the *Luftwaffe*, Erhard Milch, flew to Rome, accompanied by a host of General Staff officers, to meet Generale di Squadra Aerea Francesco Pricolo, Chief of Staff of the *Regia Aeronautica*. The meeting was held in the headquarters of the Ministry of Aeronautics, located at Via dell'Università no. 4.
2 Alessandro Ragatzu, *Luftwaffe in Sardegna* (Cagliari: Alisea Edizioni, 2010), p.12.
3 It was Geisler who accompanied Generalfeldmarschall Erwin Rommel, the 'Desert Fox', from Catania Fontanarossa to Tripoli on 11 February 1941 in anticipation of imminent German operational reconnaissance of North Africa.

A Junkers Ju 88 in North Africa, coded '7A+LH', belonging to the air reconnaissance department of the *Luftwaffe's Aufklärungsgruppe 121*. This unit was stationed at Catania Fontanarossa airport from the end of 1940 to January 1942. (US Air Force photo 23276 AC)

A *Luftwaffe* serviceman of the intelligence service looking at aerial photos taken over Malta as they dry on a rotating frame in the photographic laboratory at Comiso airfield during mid-1941. (Author's photo)

Less than a month after the start of the operational phase, on 26 January 1941, the reconnaissance department of 1.(F)/121 recorded the loss of a Ju 88 photographic scout. The aircraft, coded '7A+DH' and flown by Leutnant Helmut Fund, was intercepted at 2:30 p.m., at 10,000 feet, near the Sicilian coast by two Hurricanes while it was returning from a sortie over the central Mediterranean. A slightly better fate befell a 3.(F)/121 reconnaissance aircraft as it was able to return to Sicily with serious damage and a mortally wounded crew member.[4]

On 9 February 1941, the *Luftwaffe* further increased its presence on the island, sending 14 Messerschmitt Bf 109Es of 7./JG 26 (7th Squadron of *Jagdgeschwader* 26) to Gela Ponte Olivo air base. They were led by ace Oberleutnant Joachim Müncheberg.[5]

No. 69 Squadron and its first ops (January–April 1941)

The battle for the Mediterranean was becoming increasingly fierce; on 10 January 1941 Ju 87 Stuka dive-bombers and SM.79 torpedo bombers attacked the British convoys engaged in Operation *Excess* (the resupply of Malta, Alexandria and Greece). In the afternoon, the aircraft carrier HMS *Illustrious* was attacked by more than 40 Ju 87Bs, of II./SG 2, and long-range Ju 87Rs, of I./SG 1, led by Major Walter Enneccerus and Hauptmann Paul-Werner Hozzel respectively. Heinkel He 111s of II./KG 26 also took part in the bombing. The carrier was hit seven times. A 1,000kg bomb penetrated the armoured flight deck and exploded in the hangar. The ship was repaired in the United States and did not return to Britain until the end of the year.

On the same day, No. 431 General Reconnaissance Flight on Malta became No. 69 Squadron, with the motto 'With Vigilance We Serve'. Squadron Leader Ernest Whiteley remained in command. The following day, 11 January, a lone aircraft of the 'new' unit, Maryland I AR707, left Malta at 7:00 a.m. for a photographic sortie to Taranto. On the return flight, the pilot flew over the east coast of Sicily. Near Catania, at about 10,000 feet, the Maryland was intercepted by Tenente Pilota Antonio Palazzeschi, flying a Macchi MC.200 belonging to the *6° Gruppo Autonomo CT* (*Caccia Terrestre* – land-based fighters), and shot down.

The aircraft crashed alongside the Primosole bridge, near the city of Catania, killing the entire crew–Sergeants Renè Duvauchelle, George Taylor and Jacques Méhouas.[6] The Italian pilot mistook the aircraft for a Bristol Blenheim. Shortly after, the British intercepted an Italian radio message announcing: 'Today one of our fighters, on a patrol mission, intercepted a Blenheim type aircraft south of Catania.'[7]

On 12 January, in anticipation of an RAF night raid on Sicily,[8] 69 Squadron sent Maryland AR705 to photograph Catania and Augusta just before midday. The crew, Flying Officer J.B.

4   Cull, Galea, *Hurricanes Over Malta*, p.67.
5   Jerry Scutts, *Bf 109 Aces of North Africa and the Mediterranean* (Oxford: Osprey Publishing, 1994), p.6.
6   With the fall of France, some *Armée de l'Air* aircraft fled to British bases in the Mediterranean. On 5 July 1940, Premier-Maître (Chief Petty Officer) René Duvauchelle and his radio operator, Quartier-Maître (Quartermaster) Jacques Méhouas, arrived at Malta, from Bizerte in Tunisia, on board a Latécoère seaplane of *Escadrille 2HT*.
7   The National Archives London, Royal Air Force, Operations Record Books, 69 Squadron AIR 27/610/5.
8   To further enhance the offensive capacity of Malta, Wellington bombers had been deployed to Luqa the previous October. With a bomb load capacity of 4,500lb and a range of more than 2,500 miles, the 'Wimpy' was capable of reaching Rome.

Boys-Stones, and Sergeants Bastard and Berrett, had barely landed at Luqa (at 2:30 p.m.) when Intelligence staff rushed the film off for processing and analysis. The information gleaned from the images was transmitted to No. 148 Squadron for inclusion in the bomber crews' final briefing for the pending raid. From 6:36 p.m., two flights of Vickers Wellington Mk.IC bombers (A Flight with six bombers, B Flight with four) departed for the airfield and port at Catania.[9] An A Flight aircraft, flown by Flying Officer Osborne, was hit by anti-aircraft fire over the target and forced to land near Malta; two of the four crew members, second pilot Sergeant Hall and observer Sergeant Reardon, died from their injuries. An even more tragic fate met the five men on board Wellington 'W' T2874 of B Flight. Commanded by Pilot Officer Noble, it left last at 10:37 p.m. and never returned, crashing near Catania. The entire crew was killed. At the end of the raid, the RAF could claim the destruction of 40 aircraft and two hangars at Catania Fontanarossa. From Bollettino n. 220 of 13 January 1941:

> During the night of 12/13, the enemy made air raids … on Catania, with some damage and no casualties. In Catania, the anti-aircraft defence shot down an aircraft that crashed near the city …

To verify the extent of the damage inflicted on Catania, at 11:35 a.m. on 13 January, Whiteley sent Boys-Stones and Sergeants Alexander and Gimson to survey Catania in Maryland AR705.

At 6:50 a.m. the following day, a reconnaissance of Palermo and Catania was carried out. However, due to bad weather, Adrian Warburton and Sergeants Alexander and Moren, in AR735, were unable to photograph the latter target. The same did not apply to the area around Palermo where anti-aircraft fire was encountered at 10,000 feet. Some fighters scrambled from Palermo Boccadifalco following the alarm. The operational diary of the *I° Stormo CT, 17° Gruppo Caccia* reported:

> At 12:20 a Macchi aircraft scrambled to intercept an enemy aircraft at high altitude over Palermo. The aircraft escaped the pursuit and disappeared into the clouds.

This dangerous situation repeated itself on 15 January, on another reconnaissance flight over Catania, when Maryland I AR721, with Flying Officer Foxton and Sergeants Spiers and Gridley on board, was intercepted by an MC.200 at 14,000 feet. The Macchi, probably already airborne on a regular patrol, chased the Maryland for more than 100 miles, but was unable to shoot it down despite scoring some hits with its Breda-SAFAT machine guns.

---

9   For the period from 31 October 1940 to 28 February 1941, Catania was the airfield most bombed by 148 Squadron, with 41 sorties, followed by Comiso with seven. Among the ports, the most bombed was Messina (seven), with Palermo (three) and Syracuse and Augusta, with just one apiece, also receiving attention.

Kampfgeschwader 26 (KG 26) 'Löwengeschwader' (Bomber Wing 26, 'Lions' Wing' by virtue of its insignia) members posing in front of a Heinkel He 111 at Catania Fontanarossa. The lattice structure in the background is a hangar. (ACS 09916)

A Heinkel He 111 pilot of KG 26 talks to another officer from his 'front office'. The nose carries the famous *Gruppe* 'Löwen' badge with the Latin motto 'Vestigium Iconis'. (ACS 09919)

Surprise was great on Malta when, a few days later, 19 January, a brand-new photo-reconnaissance Spitfire (P9551, coded 'PY') landed and taxied across the rough, bomb-scarred terrain at Takali. The arrival of the Spitfire was completely unexpected. The aircraft, flown by Flight Lieutenant Peter Corbishley, had left England to reconnoitre the shores of Genoa in anticipation of Operation *Grog* (naval bombardment of Genoa). Corbishley was forced to head towards Malta due to a strong headwind. The Spitfire would be the first of its type to be used in a photographic survey of Sicily. [10]

At 8:05 on the morning of 31 January, Flying Officer Adrian Warburton, together with Sergeants Alexander and Berrett, took off in Maryland I AR705 for an aerial reconnaissance over eastern Sicily. Three warships were seen anchored in the port of Messina, unidentified fighter planes were spotted leaving Sicily for the Italian peninsula, and the port of Catania revealed little of interest besides a few modestly sized merchant ships. At Catania Fontanarossa, however, more than 100 aircraft were visible along the perimeter of the runway. Finally, at the Syracuse seaplane base, six seaplanes were seen on the buoys, while the shapes of two submarines and six seaplanes were clearly distinguishable at Augusta.

With the arrival of the German *Afrika Korps* in Libya in February 1941, British reconnaissance activity of the main ports of Sicily and southern Italy was increased. A special photo-interpretation section was created; the service, directed by Adrian Warburton, specialised in monitoring the movements of cargo ships bound for North Africa.

On 9 February, at 10:05 a.m., Warburton, with Sergeants Spires and Moren, flew Maryland I AR713 to Calitri in the province of Avellino. The sortie lasted six hours. Reconnaissance of Calitri had already been carried out on 15, 16 and 25 January but, for various reasons, both meteorological and technical, the results had been negative or inconclusive. All of this effort was in anticipation of the first deployment of British airborne troops on Italian territory, scheduled for the evening of 10 February. The raid (Operation *Colossus*, consisting of 35 men, mostly from No. 11 Special Air Service Battalion, as X Troop) left Malta on board six Armstrong-Whitworth Whitleys and reached the small town of Calitri to sabotage the imposing Apulian aqueduct, thereby hindering the Italian war effort and affecting their morale. Once the raid had been completed, the submarine HMS *Triumph* was waiting for the commandos about 60 miles away. Unfortunately, however, all of the men were captured soon after successfully destroying part of the aqueduct which was subsequently repaired in short order. Three days later, at 9:15 a.m., the same crew that had carried out the survey of Calitri on 9 February flew to the town of Avellino to photograph the results of the sabotage from 20,000 feet. No opposition was encountered.

---

10   On 2 February, Flight Lieutenant Peter Corbishley left Malta for a photographic survey of Genoa and Leghorn. He was hit by anti-aircraft fire over Viareggio. After baling out, Corbishley was taken prisoner.

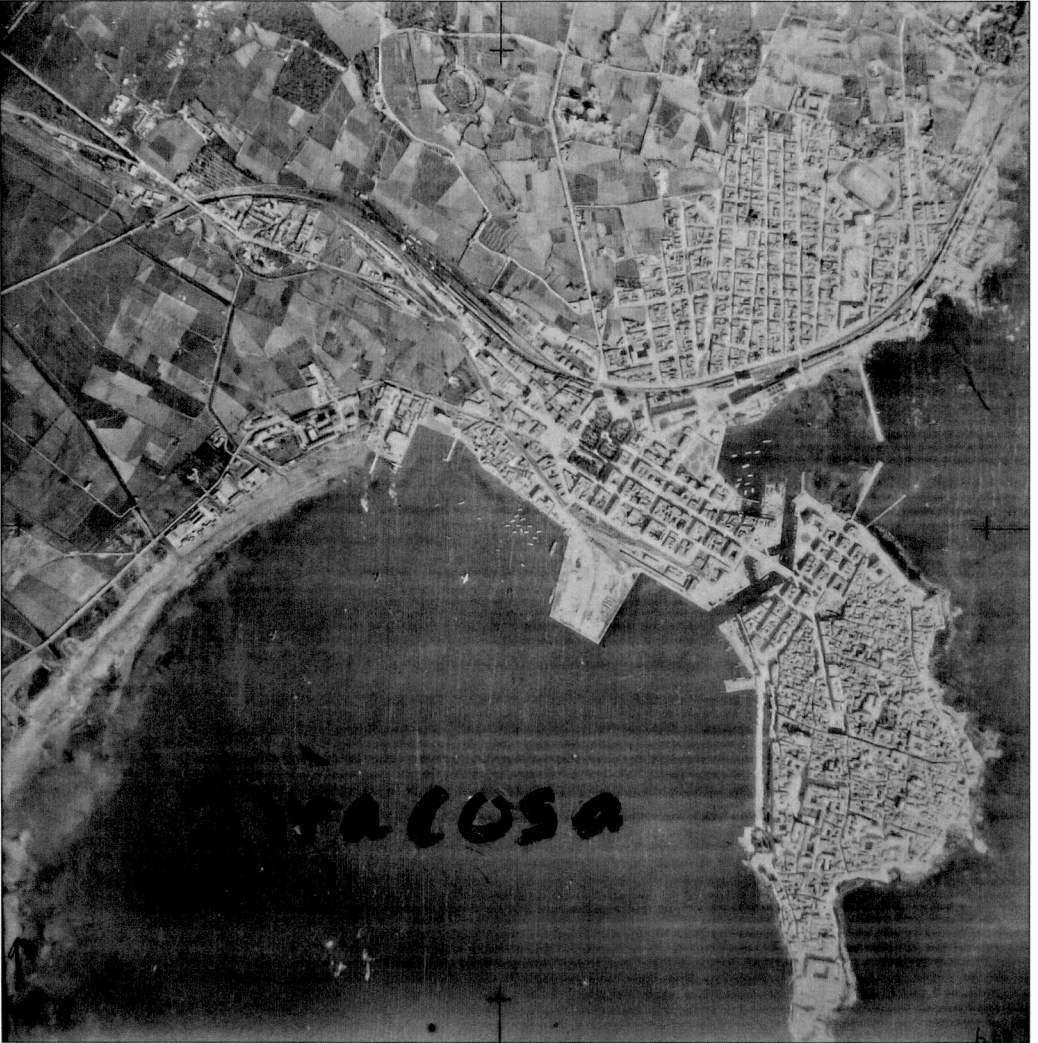

An image taken during an aerial reconnaissance of Syracuse clearly shows some seaplanes on the buoys near the port. (Author's photo)

The small fishing village of Marina di Ragusa photographed by the RAF at the beginning of the conflict. (Author's photo)

A view of Trapani Milo airfield. In addition to the fuel drums, there are some Fiat CR.42s and a Junkers Ju 87 landing on the runway. (Alessandro Ragatzu)

The failure of the Italian aircraft industry to produce a viable attack aircraft led to the use of the Junkers Ju 87 by the *Regia Aeronautica*. Flying Ju 87Bs, the *208ª Squadriglia, 101° Gruppo BaT*, was based at Lecce in March 1941 before it acquired longer-range Ju 87Rs for use against Malta from Trapani. (ACS 21952)

The sortie on 13 February was like so many more before it; Maryland I AR713 taking off at 11:40 a.m. from Luqa. The expertise of Flying Officer Williams and Sergeants Alexander and Berrett led to the discovery of a secret airfield, hidden for months, near a dense wooded area between the towns of Biscari (now Acate) and Caltagirone:

> Recco of Comiso – Gela Aerodromes. Weather Fine. Photographs taken from 2000'.
> New Aerodrome located near Biscari. Oblique photographs taken with Leica by observer very successful.[11]

In addition to this extraordinary discovery, another important sighting was made by Warburton who, during a sortie, identified the newly arrived Messerschmitt Bf 109Es of 7./JG 26 temporarily parked on the Catania Fontanarossa perimeter track.

February was characterised mainly by bad weather over Sicily, so much so as to compromise the use of photographic equipment at high altitudes; the equipment was often 'literally frozen', as reported by the crews themselves. For this reason, in many cases it became necessary to

11   The National Archives London, Royal Air Force, Operations Record Books, 69 Squadron AIR 27/606/12, p.3.

use a Leica manual camera. In total, 69 Squadron managed to perform 22 sorties, with the five Marylands available, for a total of 90 hours and five minutes of flying. A new Maryland (AR706) was also brought out from UK by Squadron Leader Whiteley, Sergeant Preater and Corporal Shephard.

In addition to the now obligatory visits to the ports of Taranto and Messina, and the airfields of Gela Ponte Olivo, Comiso and Catania, some sorties were flown to Tripoli and Sardinia.

Summary of operations carried out by Wellington bombers from Malta between 31 October 1940 and 28 February 1941					
Target	Raids	Sorties	General Purpose (lb)	Semi Armour Piercing (lb)	Incendiary (lb)
Catania Airfield	9	41	134,250	-	14,860
Tripoli Harbour	6	46	135,000	35,900	9,800
Castel Benito Airfield	4	38	87,980	-	16,520
Bari Harbour	3	18	27,500	-	3,590
Brindisi Harbour	3	13	16,750	5,000	1,680
Taranto Harbour	3	16	23,000	13,750	2,400
Augusta Harbour	1	1	2,000	-	-
Comiso Airfield	5	7	15,750	-	6,720
Crotone Chemical Works	2	2	1,750	2,750	240
Palermo Harbour	2	3	2,500	5,250	-
Capodichino Airfield	1	3	6,750	-	720
Mellaha Airfield	1	2	1,000	-	480
Messina Harbour	1	7	9,000	9,000	480
Siracusa Harbour	1	1	2,500	-	960
Torre Annunziata Arsenal	1	1	-	2,750	-
Napoli Harbour	3	21	5,000	36,250	1,360
Napoli Oil Refinery	5	10	21,500	-	6,160
Napoli Railway Station	4	9	19,250	-	1,200
Valona (Albania)	1	4	9,000	-	960
Total	56	243	520,480	110,650	68,130

Maryland I AR707 of No. 69 Squadron RAF was shot down over Catania by Tenente Pilota Antonio Palazzeschi and crashed not far from the Primosole bridge. (ACS 10033, 10034)

At 9:55 a.m. on 7 March, Maryland AR706 was sent to Taormina, the *Luftwaffe* headquarters in Sicily. On board was the experienced crew of Flying Officer Boys-Stones and Sergeants Alexander and Levy. During a pass over Taormina, at an altitude of 21,000 feet, an Italian monoplane fighter suddenly emerged from a bank of clouds less than 400 yards away. The shells from its guns did not strike home but forced the RAF men to abandon their tasking and return to Malta while outrunning the Italian. On the way back, they attacked a CANT Z.506, but only managed to damage the enemy floatplane.

Malta, warned of the danger, immediately sent Hurricane P2645 of No. 261 Squadron to the rescue; Sergeant Jessop was at the controls on his first local flight. Not far from Malta, however, an ambush awaited in the form of six 7./JG 26 Bf 109s. The Bf 109E of Oberfeldwebel Karl Kühdorf shot the unfortunate Jessop while the Maryland was attacked by Leutnant Hans Johannsen who mistook it for a Blenheim. Johannsen's well-aimed bursts set fire to one of the Pratt & Whitney engines, the Maryland falling in flames just 11 miles north of Dingli. For Boys-Stones and Levy, 22 and 27-years-old respectively, there was no escape; Alexander bailed out seriously injured.[12]

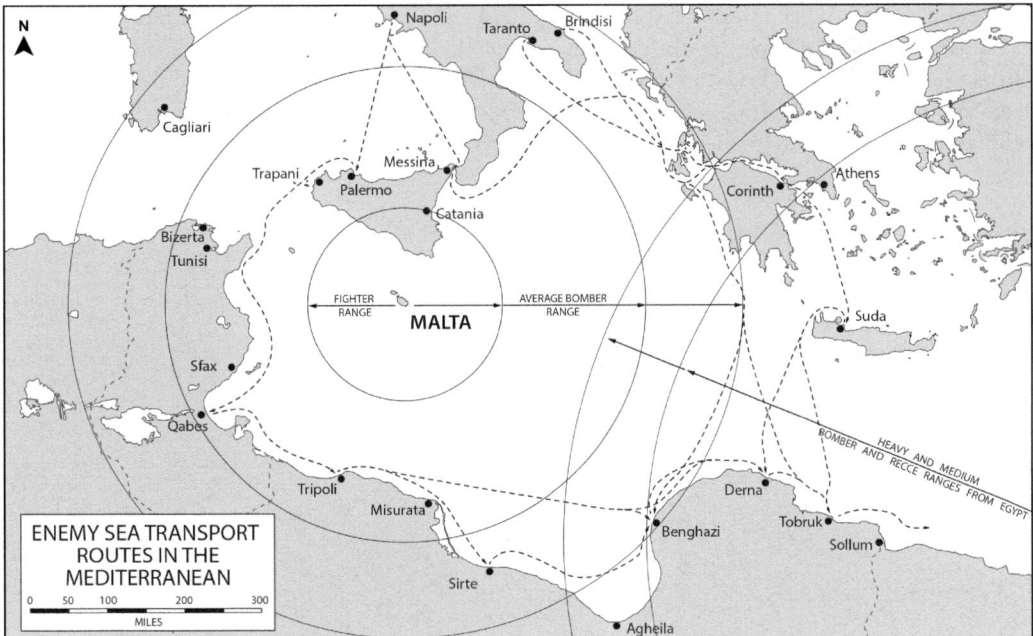

Radius of action for aircraft based on Malta. (AFHRA)

---

12   The National Archives London, Royal Air Force, Operations Record Books AIR 27/610/7.

Three days earlier, the same fate had occurred to a German reconnaissance aircraft, a Bf 110 ('4U+ZK') of 2.(F)/123, shot down 30 miles north of the island of Gozo while surveying Malta.[13] Two other aircraft of 1.(F)/121, coded '7A+GH' and '7A+BH', arrived in Catania on the 23 April.[14]

Malta, to compensate for its heavy losses, also received reinforcements. The few and precious longer-ranged photo-reconnaissance aircraft could arrive by air from Gibraltar (or direct from England). Shorter range fighters, such as the Hurricane, had to arrive in the Mediterranean on aircraft carriers, running the gauntlet of attacks on the convoys by Axis aircraft and naval forces before flying off to Malta.[15] In the late morning from 11 to 15 March, after about six hours in the air, four Marylands from England arrived without having encountered opposition on the way. Joining 69 Squadron with their crews were: AR714, Flying Officer Ainley; AR724, Flying Officer Wylde; AR727, Flying Officer Bloxam; and AR741, Pilot Officer Drew.

That same month, the MAS (*Motoscafo Armato Silurante* – Torpedo Armed Speedboats) of *II Flottiglia* left the seaplane base at Augusta to establish a base at Porto Empedocle and Trapani, thus near the waters of the Sicilian channel, in order to be able to intervene more quickly as operational needs arose. To provide assistance for this unit, at the small but important Porto Empedocle, the 3rd *Schnellboot* (fast boat) flotilla of the *Kriegsmarine* arrived in mid-December. Syracuse received the *Seenotzentrale Sirakus*, *Seenotstaffel 6*, whose He 59 seaplanes and Do 24 flying boats would provide a sea rescue service. Finally, in Augusta, almost all of the fuel storage facilities at the seaplane base, in which 2,267 tons of aviation petrol and 56 tons of lubricating oil could be stored, were made available to the Germans.[16]

13   The National Archives London, Royal Air Force, Sicily: reports on airfields and aircraft, AIR 40/1996.
14   *Ibid. Staffel* 1.(F)/121 had 15 aircraft but only nine were usable; *Staffel* 2. (F)/123 had 14 reconnaissance aircraft, seven were usable; both units were based at Catania. John Weal, *Junkers Ju 88 Kampfgeschwader in North Africa and the Mediterranean* (Oxford: Osprey Publishing, 2009), p.90.
15   German U-boats were busy patrolling the Strait of Gibraltar. On 13 November 1941, for example, the aircraft carrier HMS *Ark Royal* of Force K was hit, and sunk, by a torpedo launched by U-81 under the command of Kapitänleutnant Friedrich Guggenberger.
16   Marcon, *Augusta 1940*-1943, p.35.

Capitano Dante Ocarso, helped by a specialist, climbs into a Macchi MC.200 of the *88ª Squadriglia, 6° Gruppo, 1° Stormo CT* at Catania airfield. Note the winged archer symbol on the fuselage. (ACS 04094)

A BR.20 of the *277ª Squadriglia, 116° Gruppo BT, 37° Stormo* from Catania Fontanarossa. In October 1941, the unit carried out many night raids over Malta. (ACS 31014)

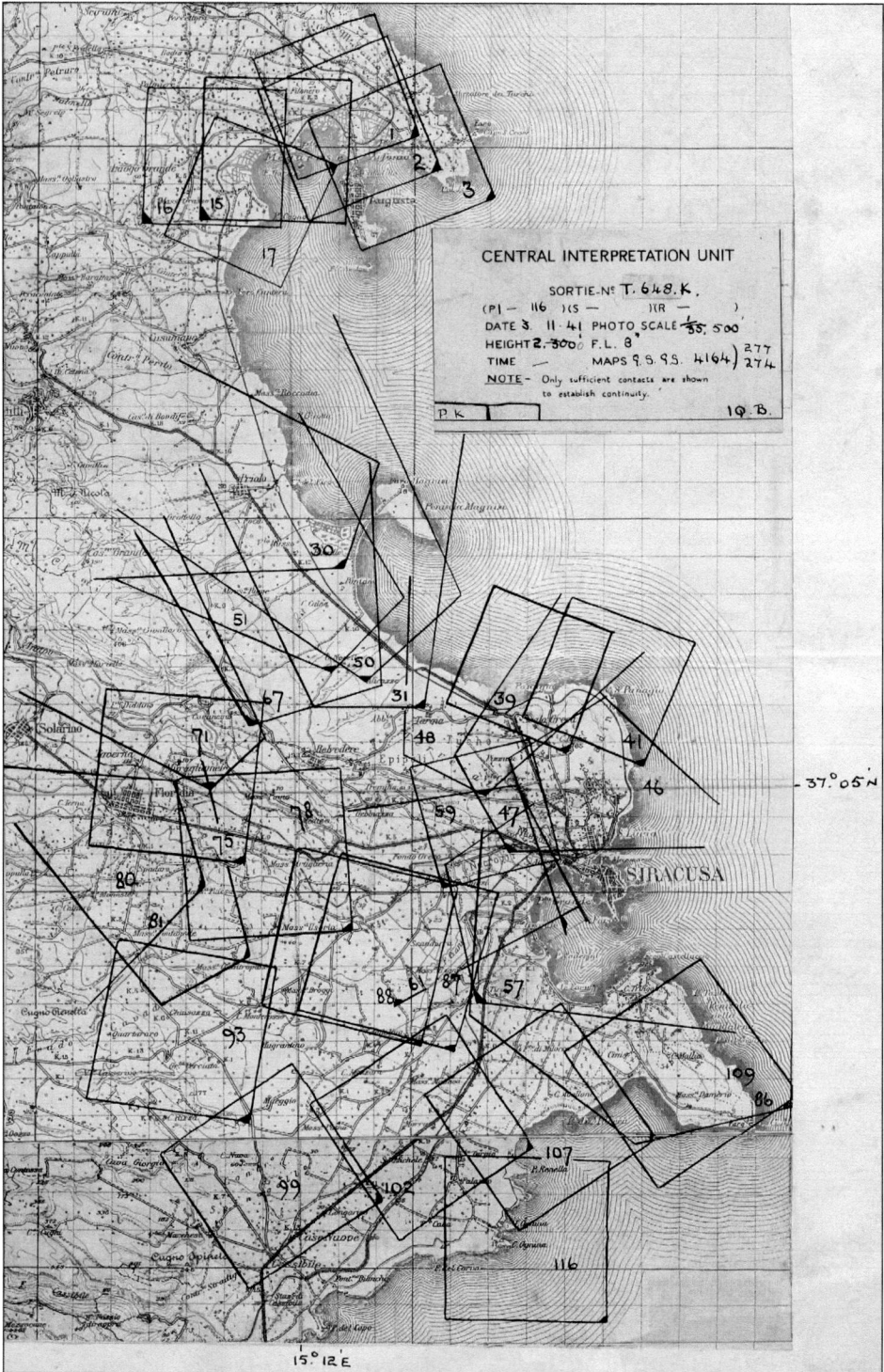

The area between Augusta and Syracuse photographed by Flight Lieutenant R.J.S. Wootton in PR
Hurricane Z3053 on 3 November 1941. (MEIU)

5

PR Hurricanes Over Sicily

Early in April, HMS *Ark Royal* sailed again towards Malta with a dozen new Hawker Hurricane IIAs which had been delivered to Gibraltar by HMS *Argus*. The Hurricanes were launched on the morning of 3 April, led by Skuas for navigation purposes. The tragedy of 7 March made the men of No. 69 Squadron think a lot about their future operations. There was the need for smaller and faster reconnaissance aircraft, able to quickly escape from the approaching enemy and, at the same time, reduce the risk of being spotted in flight.

It was decided, therefore, to modify some Hurricanes, then in use by No. 261 Squadron and other units on Malta, to perform the photo-reconnaissance role. Between late April and May 1941, 69 Squadron converted a Hurricane Mk.II.[1] Its first operation over hostile territory was carried out on 25 April from 11:10 a.m. to 12:15 p.m. The original PR Hurricane on strength (V7101), piloted by veteran Squadron Leader George Burges, headed for Gela, Syracuse and Comiso to perform vertical photographic surveys. A particular note about Comiso was placed in the squadron's diary as 38 aircraft were visible. George Burges remembered the conversion of the Hurricane into a photo-reconnaissance machine:

> We took out the guns, radio, armour plate, and anything else we could safely get rid of, and installed two cameras. Unfortunately, we didn't have the facilities to install extra fuel tanks, and so we knew its range would be restricted to Sicily. What wouldn't we have given for one of the blue Spitfires the PR chaps were using in the UK! Incidentally, we painted our Hurricane blue, mainly to enable our gunners to recognize it! I actually got this aircraft up to 36,000 feet but I think by stripping so much out it we had probably moved the centre of gravity too far back because at this height, if one wasn't careful, it whipped into a spin. I used to operate at about 30,000 feet and at this height could cover two or three targets in Sicily in one sortie.[2]

---

1   This was Hurricane Z3053 which joined Hurricane Mk.I V7101.
2   Cull, Galea, *Hurricanes Over Malta*, p.93.

Burges carried out four sorties in V7101, the flights almost always carried out over the airfields at Comiso, Gela and Catania, and on the waterways of Augusta and Syracuse, before leaving Malta in late June.[3]

In the meantime, Ultra continued to provide decrypted messages confirming movements of aircraft of the *Regia Aeronautica* to and from Sicily and North Africa. Intelligence from a message intercepted on 29 April read:

> An aircraft of the 13th Squadron, 26th Wing, 9th Bomber Regiment was identified at Sciacca on 27th April, but it is not known whether this is merely a single aircraft of this unit or whether the whole of the 13th Squadron or 26th Wing or 9th Bomber Regiment is now located in Sicily. The 9th Bomber Regiment was formerly located in Libya, from which theatre it was withdrawn at the end of January.[4]

The Marylands, which remained the most used aircraft in the squadron, were suffering reduced operational availability (only three aircraft), a delay in spare parts arriving from England forcing the other aircraft to remain on the ground. The type's operational use over the mainland was declining, however, giving way to maritime reconnaissance over the Strait of Sicily.[5]

In the late morning of 9 June, Flying Officer R.A. Hilton-Barber flew a reconnaissance over the Augusta fortress in Hurricane V7101. He saw six submarines and some CANT Z.506 and Ro.44 seaplanes. On the buoys near Syracuse were three CANT Z.501s, a Cant Z.506 and an Ro.43. Hilton-Barber was one of the original Hurricane pilots to operate from Malta and, from 11 June, was attached to the squadron from Command Headquarters, to specifically fly the PRU Hurricanes. On the 21st, Squadron Leader R.D. Welland, who had just succeeded Ernest Whiteley in command of the unit (4 June), carried out a further study over Augusta in V7101, noting 15 seaplanes moored to buoys.

At first light on 23 June, a formation of four Hurricanes of No. 46 Squadron[6], led by Squadron Leader A.C. Rabagliati DFC (a South African), performed a surprise attack on the seaplane base at Syracuse. Rabagliati wrote in his combat report:

> At 0525 attack was delivered on six Italian flying boats at moorings in the following manner. Dived to sea level in bay just south of Syracuse, pulled up over neck of land

---

3   Two other 69 Squadron pilots, Flying Officers Roger Drew and Bob Wootton, made their first flights in a PR Hurricane the same month. Hilton-Barber made 13 flights over Sicily (six with V7101 and seven with Z3053) visiting Comiso, Gela, Catania, Augusta, Syracuse, Gerbini, Messina, Trapani and Palermo. Adrian Warburton made as many flights in a PR Hurricane as he did in a Maryland during this period.

4   The National Archives London, Royal Air Force, Sicily: reports on airfields and aircraft, AIR 40/1996.

5   In April, 69 Squadron had five Maryland Is, the other two were lost (AR735 mistakenly shot down by a Hurricane on 14 April; AR705 damaged by bombing on 24 April). They specialised in observing the ports of Genoa, La Spezia, Naples and Taranto, and the coast of Tunisia.

6   Under the codename Operation *Rocket*, 43 Hurricane IIs arrived from the carriers *Ark Royal* and *Furious*. Those belonging to No. 229 Squadron, which was destined for Egypt, were exchanged for Malta's remaining Mk.Is, while those from No. 46 Squadron were to remain on Malta under command of Squadron Leader AC 'Sandy' Rabagliati DFC.

Several views of PR Hurricane Mk.IIC DG622 belonging to No. 2 PRU, RAF, at Heliopolis in Egypt. Posing on the wing, first from right, is Algernon de Blois Spurr. This aircraft operated from Malta over Sicily for a short time. (Brian Spurr)

Algernon de Blois Spurr completing the installation and adjustment of an F.24 camera on Hurricane DG622. This aircraft carried two F.24 cameras in port and starboard positions. (Brian Spurr)

between bay and machine-gunned three flying boats, barracks and blockhouse. Attack was delivered at 250mph. Turned east directly after attack and flew out to sea.[7]

Algernon de Blois Spurr holding an F.24 camera. (Brian Spurr)

Algernon de Blois Spurr inside a photographic laboratory in a trailer. The trailer was equipped with everything needed for the development of the slides. (Brian Spurr)

The Marylands Attack (June – July 1941)

The senior officers of the *Regia Marina* believed the best shipping route for the convoys loaded with supplies for North Africa was to the east, crossing the Strait of Messina, then following the Sicilian coast, thus passing east of Malta. On 25 June, Flying Officer Hilton-Barber, on board PR Hurricane Z3053, found himself, at about 10:00 a.m., over a portion of the sea between Messina and Naples trying to intercept a large naval convoy reported to have sailed. Only a few

7   Cull, Galea, *Hurricanes Over Malta*, p.113.

destroyers were seen, just west of Palmi, in Calabria, with three others spotted west of Capo Vaticano. The sortie was repeated at 4:20 p.m. by Flying Officer RR Drew who, flying the same Hurricane, spotted a large Italian naval fleet sailing south near the Strait of Messina. The sighting was recorded as:

> Recco Messina strait and harbor (3 Cruisers 8 merchant vessels); 4 merchant vessels, 7 destroyers 205 C. Spartivento 35' [degrees] Co. 205-15 kts; 2 Battleships enter in Messina straits Co. B, 20 kts.[8]

The large naval formation included the 11,398-ton *Esperia*, under the command of Capitano Emanuele Stagnaro, the *Marco Polo*, of 12,272 tons, and the large motor ships *Neptunia* (19,328 tons) and *Oceania* (19,507 tons); all were former passenger ships ideal for use as troop transports. They left Naples at 4:30 a.m., escorted by the destroyers *Aviere* (lead escort, Capitano Luciano Bigi), *Geniere*, *Vincenzo Gioberti* and *Antonio da Noli*, and the torpedo boat *Calliope*. The head of the convoy was Contrammiraglio (Rear Admiral) Luigi Aiello embarked on the *Esperia*.

The Italians did not in the least suspect that already, on 23 June, two days before their departure, the British, thanks to Ultra, had learned that a convoy formed by *Neptunia*, *Oceania*, *Marco Polo* and *Esperia*, escorted by five destroyers, would depart Naples at 3:30 a.m. direct for Tripoli, with arrival expected at 4:30 p.m. on the 27th, sailing at a speed of about 17 knots.[9] Further interceptions, also carried out on 23 June, allowed the British to learn the convoy must cross the 34th parallel at 7:00 a.m. on the 26th, would be escorted by aircraft, and that, after unloading their cargo, would return to Naples.

After crossing the Strait of Messina, the escort was reinforced by *XII Squadriglia*, the destroyers *Ascari*, *Lanciere*, *Corazziere* and *Carabiniere* and, later, from sunset, by *III Divisione*, the heavy cruisers *Trieste* and *Gorizia*, the latter leaving Messina at 7: p.m. as an indirect escort.[10] At 6:25 p.m., whilst the ships were still not far from Syracuse, 32 miles by 90° from Capo Murro di Porco to be precise, the convoy was again sighted by Pilot Officer J.R. Bloxam, and Sergeants Preater and Moses, flying Maryland AR714. Bloxam established rapid radio contact with Malta to report the exact location of the convoy. A few moments later, crews climbed into the four Marylands available to 69 Squadron, already loaded with 500lb bombs (each aircraft could carry up to 2,000lb) in anticipation for a shipping attack. These aircraft included AR741 (Warburton and Sergeants Bastard and Moren), AR726 (Flight Sergeants B.P. Hanson, Bolton and Gimson), AR733 (Squadron Leader Welland, Flying Officer M.L. Walls and Sergeant Wilkins), and AR729 (Flight Sergeant JW Bibby, Sub-lieutenant Cook and Sergeant Lawson). They had just spotted the silhouettes of the convoy, when AR726 was suddenly attacked and shot down by a Macchi MC.200, of the *84ª Squadriglia*, *10° Gruppo*, *4° Stormo CT* (*Caccia Terrestre* – land-based fighters), flown by Sergente Roberto Steppi who had seen the British plane over the canal at about 8,000 feet.[11] On board the ships, the air raid alarms sounded;

---

8   The National Archives London, Royal Air Force, Operations Record Books AIR 27/606/18.

9   In fact, the British initially make a mistake and identified the fourth ship as *Victoria*, but the mistake was promptly corrected on 24 June.

10   Other sources report that *Lanciere* was part of the direct escort from the start of the voyage.

11   Shortly before, at 8:20 p.m., the air escort of two SM.79 bombers and four Macchi MC.200 fighters had left, leaving the convoy without aerial protection, with the exception of Steppi's aircraft.

both the merchant ships and the destroyers immediately opening fire. The Marylands dropped their bombs from medium altitude above the convoy. As confirmed by a spotter aircraft, only Warburton managed a single hit.

Meanwhile, two formations from 830 Naval Air Squadron (NAS), each made up of three torpedo-armed Fairey Swordfish, took off from Delimara Point, Malta. They found the convoy at 8:40 p.m.; approaching from starboard, they were greeted by anti-aircraft fire from the escort ships. The Swordfish fired machine gun bursts but left without delivering their torpedoes.

At 9:10 p.m. a flare ignited ahead of the convoy, at about 10,000 feet, and illuminated the area for about 8–9 minutes. The experience of the crews on the ships had taught them this was the prelude to an attack by torpedo bombers; the escort ships began to emit smoke screens in an attempt to conceal the convoy. As expected, torpedo bombers attacked at 9:29; coming from starboard and remaining in formation, they passed ahead of the convoy and then separated to attack from both bow quarters. The ships opened fire but at least four torpedoes were launched. One passed astern of the *Esperia*, the ship having avoided it, and exploded.

While the torpedo attack was still underway, at 9:37, three flares were launched. T25wo went out almost immediately, but the third remained lit for a couple of minutes, illuminating the convoy with its very strong yellow light. The ships spread out and spotted the navigation lights of other aircraft, against which they fired all weapons that could be brought to bear. The aircraft dropped large bombs; none hit, but one exploded just to starboard of the *Esperia*, at the height of the ship's number nine launch. The displacement of air caused by the detonation damaged the superstructure of the steamer, which was also hit by bursts of machine gun fire. A machine-gunner, 21-year-old Sergente Universitario Michele Romano, was killed while two German non-commissioned officers were seriously injured, and 17 crew members slightly injured. At 9:45 p.m., the aircraft departed, chased by defensive fire from the ships. One 830 NAS Swordfish was shot down; its crew, Sub-lieutenant D.A.R. Holmes and Leading Seaman J.R. Smith, were listed as missing in action.

On 22 July 1941, a seaplane of the *Nucleo Comunicazioni dell'Ala Littoria* (Communications Unit of the airline Ala Littoria) took off from Syracuse for Benghazi. CANT Z.506C (MM60468) was flown by Annibale Pecoroni and Aldo Gabucci. On board were radio operator Sottotenente Bruno Zigam, Motorista Sergente Maggiore Cristoforo Zevola and, among the passengers, Agostino Tagliaferri and Antonio Freschi, officers of the Italian Army. The crew was not informed in time of an air alarm in progress so, after just 12 minutes of flight, they were intercepted by Maryland BJ427, piloted by Flying Officer Adrian Warburton, with Sergeants Moren and Bastard, returning from a mission to Taranto. The Maryland quickly got on the tail of the seaplane, immediately damaging the left engine and the wings.

The aircraft immediately landed after launching a distress signal. According to the Italian version, Warburton returned, strafing the seaplane, which was now in flames with some of its occupants already in the water. Zevola was killed at this time. The survivors were recovered a few hours later by a trawler and an air-sea rescue CANT Z.506 of the *612ª Squadriglia* from Syracuse.

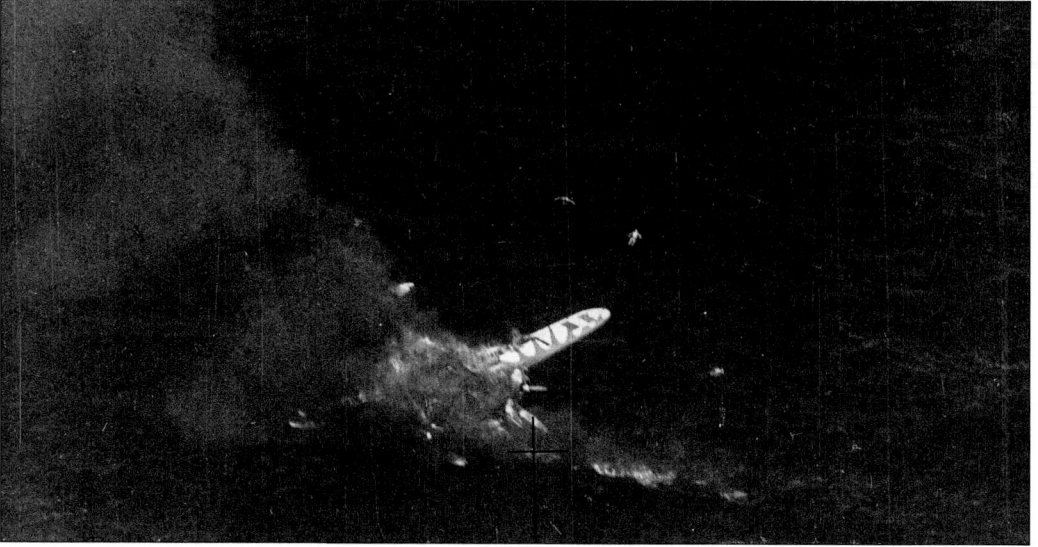

The *Nucleo Comunicazioni dell'Ala Littoria* CANT Z.506C in flames after being shot down by Adrian Warburton on 22 July 1941. Note the silhouettes of some of the crew in the water. (Frank Bastard)

Damage to some buildings at Catania Fontanarossa, caused by bombing during the summer of 1941. Some Italian officers can be seen, along with a German soldier on the right. In the background is the silhouette of a twin-engine aircraft. (Author's photo)

Maltese Offensive (August – September 1941)

The Vickers Wellingtons of No. 38 Squadron (with operational headquarters at Shallufa in Egypt, but some detached to Luqa from the previous August), having systematically bombing Tripoli and Benghazi from the beginning of the month, and even attacking the Corinth canal in Greece, launched heavy and repeated raids against the airfields of the major Sicilian cities which provided logistical support to transport aircraft and merchant ships destined for North Africa. The Wellingtons had been absent from Maltese and Sicilian skies following the arrival of *X Fliegerkorps* and the Bf 109s of 7./JG 26 led by ace Oberleutnant Joachim Müncheberg. During the *Staffel's* stay in Gela Ponte Olivo, before being transferred to the Greek front and then North Africa[12], it provided exceptional air protection and extraordinary offensive capacity alongside similar Italian units. The airfields and ports, and consequently the cities near them, experienced a period of surreal tranquility after the incessant RAF bombings between the fourth quarter of 1940 and the first two months of 1941.

The survey on 1 August of Catania Fontanarossa and Gerbini, by Flying Officer Hilton-Barber in Hurricane V7101, proved fruitful. Moored at Catania were six large merchant ships; at Fontanarossa, 12 Ju 52/3m transports, 22 SM.79 and BR.20M bombers, and 15 fighters; on the airfield at Gerbini were six SM.79s, 15 BR.20Ms and seven fighters; finally, Comiso was found to be hosting 52 fighters and a large transport aircraft.[13]

By mid-May, *X Fliegerkorps* had completed its transfer to the Greek front and, at the same time, many assets of the *Regia Aeronautica*, especially fighters, were operational in North Africa. For a few months, therefore, Malta had the opportunity to regroup and strike back. On the night of 5/6 August, 830 NAS of the Fleet Air Arm sent five Swordfish from Hal Far to dive-bomb the submarine depot and oil storage tanks at Augusta.

Kenneth Poolman, in his *Night Strike from Malta*, observed:

> After an hour's flying [Sub-Lieutenant] Cotton's aircraft fell out of the formation with engine trouble, but with great determination he pressed on to the target, ably navigated through the sea mist and ground haze by the experienced [Sub-Lieutenant] Robertson in the observer's office. Augusta was not too difficult to find as the moon was up and the main striking force had started several large fires which were still burning when Cotton arrived an hour late. Black smoke was rising from a very bad fire on the submarine jetty and there was another big conflagration near the Nafta storage tanks. Cotton added his eight incendiaries and two 500-pounders to blaze.

Tullio Marcon, in his book *Augusta 1940-1943 Cronache di una piazzaforte* (Chronicles of a Stronghold), reconstructed the attack:

---

12   In Molaoi, Greece, from 25 May to 14 June, and subsequently in Libya, to Ain-el-Gazala, from 14 June to 24 September 1941.
13   The Fiat BR.20M Cicogna (Stork) had been in Sicily since May, when the *55° and 99° Gruppo BT* (*Bombardamento Terrestre* – land-based bombers) had deployed to Gerbini to fly night raids. They were supplemented, on 6 October, when the *37° Stormo BT, 116° Gruppo,* deployed *Squadriglie 276ᵃ and 277ᵃ*.

Three aircraft dropped eleven bombs: seven went into the sea, sinking a motor sailboat at the dock, one fell into an attic in via Principe Umberto but did not explode, three hit the lumber stores in via Capitaneria, setting them on fire, and the last one ended up in a house at n .314 in via Marina Ponente [via X Ottobre], where Mariano Licciardello, a 33-year-old carter, was sleeping. The bomb broke through the roof without exploding but fell on the bed, claiming the first civilian victim in Augusta [at 1:00 a.m.]. In the glow of the flames at the dock, the illusion of seeing Malta annihilated burnt along with the stacks of timber.[14]

In July, the Malta Night Fighter Unit (MNFU) was formed at Takali with eight Hurricane IICs and four IIBs. This relieved the pressure on the soon to be disbanded Independent Night Fighting Unit whose Fulmars, though hardly suitable for the role, would be used for nocturnal intruder sorties over Sicily.

At the same time, two Fulmars of the new MNFU were sent on a regular night sortie to disrupt activities on the airfields at Catania Fontanarossa and Gerbini; some incendiary devices were dropped on the latter. One of the Fulmars then headed to Augusta to strafe some searchlights.

The MNFU also achieved its first success during the night of 5/6 August when eight BR.20s from *43° Stormo BT* (*Bombardamento Terrestre* – land-based bombers) raided Grand Harbour. Flying Officer Cassidy and Pilot Officer Barnwell, flying Hurricanes, intercepted and shot down two Italian bombers. Bollettino di Guerra n. 429 of 7 August 1941 reported that 'On the night of the 6th, British aircraft dropped some bombs on Augusta and Catania: one dead and some injured.'

Late in the afternoon of the 9th, between 5:30 and 8:35 p.m., Maryland I AR739, flown by Flying Officer Adrian Warburton, with Pilot Officer Bastard and Sergeant Moren, carried out a reconnaissance sortie over the seaplane base at Augusta. Some of the photos taken recorded 20 seaplanes moored to the buoys, and three merchant ships, all protected by a substantial barrage of 14 tethered balloons. After completing the photographic run, the crew dropped two 500lb bombs on the seaplane base, scoring a direct hit on a building.

A few days later, the focus was on a large number of merchant ships sighted between Catania and Syracuse at around 12:00 p.m. on 14 August by Maryland AH294 of 69 Squadron (flown by Sergeant Edmond, Sergeant Southorn and Flight Sergeant Harris). Further study of the same area was carried out at 2:00 p.m. Squadron Leader Eric Tennant, the new commanding officer of the unit, in PR Hurricane V7101. He first flew to Catania, where 11 Ju 52/3m transports and 28 fighters were spotted on the airfield at Fontanarossa, then to the Augusta seaplane base, where 19 moored seaplanes were observed, along with some merchant ships and two small boats, protected by the inevitable balloon barrage.

At 8:25 p.m. the same day, four Vickers Wellingtons of 38 Squadron, commanded by Sergeants Norris, Brine, Hewitt and Colvin, departed Luqa; in the bomb bays they carried a total of thirty-six 250lb General Purpose (GP) bombs and thirty-two 40lb incendiaries, all destined for the port of Catania. Sergeants Norris and Hewitt identified the target between

14   Marcon, *Augusta 1940*-1943, p.43. However, the author erroneously reports the bombing was carried out on 5 June, while the death certificate from the municipality of Augusta, drawn up on 13 August 1941, records the death of Mariano Licciardello at 1:00 a.m. on 6 August.

A balloon barrage near the port of Messina. (Author's photo)

10:20 and 10:30 p.m. thanks to the launch of some flares that, from a height of 8,000 feet, illuminated the port.

The anti-aircraft response was rapid, but there was no assistance from supporting searchlight batteries. According to a prefecture report, the air raid alarm in the city sounded at 9:30 p.m. and 10 bombs were dropped, of which seven fell into the water inside the port. The other three hit the east wall, but the damage was insignificant. In the meantime, the other two bombers, those of Sergeants Colvin and Brine, were unable to locate the target, so headed towards Augusta, dropping bombs north of the town and, south, on the railway link. Here the anti-aircraft response was immediate, and of moderate intensity, and came, according to reports from the pilots themselves, from ships moored in the port. Fourteen searchlights contributed to the defence. All bombers and crews returned to Malta between 11:10 and 11:50 p.m. without reporting any damage or injury.

Considering that the port of Catania, the main target, had been missed by half of the bombers, and that the damage inflicted by only two aircraft had been slight, at 3:20 a.m. the same night, the same aircraft and crews returned, this time with forty-eight 250lb bombs between them. Cozzo Spadaro, near Portopalo, raised the alarm, informing the prefecture of Catania that a formation of bombers heading north had been spotted. The air raid sirens sounded again over Catania. This time, bright moonlight helped the Wellingtons locate the port. Bombs were dropped from 6,500 feet between 4:25 and 5:10 a.m. Some hit merchant ships and the east pier, while others intended for railway infrastructure missed the target and fell on Piazza Giovanni Bovio. The Bollettino n. 437 of 15 August reported:

British aircraft attacked Catania and Augusta last night; in Catania 3 dead and 20 wounded. The immediate and intense reaction of our anti-aircraft defence forced the enemy to drop most of the bombs offshore. One of the planes was shot down and crashed into the sea.

The following day, Pilot Officer H.S. Smith of 69 Squadron was charged with checking the damage to Catania, and, in the late August afternoon, flew over the city taking photos from Hurricane V7101. The Intelligence specialists analysing the resulting images judged the damage to be insufficient, so much so another raid on Catania was scheduled that evening, again using the Wellingtons across two distinct raids of four and five aircraft respectively, for a total of nine sorties. The Wellingtons of 38 Squadron, that flew two sorties each, were flown by Flight Lieutenant Rollinson, Flying Officer Day and Sergeant Jones, while Squadron Leader Ross, Flying Officer Pascall and Sergeant Rane led their crews on one sortie. During the first raid, the bombers were over the target from 9:45 to 10:30 p.m., dropping 9,000lbs of GP bombs and 6,480lbs of incendiaries, hitting the north part of the central pier. During the second raid, 14,250lbs of GP bombs and 720lbs of incendiaries were dropped. The bombs, according to reports collected from the crews during their debriefings, hit the northern part of the port, near the railway station, the central pier, and the railway line. Two large fires remained visible for three quarters of an hour. One of them was triggered by bombs from Day's aircraft; intermittent explosions from a fuel depot were visible up to 60–70 miles away.

The prefecture's report spoke of these two incursions, which took place from 9:36 to 11:11 p.m. and from 3:37 to 5:25 a.m., as the most tragic in Catania, due to the destruction caused and the number of deaths since the beginning of the war. For the second raid, regarded as the most devastating, the alarm was again raised by Cozzo Spadaro's observation point eight minutes before the bombers reached Catania. The vast fire to which Flying Officer Day referred was from the warehouse of the tobacco factory located in via del Faro, near the port.

The fire, as reported by the prefect's report, "was violent and took on vast proportions, so that the flames were noticeable from every point of the city. After about six hours, the firefighters managed to suffocate the fire. The damage was over a million lire. The removal of debris continued for several days. During the battle to extinguish the fire, a fireman, due to the absorption of nicotine, was poisoned and hospitalised with a critical condition. He was subsequently declared out of danger." It took several days to compile the complete list of victims, however, the definitive report of the prefect to the ministry of the interior, dated 4 September 1941, summarised: "26 dead, 36 injured." The number of deaths was subsequently increased to 27.[15]

---

15 Salvatore Nicolosi, *La guerra a Catania* (Catania: Tringali editore, 1984), p.55. A little further on, the author adds: 'On the morning of August 17, on the surviving but fragmented wall of a house demolished by the bombing, charcoal writing was found of a phrase that went down in history: 'U sicilianu avi cori and sapi pavari' ('The Sicilian has courage and knows how to repay'). It was never known who wrote it, but someone photographed it and, just over a year later, thousands of photographs were printed and offered for sale by the fascist federation of Catania.'

Six Blenheims by No. 105 Squadron RAF attacking a power station and chemical factory in Licata.
(Alessandro Emanuele)

At 10:05 a.m. on 16 August, Flying Officer Drew, in Hurricane V7101, visited the tormented city to perform the usual photographic surveys and check the damage caused.

In anticipation of a future British offensive in North Africa, scheduled for November, the future Operation *Crusader*, British commanders sent reinforcements to Malta by sea in mid-September (Operation *Halberd*). Because of this, it was incredibly important to obtain an up-to-date picture of the main Sicilian ports and airfields. On 19 August, the first two Bristol Beauforts (with Sergeant E.J. Harvey as pilot of L9875 and Pilot Officer S.W. Gooch flying W6518) arrived at 69 Squadron to be used almost exclusively for maritime reconnaissance.[16]

On 5 September, two separate reconnaissance runs were made by the squadron. The first was entrusted to Squadron Leader Tennant who, taking off in Hurricane V7101 at 8:41 a.m., spent two hours photographing the ports of Augusta and Catania and the airfields at Catania Fontanarossa and Gerbini. Two large merchant ships were identified at Catania and 54 aircraft were located at Fontanarossa. At anchor at the Augusta seaplane base were a hospital ship, a merchant ship, three small boats, and 15 CANT Z.501 flying boats and 14 CANT Z.506

16   As of 31 August, only one Maryland was operational. Another nine were unserviceable at the time.

floatplanes, all protected by seven tethered balloons. The second sortie was carried out from 10:00 a.m. to 12:05 p.m. by Flying Officer R.J.S. Wootton, this time in Hurricane Z3053, over the Palermo airfield area. Near the port, Wootton identified some units of the *Regia Marina* belonging to VIII Division, including the light cruisers *Raimondo Montecuccoli* and *Muzio Attendolo*, surrounded by several escort destroyers and a fairly large number of merchant ships. Twenty-nine aircraft were seen on the airfield at Palermo Boccadifalco.

On the night of 7/8 September, nine Wellingtons of 38 Squadron, under the command of Squadron Leader Bamber, attacked the port and military installations near Palermo three times between 11:55 p.m. and 4:00 a.m. The first two raids took place from the north-west, from the sea, while the third approached from the east, flying over Licata. All three were separated by two hours. The bombers unloaded 34,250lbs of high explosive bombs and 2,100lbs of incendiaries. The 8,875-ton light cruiser *Raimondo Montecuccoli* was hit by shrapnel from bombs that exploded nearby; another device damaged the stern of the 5,247-ton steamship *Campania*, killing two people and injuring three others. A fire flared up in a shipyard workshop, while adjacent warehouses of the Tirrenia shipping company were damaged by two bombs. Some of the maritime railway yard infrastructure was also damaged. The *11ª Batteria Contraerea* (anti-aircraft battery) was hit, with four injured and one dead.

The following morning the survey ascertained the continued presence of the naval units at Palermo and, given the poor results obtained by the three raids, the Wellingtons returned the following night, between 11:20 p.m. and 4:40 a.m., using the same pattern of attacks. The nine aircraft of 38 Squadron, this time led by Rollinson, carried 33,750lbs of GP bombs between them. The anti-aircraft batteries awaiting them opened up with intense and accurate fire and were joined by a light barrage from the three piers. Disrupted by the anti-aircraft fire, several bombers dropped off target, hitting some residential parts of the city. The alarm issued to various Italian military units allowed two fighters to take off. These were probably MC.200s of the *23° Gruppo CT*, flown by the *Gruppo*'s commander, Maggiore Tito Falconi, and Tenente Claudio Solaro, commander of the *70ª Squadriglia*, that, due to the regular night raids on Palermo by the RAF, carried out night hunting sorties from September to December. They were not able to reach the bombers but were seen approaching by some of the crews.

Regia Aeronautica pilot Corrado Ricci remembered some of the difficulties encountered flying day fighters at night:

> The aircraft were normal single-seaters, single-engine day fighters, and with them we were running around the dark sky without, obviously, being able to see neither friends nor enemies. On some planes we also had a radio, but [it was] very inefficient and with a maximum range of about ten kilometres; however, they were of little use because no one could ever tell us news to intercept the raiders.[17]

Assaults like these were repeated throughout the month, mainly on the ports of Tripoli, Palermo and Messina. From Bollettino n. 462 of 9 September:

---

17   Alessandro Bellomo, *Bombe su Palermo: Cronaca degli attacchi aerei 1940-1943* [Bombs on Palermo: A Chronicle of the Air Attacks 1940-1943] (Zanica (BG): Soldiershop, 2016), p.47.

Tonight [8/9], enemy aircraft flew over Palermo again, dropping some bombs, almost all of which fell into the sea. Little damage and no casualties. The losses among the Palermo population, caused by last night's [7/8] air raid, rose to 27 dead and 58 injured.[18] The calm and disciplined demeanour of the population was exemplary.

On 22 September, Flying Officer Wootton, flying Hurricane Z2332, performed a long sortie, from 10:45 a.m. to 1:30 p.m., over almost all of Sicily, despite the worsening weather, and using the six-inch camera, took photos of Palermo revealing two cruisers, three destroyers and seven merchant ships in port. Catania was noted to be hosting four merchant ships while 67 aircraft were dispersed around the airfield at Catania Fontanarossa. A single merchant ship and three minesweepers were moored at Augusta and a CANT Z.506 and 10 CANT Z.501s were seen at the seaplane base at Marsala. The port of Trapani had a barrage of six tethered balloons. Wootton dropped leaflets over Marsala, Palermo and Catania.

Biscari Santo Pietro airfield, near Caltagirone. Several aircraft are visible on the runway, including a large transport. The airfield, surrounded by dense vegetation, remained hidden for some time from Allied photo-reconnaissance. (US Air Force)

18　The news was subsequently corrected to 41 dead and 56 injured on 12 September by the *Giornale di Sicilia*.

Meanwhile the first Spitfire PR.IV assigned to Malta arrived on 22 September 1941. It was flown there by Squadron Leader Norman Henry Edward Messervy, an Australian from Point Cook, Victoria, from No. 1 Photographic Reconnaissance Unit (PRU) in the UK. Messervy flew photo-reconnaissance sorties over Italian ports, prior Operation *Halberd*, the latest Malta resupply effort at the time. Tyre damage on landing grounded the aircraft on Malta for nearly three weeks until replacement parts could be flown out from Britain. With the Spitfire unavailable, Messervy carried out sorties over Sicily and Tripoli in Hurricane Z3053. The Spitfire eventually flew 11 successful sorties from the island before returning to Benson on 3 November.

It had just passed 7:00 a.m., on Wednesday 24 September 1941, and Maryland BS763 of 69 Squadron was flying the now usual maritime reconnaissance in search of enemy shipping on the Ionian Sea. Unexpectedly, the Warburton, Bastard and Moren crew found a CANT Z.506B floatplane (MM45318 '170-5' of the *170ª Squadriglia RM*) that had taken off from the Augusta seaplane base for a reconnaissance of the central Mediterranean. The Italian crew included Tenente Pierluigi Colli, Sergente Pilota Carlo Pirotta, Tenente di Vascello Osservatore Leonardo Madoni, 1° Aviere Motorista Enrico Miola, 1° Aviere Radio Telegrafista Salvatore Capuano, and 1° Aviere Scelto Armiere Luigi Scattolini. In the clash, the CANT, hit heavily by bursts from the Maryland's four Browning 0.303in calibre machine guns, was forced to ditch; it sank in the afternoon. Most of the crew, seriously injured, managed to escape, but one man was trapped inside the seaplane and died shortly after. Rescue was not long in coming: a CANT Z.506B of the *186ª Squadriglia RM* (*Ricognizione Marittima* – maritime reconnaissance) was called by radio and arrived from Augusta under the command of Tenente Pilota Mario Bellotto; it was joined by two other seaplanes from Benghazi and Taranto. Meanwhile, Warburton and his crew returned unscathed to Malta at 12:00 p.m.

That night, six Wellingtons of 38 Squadron headed towards Palermo at about 10:00 p.m. The formation was led by Flying Officer Loweth with Pilot Officers Freeman and Cooper, Sergeants Hawes and McManus, and Flying Officer Fell in command of the remaining bombers. The attack was concentrated on the piers, the Wellingtons delivering 19,000lbs of bombs. Unfortunately for them, the cruiser *Muzio Attendolo*, the real target of the raid, has already left port. Two bombs hit the bow of the German steamer *Ruhr* and sank the oceangoing tugboat *Salvatore Primo*; fires were also recorded along the wharves, and a fuel depot was hit near Calata Quattroventi. Slight damage to the dry dock was also reported.

September marked an important milestone for Flying Officer Adrian Warburton who, since setting foot on Malta, had flown 155 reconnaissance sorties (eight in a PR Hurricane), shot down several aircraft (especially seaplanes), and bombed Pantelleria. His photographic surveys had ranged from 12,000 feet over Palermo and to just 50 feet over the port of Messina. His notoriety took him away from Malta and Sicily temporarily as the RAF assigned him to No. 223 Squadron in Heliopolis, Egypt, as a flying instructor for the squadron's new Marylands.

Air Vice-Marshal Hugh Pughe Lloyd assumed command of the air forces on Malta from 1 June. In an interview after the war, he said:

> Warburton was the absolute king of photographic reconnaissance, the Pearl of the Mediterranean. If I wanted photographs of Naples, Tripoli or any other Axis port he would say: "Yes sir," and go out and get them at no matter what cost. Thanks to him

and the other reconnaissance pilots, I knew every time the German or Italians moved a boat.[19]

The fruitful reconnaissance activities carried out during the four months from mid-June to mid-October 1941 allowed the Wellingtons of the various units operating from Malta to fly 357 sorties. Of these, 170 were against airfields in Sicily and southern Italy, while Tripoli was attacked 72 times. From the main bases in Egypt, the Wellingtons raided targets such as Benghazi, attacking it 102 times, for a total of 578 sorties, which represented an average of 5–6 bombers per night for six nights a week. All of this was thanks to aerial reconnaissance reporting the objectives in near real time.

A Savoia-Marchetti SM.81 'Pipistrello' destroyed on the ground at Catania Fontanarossa by RAF bombing towards the end of 1941. (Author's photo)

19 Tony Spooner, *Warburton's War: The Life of Maverick Ace Adrian Warburton* (Manchester: Crécy Publishing, 2003), p.67.

The arrival of German vehicles and supplies at the port of Catania. (Author's photo)

Italian Thunderbolts over Malta (October–December 1941)

Since the end of September there had been several attacks against objectives not directly of a military nature; these were repeated throughout the month of October. Worthy of note were the offensive raids successfully carried out by Malta-based Blenheims of Nos. 18, 105 and 107 Squadrons on the Porto Empedocle power station, the sulphur refinery in Licata, and on the railway switches at Syracuse and Catania.

Porto Empedocle, in particular, had already been attacked on 27 September at 4:25 p.m. by six Blenheim Ivs of 105 Squadron. On that occasion, the violent reaction from Italian anti-aircraft fire had damaged two aircraft, those of the Sergeants Hopkinson and Broom.[20] *La Milizia marittima di artiglieria* (*MILMART*[21]) reported:

20   In fact, the initial objective of the mission was Trapani Bo Rizzo airport, but due to bad weather the six Blenheims of 105 Squadron aimed for an alternative target. The National Archives London, Royal Air Force, Operations Record Books AIR 27/826/36.

21   The Maritime Artillery Militia or *MILMART* was an artillery specialty of the Voluntary Homeland Security Militia.

The power plant was hit by at least one bomb which exploded causing the collapse of an adjacent building and the death of three workers ... The reaction of the anti-aircraft attacked by the enemy, however, was determined: during the airstrike the Milmart weapons fired 2,480 13.2 mm shells and 1,738 20 mm shells for a total of 4,218 machine gun shells with an additional 81 76/40 anti-aircraft shells.[22]

Porto Empedocle was subsequently photographed on the morning of 30 September by Flying Officer Wootton, who also reported encountering anti-aircraft fire. In addition to the Blenheim sorties, the Albacores of 828 NAS successfully attacked railway connections near Canicattì and the sulphur refinery at Licata.

At 10:10 a.m. on 17 October, Flying Officer Drew was over Sicily at the controls of Hurricane Z3053. Coming from Gela Ponte Olivo, he headed towards Comiso and its new runway, earlier identified on 13 February. This new airfield has been named Biscari. Still under construction, it had remained hidden thanks to the dense vegetation of the area, mostly consisting of cork and oak trees. Drew's report in the squadron's Operations Record Book (ORB) observed:

> Recco Borizzo (16 aircraft). Castel Vetrano (16 aircraft). Gela (26 aircraft). Comiso, 25 aircraft. A new aerodrome in Biscari under construction was photographed.[23]

On balance, October did not record many surveys over Sicily, but they did provide fruitful results. On 31 October, 69 Squadron closed its ORB with a maritime reconnaissance over the islands of Pantelleria and Marettimo by Maryland I AR725. Sergeants Macdonald, Hall, Cameron and Willson sighted, just north of Pantelleria, what appeared to be three SM.79s heading for North Africa. This type of sighting was not new. Despite 69 Squadron having just seven of the 14 Marylands on hand operational (along with the two Hurricanes), it had been very active in maritime reconnaissance during October, especially over the stretch of sea west of Sicily. The Marylands had even come close to the coast of Sardinia, on three different occasions encountering Ju 52/3m transports of III./KGrzbV 1 and, as occurred on 20 October, managing to damage one of them.

On the morning of 6 November, the squadron ORB recorded the first reconnaissance carried out by a Mosquito (PR.I W4055) of No. 1 PRU (Photographic Reconnaissance Unit) from the UK; it was flown by Squadron Leader Alastair Lennox "Ice" Taylor DFC and Bar and Sergeant Horsfall on a 'Special photographic task'.[24]

On 10 November, the Maryland (AR725) of Pilot Officer R.G. Fox and Sergeants McKenzie, Windebank and Turner left Malta at 11:20 a.m. on a sea reconnaissance along the coast north of Sicily, observing a large naval presence off Messina consisting of three cruisers, eight destroyers, four small boats, two railway ferries, four merchant ships and a hospital ship in transit near Capo Spartivento. Off Stromboli, three other cruisers and a destroyer were identified at an estimated

22   Calogero Conigliaro, *I corsari del terzo Reich e i segreti di Husky. Sicilia 1940-1943* [Privateers of the Third Reich and Husky's Secrets. Sicily 1940-1943] (Gorizia: Libreria Editrice Goriziana, 2017), pp.29–30.
23   The National Archives London, Royal Air Force, Operations Record Books AIR 27/606/24.
24   The National Archives London, Royal Air Force, Operations Record Books, 69 Squadron AIR 27/610/15.

cruising speed of around 23 knots. For further analysis, 69 Squadron sent another reconnaissance aircraft to the same area early in the morning the next day. On board Maryland BS760 were Flight Lieutenant Williams and Pilot Officers Wiseman and Berrett. After scouring the coasts of Sardinia, the port of Cagliari and the airfield at Elmas, they headed towards Palermo where they witnessed the arrival of four merchant ships and three coastal vessels. Shortly afterwards, over the port of Trapani, six merchant ships were observed and photographed as they completed docking operations; the steamer *Le Tre Marie* of 1,086 tons and the small *Sant'Antonio*, only 374 tons, were ready to sail from Trapani at 7:30 p.m. escorted by the torpedo boat *Prestinari* at a cruising speed of 7 knots. Between them they were carrying 3,000 tons of food and materials for Italian troops in Libya. Another convoy making its way west at an estimated cruising speed of 10 knots was located near San Vito Lo Capo and comprised two destroyers and three merchant ships. On the other side of Sicily, Flying Officer Drew in Hurricane Z2332 was carrying out photographic surveys of the coastline between Aci Castello, Letojanni and Gallodoro.

Meantime, from Malta, eight Wellingtons from No. 40 Squadron and nine from No. 104 Squadron took off to attack Naples. In the darkness, Lieutenant Commander Hunt led a formation of seven 830 NAS Swordfish towards Sicily to intercept the previously reported vessels. His aircraft was the only one not armed to attack the ships as it was equipped with ASV (Air-to-Surface Vessel) radar. An intense Sirocco wind, with gusts exceeding 30 knots slowed the biplanes' progress. Three aircraft soon aborted due to mechanical problems, while the other four headed towards Pantelleria intent on intercepting the convoy. With nothing showing on the radar, they flew the usual route towards Trapani and then turned east to Palermo. Still not finding anything, they returned to Pantelleria. By this time the Swordfish had been flying for about four hours and travelled more than 400 miles. Their full war load included about 170 gallons of fuel, giving a nominal range of over 500 miles, but, on this occasion, they had embarked another 60 gallons in a third tank positioned behind the pilot in the space usually occupied by the observer. At some point, the Swordfish found themselves out of radio contact with Malta and, completely off course, became lost. Some sources speculated they reached the Gulf of Gabès, Tunisia. Having lost all hope of reaching Malta, the crews got rid of their torpedoes so as to make emergency landings. They went beyond what they identified as Palermo and, at Cefalù, found a stretch of beach that appeared possible to land on. One of the aircraft, that of Sub-lieutenant Taylor, managed to land on the beach, ending upside down with its nose stuck in the sand; Lieutenant Osborn and Sub-lieutenant Campbell, however, were forced down by Italian anti-aircraft fire while the fourth Swordfish tragically exploded when it made contact with the sea.

Not seeing the Swordfish return to Malta, at 7:10 the following morning, Maryland BJ427, piloted by Wing Commander Dowland, with Pilot Officer Potter and Flight Sergeant Harris as crew, flew to the west coast of Sicily in the hope of locating the four Swordfish. Finding nothing, the Maryland returned at 12:05 p.m.

On balance, 830 NAS had been almost decimated. It was not the first time this month a Swordfish had not returned and that a reconnaissance aircraft of 69 Squadron had attempted to locate it; it had already happened on the night of ½ November when a Swordfish disappeared between Tripoli and the Kerkennah Islands in Tunisia.

Bollettino n. 528 of 12 November 12 reported:

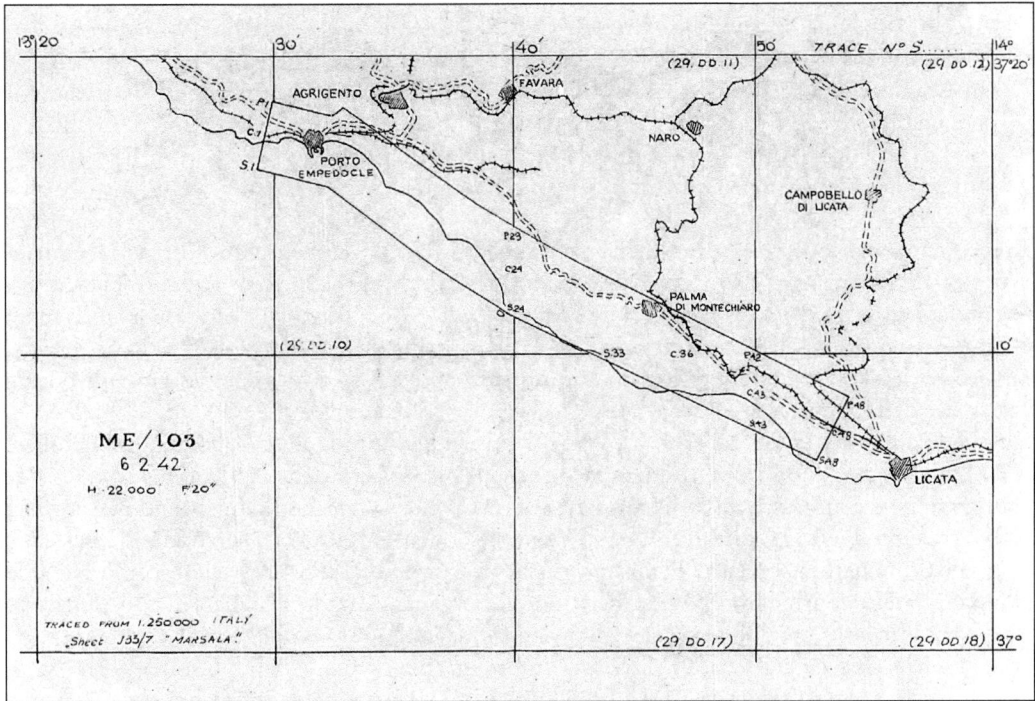

A map of the route taken by Flying Officer Cox in PR Hurricane Mk.IIC DG622 from No. 2 PRU. This aircraft arrived on Malta in January 1942 for some special sorties. (MEIU)

The enemy's air force has made other raids on southern Italy and Sicily. Yesterday afternoon a reconnaissance aircraft was shot down by our fighters near Capri. Tonight, explosive and incendiary bombs were dropped on the city of Naples in various waves: there was damage to civil buildings, but the fires were soon tamed; 6 people were killed and around 30 injured. The demeanour of the population is always calm and disciplined. In the early hours of this morning, in Sicily, 3 British aircraft were shot down: one by anti-aircraft defence and two by our fighters. The crew of another enemy plane crashed into the sea and was captured. Also, in the early hours of this morning, four British heavy fighters, intercepted by our forces, fell in the Cefalù area. Three disappeared into the sea, the fourth fell ashore and the officer who flew it was taken prisoner.

From 12 to 17 November, 69 Squadron, due to bad weather, was unable to carry out photographic reconnaissance over Sicily, falling back to the localities of Kefalonia, Corfu, Kalamata and Zante. The Wellingtons, on the other hand, continued to bomb Sicily, braving the uncertain weather. Between 7:55 p.m. on the 14th and 2:02 a.m. on the 15th, 12 Wellingtons from 40 Squadron and seven from 104 Squadron left Malta to attack Catania and surrounding areas. Bollettini n. 531 of 15 November and n. 532 of 16 November reported respectively:

Enemy air raids on Catania, Acireale and Brindisi, with the dropping of explosive and incendiary bombs: some civilian homes were damaged; 17 dead and 12 wounded in Catania and 12 dead and 8 wounded in Acireale. Exemplary attitude from the population. In Sicily, at Acireale, the losses caused by the British air force, in the night's raid on the 15th, increased to 21 dead and 29 injured. On the coast, the crew of three non-commissioned officers of a plane shot down at sea was captured.

The reconnaissance sorties over Sicily resumed on 18 November with Flight Lieutenant Wootton, in Hurricane Z2332, departing at 9:00 a.m. to cover the Sicilian airfields. He has just photographed Castelvetrano (15 aircraft visible), Trapani Bo Rizzo (14 aircraft) and Trapani Milo (57 aircraft) when, after spotting three minesweepers near the port of Sciacca, he was warned by Maltese radio control of the imminent approach of two enemy aircraft; Wootton wisely decided to return to Malta.

At 8:00 a.m. on 21 November 1941, Wing Commander John Dowland, commanding officer of 69 Squadron, took off from Malta in Hurricane Z3053 to carry out a dangerous low-altitude photographic reconnaissance of the airfields at Gela Ponte Olivo and Comiso, and new airfield at Biscari Santo Pietro. While over Comiso, he was suddenly attacked by three Macchi MC.202 Folgores (Thunderbolts), of the *9º Gruppo* of the *4º Stormo CT*, flown by Maresciallo Rinaldo Damiani, Sergente Maggiore Otello Perroti and Sergente Alfredo Bombardini. In the clash, which continued to the Maltese coast, Dowland's machine was completely riddled by gunfire from the Macchis' Breda-SAFAT 12.7mm calibre machine guns. About 30 miles north of St. Paul's Bay, in the northern area of the island of Malta, with a rapidly failing aircraft, Dowland managed to bail out into the sea, saving himself, but losing the squadron's third PR Hurricane.

There was an immediate search, during which he was spotted by Pilot Officer Oliver of No. 185 Squadron, and he was rescued an hour later by Kalafrana's Swordfish floatplane flown by Sub-lieutenant Hurle-Hobbs. At Kalafrana, LAC Phil Chandler recorded:

> … the Swordfish rescue seaplane took off. We heard him coming in not very long afterwards and at the same time saw the ambulance pull up on the slipway. We dashed out on to the armoury roof. There were three people in the seaplane and only two had gone up. As the third man, who was wrapped in a blanket, was being helped out of the cockpit, our flight sergeant who had the binoculars trained on the scene, recognised him as a Wing Commander from Luqa. I don't know whether he was shot down in the earlier dogfight or crashed by accident. He seemed not much the worse, however; was carried ashore pick-a-back by one of the groundcrew and walked to the ambulance, with a word with some of our officers who had come on the scene. The Swordfish went out again early this evening but was soon back.[25]

Due to the fierce fighting in North Africa, Italian fighter units left Comiso towards the end of November and were soon replaced by Luftwaffe units. On 23 November, the *Forza Aerea di Sicilia* gave the order to transfer 18 MC.202s, of the *96ª* and *97ª Squadriglie, 9º Gruppo, 4º Stormo*, from Comiso to Pantelleria, the first stop on the way to the African front.

25   Cull, Galea, *Hurricanes Over Malta*, p.160.

On 16 December, the *23° Gruppo Autonomo CT* received orders to leave Sicily and return to Libya. It took off from Comiso at 10:55 a.m. the same day with 21 Fiat CR.42s, and three Caproni Ca.133s, from its three units, *70ª*, *74ª* and *75ª Squadriglia*.

In order to better analyse the movements of the enemy, the RAF sent out Hurricane Z3173 at 11:30 a.m. on 23 December.[26] Flying Officer H.S. Smith was flying over Trapani Bo Rizzo to capture the final photographs of the sortie when he was attacked by an MC.202. He managed to evade the Italian, diving from 23,000 feet to 8,000 feet, and, taking advantage of a cloud bank, returned to Malta unscathed. Smith had earlier flown over Catania, at around 10:00 a.m., just as five large merchant ships were entering the port. At Catania Fontanarossa, he spotted 76 clearly visible aircraft.

To confirm what Ultra intercepted regarding the arrival of German units in Sicily, more than 100 trucks carrying weapons, ammunition and equipment had already left Naples on 17 December on board a fleet of ferries. The Neapolitan city and its port had been the subject of careful photographic reconnaissance on 15 November when Wootton, who had photographed the Acerra and Capodichino airfields during the same sortie, recorded the presence of at least 106 aircraft.

The port of Tripoli photographed on the morning of 6 February 1942 by Flight Lieutenant Adrian Warburton and LAC Shirley in Beaufighter T4705 of No. 69 Squadron RAF. (IBCC Digital Archive PClarkD1506)

26   Hurricane Z3173 had replaced Z3053, which had been lost the previous month. The squadron also lost Z2332 destroyed on the ground during an Italian raid on Malta. The aircraft flew its final sortie on 23 November over Gerbini. Just seven Marylands and one Hurricane (Z3173) were now available to 69 Squadron. Of the approximately 126 reconnaissance sorties carried out in December, most were flown in search of the Italian fleet in the Mediterranean. In particular, 45 sorties covered Tunis, the Gulf of Hammamet and Libya, and almost the same number covered Greece, Lampedusa and Pantelleria; only a very low percentage concerned Sicilian airfields (Gerbini, Catania Fontanarossa and Gela Ponte Olivo were the most visited).

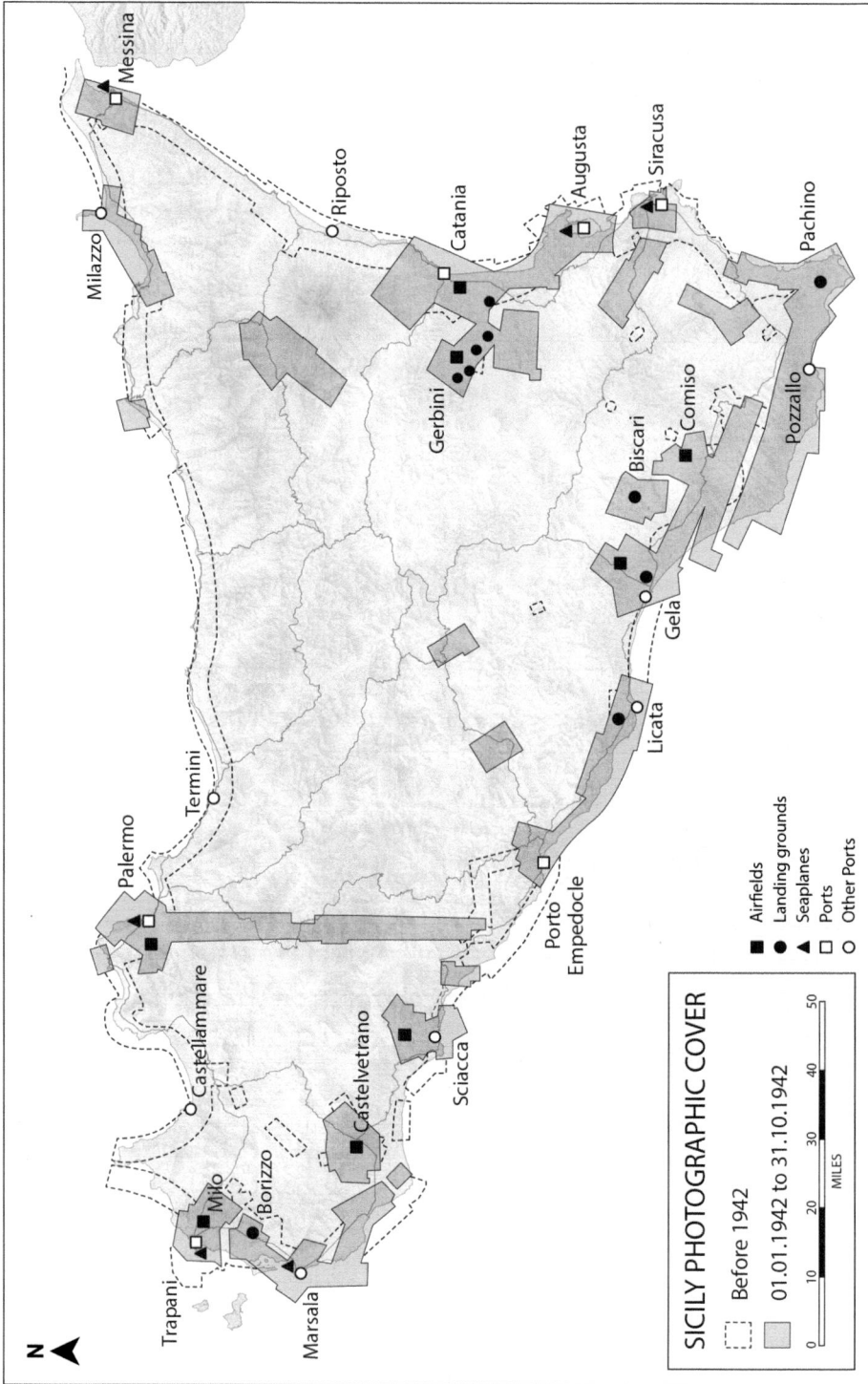

Primary targets photographed by Malta reconnaissance. (AFHRA)

6

1942
German Supremacy and the Year of the PR Spitfires

The Arrival of *II Fliegerkorps* (December 1941)

On 23 December, the British intercepted a German radio communication announcing the arrival in Sicily of *II Fliegerkorps*, which entailed a significant increase in vehicles and aircraft. After the departure of the last German echelons of *X CAT* (*Corpo Aereo Tedesco* – German Air Corps) from Italy in October 1941, Hitler proposed to Mussolini to replace it with another large air unit, *II CAT*, commanded since 11 October 1939 by General der Flieger Bruno Löerzer. Returning from the Eastern front, *II CAT* was part of Generalfeldmarschall Albert Kesselring's *Luftflotte 2* (2nd Air Fleet).

With the changing of the German guard, the strength of Luftwaffe reconnaissance units increased with two *Staffels*, 1.(F)/122 and 2.(F)/122, spread between Gerbini, Catania and Trapani.[1] Messerschmitt Bf 109 F-4/R3s, based at Catania Fontanarossa, supplemented the Ju 88s. The two land-based *Staffels* made up for the difficulties encountered by the maritime reconnaissance units operating mainly from the waterways of Augusta and Marsala.

Luftflotte 2 established its headquarters in Frascati while Löerzer maintained his command at Taormina. The Luftwaffe's objectives were to achieve maritime supremacy between southern Italy and northern Africa, in collaboration with Italian units, and to neutralise Malta, which also entailed attacking maritime traffic.

Still under siege, especially from the air, Malta, and consequently all of its population, was exhausted from 18 months of war. In the first three months of 1942, about 2,000 raids occurred, more than 20 per day. A thousand bombs were dropped in February 1942. A study carried out post-war established that more bombs fell on Malta from February to April than RAF Bomber Command dropped on Germany throughout 1942. The same study showed the extent of the raids carried out in March far exceeded those carried out on English cities by the *Luftwaffe* during the whole war.

---

1   Long-range reconnaissance units were known as *Fernaufklärungsstaffeln* or *Aufklärungsstaffeln* (F), abbreviated as Aufkl./(F) or (F).

Rumours of a possible Italian-German landing reached London, together with the fear, certainly well founded, the small island could not withstand such an offensive. Massive enemy deployments of air, land and sea forces were flowing into Sicily, or about to do so, to prepare for the Axis offensive (codenamed Operation *C3*, Operation *Herkules* for the Germans).[2]

A curious episode, during one of the reconnaissance sorties of this period, was recounted by Jonny Spires, Adrian Warburton's inseparable colleague, when he was interviewed by Roy Nash of *The Daily Star* in March 1958:

> We were always on the lookout for gliders. Malta was in daily anxiety about an airborne invasion. We saw the airfield, Catania, through the clouds and Warby decided to have a closer look. As we swept round, Warby found that we were on the circuit for a landing. Said Warby: 'We've got a green. I'm going in.' He then put down the wheels and made a normal circuit to approach the centre of the airfield. I was flabbergasted: 'What the hell do you think you are doing. This is Catania not Luqa.' I know,' Warby

Several Junkers Ju 88s at Catania Fontanarossa. The *Luftwaffe* crews are taking a moment to rest before the sortie. (Author's photo)

2   Operation *C3* provided for 270 landing craft and about 50 other vessels, escorted by about 30 torpedo boats, while the rest of the Italian fleet would have been ready to intervene from the ports of Messina, Reggio Calabria, Augusta, Naples and Cagliari. The use of nine German and 51 Italian battalions was also planned, with 1,600 vehicles and 700 artillery pieces transported on 33 large ships with adequate supplies, and hundreds of German gliders supported by 1,500 aircraft, including 600 of the *Luftwaffe*. The operation was never implemented due to events during the North African campaign, particularly after the siege of Tobruk, which cost Axis forces the city.

A Junkers Ju 88 landing at Catania. In the background is the snow-covered Etna. (Author's photo)

replied, 'now watch.' He told Paddy to get ready to strafe the Huns. There were lots of transports lined up on the tarmac, like rows of soldiers. He went straight out to sea leaving a bunch of very surprised Germans behind.[3]

PR Mosquitos and Beaufighters over Sicily (January – February 1942)

The new year saw the arrival in Malta from the Middle East of new aircraft suitable for photo-reconnaissance: two PR Beaufighters (T3301 and T4705) and two PR Hurricanes, belonging to No. 2 Photographic Reconnaissance Unit (PRU) at Heliopolis, Egypt, which were to be used in special reconnaissance sorties over Sicily.[4] On board these aircraft were the following pilots: Squadron Leader Walker, Flight Lieutenant Stephenson, Flight Lieutenant White, Flying Officer Cox, and Flying Officer Adrian Warburton returning to Malta.

---

3   Spooner, *Warburton's War*, pp.64–65.
4   T Flight 2 PRU left Heliopolis bound for Malta on 29 December 1941 with Warby taking both Norman Shirley and his great friend LAC Ron Hadden in T4705. Johnny Walker took Flying Officer Benjie White and the third camera operator Corporal Liebert. En route to Malta both planes stopped at Timimi, west of Tobruk, to refuel. Spooner, *Warburton's War*, p.88.

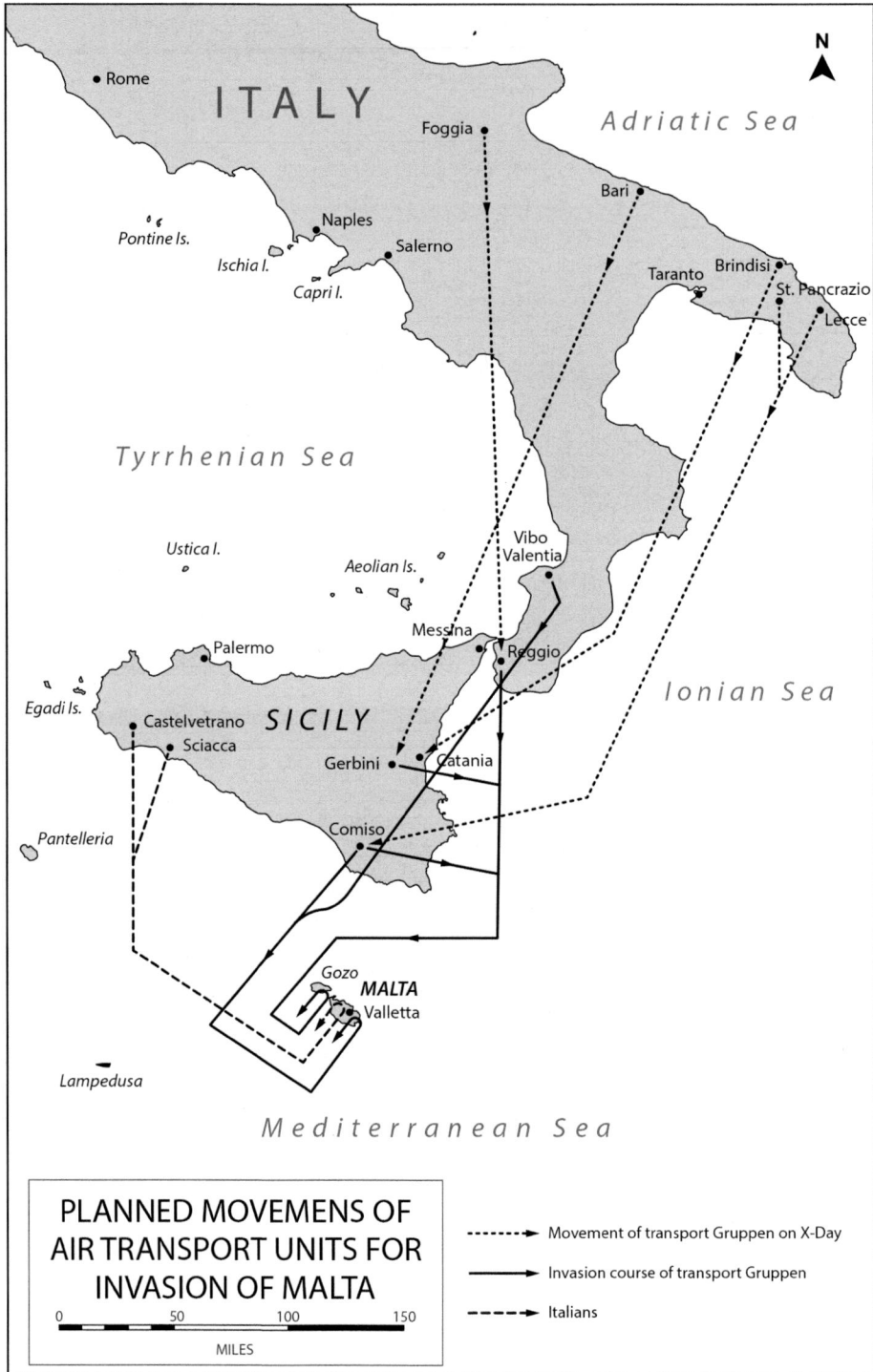

Aerial plan for Operation *C3*. (USSMA)

On 3 January, from 1:00 to 3:00 p.m., Beaufighter T4705 was baptised over Sicily as Warburton and Leading Aircraftman Shirley carried out a quick photographic survey of the airfields in the west of the island. They recorded:
Recco Castel Vetrano (75 Bombers 13 fighters); Trapani (33 aircraft); Borizzo (3 u/s aircraft); Marsala (11 seaplanes 3 small craft); Palermo (1 T.B. floating unit arrived, 1 tanker departed, 1 seaplane) and Trapani harbour (no change). No photo of Comiso owing cloud.[5]

Following the usual script, the following day Malta prepared to attack the airfields just photographed. A formation consisting of four Blenheims from No. 107 Squadron, led by Pilot Officer Williamson, and six Blenheims from No. 18 Squadron, attacked the aircraft identified on the ground at Castelvetrano. The Blenheims, arranged in three formations, struck from a very low height, 'between 25 and 100 feet', machine-gunning and bombing a large number of German Ju 52/3m transports and Italian BR.20Ms. The bombing caused a column of smoke to rise to 1,000 feet, enough to be visible 40 miles away. Despite the immediate response by the anti-aircraft batteries, all of the Blenheims returned to base unscathed. In the late evening, five Vickers Wellingtons of Nos. 40 and 104 Squadrons headed to Castelvetrano between 8:41 and 10:00 p.m. Four of them, just returned from the first raid, re-armed and refueled to return between 3:57 and 5:25 a.m. The attackers claimed the destruction of 12 aircraft on the ground: six SM.82s (one of which was used by the *Luftwaffe*), four CANT Z.1007bis, a CR.42 and a Ju 52/3m; in addition, at least 42 more aircraft were damaged, including 22 SM.82s, 15 CANT Z.1007bis, two FN305s, two CR.42s and an MC.200.[6]

More than 100 fuel drums went up in flames, vehicles and buildings were damaged and eight deaths occurred among the base staff. The raid, however, cost 40 Squadron Wellington IC Z9036 flown by Flight Sergeant Lewthwaite, with Sergeants Pick, Chalmers, Bryan, James and Lill on board. The Bollettino n. 582 of 5 January 1942 reported:

> Last night the enemy made a raid on Castelvetrano causing minor damage: eight dead and 15 injured; an enemy bomber, hit by anti-aircraft fire, was shot down.

On 13 January, at 12:45 p.m., No. 69 Squadron suffered a heavy loss: Wing Commander John Noel Dowland and his wireless operator, Pilot Officer Robert Victor Gridley, lost their lives when their Maryland (AR721) was attacked by *Luftwaffe* fighters off the Maltese coast near Tigné as they are returned from a sortie over Cape Bon. Before losing his life, Dowland managed to shoot down one of his attackers. Only the observer, Pilot Officer Arnold Potter, escaped by baling out. The German fighters were Bf 109s from JG 53, one of which was flown by Leutnant Hans-Volkmar Müller, of 5./JG 53, who claimed the destruction of the Maryland. Command of 69 Squadron passed back to Wing Commander Eric Tennant.

5   The National Archives London, Royal Air Force, Operations Record Books, 69 Squadron AIR 27/607/1.
6   Nicola Malizia, Inferno su Malta: La più lunga battaglia aeronavale nel Mediterraneo. 1940-1943 [Hell over Malta: The longest air-naval battle in the Mediterranean. 1940-1943] (Milano: Ugo Mursia Editore, 2015), p.223.

Beaufighter T3301 of No. 2 PRU at Heliopolis, Egypt. This aircraft was used by No. 69 Squadron RAF over Sicily and the Mediterranean. (Brian Spurr)

On 14 January, at exactly 12:05 p.m., Flight Lieutenant Wootton, in Hurricane Z3173, flew over Pantelleria where three sailing vessels and 20 small boats were anchored near the port. 12 aircraft were noted on the airfield. Meanwhile, at sea a little further north, an MAS (Motoscafo Armato Silurante – torpedo-armed speedboat) was sighted trying to reach port.

Important air and sea movements were recorded on 17 January. Warburton and Corporal Liebert, on a sortie to Sicily from 8:30 to 10:45 a.m. in Beaufighter T4705, reported:

> Recco Sicilian aerodromes. Palermo (1 Cruiser, 5 Destroyer, 1 Torpedo boat, 17 merchant vessels, and 8 Float units) Bocca di Falco (71 aircraft) Messina (3 Cruiser, 4 Destroyers, 2 Torpedo boats, 4 Submarine, 4 Train ferries 2 oilers) Reggio di Calabria (27 aircraft). Gela (42 aircraft) Comiso (50 aircraft) Catania (70 aircraft) Gerbini (1 aircraft visible) Vibo Valentia obscured by cloud. Considerable A.A. from all aerodromes, particularly Gela, Comiso and Gerbini. Intense and accurate A.A. at Messina.[7]

Wootton, during a reconnaissance on the 25th, spotted the unmistakable path of a steam train at around 12:05 p.m. (near Syracuse, exactly 30 degrees to the east), the trail of smoke from the funnel visible even from an altitude of 18,000 feet.

Luftwaffe Generalleutnant Gottlob Müller during a visit to Catania Fontanarossa in 1942. (Author's photo)

7   The National Archives London, Royal Air Force, Operations Record Books AIR 27/607/1.

Meantime, a No. 1 PRU de Havilland Mosquito PR.I (W4051) had arrived from Benson, England, for testing in the Mediterranean. However, the Mosquito, flown by Pilot Officer P.J. Kelly, was seriously damaged in a ruinous landing off the runway at Luqa. A second PR.I (W4063), flown by Pilot Officer R.E. Walker, arrived safely in Malta on 17 January although, after a series of sorties over Italy, it was eventually lost on 31 March, returning from a flight over Sicily, due to the damage inflicted by a Bf 109.[8]

At 8:20 a.m. on 28 January, Hurricane Z3173, thanks to additional fuel tanks, managed to cover Catanzaro. Flown by Sergeant R. Ballantyne, it was hit by anti-aircraft fire. The pilot, forced to bale out near Marcellinara, Catanzaro, was captured and taken prisoner as reported in Bollettino n. 606 of 29 January.

The run of losses for the squadron, which began with the new year, showed little sign of stopping. The skies over Castelvetrano proved treacherous on 7 February for Flight Lieutenant White and Leading Aircraftman Shirley in Beaufighter T3301. With a tip off from Maltese Intelligence, they left at 7:45 a.m. to perform photographic surveys of the airfields at Castelvetrano, Trapani Bo Rizzo and Trapani Milo. Immediately after photographing 14 aircraft over the first target, White and Shirley saw two Bf 109s diving on them. The Germans' fire hit White in the shoulder and foot and set fire to the cockpit. Shirley, with a severe groin wound, managed to extinguish the fire and bring the aircraft back to Malta. His gallantry was recognised by the award of a Distinguished Flying Medal.

Noteworthy data from the sortie over Taranto and Messina on the 13th was acquired the hard way: newly promoted Flight Lieutenant Adrian Warburton and Corporal Hadden lost an engine on Beaufighter T4705, and were threatened by four Italian fighters, but managed to return safely:

> Recce Taranto (2 Battleships, 9 Submarines, 2 Destroyers, 1 Torpedo Boat, 1 Hospital ship, 1 merchant vessel by photo – visually 4 Battleships, 4 Cruisers, 6–8 Destroyers, 5 merchant vessels); Messina (3 Cruisers, 4 Destroyers, 5 merchant vessels). Intense light A.A. fire from Taranto. Aircraft chased by 4 Macchi 202 but evade. 1 Hospital ship 10° south of Reggio di Calabria, Co 1600/5–6kts, slight heavy A.A. from Messina. Port engine shut off over Taranto owing to oil failure, Messina being covered with one engine.[9]

On the 16th, a clear sky over Palermo assisted Sergeants Macdonald, Hall, Cameron and Delehaunt on board Maryland AR709 in their task, having departed Malta at 12:15 p.m. for a maritime reconnaissance over Capo Spartivento. Scrambled from Boccadifalco airport, an MC.200 of the *167ª Squadriglia*, *16° Gruppo, 54° Stormo CT* (*Caccia Terrestre* – land-based fighters), took off to intercept the Maryland. The pilot, Tenente Pilota Cesare Tramontini, claimed the RAF aircraft shot down after a long chase.[10] However, this claim is completely unfounded; the Maryland landed at Luqa at 4:30 p.m. without reporting any damage.

8   Martin Bowman, *Mosquito Photo-Reconnaissance Units of World War 2* (Oxford: Osprey Publishing, 1999), p.10.
9   The National Archives London, Royal Air Force, Operations Record Book AIR 27/607/2.
10   Malizia, *Inferno su Malta*, p.229.

What remains of Hurricane BE347, at the controls of which was Pilot Officer James E. Wood (120504), from No. 1435 (Night Fighter) Flight based on Malta. The moon was three-quarters full when, on the night of 27/28 April, the 21-year-old flew a sortie to Sicily. The young pilot, who grew up in Yorkshire in England, was hit by anti-aircraft fire and crashed near Gerbini. He was buried in the Catania War Cemetery. (ACS 45267, 45268)

The PR Spitfire over Sicily (March – June 1942)

March began with a dangerous reconnaissance sortie over Sicily, heralding a night raid. In the early afternoon of the 1st, Warburton and Leading Aircraftman Hadden flew Beaufighter T4705 low over Palermo, between 500 and 1,000 feet. An intense and accurate anti-aircraft barrage was put from the port, and some splinters hit the Beaufighter, but did little to stop the crew returning home.

The following day the sortie was repeated with the same aircraft and crew. While they were intent on observing the area near Palermo, due to the consistent presence of merchant ships, two formations (five and seven aircraft) of Bf 109s tried to intercept. The Messerschmitts were not successful and the Beaufighter returned without suffering any damage.

On the night of 2/3 March, in what was the first of three raids, nine Wellingtons from No. 37 Squadron received orders to depart between 9:00 and 11:00 p.m. to bomb the ships moored at Palermo. The formation was led by Squadron Leader Tomkins, who was flying with his crew in Wellington IC D9111. According to British reports, bombs hit the piers and ships, creating numerous explosions. Sergeant Steward reported having hit the buildings in the area north-west of the port. Due to intense enemy fire, Tomkins's aircraft was hit by anti-aircraft fire, which he referred to as 'spasmodic', forcing him to return for an emergency landing on the Luqa runway.[11] The sorties over Palermo ended at 6:20 a.m. on the 3rd when the last bomber, Wellington IC Z9938, flown by Flight Sergeant Morrison, landed at Luqa; the crew reported it had dropped its stick of bombs from 8,500 feet and caused a flashy green explosion.[12]

The damage to Palermo's port installations was reported as follows:

> The following were sunk: *Cuna* (ex *Australien*), a German transport vessel of 6,652 T., loaded with ammunition, aerial bombs, petrol drums, 480 T. of diesel fuel, vehicles, tanks and spare parts for the Afrika Korps; *Securitas*, Italian steamer of 5,366 T., later recovered; *Tricolore*, Italian tanker ship of 179 T.; *Le Tre Marie* Italian requisitioned steamer of 1,086 T.; G.R.42 (bettolina) military barge. All units were moored along the head of the north pier. Damaged: 39 other vessels. Extensive damage in the city … In the phonogram subsequently sent by Prefect A. Mariano to the News Collection Office of the Ministry of War in Rome, it is reported that the dead are 30, of which 24 are military, and 235 wounded, of which 108 are civilians and 127 military.[13]

11   'One night in March 1942, Squadron Leader Tomkins, as senior captain of the aircraft, participated in a successful attack on Palermo. He spent a considerable time over the harbour, in the face of intense anti-aircraft fire, before making his attack. He succeeded in setting a large enemy merchant vessel on fire, thereby assisting other aircraft in locating the target area in subsequent attacks. As a result of the operation, 2 enemy vessels of 6,000 tons were sunk and one 9,000-ton vessel was severely damaged. Considerable damage was also caused to harbour installations. The successes achieved were largely due to Squadron Leader Tomkins's courage and determination.' ('Distinguished Flying Cross', *The London Gazette*, 20 March 1942, p.1275).

12   A standard bomb load carried by Wellingtons during this period included 5–7 250 or 500lb bombs with SBCs (Small Bomb Containers – incendiaries) taking up the remaining space in the bomb bay.

13   Bellomo, *Bombe su Palermo*, p.77.

Around 11:00 in the morning of the following day, the alarm raised for Palermo saw a Macchi MC.200, flown by Tenente Cesare Tramontini of the *167ª Squadriglia*, scramble to intercept a twin-engine aircraft, identified as a Bristol Blenheim, on a reconnaissance flight over Palermo, probably, according to local senior officers of the *Regia Aeronautica*, to assess the raid of the previous night. The British aircraft was attacked but without any definite result. Adrian Warburton and Corporal Liebert, on board Beaufighter T4705, reported having been intercepted at 4,000 feet by two Bf 109s during their first pass over the city.

On 7 March, after a few days of travel, Spitfire PR.IV AB300, flown by Pilot Officer 'Harry' Coldbeck (a New Zealander), arrived at Takali from Benson. After a few days, another reconnaissance pilot, Sergeant Leslie R. Colquhoun, with Spitfire PR.IV BP885, also arrived from the United Kingdom. The two PR.IVs would make up B Flight, 69 Squadron. Also on 7 March, 15 new Spitfire Mk.Vcs launched for Malta from the aircraft carrier HMS *Eagle*.

At 12:15 p.m. on 12 March, Pilot Officer Kelly baptised AB300 over Sicily. The sortie covered almost the entire island, as reported by Kelly in the squadron's Operations Record Book:

Recce Sicilian aerodromes Trapani (1 destroyer, 1 T.B., 1 liner, 9 merchant vessels left, 4 merchant vessels arrived) and aerodrome (18 aircraft). Palermo (1 merchant vessel left, 9 merchant vessels arrived) Bocca di Falco (16 aircraft) Messina (1 tanker, 1 merchant vessel left, 1 merchant vessel arrived) Gerbini (15 aircraft). No photo of Catania or Gela.[14]

As reported by Coldbeck on 27 March, a large number of aircraft, 103 and 43 respectively, were sighted at Catania Fontanarossa and Gerbini

March saw the squadron lose two Marylands, with three more damaged during air raids on Malta. Due to the continuous enemy incursions over the islands, the squadron, like other units during this period, was having a difficult time. Despite the obvious operational difficulties, it managed to fly just 14 reconnaissance sorties. Such a low number had not been recorded since the beginning of the conflict.

On 20 March 1942, a Distinguished Service Order was awarded to Adrian Warburton, the reasons for which were published in *The London Gazette*:

This officer has carried out many missions each of which has demanded the highest degree of courage and skill. On one occasion whilst carrying out a reconnaissance of Taranto, Flight Lieutenant Warburton made 2 attempts to penetrate the harbour, although as there was much low cloud this entailed flying at a height of 50 feet over an enemy battleship. In spite of the failure of his port engine and repeated attacks from enemy aircraft, he completed his mission and made a safe return. On another occasion he obtained photographs of Tripoli in spite of enemy fighter patrols over the harbour. In March, 1942, Flight Lieutenant Warburton carried out a reconnaissance of Palermo and obtained photographs - revealing the damage caused by our attacks. This officer has never failed to obtain photographs from a very low altitude, regardless

---

14 The National Archives London, Royal Air Force, Operations Record Books AIR 27/607/1.

An aerial photo of Avola taken by a PRU aircraft flying from England to Malta to carry out special coverage of Sicilian locations of strategic interest. (US Air Force)

of enemy opposition. His work has been most valuable and he has displayed great skill and tenacity.

At 4:10 p.m. on 10 April, Coldbeck and Colquhoun flew two very dangerous sorties over the airfields at Castelvetrano and Sciacca and over targets in eastern Sicily. At the same time, a heavy *Luftwaffe* offensive by 64 Ju 88 and 21 Ju 87 bombers escorted by 13 Bf 109s was underway over Malta. Colquhoun noted:

Recco of Sicilian aerodromes. – Augusta = 1 Hospital ship. Photo of Comiso 22 bombers 71 fighters – Biscari = 33 aircraft. No photo of Catania Reggio di Calabria or Vibo Valentia owing to cloud.[15]

On 12 April, two more PR Spitfires arrived on Malta, Flight Sergeant John O. Dalley and Sergeant Frank R. Gillions doing the honours. During April, other PR Spitfires would stopover before carrying on to other destinations in the Middle East.

A naval convoy of the *Regia Marina* escorted by a CANT Z.501 carrying a 160kg anti-submarine bomb. (ACS 16366)

The *Regia Aeronautica*, meanwhile, strengthened its presence in Sicily, anticipating the final annihilation of Malta. On 12 April, 26 new MC.202s of the *4° Stormo* were preparing to deploy to Sicily. They were from the *10° Gruppo CT*, with the *84ᵃ*, *90ᵃ*, and *91ᵃ Squadriglie*, which called Sciacca home on 15 April, and the *9° Gruppo CT* (*73ᵃ*, *96ᵃ* and *97ᵃ Squadriglie*) which spread itself between Castelvetrano and Sciacca on the 23rd. Soon after, *4° Gruppo BT* (*Bombardamento Terrestre* – land-based bombers), and its SM.84 three-engine torpedo bombers with the *14ᵃ* and *15ᵃ Squadriglia*, arrived. On 4 May, the Re.2001 fighters of the *2° Gruppo Autonomo CT*,

15   The National Archives London, Royal Air Force, Operations Record Books AIR 27/607/4.

comprising the *150ª, 152ª* and *358ª Squadriglie*, landed at Biscari Santo Pietro. The *102° Gruppo BaT* (*Bombardamento a Tuffo* – dive-bombing), of the *5° Stormo*, under the command of Maggiore Pilota Giuseppe Cenni, arrived at Gela Ponte Olivo airfield on 24 May with the *209ª* and *239ª Squadriglie*. The unit was equipped with 16 Ju 87B and R5 Stukas. On the afternoon of 1 June, the MC.202s, of the *155ª Gruppo CT, 51° Stormo CT*, arrived from Ciampino Sud. The *33° Gruppo* of the *9° Stormo BT*, coming from Viterbo, also deployed to Trapani Chinisia. The *59ª* and *60ª Squadriglie* were equipped with the CANT Z.1007bis.

Spitfire PR.IV BP888. (Ken Delve)

The reaction from Malta was not long in coming and, on the evening of 20 April, eight Wellington ICs of No. 148 Squadron arrived at Luqa, after a flight from Kabrit, Egypt (including a technical stop at Landing Ground 106 on the Egyptian coast). Two more bombers arrived on the night of the 22nd.

At 11:20 a.m. on 21 April, Colquhoun was sent out to reconnoitre the airfields at Comiso, Catania Fontanarossa, Gerbini, Gela Ponte Olivo and Biscari Santo Pietro.

At 8:40 that same evening, Wellington 'Q' (BB483) of Squadron Leader Prickett and Pilot Officer Pelletier's 'O' (DV573) carried out the first raid on Comiso, returning at 10:45 p.m. After reloading, they departed again at about 12:40 a.m. to repeat the effort. Meanwhile, 10 minutes before, three other Wellingtons headed to Comiso, returning at 3:20 a.m.. These were 'C2' (ES984) of Flight Sergeant Vertican, 'K' (DV505) flown by Pilot Officer Crump, and 'O'

(DV573) with Sergeant Elcoate at the controls. A solitary Wellington, 'F' (DV487) flown by Sergeant Clark, took off at 2:10 a.m. to carry out the final bombing sortie of the night. The Bollettino n. 691 of 23 April reported:

> Last night British planes dropped some bombs on Ragusa and again on Comiso: no casualties among the population, insignificant damage to Comiso.

Meantime, Malta was subjected to yet another heavy raid by Axis aircraft. Although the hopes of survival for the British on Malta were now at an all-time low, the few surviving bombers on the island did not give up and attacks on nearby Comiso continued. At 8:40 p.m. on 23 April, until 5:25 a.m. the following day, five Wellingtons of 148 Squadron flew nine sorties. The offensive action cost Wellington 'Q' (BB483), flown by Flight Lieutenant Hayter, and Flying Officer Harper's Wellington 'O' (DV573). The Bollettino n. 692 of 24 April reported:

> Last night the enemy made a double raid on Comiso without causing damage or victims; two of the bombers participating in the action were hit and destroyed by anti-aircraft artillery near Vittoria and around Acate. Bombs dropped on the town of Vittoria (Ragusa) injured a girl and damaged some buildings.

On the following night, from 12:37 to 4:28 a.m., a solitary Wellington ('K', DV505) flew two more sorties to Comiso.[16]

During the month of April, 6,728 tons of bombs were dropped on Malta. Most of them fell upon a handful of targets situated within a few miles of each other. The distribution was:

Dockyard area	3,156 tons
Luqa airfield	805 tons
Takali airfield	841 tons
Hal Far airfield	750 tons
Kalafrana seaplane base	196 tons
Elsewhere	980 tons

The dockyard district included the densely populated areas of the Three Cities and Valetta surrounding the vital harbour.

Whilst the inhabitants took to the cliffs and caves, their homes, churches and historic buildings, together with military objectives, were pounded and demolished. The loss of civilian life during this black month rose to 300 people, the highest figure for any month, but still relatively low owing to the unassailable rock shelters many people were spending their lives in.

---

16   From the 25th to the 30th, the eight surviving Wellingtons returned to their bases at Kabrit and Fayid in Egypt. The bomber squadrons on Malta operated on 99 of the 224 nights between 14 October 1941 and 25 May 1942, performing 865 sorties, an average of nearly nine sorties per night. Although Axis aircraft bombed incessantly day and night, Malta never lost the ability to fight. Ports and ships were the main targets for 608 sorties, an average of 70%; 189 sorties were assigned to Axis airfields (22%). This *modus operandi* managed to cause delays in supplies of more than five days to the Axis armies in North Africa, something Rommel could not afford. As a result, the *Luftwaffe* intensified its attacks on Malta.

A CANT Z.1007 undergoing maintenance at Sciacca. (Alessandro Ragatzu)

By March, there was already sheltered accommodation for some 440,000 (nearly double the estimated population), but over 10,000 buildings were destroyed or damaged during April.

As April drew to a close the situation on Malta was nearly desperate. Though in that month the guns and fighters had destroyed or probably destroyed 200 of the attackers, the defenders had lost 23 Spitfires (57 damaged) and 18 Hurricanes (30 damaged). The serviceability of the fighters dropped; some days the air force was virtually grounded; while the anti-aircraft gunners had their ammunition rationed, these losses could be ill-afforded.

In 1944, the Air Ministry published *The air battle of Malta: The Official Account of the R.A.F. in Malta, June 1940 to November 1942*, highlighting the identification of satellite fields near Gerbini:

On 21st April, when the offensive was at its height, attention was drawn to a feature which had appeared to the west of Gerbini airfield, one of the enemy's main bomber airfields in Sicily. It consisted of a rectangle marked out on the ground by a plough. On 24th April more photographs were taken of the same area, and it was observed that the ground enclosed in the rectangle had undergone a change. The vegetation had been cut short and small hollows and mounds had been levelled. The rectangle measured some 1,500 yards long by 400 yards wide. The immediate interpretation put upon it was that the enemy had found the existing bomber airfields, Gerbini, Catania and Comiso, inadequate and were preparing a satellite landing ground. This theory was not accepted for long. By the end of April two other strips were found in the same vicinity, one of which was nearly complete when first photographed. The new satellites were about the same size as the first, and all three ran parallel to the runway of Gerbini airfield–that is, roughly west to east, the direction of the prevailing wind. It was also observed that each strip had been laid out within easy reach of a railway station, and that at four of these stations new sidings were under construction. It became evident that there was a second and more disturbing explanation of the strips, namely that they might be intended not to provide additional dispersal for bomber aircraft but to accommodate a large number of gliders for an airborne invasion of Malta. The Vale of Catania, where the strips were found, is a flat tract of open land, nearly a hundred miles square. It is only about a hundred miles from Malta and would be an ideal site for the purpose. The satellites could be prepared with the minimum of time and labour, and each would be within easy access of its railway station, of which the significance was that the two most common of the German gliders, the Gotha 242 and the D.F.S. 230, are built in sections which can be easily transported and rapidly assembled. The sections could be brought from Italy by rail the whole way, over the Messina train ferry, to the strips.

Following their customary plan of surprise, the Germans could bring down their gliders in sections, and need not assemble them until a day or two before the operation was due to begin. Though it is possible on air photographs to distinguish glider components on an open landing ground, the parts could easily be concealed under trees or camouflaged. The invasion troops could be accommodated in the large camps already existing farther afield until they were required. Obviously, large quantities of stores and ammunition would be required, but any increase in the size of the existing dumps in the vicinity may well have been interpreted as heralding an even greater air bombardment of Malta. It is probable that the enemy intended to give this impression and hoped that the new satellites would be regarded as take-off strips for more bombers. Their real intention would not be fully proved until the assembled gliders themselves appeared at the last minute. On the discovery of the three strips, the Royal Air Force photographic reconnaissance staff considered in what areas further strips could be built, and aircraft were sent out to photograph these areas, As a result, photographs were obtained of the whole of the Vale of Catania, and other areas in southern Sicily. In all, about 300 square miles of country were photographed, but no further strips were discovered. It seemed that the enemy thought that the three existing strips were enough. Regular reconnaissance was therefore made every other day, and progress closely observed. New huts were erected. Underground cables were laid. By 10th May, all three satellites were complete. A close watch was kept for any increases in stores, or the arrival of anything resembling glider components, but no further developments occurred and no anti-aircraft defences appeared to have been prepared.[17]

In the early afternoon of 9 May, a PR Spitfire flew to Messina in search of the Italian naval fleet. Sergeant Colquhoun sighted a cruiser and a large merchant ship, along with other small

---

17   Air Ministry, *The air battle of Malta: The Official Account of the R.A.F. in Malta, June 1940 to November 1942* (London: 1944) p.64.

merchant ships, just outside the port. Three other cruisers and an unknown number of warships were still anchored inside the port, four destroyers included. The nearby port of Reggio Calabria, hosting three destroyers, also received attention. A new sortie was proposed the next day; this time it was up to 'Harry' Coldbeck in Spitfire BP885 to confirm the presence of the Italian naval fleet.[18] Little reassuring news came from the reconnaissance on 26 May: Colquhoun, surveying Comiso, identified 15 Ju 87 Stukas but also noted the number of Ju 88s on the aerodrome has decreased from the 49 in late April to just 10. The offensive capacity of the airfield remained strong, however, being the main operational headquarters of the Bf 109s of JG 53 'Pik As'. The latter decreased from 58 aircraft in April to 34 after the air battles of 10 May, but, by the end of the month, the survey ascertained the unit had rebuilt its strength to about 62 aircraft.

Just three days later, Leslie Colquhoun, on a sea reconnaissance, spotted an enemy convoy consisting of three merchant ships and three destroyers just south of Pantelleria. The photos revealed their freight to be various types of vehicles and materials.

A stereophoto of the port of Marsala. The silhouettes of several seaplanes can be clearly seen on the water. (Alessandro Ragatzu)

On the night of 26 May, from 9:00 p.m. to 1:00 a.m., seven 104 Squadron Wellingtons flew over Messina to carry out a bombing raid on the railway station and port area. Most of the bombs hit the targets, with some falling just south of the port. From 1:24 to 4:34 a.m., a second raid by two bombers returned to the same target. Bollettino n. 726 of 27 May reported:

Last night the enemy attacked Messina with two waves of bombers. The dropped bombs were explosive and incendiary. Significant damage was caused to the Duomo, to

18   The only two Spitfire PR.IVs operating at the time were BP908 and BP885. Spitfire AB300 was unserviceable. With only two aircraft operating, Colquhoun and Coldbeck flew most of the sorties over Sicily during the month (12 and 18 respectively).

the R. University and to some private homes. So far 7 deaths and 19 injuries have been ascertained among the civilian population while the clearing of the rubble continues. There are also 7 injured sailors. An aircraft hit by the anti-aircraft defence crashed into the sea. The demeanour of the population was calm and disciplined.

Other raids were made on the airfield at Catania Fontanarossa on the nights of 28/29 and 29/30 May. In both cases, the bombs were dropped on the runway and between the buildings. During the attack on the 29th, the crew of a 104 Squadron Wellington was hit by anti-aircraft fire, one of its engines failing before it dropped its bombs. The crew reported they decided to lighten the load, jettisoning all of the bombs into the sea, in an attempt to maintain an altitude high enough to allow them to return to Malta. At Luqa, the bomber made a disastrous landing; three crew members died in the crash and the second pilot passed away in hospital a few days later.[19] On the night of 30/31 May, three Wellingtons returned to Messina, although one aborted early due to mechanical problems. An oil tanker was hit by some of the 4,000lbs of bombs dropped, generating a vast blanket of smoke. Another seven bombers returned the following night. In this latest attack, however, one of the bombers, struck by anti-aircraft fire, ditched into the sea about three miles from Malta; the entire crew was recovered. Another bomber performed an emergency landing at Luqa on one engine. Bollettino n. 731 of 1 June reported:

> Last night the British air force made a new incursion, with successive waves and with considerable force, on the city of Messina: one dead and thirteen injured in the civilian population, considerable damage to some buildings including the Principe di Piemonte hospital where 40 hospitalized were injured. Two bombers, hit hard by the anti-aircraft defence, fell into the sea: one between Villa S. Giovanni and the Riviera del Faro, the other between Gallina and Catona.

On the nights between 1 and 11 June, the airfields of the province of Catania, and the cities of Augusta and Syracuse, were hit again by the bombers of 104 Squadron, with 12 sorties across two distinct attacks. The Augusta seaplane base suffered an attack of three aircraft on 1 June. In the raid of 5 June, unable to locate the airfield at Catania due to unfavourable weather conditions, the Wellingtons held on to their bombs, two of them heading towards Syracuse, which was bombed between 12:22 and 3:55 a.m. The Bollettino n. 735 of June 5 reported: 'British bombers attacked the city of Syracuse tonight: limited material damage, no casualties among the civilian population.'

---

19   It is very probable the bomber dropped the bombs on the area of Misterbianco, not in the sea, causing the death of eight people and wounding 12 others, all civilians.

German Field Marshal Erwin Rommel, known as the 'Desert Fox'. In February 1941, Rommel was appointed commander of the German troops dispatched to aid the all-but-defeated Italian army in Libya. At the end of October 1942, he was defeated in the second Battle of El Alamein and had to withdraw to the German bridgehead in Tunis. In March 1943, Hitler ordered him home. (ACS 42968)

Reconnaissance Aircraft over the Mediterranean (June – August 1942)

When, in late May 1942, Rommel began his advance in Libya, winning the great battle of Ain el-Gazala, which took him to El Alamein, Churchill and the military leaders in London immediately identified the cause of his success: the *Afrika Korps*, supplied by largely unopposed Italian merchant traffic, had been able to rebuild its supply reserves and strengthen the armoured divisions. An efficient tool of war had returned after the crisis of the previous autumn. This had happened because aircraft, ships and submarines could no longer leave besieged Malta to intercept the valuable convoys. Now that the attacks on the island by Kesselring's aircraft were declining, a robust reinforcement for the vital Mediterranean outpost could be considered.

The new directives imposed in this period by Admiral Sir Andrew Cunningham required aerial reconnaissance, especially from Malta, to constantly monitor the Mediterranean from Gibraltar to Corfu and Kefalonia. For these activities, six Martin Baltimore crews from the Middle East arrived to join 69 Squadron.

Here, therefore, Cunningham gave life to a complex and articulated operation, already attempted several times before, involving the simultaneous dispatch from Gibraltar and Alexandria of two strongly escorted convoys, Operations *Harpoon* and *Vigorous* respectively, to resupply Malta. In the meantime, at 4:00 p.m. on 13 June, the *Regia Marina*'s VII Cruiser Division set sail from Cagliari. The Italian units, not having spotted any enemy ships, headed towards Palermo, unaware of the fact they were observed by Colquhoun's PR Spitfire. The next day, at the same time, IX Naval Division, together with the cruisers of VIII Division, was preparing to leave Taranto. This time 'Harry' Coldbeck's Spitfire PR.IV (BP908) took off at 1:30 p.m. to find them.

Portopalo immortalised by the RAF during mapping operations. (US Air Force)

The operating directives of the *Regia Marina* provided that, on the evening of 14 June, the cruisers *Eugenio di Savoia* and *Raimondo Montecuccoli*, both of 7,000 tons, and seven destroyers were to sail from Palermo under the command of Admiral Alberto da Zara. Their purpose was to intercept, starting at dawn on the 15th, British ships in transit in the waters around Pantelleria. In the early afternoon, on the 14th, Admiral Angelo Iachino left Taranto with a powerful formation comprising two battleships, *Littorio* and *Vittorio Veneto*, four cruisers (*Giuseppe Garibaldi*, *Emanuele Filiberto Duca d'Aosta*, *Gorizia* and *Trento*) and 10 destroyers, and headed towards the waters west of Crete to intercept the convoy from Alexandria. At 5:00 p.m., John Dalley flew over Palermo at 25,000 feet, confirming the Italian fleet at berth, but at 7:15 p.m., threatened by enemy fighters rapidly climbing from 5,000 feet, he turned for Malta.

Italian SM.79 bombers captured during an attack on a convoy in the Mediterranean. Note the large torpedo attached to the belly of the bomber. (ACS 43084)

On the late evening of 14 June, as fading daylight prevented photos from being taken, Leslie Colquhoun observed two cruisers and four destroyers just outside the port of Palermo. This information allowed a Royal Navy submarine to later damage a cruiser and Wellington bombers from Malta to torpedo *Littorio* in the late evening of the 15th.[20] The next day, the squadron flew 10 reconnaissance sorties with several Baltimores looking for the Italian naval units.[21]

20   Conigliaro, *I corsari del terzo Reich e i segreti di Husky*, p.57.
21   One of these sorties met a tragic end. On board Baltimore AG715 were Pilot Officer Arthur Hedley Patrick, Flight Sergeant Allen Dawe Harris (RAAF), Sergeant William Dennis Warburton and

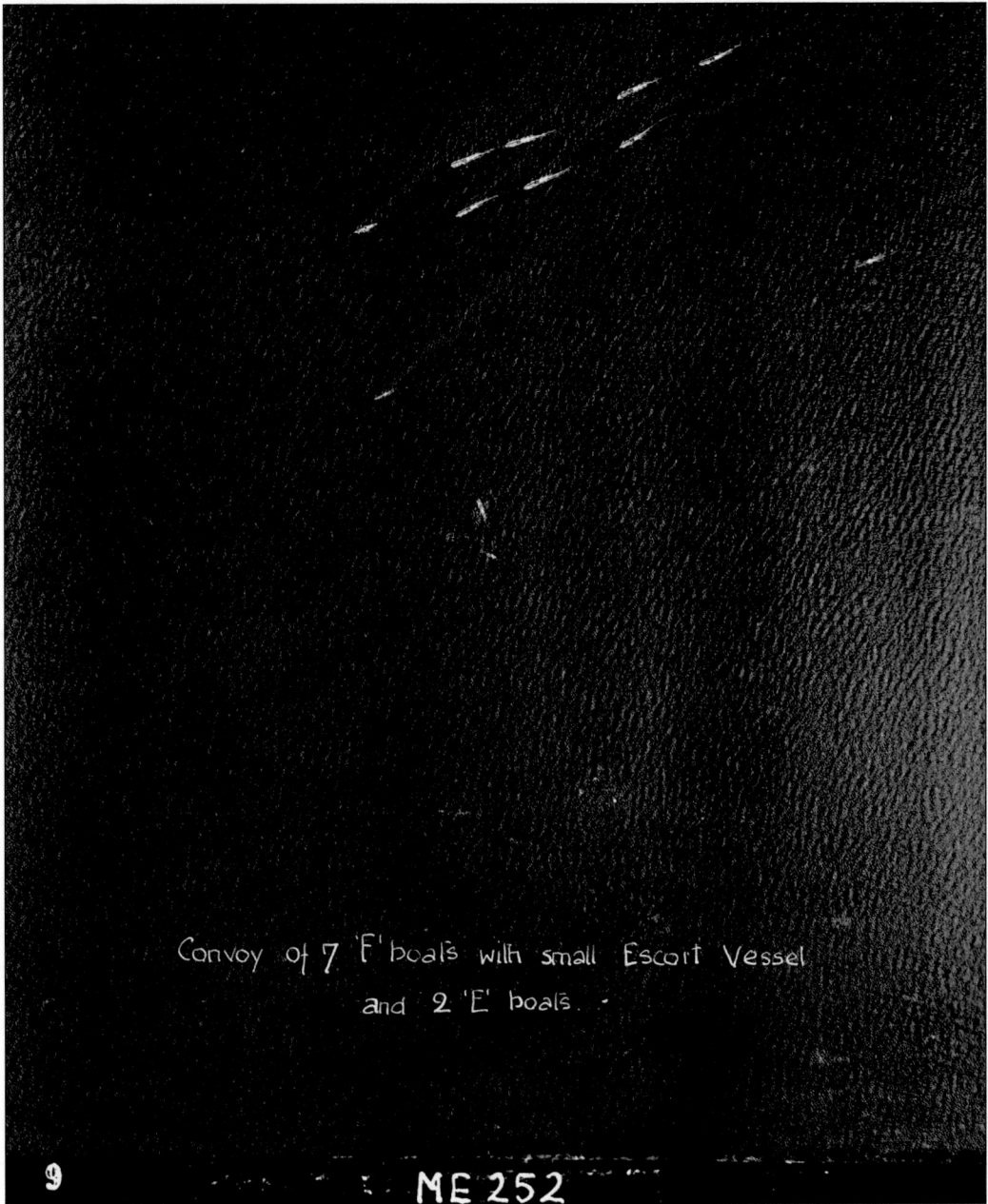

Convoy of 7 'F' boats with small Escort Vessel
and 2 'E' boats.

ME 252

Maritime reconnaissance of the eastern Mediterranean by No. 2 PRU. (Author's photo)

Top: A Macchi MC.202, coded '378-10' of the *378ª Squadriglia, 155° Gruppo, 51° Stormo CT*, at Gela Ponte Olivo during operations against Malta. Bottom: Maresciallo G. Gambari, speaking with other pilots before climbing into his fighter and heading for Malta. (ACS 44179, 44183)

In July, the PR Spitfires operated without loss. However, on the morning of the 11th, A Flight lost Sergeant Corbett, Pilot Officer Stark, Sergeant Woolley and Flight Sergeant Wathern when their Baltimore (AG700) did not return from a reconnaissance of Lampedusa and Cape Bon.[22]

Towards the end of the month, the careful analysis carried out by Maltese Intelligence, of the photos taken by PR aircraft, revealed the number of aircraft in the Gerbini area now included 23 Ju 88 bombers, double that noted in previous observations. One of its satellite runways in use hosted 12 fighters. Two other runways were under construction in addition to the three satellites previously identified.

An unusual sortie was proposed in the afternoon of 9 August. Coldbeck received a note directly from Air Headquarters Malta accompanied by a medium-sized package; on the package was written 'To the Regia Aeronautica in Sicily'. Coldbeck was asked to drop the package over Catania Fontanarossa. He knew Catania well, especially since it was home to a large number of aircraft, many of which were ready to react to RAF incursions. At 7:05 a.m. on 10 August, Coldbeck and the package took off in Spitfire BP915 for Catania Fontanarossa and, subsequently, Naples. Below is an excerpt from his logbook:

Photo Recco of Messina and Naples. Average height flown 23,000 feet. Sighted Merchant Vessel (5-6,000 tons) and 1 Destroyer 260° Cape Spartivento 10 miles, course west (2 hours later the same convoy was sighted 8 miles off Taormina going south. Messina: 2 Cruisers, 4 Destroyers, 2,000 ton Merchant Vessel with small unidentified craft leaving Messina, heading south. Weather condition poor. 10/10 cloud at 20,000 feet, north of Sicily and upwards. Broken cloud at 10,000 feet. One Italian P. of W. Mail package dropped on Catania aerodrome.[23]

Coldbeck later wrote about the mystery package in his autobiography:

> I had discovered from the Intelligence section, that this packet contains letters and other keepsakes of the Italian crew of the Cant float-plane [CANT Z.506B, '139-13', MM45432] which the South African Air Force officer, Lt Strever and his crew, comprising an English RAF Officer and two Royal New Zealand Air Force NCOs had captured while they were being transferred as prisoners-of-war from the vicinity of the island of Corfu to the Italian mainland at Taranto. … The crew had been rescued by Italian Cant float-plane [on 29 July] and had been taken as prisoners of war to its base at Prevesa where they were extremely well treated …[24]

Sergeant Ernest Charles. They departed Luqa at 6:50 a.m. but did not return, mysteriously disappearing over the central Ionian Sea.

22 This loss left the squadron with just one serviceable Baltimore (AG734). The other aircraft, AG746, required urgent maintenance and spare parts. Squadron members, including Pilot Officers Foster and Mackay, travelled to Egypt to acquire what was so desperately needed.

23 The National Archives London, Royal Air Force, Operations Record Books AIR 27/607/8.

24 Harry Coldbeck, *The Maltese Spitfire. One Pilot, One Plane – Find Enemy Forces on Land and Sea* (Shrewsbury: Airlife Publishing Ltd, 1997), p.76. Such efforts were not unique. At least one other occasion was recorded, which took place on 8 November 1941, when Italian fighters from Sicily sent a message to Malta, enclosed in a container, requesting information on the fate of two pilots of the *Cavallino Rampante* who had disappeared over Malta. Further details in the text of Malizia, *Inferno su Malta*, p.204.

On 11 August, a Spitfire PR.IV (BP883), flown by Flight Lieutenant Day, arrived at Luqa from the Middle East and, on 12 August, another three Spitfire PR.IVs (BR653, Sergeant A.G.D. Terret; BR665, Pilot Officer W.S. Backen; and BR662, Pilot Officer M.G. Brown) arrived on Malta after a stopover at Gibraltar. On the 13th, Pilot Officer G.H.E. Maloney and BR663 arrived from the UK via Gibraltar, the same day two other aircraft passed through on their way to 2 PRU at Heliopolis, Egypt.

Capitano Giuseppe Cenni, second from right, the Italian Ju 87 Stuka ace. During his stay on Sicily, he operated against Malta and the British fleet in the Mediterranean. In June 1942, he personally led a formation of 17 Picchiatelli attacking the *Harpoon* convoy. (ACS 19844)

At 8:20 a.m. on 17 August, Coldbeck was flying a routine recce to Trapani in Spitfire BR665:

Having completed my Photographic Reconnaissance there of Cagliari, Elmas, Deccimomanu and San Pietro Island on the south-west corner of Sardinia, I set off for Malta again on the direct route through the Sicilian Straits area. Approaching the island of Pantelleria, I sighted a merchant vessel which I estimated to be about 7000 tons, accompanied in convoy by two destroyers; 320° Pantellaria 4 miles. Having photographed the convoy I resumed my homeward course. Flying time on landing was four hours ten minutes. That same day I was in the same aircraft, refuelled and camera magazines changed, on my way back to find the convoy again, or what was left of it, the Beaufort torpedo-bombers having attacked it after I was there earlier that day. I photographed the now stationary smoking vessel which I recorded was down by the bow and I noted one of the destroyers leaving for the north, (Sicily). The whole area of the operation had moved south and east to the vicinity of Lampedusa, 290° 45 miles. There were now several enemy aircraft present and I noted six fighters and four Ju88s. There was an element of mystery about the enemy aircraft which had now appeared and were flying around the ship and the retreating destroyer. They didn't seem interested in chasing me who was above them and could view them easily. Perhaps they had been sent on anti-submarine duties and didn't really expect a Spitfire out there in the wide open ocean so far from Malta, (150 miles). ... Completing my photography for the second time, I moved off back to Malta. Flying time from take-off to landing – two hours.[25]

Coldbeck mentioned the attack by six Bristol Beauforts from No. 86 Squadron and the subsequent sinking, by the submarine HMS *United*, of the motor ship *Rosolino Pilo* (8,326 tons) which had left Naples the day before with a cargo of 3,429 tons, 112 vehicles and 101 German military personnel, escorted by the destroyers *Maestrale* and *Vincenzo Gioberti*. The destroyers were also damaged.

On the 26th, Warburton, during a reconnaissance of Corinth in a Spitfire, landed at Burg-el-Arab, in Egypt. He returned to Malta the next day.

On 25 August, two Wellingtons operated for the first time with 69 Squadron, making up C Flight, attacking some oil tankers near Corfu.

25 Coldbeck, *The Maltese Spitfire*, p.74.

What remains of Spitfire Mk.V EP339 flown by Group Captain Churchill DSO DFC. He planned the first offensive sweeps over Sicily and led the first one on 23 August 1942. Four days later, leading the second sweep, he was killed when his Spitfire was hit by flak and crashed in flames near Biscari airfield. (ACS 50009, 50003)

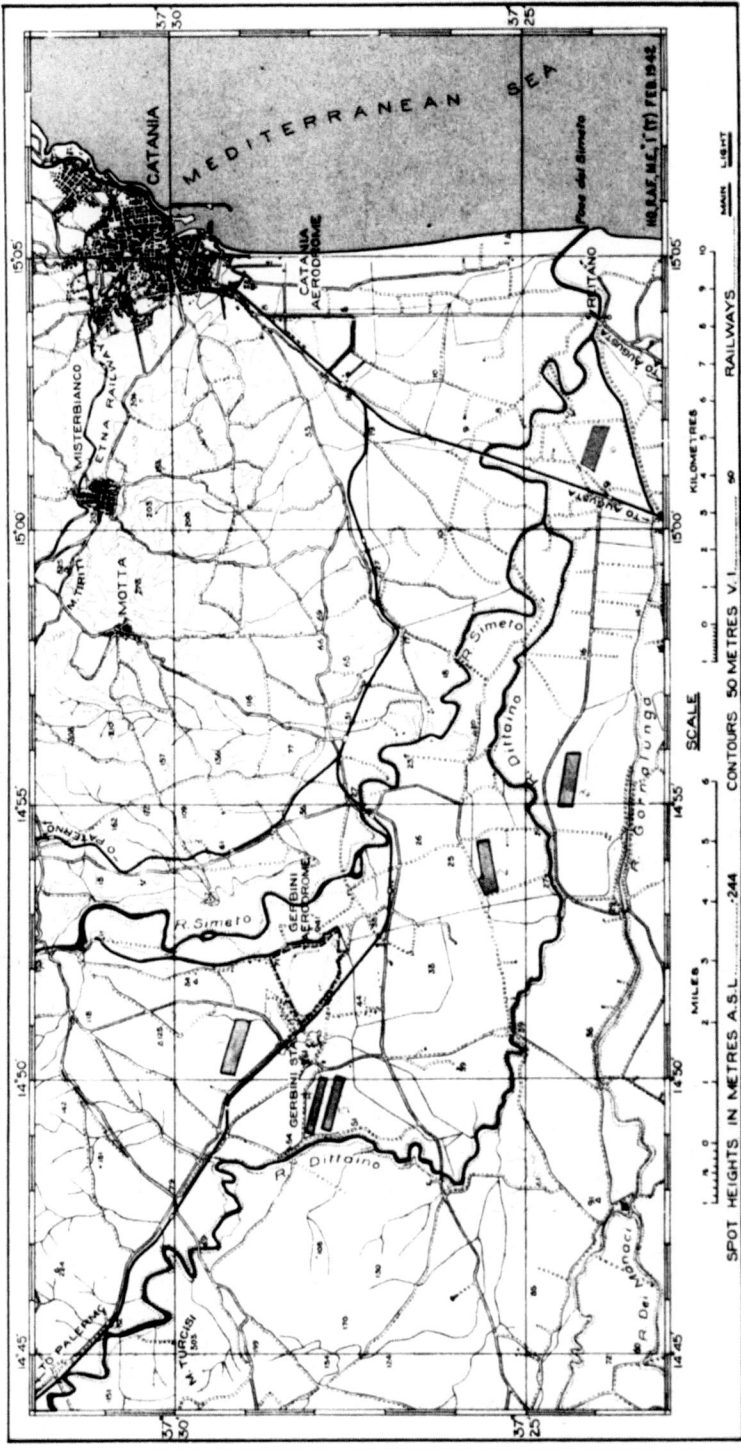

Gerbini aerodrome complex, August 1942. (AFHRA)

7

Sicilian Dangers

The great naval and air battles of the Mediterranean ended with a clear victory for the Axis, especially the sinking of the aircraft carrier HMS *Eagle* by the German submarine U-73, but with concrete strategic results for the British. The latter, in fact, with some supplies miraculously reaching their destination, thanks to Operation *Pedestal*, could now hinder the movement of supplies required by the *Afrika Korps*, whose offensive had ground to a halt near El Alamein, and increase reconnaissance sorties over Sicily and the rest of southern Italy.

At 3:40 p.m. on 4 September, Flight Sergeant J.O. Dalley was flying a routine recce to North Africa in Spitfire BR665:

> Photo recco. Capo Bon to Kelibia to look for minesweepers, also South of Gabes and West of Zuara to search for new constructional activity … Group buildings 1½ miles south of Gabes … Watercourse and strong defensive position. East of Arrum and road between Gabes and Medanine. Apparently defended position where road between Medanine and Ben Gardane crosses watercourse …

Meanwhile the Wellingtons of No. 69 Squadron carried out maritime reconnaissance near the island of Corfu, attacking enemy convoys, with the Baltimore engaged between Cephalonia and the heel of Italy.

About this time, 'Harry' Coldbeck recalled:

> A typical landfall would be the Greek island of Zante; a shallow turn south would enable the search to be made, looking over the starboard wing along the increasingly sunlit sea, in the hope of seeing the telltale arrowhead pattern on the surface which we had come to expect a convoy in motion to make. Without that pattern to guide the eye, stationary vessels were very difficult, if not impossible, to spot from 25,000 feet in this early light. Proceeding parallel to the distant coast and along the north/south axis of Zante, a thorough search of the glistening sea surface could be made, looking as far as possible under any broken cloud, for signs of a quarry. Quite often this arrowhead pattern would be partly obscured by these broken clouds so that two converging lines might be spotted between two clouds. By following the direction of convergence, with luck the tip of the arrow might be found in the open, beyond the cloud cover. Embedded within the arrowhead would be the plan shapes of the vessels and as time

Pilot Officer Henry Coldbeck writes his photographic report on his Spitfire's wing in March 1942. Camera staff were waiting to take the camera magazines to Valletta. (Harry Coldbeck, *The Maltese Spitfire*)

Luqa in late 1942. Lieutenant John Tucker of the Dorset Regiment, seated, and Pilot Officer John Dalley, later group captain. Regretfully, John Tucker lost his life during the invasion of Sicily the following year. (Harry Coldbeck, *The Maltese Spitfire*.)

had passed in this job, those of us now comprising the flight had learned to recognise, with the help of the photographic interpreters, Colvin and Herschel, what these plan shapes meant: merchant vessels and their tonnage; naval cruisers; destroyers; E-boats, etc. we could tell what vessels we were looking down on, as a whole convoy and escort ploughed its way towards the south where the Axis forces on the African continent waited for their supplies of fuel, ammunition, rations and transport.[1]

Two days later, 6 September, Warburton, with Sergeants Hemming, Cliffe and Covich, was flying a strike cover sortie near Cape Lefkada to verify the results of an attack on a large convoy by RAF Beauforts.

A German 20-mm Flak 30 cannon (Flugzeugabwehrkanone 30) on a building at Catania Fontanarossa. (Author's photo)

On 15 September, a signal decrypted at Bletchley Park revealed that the merchant vessel *Carbonia* (1,237 tons) had left Naples three days before. At this stage her destination was not known but the following day a further decryption indicated she had arrived in Tunis and was scheduled to leave that port the same evening, headed for Tripoli. She was not escorted, for the Italians sometimes hoped that smaller ships could slip through the blockade unobserved; indeed, so far, she had been successful.

---

1   Coldbeck, *The Maltese Spitfire*, p.72.

A German 88-mm anti-aircraft gun positioned on the coast near Catania. It is firing during a night raid on the city's military facilities. (Umberto Lugnan)

On the afternoon of 17 September, at around 1:00 p.m., Warburton and Spitfire BR665, carrying out a 'shipping search', spotted the ship sailing near Tunis. At 4:15 p.m., Squadron Leader William C. Wigmore of No. 227 Squadron took off at the head of six Beaufighters, each carrying two 250lb bombs. The formation hunted along the coast until, two hours later, the aircrews spotted and attacked the *Carbonia* in the Gulf of Hammamet.

On the morning of 19 September, 69 Squadron Spitfire PR.IV (AB300), flown by Sergeant Frank Gillions, was sent to Sicily for the now customary sortie over the ports and airfields in the west of the island. At 10:33 a.m., while photographing Castelvetrano, Gillions made his last radio communication with Malta, 'Are you receiving me?' to warn the engine of his Spitfire had problems. He tried to return to Luqa but was forced to bail out of the uncontrollable Spitfire near Agrigento. He was captured by the Italian military as reported in Bollettino n. 846 of 20 September 1942:

An enemy aircraft crashed in flames at Cattolica Eraclea (Agrigento): one of the airmen – New Zealand born – parachuted to the ground and was captured.

The reconnaissance activity during September was intense; on the 24th, two sorties were performed in succession over Sicily by 69 Squadron. The first was entrusted to Dalley who left Luqa at the controls of Spitfire BR431 at 7:00 a.m. to photograph the Capo Stilo and Messina areas. At 8:30 a.m., from 24,000 feet, a 2,000-ton hospital ship was photographed five miles

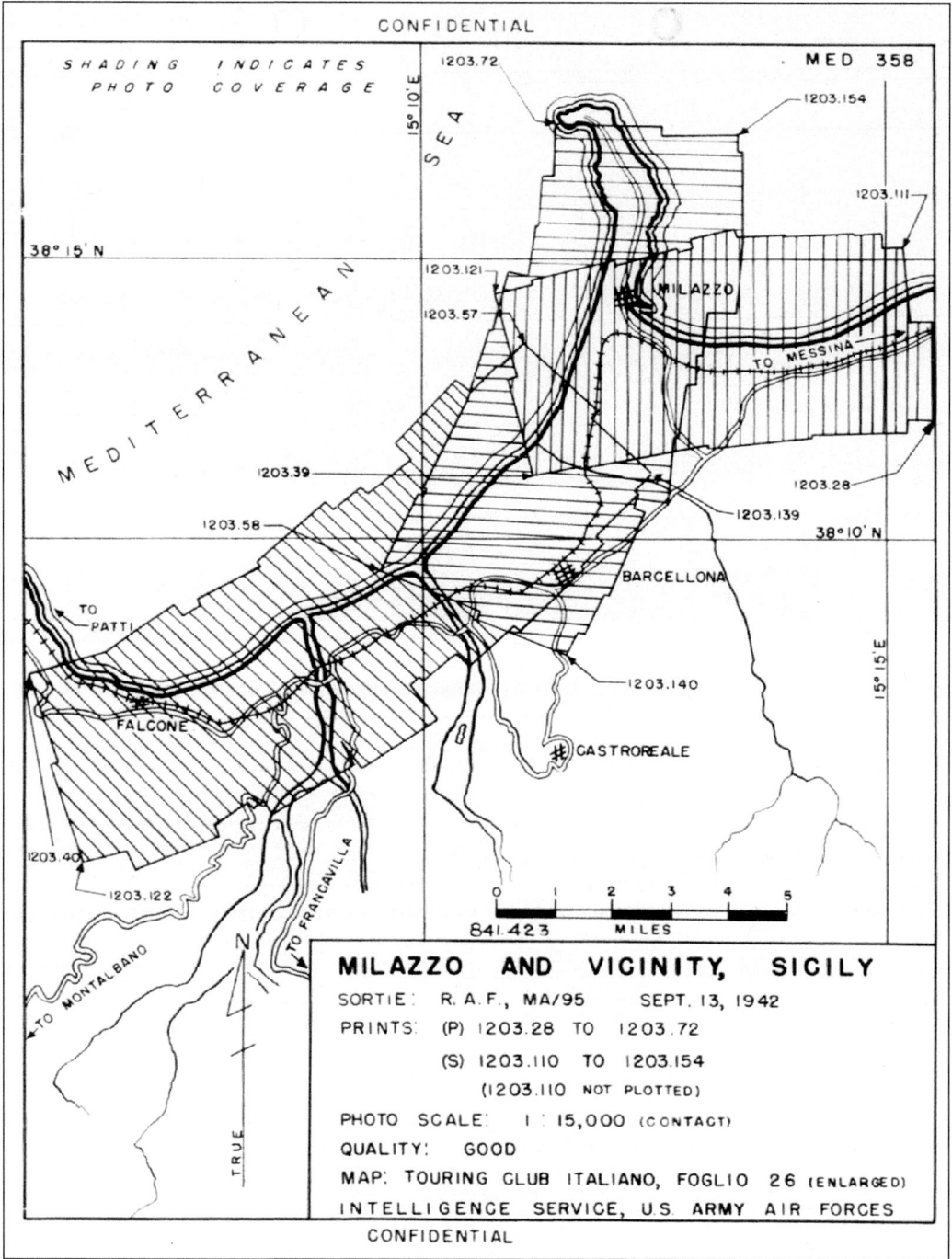

Coverage plots for Milazzo, 13 September 1942. This sortie was flown by Squadron Leader Adrian Warburton. (AFHRA)

Luftwaffe groundcrew maintain the weapons of a Bf 109E-7/Trop of *Jagdgeschwader 27 Afrika*. It was the unit of ace Hauptmann Hans-Joachim Marseille who died in North Africa at the age of 22, having amassed 158 victories. In Sicily, this *Jagdgeschwader* operated against Malta from various airfields including Comiso, Gela Ponte Olivo and Pachino. (ACS 21885, 21884)

from Capo d'Armi. At Messina, 10 minutes later, despite cloud cover obscuring some of the port facilities, four large merchant ships of 4,000 tons each, and three warships, were photographed. Dalley completed the sortie at 9:24 a.m.. At 8:45 the second sortie of the day had followed him out; Spitfire BR662, with Coldbeck at the controls, covering Augusta, Catania and Messina. Dense cloud cover over Palermo prevented photographs from being taken and no large vessels were reported at Trapani. Small boats at Porto Empedocle and Licata were identified and, finally, over Lampedusa, Coldbeck descended to 14,000 feet to photograph two 1,000-ton merchant ships. He then resumed the return flight to Malta, landing at 12:00 p.m. The day after, Warburton departed in Spitfire BR665, covering Messina and Capo Stilo in search of a large merchant ship which was ultimately found a mile from Capo d'Armi at 2:25 p.m. The ship was escorted by five warships, one of which was equipped with an anti-aircraft defence system.

A photo of Comiso airport taken on 14 September 1942 by Pilot Officer L.R. Colquhoun in Spitfire PR.IV BR653. (US Air Force)

That afternoon, the hospital ship spotted earlier was photographed, by Dalley from 17,500 feet, entering the port of Lampedusa with four 1,000-ton merchant ships. Dalley also photographed eight torpedo boats moored at Porto Empedocle where heavy anti-aircraft fire came close to hitting him.

Since 25 August, 69 Squadron's C Flight had been flying, mainly at night, several Vickers Wellington Mk.VIII bombers to search for, and attack, enemy ships. Between 28 and 29 September, the moon was three-quarters full and visibility excellent. On board Wellington HX604 'X' were Flying Officer Fitzgerald and Sergeants Langford, Shierlaw, Sugden, Wildman and Sweeny. They took off from Luqa at 9:20 p.m. and headed to Messina in search of large vessels reported by the previous recce. The Wellington reached Capo Spartivento at 10:41 p.m. At 11:05, while over Messina, a heavy barrage of anti-aircraft fire, supported by 10 searchlights, which illuminated the sky as though it were daytime, challenged the RAF bomber. Fitzgerald miraculously managed to get out of range, heading towards Capo d'Armi. Midnight had just passed when a large 4,000-ton merchant ship was sighted, escorted by three other vessels. The Wellington dived to 3,000 feet, dropping four 500lb bombs that hit the ship. Two of the escorts opened up with light anti-aircraft fire, but they were unable to hit the Wellington which landed safely back at Luqa at 2:55 a.m..

It was just on dawn the following day, when Coldbeck, in Spitfire BR653[2], flew to Messina to assess the damage caused the previous night. Near Capo d'Armi, he spotted a 7,000-ton merchant ship escorted by three small boats. In addition, three Axis aircraft were seen protecting the vessels.

On 1 October, the work to extend the runway at Comiso was recorded. The same thing was happening at Gerbini. The next day, 69 Squadron's Flying Officer A.W. Gubb, intent on photographing Gela Ponte Olivo from 25,000 feet, noticed two Re.2001 fighters at 22,000 feet on their way up to intercept him. He changed course and headed towards Comiso where he spotted more fighters at 5,000 feet. It was a wise decision to return to Malta.

The arrival of Pilot Officer Fred McKay and Flight Sergeant 'Paddy' Hope of No. 540 Squadron (No. 1 Photographic Reconnaissance Unit) from Benson on board a PR Mosquito (DK320) was very welcome.[3] They were part of the Gibraltar detachment of 540 Squadron. During their transit, more than 800 photographs were taken over Venice, Trieste, Fiume, Pola, Rome, Littorio aerodrome and Palermo, a performance for which they received a special telegram from the commander of No. 16 Group:

> Congratulations to P/O McKay and F/S Hope on their very fine reconnaissance on 2/10, which was outstanding in every way.

A very delicate sortie was flown on 8 October by Squadron Leader Adrian Warburton who had become commanding officer of 69 Squadron in August. The task was to investigate, and take low-altitude photos of, the German RDF (Range and Direction Finding – radar) station at Noto, installed near a country property called Villa Oliva, in the Testa dell'Acqua district. The area was defended. In fact, in the immediate vicinity, the Germans had placed numerous

---

2   For the month of September, there are some differences in data (aircraft serials and dates) between the ORB and Appendices of 69 Squadron.

3   McKay, after conducting several sorties from Malta, returned to Benson just three days later.

88mm heavy anti-aircraft guns, the so-called heavy flak, to defend the station.[4] At 9:45 a.m., Warburton left Luqa for Noto, flying over the area at 3,000 feet. He wrote:

> Flew over Noto turn back over the R.D.F. station, 180° Testa dell'Acqua 2¼miles. Square building with nine masts, 4 on either side and one at end. Orbited and made second run Photographs taken. Two Me 109's [sic] orbiting at 3,000' over Noto. One pursuing the Spitfire [BR665] for several minutes. Set course for base. Two more Me 109's [sic] sighted at 3,000' over Cape Passero flying on course of 360°. These paid no attention to the Spitfire much proceeded on their course. Map reference Ragusa 1/250.000 sheet J.33/11.[5]

On 9 October, Ultra intercepted a German message announcing the arrival from Bari of 25 Bf109s of I/JG 27 at Pachino airfield between 1:30 and 3:00 p.m. that day.

On 13 October, Coldbeck was sent to the area and spotted the Bf 109s of JG 27 'Afrika' parked on the runway at Pachino; photos were taken from 8,000 feet despite the threat of enemy fighters. The German unit ended its stay at this airfield on 23 October when it moved to North Africa.

The morning of 14 October, three Beaufighters of 227 Squadron, led by Squadron Leader Peter L. Underwood, left Luqa to attack a small convoy consisting of the German merchant vessel *Trapani* (1,855 tons) escorted by the torpedo boat *Medici*. These two vessels had left Tripoli in the early morning and were headed along the coast of North Africa to Benghazi. Two Macchi fighters circled overhead.

The three Beaufighters reached the enemy convoy at 12:30 p.m. and attacked. The results were described in a report written by the commander of the torpedo boat, Tenente di Vascello Antonio Furlan:

> At 1237 hours the convoy was attacked at very low level by three bombers. The first bomber attempted to fly across the merchant ship from port to starboard but was too low. Probably hit by machine gun fire, it hit the mast at the stem, crashed into the sea on the starboard side, and exploded. The second aircraft tried a similar manoeuvre from the opposite direction but, noticing that it was too low, tried to turn away and dropped two bombs on the starboard side, neither of which exploded. At the same time, it was firing its machine guns. Caught between fire from Trapani and Medici (which was well within range, being only 300 metres away), the aircraft was hit in the engines. It lost height as it flew off and was seen to crash into the sea. The third bomber did not carry out an attack but was chased and overtaken by the escorting

---

4   Based on direct agreements between the Undersecretary for the Air Force and Kesselring, it had been decided that the CD1(*Centri di Disturbo*, Radio Interference Centres) at Noto would remain controlled by the Germans and that the Italians would construct CD2 in Monte Renna, CD3 in Santa Maria di Leuca, CD4 in Kefalonia, CD5 in Ustica and CD6 in Ischia. Already, by 20 July 1942, CD1 and the CD2 were in operation. Giuseppe Pesce, *Guerra attraverso l'etere. Il radar durante il secondo conflitto mondiale* [*War across the ether: Radar during the Second World War*] (Modena, Mucchi, 1978), p.153.

5   The National Archives London, Royal Air Force, Operations Record Books Appendices Air 27/611-2, Sortie Report 109, p.27.

fighters, which shot it down. I steered towards the position where the second aircraft had crashed into the sea, this position having been indicated to me by an escorting fighter [Warburton's Spitfire]. I spotted a rubber dinghy and rescued the crew, which consisted of an officer and a sergeant …[6]

Adrian Warburton followed the Beaufighters in Spitfire BR665 and was an eyewitness to the attack, summarising it in his report:

A/C 'Q' attacked with cannons from mast height but his bombs hung up and the aircraft exploded in the air150/200 yards after flying past the M/V.
A/C 'Y' attacked next and his cannon fire was observed straddling the M/V's deck but his bombs overshot.
'Y', after the attack, rapidly lost height and went in the sea. A dinghy with two occupants was observed some 5 to 10 miles North North West of the convoy on a bearing of 350°.
A/C 'H' attacked last and cannon fire hits were observed straddling the M/V's deck amidships but no bombs were seen dropping from the aircraft.
'H' made a second run and dropped his bombs from mast height. Bombs undershot.
Repeatedly dived and flew alongside the D/r at 0 feet waggling wings in an attempt to guide the D/r towards the dinghy.
Light flak experienced from D/r during first two runs.
After some 20 minutes the D/r apparently understood the meaning of my unusual tactics and course for the dinghy. Circled over dinghy to indicate correct position to D/r when six Macchi 200 presumably from Mellaha, attempted to intercept me.
Macchis got on my tail four times but I managed to shake them off. Relying on my superior speed, I took evasive action and remained in the vicinity of the dinghy until I saw the D/r pick up the dinghy with its two occupants.[7]

The first Beaufighter was flown by Underwood, who was by then a flight commander and nearing the end of his operational tour. He was noted for the determination of his attacks, as well as for his frequent support of Beauforts in difficulties. Both he and his navigator, Flight Sergeant Ivor R. Miller, lost their lives. The second Beaufighter was flown by Pilot Officer J.M. Bryce and navigated by Flight Sergeant S.W. Cole. Fortunately, they were picked up by the *Medici* and became PoWs. The third Beaufighter was not shot down and in fact made two attacks on the *Trapani*. The bombs hung up on the first occasion and they overshot on the second. The Beaufighter, flown by Pilot Officer Tom St B. Freer, was badly hit and the hydraulics were shot away, but the pilot nursed it back to a crash-landing at Luqa. By this time, the strength of 227 Squadron was reduced to six Beaufighters, of which only three were serviceable. This was the period known as the 'mini-blitz' when Malta came under renewed attack from Sicily. One of these machines was burnt out in a blast pen on 17 October following an air raid.

6   Roy Conyers Nesbit. *The Armed Rovers: Beauforts and Beaufighters over the Mediterranean* (Shrewsbury: Airlife Publishing Ltd, 1995), p.85.
7   The National Archives London, Royal Air Force, Operations Record Books Appendices Air 27/611-2, p.58.

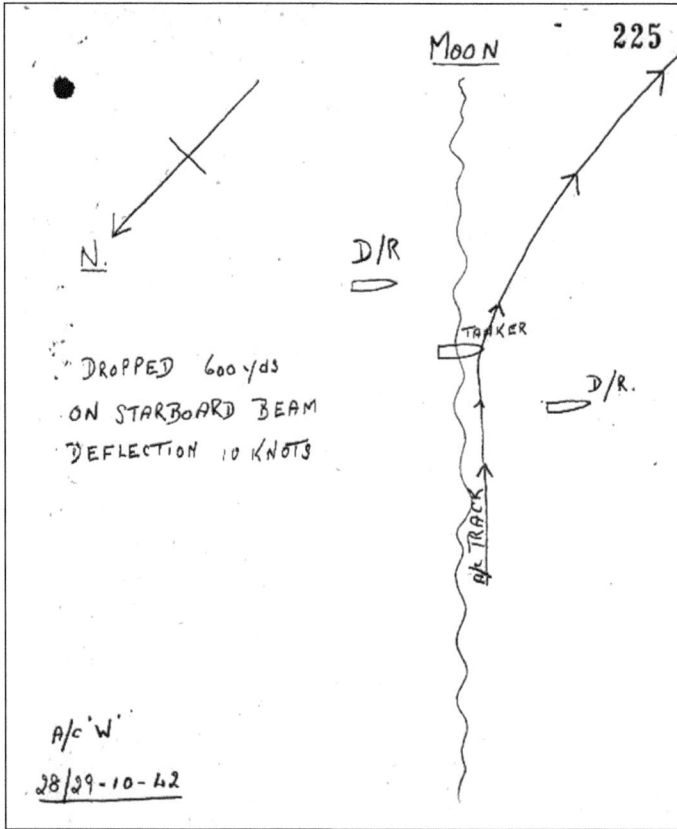

Drawing of the attack on the tanker reported by Adrian Warburton. (TNA)

The most delicate sorties, especially the dangerous ones flown at low altitude, were entrusted to experienced pilots. An example of this occurred on 19 October when Warburton flew to the *Luftwaffe* HQ at Taormina. Taking off at 3:00 p.m. at the controls of Spitfire BR665, he flew over the target several times, at an altitude between 3,000 and 3,500 feet, without taking any photos due to a dense bank of clouds. On the return flight, the 24-year-old English pilot was tracked near Comiso by an Italian-German RDF station which directed four fighters to intercept him. Warburton returned safely to Malta at 5:00 p.m.

In the meantime, Leslie Colquhoun had finished his tour. He had carried out 154 photo-reconnaissance sorties over hostile territory, flying 475 hours.[8] An anecdote of note is taken from his memoirs, collected by Jane Wilson in *On Wing and Water: The life of Leslie R. Colquhoun, war hero, test pilot and hovercraft pioneer*:

Although there must have been many dangerous moments and narrow squeaks during his time in Malta, Les admits to one incident which upset him, on a flight over Sicily. His squadron had just received a consignment of chocolate, which was considered

8   The veteran pilot returned to England. The following year he was assigned to No. 682 Squadron to operate from North Africa.

almost as valuable as gold. Les took a packet with him to eat during the flight. "I was flying over Cape Passero, the south eastern extremity of Sicily, and came down to 16,000 ft. to take off my oxygen mask to eat some chocolate before setting course for Malta. Suddenly I saw a shadow and just behind me almost in formation was an ME109. His guns must have jammed, or he was out of ammunition, or was a pupil on a training flight, for he did not fire at me, and of course I had no guns. I called up Luqa madly for help, but the 109 flew away and all ended well – for me!" Maybe that was one moment when chocolate did not taste so good.[9]

In October, Lieutenant W.S. Clark, officer commanding Wellington C Flight was appointed temporary captain. 'Harry' Coldbeck, on taking charge of the PRU Spitfires of B Flight, was appointed acting flight lieutenant, as was MacKay, now commanding the Baltimores of A Flight. Meanwhile the Squadron Leader Warburton DSO DFC was awarded a second bar to his DFC.

In the late afternoon of 28 October, a formation of Wellingtons from 69 Squadron was sent to attack a naval convoy near Navarino, Greece. The convoy had been located by a Baltimore squadron during the morning of the previous day. Wellington MX565 W', piloted by Pilot Officer Donkersley, torpedoed an oil tanker.

German SC1000 bombs at Comiso. Inside the hangar can be seen the silhouette of a Messerschmitt Me 210. (Author's photo)

9   J. Wilson, *On Wing and Water: The life of Leslie R Colquhoun, war hero, test pilot and hovercraft pioneer* (Cirencester, UK: Mereo Books, 2014).

Part of a mosaic of southern Sicily. The photo was taken from 26,000 feet, between 11:30 a.m. and 12:15 p.m., of the Pozzallo, Ragusa and Gela area. The sortie was flown by Coldbeck in Spitfire PR.IV BR431. The shot shows the city of Vittoria near Ragusa. (US Air Force)

October saw a significant increase, compared to previous months, in photo-reconnaissance sorties. The Spitfires flew 162 hours and 45 minutes, the Baltimores 98 hours and 35 minutes, and the Wellingtons 237 hours and 20 minutes.

The following month proved decisive and unforgettable for one of the pilots who had distinguished himself recently. At 1:44 p.m. on 10 November, Harry Coldbeck lifted off from Luqa in Spitfire BS367 for a routine sortie to Taranto, Messina and Augusta. It proved to be his final operational flight of the war in Europe. He was shot down by anti-aircraft fire near Augusta but managed to bail out into the sea. Recovered and taken prisoner by the Italian Navy, he was transferred to various prison camps, after receiving treatment for his injuries, first in Italy and then to the famous Stalag Luft III, in Żagań, Poland. He was released in 1945.[10] His account of that unforgettable day, taken from his autobiography *The Maltese Spitfire. One Pilot, One Plane – Find Enemy Forces on Land and Sea*, highlights how lucky he was to survive:

After several circuits counting the battleships and cruisers, using my verticals as well as the oblique camera, with which this new aircraft was fitted, I vacated the area and made my way, climbing from under 8,000 feet on the way to Messina. There was a cruiser there, which I just had to sight, at Messina and their gunners too, were keen to deter me. Eventually, a hole in the cloud, at about 5,000 feet let me see it and note it. Next stop Augusta! On my way past Mt Etna, I was climbing again for there were three cruisers there which had been confirmed in Augusta on previous thrice-daily sorties. They had moved over from Navarino in Greece where we had been watching them. Once again my altimeter began to unwind as I descended below the first layer of cloud, looking for a hole to observe the three cruisers. Another layer of cloud over the harbour saw me south of Augusta looking north through a hole in that cloud layer and my luck was in, for the moment. There were the three cruisers; I was free to go home. Now! I had just rounded out, at 4,000 feet, and my speed was approximately 400 miles an hour. There was a loud crunching noise from the rear of the aircraft and the nose went violently down as in a bunt. Simultaneously, I had a glimpse of the Perspex windscreen distorting in front of me before I lost consciousness. I came to, outside the aircraft, falling freely through the air. I looked down as I felt the air rushing past my ears. My helmet had gone and there was a swirling turbulent circle of sea below where, presumably, the Spitfire had gone in. I looked down again and found the rip-cord misplaced down my body and although there didn't seem to be any urgency, I pulled it and the parachute opened with a jerk and I was in the sea. In parachute drill, the recommended way to enter the water is to rotate a disc on the front of the quick release box so that on entering the water a blow with the fist will free the parachute. There had

10 Flight Lieutenant Henry Gift Coldbeck (NZ405235) of the Royal New Zealand Air Force, 69 Squadron RAF, was awarded the Distinguished Flying Cross. 'This officer has performed outstanding work in Malta and the successes achieved against enemy shipping lately are largely due to his courage and skill in locating enemy convoys. On many occasions he has flown low over heavily defended areas and the resulting excellent information has been of invaluable assistance. On one occasion, although attacked by 3 enemy fighters, he flew over Palermo at 5,000 feet and located a large enemy tanker destined for North Africa. Flight Lieutenant Coldbeck is a resolute and fearless pilot whose exceptional skill has been invaluable in obtaining reports of enemy shipping movements and the dispositions of aircraft.' In *The London Gazette*, 17 November 1943.

been no time for such action and on my landing in the sea, the parachute proceeded to pull me along like an aquaplane, further out to sea. It was now so quiet with only the lapping of the waves to be heard. I was overcome with sorrow as I believed this was the end of my flying career. It was getting quite dark now on the water as I undid the dinghy pack which the lanyard, attached to my life-jacket, had pulled away from the parachute when I let it go. I was glad we had practiced this sort of thing in swimming baths in the United Kingdom[11].

After flying armed reconnaissances in the Mersa Matruh area, in Egypt, No. 46 Squadron entered the scene over Sicily, transferring some of its Bristol Beaufighter Mk.VI aircraft to Malta. The first three Beaufighters were sent on 15 November, but none reached the island. The last radio contact was established 40 miles from the coast, after which they disappeared into thin air, so much so they are still missing in action. Other Beaufighters, however, managed to reach Malta in the following days. In the late evening of the 19th, eight of them went into action, carrying out an armed reconnaissance over various parts of Sicily. The airfields at Trapani and Comiso were among the targets and several aircraft were machine-gunned on the ground.

Three Beaufighters from 46 Squadron left Malta at 6:00 p.m. the next day (20th) to attack Trapani. Pilot Officer Atkins and Sergeant Mayo took part in the operation in Beaufighter '7809', summarising their part in it as follows:

> Night strafing of Trapani A/D. On initial run over A/D pilot saw 5 or 6 JU 52's [sic] in a line on the runway. In all our A/C made 6 runs strafing the E/A. the 2nd run in at about 200ft, 3rd run strafing from 500ft down to about 100ft, 4th, 5th, and 6th runs at about 30ft firing through the line of E/A and concentrating on the last A/C in which a fire was started. … Two light Enemy A/A guns were firing at our A/C …[12]

Struck by bursts from anti-aircraft machine guns, Beaufighter '7760', crewed by Flying Officer Kemp and Flight Sergeant Bonner, managed to return to Malta on one engine. A more tragic fate befell Beaufighter '8137' as it was shot down near Calatafimi, killing Flying Officer Bate while Flight Sergeant Vineburg survived to be taken prisoner. That evening, three Wellingtons from No. 104 Squadron carried out five sorties, from 5:45 p.m. to 4:30 a.m. the next day, against Trapani, dropping 4,000lbs of bombs there. The same squadron also bombed Gerbini the following night.

On 21 November, Sergeant Keith Durbidge took some photos of Castelvetrano, capturing the presence of 30 large aircraft and 10 probable fighters. At the Trapani complex, he identified 30 large aircraft and 20 fighters, while over Palermo Boccadifalco oblique photos were taken, from 24,000 feet, revealing the silhouettes of 20 large aircraft parked in the area north-west of the runway.

11   Coldbeck, *The Maltese Spitfire*, p.81.
12   The National Archives London, Royal Air Force, Operations Record Books AIR 27/460/51.

1942	Photo-Recce	Photo-Recce Navy/Convoy	Visual Recce	Fighters[13]	AA	Times two sorties in one day	Total
Sorties carried out by Coldbeck							
Mar	4			1	2		4
Apr	12				1		12
May	16					2	16
June	10	12	2	1		5	24
July	7	12		1	3	2	19
Aug	11	14		2		3	25
Sept	8	17	1	1	2	3	26
Oct	8	9		2	2		17
Nov	4	6			3	3	10
Total	80	70	3	8	13	18	153

Period	Shipping	Submarine (Area and Close Cover)
Reconnaissance - Sea from Malta between 19/20 May – 29 December 1942		
19/20 May – 2 June	56	
2/3 - 16 June	43	
16/17 - 30 June	47	
30 June/1 – 14 July	27	
14/15 – 28 July	23	
28/29 July – 11 Aug.	22	
11/12 – 25 Aug.	61	
25/26 Aug. – 8 Sept.	17	
8/9 – 22 Sept	28	
22/23 Sept. – 6 Oct.	35	
6/7 – 20 Oct.	22	
20/21 Oct. – 3 Nov.	32	2
3/4 – 17 Nov.	71	
17/18 Nov. – 1 Dec.	78	1
1/2 - 15 Dec.	119	8
15/16 – 29 Dec.	52	10
Total	**733**	**21**

13   Sorties where Flight Lieutenant Henry Gift Coldbeck was intercepted by fighters or subjected to anti-aircraft fire.

The area covered operationally by PR Spitfires from Malta. (TNA)

American Reconnaissance Aircraft and Operation *Torch*

In the late morning of 4 November, Flying Officer A. Gubb, in Spitfire PR.IV (BR653), photographed the runway at Sciacca, despite the airfield being well hidden and the aircraft sheltered under the centuries-old olive trees. A large number of twin-engine aircraft were visible. Recent sorties had also paid particular and constant attention to the large number of E-boats moored near Porto Empedocle; there were 10 of them on 6 November.[14] Significant movements were recorded the same day at Catania Fontanarossa where 15 Ju 88s of KG 54 had just landed from Heraklion. Two days later, 13 Ju 88s of LG 1 (*Lehrgeschwader* – training squadron) also arrived from Heraklion, in addition to five Bf 110s from Araxos, 12 from Kastelli, and further Ju 88s from various parts of Italy. On 18 November, 22 He 111 bombers of KG 26 arrived at Catania Fontanarossa from Grosseto.

In a broader context, a progressive increase in aircraft was evident, including at Trapani, Castelvetrano and Gerbini. On the former, 30 large aircraft were observed on the runway and on the northern part of the airfield's dispersal area. In the Castelvetrano area, 20 Ju 88s were identified parked on the northern side. Reconstruction works were observed in the south-west

A pilot of the *Regia Aeronautica* looks out of his Caproni Ca.314. Note the extensive nose glazing. From October 1942, the *173ᵃ Squadriglia RST* received several Ca.314s. Operating from Palermo, the unit patrolled the seas north of Sicily, escorting convoys and observing enemy ships. (ACS 40210)

14 These were the Schnellbootes of the 3rd *Kriegsmarine* Flotilla, about to leave Porto Empedocle for Trapani. They were S-30, S-33, S-35, S-36, S-54, S-56, S-57, S-59, S-60, S-61, while two other S-Bootes, S-55 and S-58, were based at Palermo. Alberto Santoni, Francesco Mattesini, *La partecipazione tedesca alla guerra aeronavale nel Mediterraneo* [*German participation in the air and naval war in the Mediterranean*] *(1940-1945)* (Parma: Albertelli Edizioni Speciali, 2005), p.286.

sector of the airfield at Biscari Santo Pietro. Palermo Boccadifalco was home to 12 Bf 110s of 7./ZG 26, waiting to be transferred to Kastelli, in Greece, on the 21st. Maritime traffic between Sicily and the ports of Tunis and Tripoli was significant. The British were also sufficiently alarmed by the arrival in Sicily of some Tiger and Panzer III tanks, of the *Panzer-Abteilung 501*, waiting to be loaded for the sea voyage to Tunisia. They arrived at Trapani via a rail service from Fallingbostel, a town in Lower Saxony, Germany.[15]

On 8 November, Anglo-American forces landed in Casablanca (Morocco), Oran and Algiers (Algeria), starting Operation *Torch*. While in Morocco, the Americans had only to deal with the relatively superficial resistance posed by the Vichy French air force. In Algeria, having eliminated the few French machines, the Americans found themselves facing harsher resistance in the air, in the form of Italian-German attacks, as the entire Algerian area fell within range of the Axis aircraft. The Allied landings in the Mediterranean had not taken the Germans by surprise as, as early as October 1942, reconnaissance carried out near Gibraltar reported the continuous deployment of substantial Allied air and naval forces.

On 7 November, Sergeants Durbidge and Howard had left England to deliver two PR Spitfires to Malta, joining 69 Squadron in the process. Unexpectedly, they found themselves witnessing the Allied offensive in North Africa. Keith Durbidge remembered that day:

> Howard and I flew down to R.A.F. Portreath in Cornwall in brand new Mark IV Spitfires and after a day's delay due to bad weather took off separately for Gibraltar. The airfield at Gibraltar was completely stacked out with aircraft of all shapes, size and types, thus leaving a narrow corridor in which to land. The reason for this became apparent the next morning when we flew direct to Malta. It was November 7th and the start of the Allied attack on German and pro-Axis forces in North-West Africa. Scenes of fighting were clearly visible along the coasts of Morocco, Algeria and Tunisia, A few weeks after joining No. 69 Squadron … I was hospitalized … with an ear infection which stopped me flying. While I was away from the Squadron, Howard was shot down returning from a sortie … The principal task was to provide regular visual and photographic coverage of the enemy's land, sea and air forces; their strengths; their movements; and their lines of communication. A close eye was kept on a regular basis for any ship heading to or from the North African coast where the German and Italian armies, under Field Marshal Rommel, opposed Montgomery's 8th army in the East. … Whenever [an] Allied convoy to Malta was planned or was in passage from Alexandria or Gibraltar, the Squadron was required to obtain, regardless of weather conditions, coverage of the three main Italian naval bases of Taranto, Naples and Messina where at least five battleships and 12 cruisers were stationed. Each day, three sorties were flown, one at first photographic light, one at noon, and a final one at last light, to ensure a convoy's safety, at least from large surface craft. Pilots on these particular sorties were authorized to disregard the instructions to maintain radio silence. They were to report 'in the clear' and, of course, in code, any capital ship that was absent from its usual moorings. On this information, whole convoys could be ordered to turn back.[16]

15   George Forty, *Tiger Tank Battalions in World War II* (Minneapolis, USA: Zenith Press, 2008), p.33.
16   Keith Durbidge, *Memoirs of a High Flyer* (England: Lulu.com, 2013), p.35.

The aftermath of Heinkel He 111s of II./KG 100 bombing the English airfield near the oasis of Kufra, in Libya. The photo was taken shortly after by a *Luftwaffe* photo-reconnaissance machine. In the air raid, three Bristol Bombays of No. 216 Squadron were destroyed on the ground. (Pier Ferrari)

In support of the Allied invasion of North Africa, No. 4 Photographic Reconnaissance Unit (PRU) was the only photo-reconnaissance unit available to meet the needs of the Anglo-American forces engaged in Operation *Torch*. Based at Gibraltar, it performed most of the aerial photographic sorties in the North African area.

At 1:05 p.m. on 14 November, John Dalley left Luqa for a shipping search in the western Mediterranean Sea, flying over Sardinia. He subsequently wrote:

Top: Sergeant Peter Morris, of No. 682 Squadron, in the cockpit of a Spitfire PR.XI.
Bottom: Morris's Spitfire made an emergency landing at La Marsa after being hit by anti-aircraft fire.
Both images were taken in mid-1943. (Alessandro Ragatzu)

Decimomannu. Whilst photographic East dispersal of drome at 6500' I observed 2 ME.202's [sic] at 2 O'clock at 500 above and ½ mile distance and a second or two later saw section of 4 ME.202's [sic] in a straggling line ahead climbing to my port quarter, the leader being 4/500 yds away at 9 O'clock. I immediately turned cameras off, selected fully fine and opened full out, as I had been taking photos at only 165 indicated. The aircraft at 2 O'clock peeled off into a head-on attack, the leader opening up at what must have been 500 yards. I put on full right rudder, banging my head violently against the left hood blister. White streaks were observed passing over my port wing and further out. Immediately the aircraft had passed overhead, the second of which did not fire, I went into a steep climb turn toward the other 4, the leader of which was roughly 200 yards away and firing. He followed me round but was unable to obtain sufficient deflection to hit my aircraft. I maintained the tight climbing turn and experienced no difficulty in outclimbing them and outturning them and escaped into cloud cover. The ME.202's [sic] were camouflaged Brown-Green, on the upper surface with dark belly, and duck egg blue spinners, and a white band just forward of the tail unit. Their armament appeared to be 2 machine guns in either wing/outside the propellor.[17]

On 13 November 1942, the newly formed 4 PRU[18] arrived at Maison Blanche in Algeria, from Portreath, England. The unit consisted of six Spitfire PR.IVs under the command of Squadron Leader Alfred H.W. 'Freddy' Ball, Eastern Air Command. Thus, the area of Algiers and Oran began to be covered, as well as the north-western coast to Casablanca. A few days after arriving, however, the unit lost several Spitfires and much photographic equipment in a disastrous *Luftwaffe* attack on the airfield. The first mission from the new airfield was carried out on the 17th by Flying Officer McKenzie who covered Bizerte and Tunis.

The Spitfires were soon replaced, via Gibraltar, but ground-based photographers had to improvise and modify much of their equipment to carry on the unit's activities. On 23 November, the French forces in West Africa decided to join the Allied cause and the operations of the RAF photographic contingent consequently ended a few months later.

Transferred, on 24 November, from Oran–Tafaraoui to Algiers–Maison Blanche, the American photographic staff of the 3rd Photographic Group (PG) operated for the first time four days later. Over the following two and a half months, the British and American units cooperated increasingly to avoid duplication of their efforts; this would also occur over Sicily and western Europe in the near future.

Although the remaining staff belonging to the 3rd PG arrived in Algiers in December, with the 12th Photographic Reconnaissance Squadron (PRS) ground echelon arriving in Casablanca direct from the United States, most of the activity during this period was carried out by the 5th PRS.

The first interpretation report of the areas of North Africa was issued on 17 November by the NACIU (Northwest African Central Interpretation Unit). Delivered to 395 recipients, it included 21 different types of reports which were divided into several main categories, including:

---

17 The National Archives London, Royal Air Force, Operations Record Books AIR 27/607/11-1, p.33.
18 The unit formed at RAF Benson on 10 September 1942.

Differences in altitude, attitude, or airspeed changed image overlap and could deny stereo coverage from a British Middle East Intelligence Unit report. (MEIU)

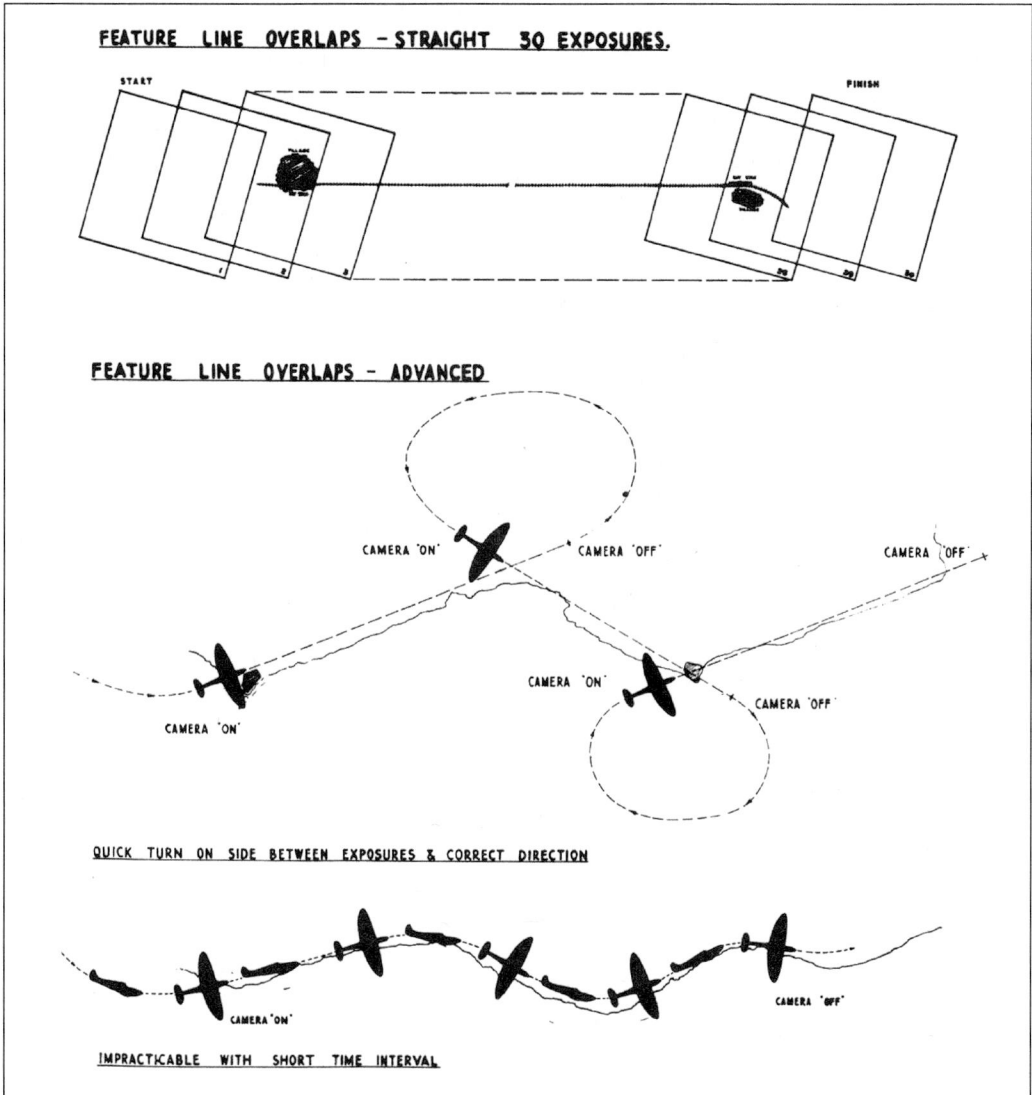

FEATURE LINE OVERLAPS - STRAIGHT 30 EXPOSURES.

FEATURE LINE OVERLAPS - ADVANCED

QUICK TURN ON SIDE BETWEEN EXPOSURES & CORRECT DIRECTION

IMPRACTICABLE WITH SHORT TIME INTERVAL

Top: Coverage of a straight-line segment showing exposure overlap with about a 15° crosswind correction to the right. Centre: Flying pattern to divide an irregular coastline into a series of straight-line segments – or legs – to save film and avoid picture distortion in extreme turns. Bottom: Snap roll turns to make small course corrections when following a nearly straight linear objective. (MEIU)

plants, naval and naval units, defences and land forces, airfields and aircraft, evaluation of damage from bombing, anti-aircraft defences, objectives industrial and special, radar and radio, night bombing reports, daily survey of ships, airfields, and communication routes.

The First American Reconnaissance over Sicily

On 5 December, almost a year after 11 December 1941, the day on which Italy and Germany declared war on the United States of America, a senior American officer, Lieutenant Colonel Harry T. Eidson, of the 3rd PG, flew to Sicily for the first time on board an American F-4A (the photographic version of the Lockheed P-38 Lightning). This was mission number '3PG18'. Eidson reported an intense anti-aircraft artillery barrage from Palermo Boccadifalco airfield and photographed the airfields at Trapani Bo Rizzo and Trapani Milo. On the night of 11/12 December, Palermo was raided by five Wellingtons of No. 40 Squadron from Malta. Strong raids were also recorded in Naples, with significant damage to the port area and city centre. The confirmed losses among the civilian population were 57 dead and 138 injured.

In the meantime, Ultra revealed the arrival at Castelvetrano of 27 German Ju 52/3m transports from Castel Benito on 14 December and another 19 in the early morning of the 18th, between 3:00 and 4:05 a.m. In addition, an Me 323, coming from Pomigliano in Campania and bound for North Africa, landed for technical reasons at 3:45 p.m. on the 17th. At 8:00 a.m. on 18 December, Sergeant D. Howard of 69 Squadron took off from Malta and pointed the nose of Spitfire BR426 towards the naval bases of Taranto and Augusta. Tragically, he did not return and was found dead in his lifeboat adrift in the Mediterranean. A similar epilogue also awaited Pilot Officer W.F. Rains, of 4 PRU, who left at 9:00 a.m. in Spitfire BS649 for the Tunis area. A PR Spitfire was possibly shot down north of Valletta by Unteroffizier Bahnesen of 8./JG 53 at 8:41; it is probable this was Howard. Another pilot of the same *Staffel*, based in Sicily, was credited with shooting down another Spitfire over Marsa Scirocco at 11:02 a.m.; this was most likely BS649 of Rains.

In the early afternoon of 23 December, after taking photos of Venice, Trieste, Fiume, Ancona and then down Italy to Naples and Sicily, PR Mosquito DZ382 of No. 540 Squadron landed in Malta from Benson. The aircraft, piloted by Flight Lieutenant M.D.S. Hood and Pilot Officer T.H. Burdett, returned to Benson the next day. Another 540 Squadron Mosquito, DK320 flown by Flying Officer W. Payne and Sergeant A.J. Kent, had flown to Maison Blanche from Gibraltar on 4 December.[19]

At the close of the year, 31 December, a few hours apart, 69 Squadron sent off four of its pilots on sorties. The first was Pilot Officer J.A. Frazer who, at 9:51 a.m., took off to head towards Sfax, Tunisia; he was followed at 12:15 p.m. by Wing Commander Adrian Warburton who diverted towards the Strait of Messina to photograph a northbound 10,000-ton hospital ship. At 1:35 p.m., it was Pilot Officer Laurie E. Philpotts's turn to fly over Taranto and Isola di Capo Rizzuto, sighting and photographing the hospital ship near Capo Vaticano. At the same time, the cities of Palermo and Naples were being photographed by Flying Officer M.G. Brown.

19   The National Archives London, Royal Air Force, Operations Record Books AIR 27/2007.

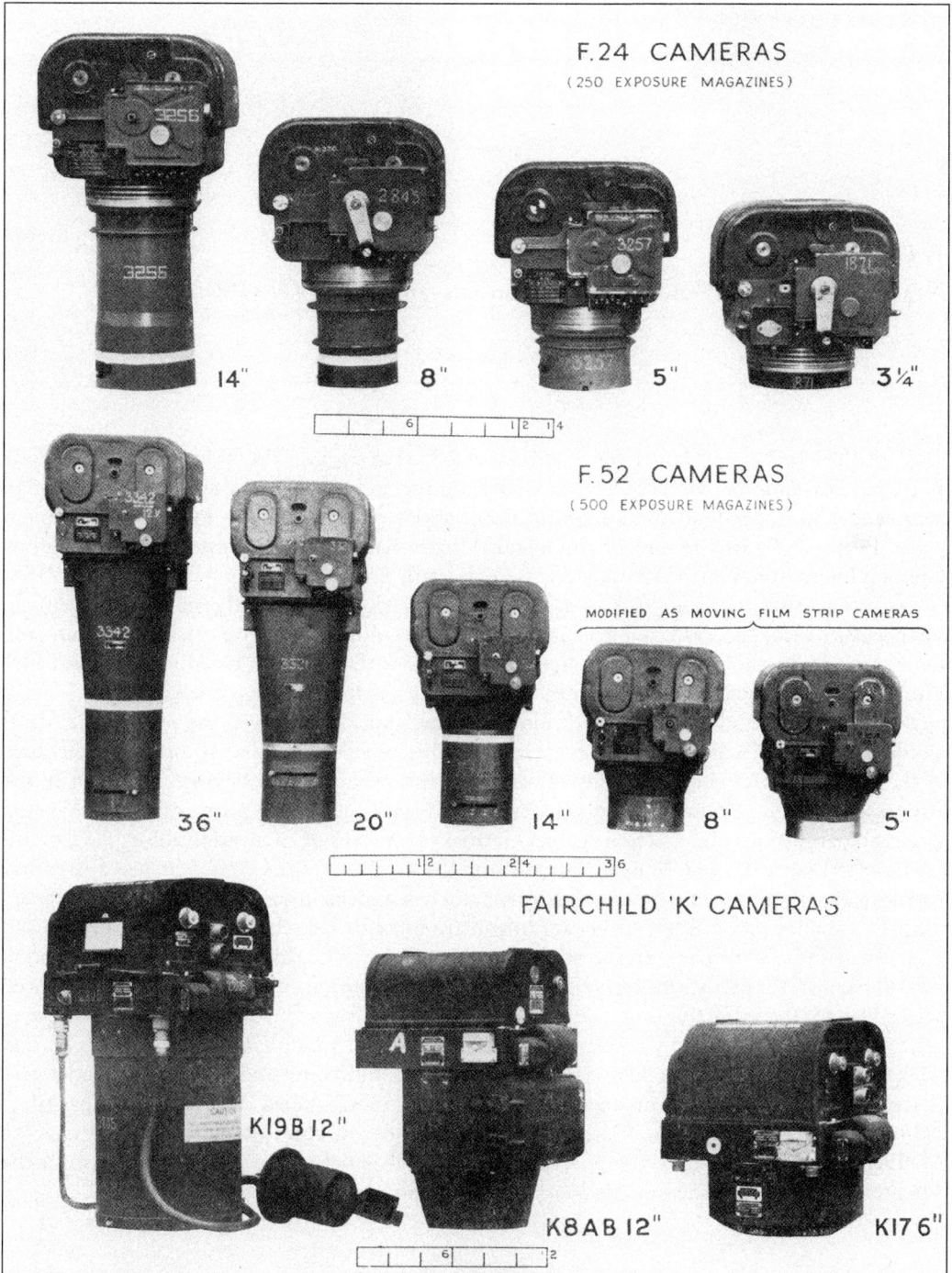

F.24 CAMERAS
(250 EXPOSURE MAGAZINES)

14"   8"   5"   3¼"

F.52 CAMERAS
(500 EXPOSURE MAGAZINES)

MODIFIED AS MOVING FILM STRIP CAMERAS

36"   20"   14"   8"   5"

FAIRCHILD 'K' CAMERAS

K19B 12"   K8AB 12"   K17 6"

Second World War British cameras. Note the middle row is shown at a smaller scale. Exposure sizes for each row are 5, 7, and 9-in. width respectively, with U.S. cameras in the bottom row. (AFHRA)

8

1943
Northwest African Photographic Reconnaissance Wing (NAPRW)

The British victory at El Alamein on 4 November led to strategic results far beyond its immediate consequences. Among them, the first major defeat suffered by Rommel, the only senior German commander to understand the long-term implications of El Alamein, deserves a prominent place. Precisely for this reason, the Generalfeldmarschall had long insisted Hitler withdraw German forces from North Africa while there was still time.

Operation *Torch*, the Anglo-American invasion of Morocco and Algeria on 8 November, further sealed the fate of Axis forces in North Africa. While Montgomery chased Rommel's forces to Tripoli, the Allied Task Force led by General Dwight D. Eisenhower moved into Tunisia where the two sides fought to the limit during the first months of 1943.

To the German and Italian high commands, it was very clear, given the massive air, naval and land forces the Allies had available, that the Allies would immediately attack another area of the Mediterranean once the Tunisian campaign was over. General George C. Marshall, the American strategic architect who disagreed strongly with the British prime minister, Winston Churchill, argued for direct action against Germany by means of an invasion across the English Channel to France in 1943. When Churchill and the President of the United States of America, Franklin Delano Roosevelt, met in Casablanca, there was deep uncertainty as to which strategy the Allies should adopt. After strong arguments from the British chiefs of staff on one side and their American counterparts on the other, a compromise was finally reached. The US agreed to British requests for further military operations in the Mediterranean in exchange for a renewed action plan for the inevitable Channel crossing, which would soon be called Operation *Overlord*.

The decision was made in Casablanca to invade Sicily (Operation *Husky*). General Sir Harold Alexander was appointed deputy commander-in-chief and commander of the ground forces (Eisenhower was overall commander). The command of all Allied naval forces belonged to Admiral Sir Andrew Browne Cunningham, commander-in-chief of the Royal Navy in the Mediterranean. For aviation, the post of commander-in-chief of the Allied Air Forces in the Mediterranean was assigned to Air Marshal Sir Arthur Tedder.

From left to right: General Carl B. Spaatz, Colonel Elliott Roosevelt, General Alexander, (?), and Group Captain Humphreys analyse aerial photos of Sicily before agreeing on further action. (US Air Force photo 26214 AC)

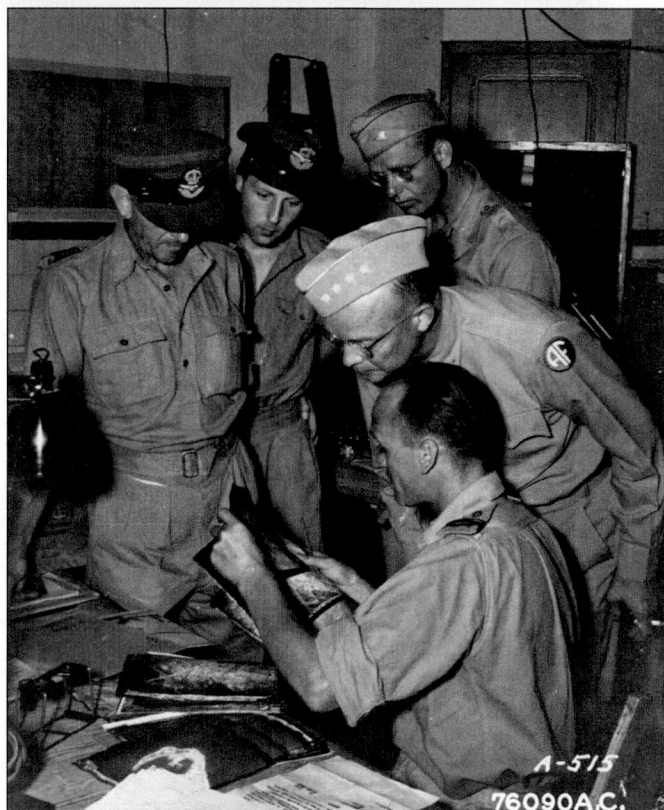

General Dwight D. Eisenhower observes some images taken by a photo-reconnaissance aircraft over Messina. (US Air Force photo 76090 AC)

The 3rd Photographic Group USAAF

The 3rd Photographic Group (PG), made up of the 5th, 12th and 15th Photographic Reconnaissance Squadrons (PRS), under the command of Colonel Elliott Roosevelt (son of the American president), operated from the airfield at Maison Blanche in Algeria with three Boeing B-17 Flying Fortresses (the F-9 photo-reconnaissance variant) and about 10 F-4 and F-4A Lightnings. The operational sorties were mainly carried out by the Lightnings as the F-9 was unsatisfactory for mapping of enemy territory. The four-engine aircraft were instead used for courier services within the theatre and to Great Britain.

On 18 February 1943, with the consolidation of the 12th Air Force and the RAF's Eastern Air Command, the 3rd PG and No. 4 Photographic Reconnaissance Unit (PRU) were brought together as the Northwest African Photographic Reconnaissance Wing (NAPRW) under the leadership of Roosevelt and his second in command, Eric Fuller, head of the 3rd PG. The RAF posted some of its most' experienced photo interpreters of the North African Central Interpretation Unit (NACIU) to the wing under the supervision of Squadron Leader E.A. Tilling (previously the head of the photographic interpretation section of Bomber Command). Squadron Leader Alfred Ball became commander of No. 682 Squadron, previously 4 PRU, with its main operational headquarters also at Maison Blanche.

The new NAPRW was entrusted with the direction of all aerial photographic operations in the western Mediterranean, avoiding the duplication of sorties. The interpretation section was responsible for compiling daily reports relating to the surveys of airfield and port activities, and communication lines, as well as detailed reports on shipping, coastal and anti-aircraft defence systems, planning sorties to assess bombing damage, the identification of radar positions, and the analysis of photos taken by bomber crews as they released their loads over targets. Some recces were carried out at night; it was easier to identify the exact location of anti-aircraft batteries when they fired. The central operational office of the NAPRW, in a period of maximum activity, went as far as to request 34 daily flights. On several occasions, NAPRW aircraft preceded the bombers, took photos before the attack, circled while awaiting the release of the bombs, before flying over the target again to take pictures of the damage. This provided interpreters with an excellent basis to compare photos for damage assessment, and for planning any subsequent targeted bombing.

Although the operation of the NAPRW was limited by the small number of aircraft supplied for photo-reconnaissance, it proved to be up to the task and managed to honour its commitments. In fact, it covered almost the entire western Mediterranean and part of the eastern sector.[1] To lend a hand, on 5 March 1943, the first complete advanced photographic unit for the 3rd

---

1   On 15 March, the NAPRW expressly requested the Air Ministry, through the AHQ of Malta, allocate a Mosquito equipped with a 36-inch focal length camera to cover Catania, Licata, Sciacca, Marsala, San Vito Lo Capo and Termini Imerese. In the absence of such equipment, the Mosquito would also be accepted with 14-inch focal length cameras. On 29 March, another request was sent to the Air Ministry, by the RAF's Air Vice-Marshal Robb, for six PR Mosquitos equipped with 36-inch lenses, extremely necessary to cover some targets in Sicily. Operating from Maison Blanche, 682 Squadron only had five Spitfire PR.IVs that could be used for targets outside North Africa (four PR.XIs were due to arrive). The 3rd PG also operated with limitations; by the express will of Air Marshal Sir Arthur Tedder, it was not allowed to fly over enemy territory due to inadequacies of the F-4 and F-4A aircraft. Soon, however, 13 new F-5A Lightnings would be available. AFHRA, IRISREF MAAF 257, p.1287.

PG was set up in Telergma, Algeria, to operate at the request of the USAAF; it replaced the experimental field unit that had operated until then at the same airport, set up in an old French Potez 540 transport aircraft.

Aircraft suitable for photo-reconnaissance in the Mediterranean area on 24 February 1943	
One squadron of 12 Spitfires	Middle East Command
One squadron of 12 Spitfires	Malta Command
One squadron of 12 Spitfires	North West Mediterranean Command
3rd PG with 26 Lightnings	North West Mediterranean Command

A photo of Gela Ponte Olivo taken on 13 February 1943 by Sergeant Snowden. During the same sortie, reconnaissance was carried out over Comiso, Biscari, Gerbini, Avola and Pozzallo; a mosaic was also made of the Pachino area. (US Air Force)

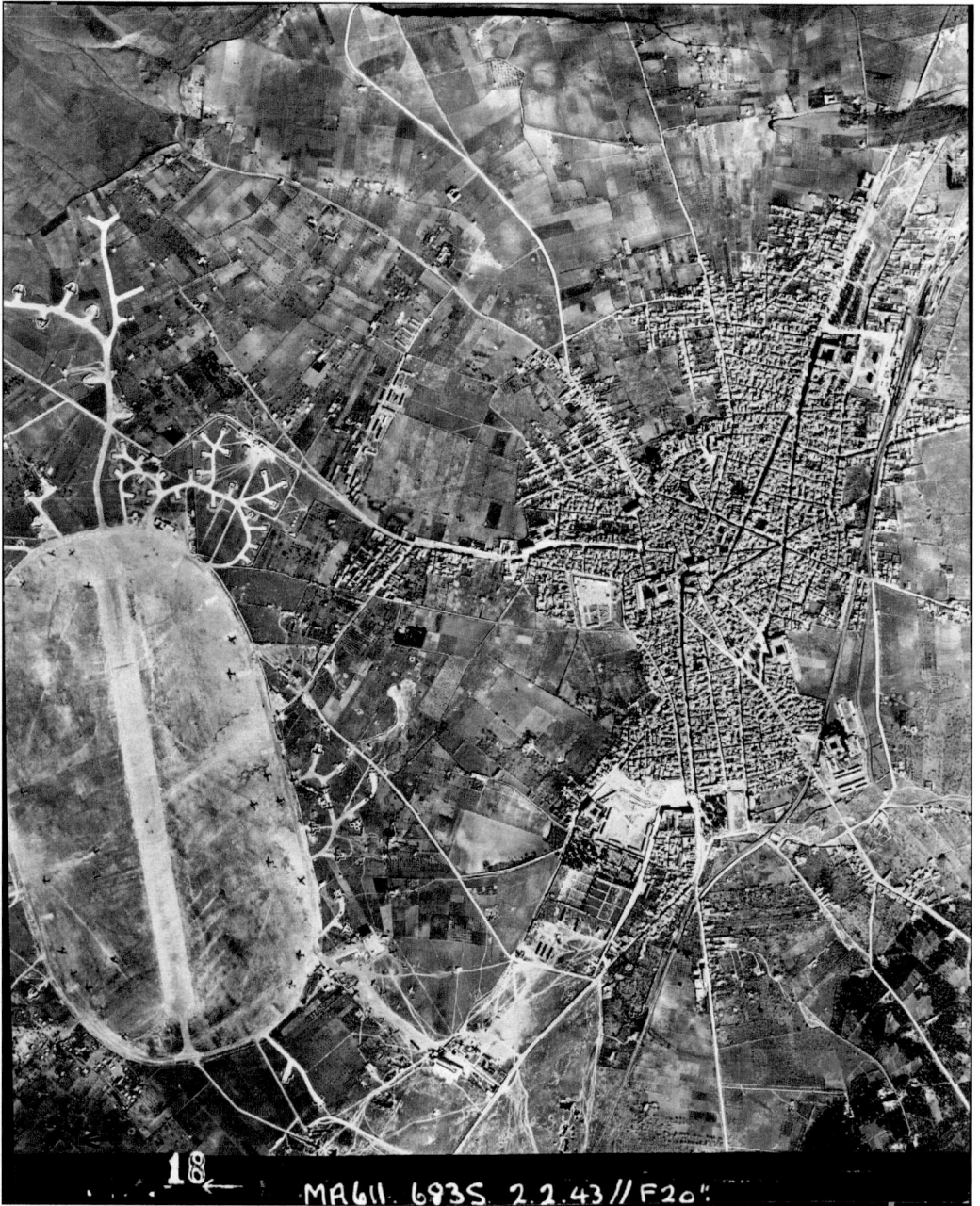

A photo of Castelvetrano taken by Sergeant Keith Durbidge on the morning of 2 February 1943. The No. 683 Squadron pilot, flying a Spitfire PR.IV, also captured the airfields at Palermo, Sciacca, Trapani Bo Rizzo and Pantelleria. (US Air Force)

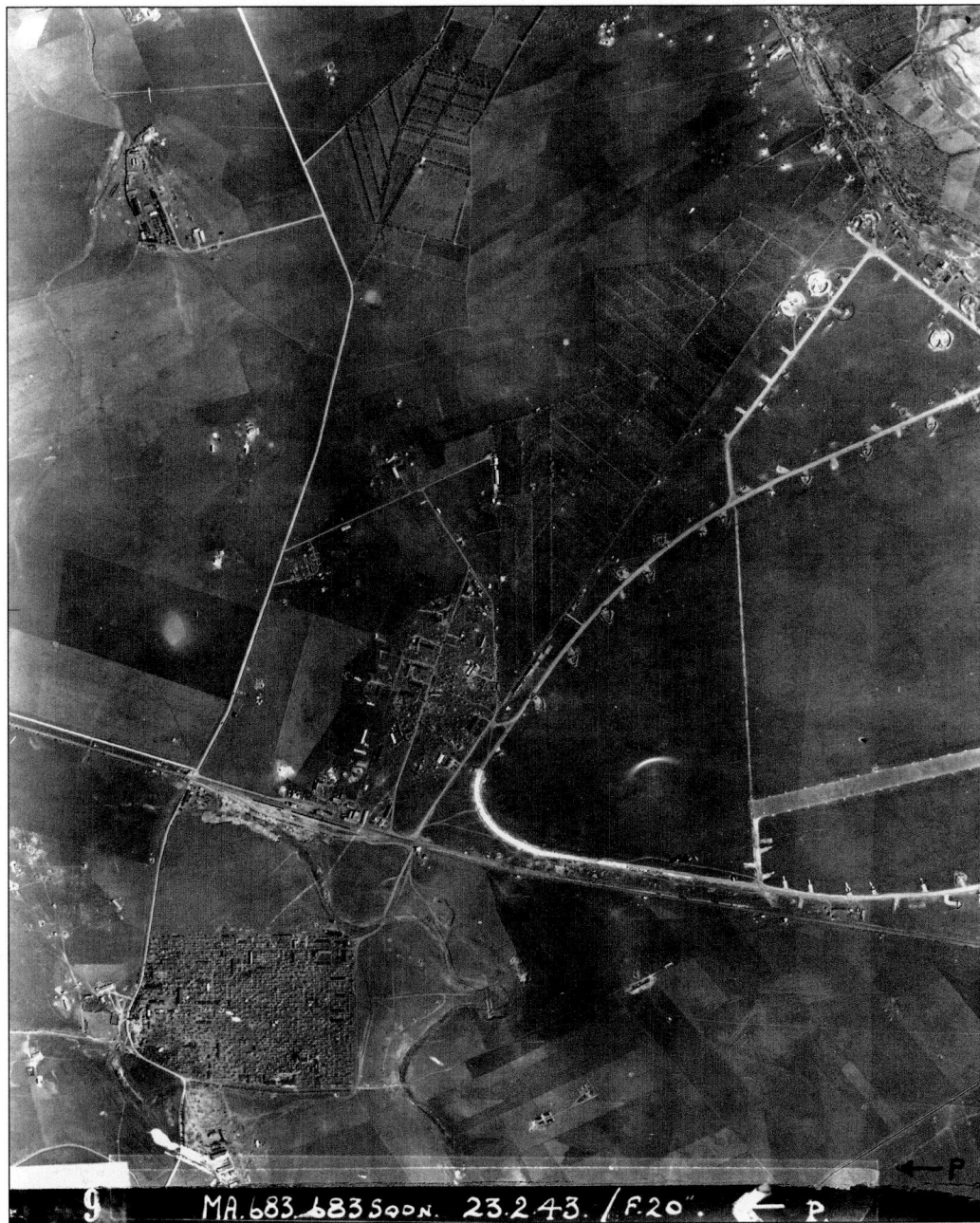

Gerbini Main captured by the camera of Spitfire PR.IV BS905 flown by Sergeant Keith Durbidge. (Alessandro Emanuele)

Aerial Defences in Sicily at the beginning of 1943

At the beginning of the year, the *Luftwaffe's II Fliegerkorps*, with its fighters and fighter-bombers, consolidated its presence in Sicily, with 60 Bf 109Gs and 77 Bf 110Cs, plus about 14 Ju 88C night fighters. The total number of *Luftwaffe* bombers was approximately 260 Ju 88s, mainly located at Comiso, Gerbini and Catania, which included I./KG 26 (equipped with the He 111), III./KG 26, III./ KG 30, II./KG 76, II./KG 77, and elements of KG 60. Reconnaissance was entrusted to 2.(F)/122 Ju 88s at Trapani. In addition to these groups, there were eight other *Luftwaffe Gruppen* using transport aircraft, mainly on the Sicily–Tunisia route; these were mainly operational from Trapani Milo, Trapani Bo Rizzo and Castelvetrano, and consisted of KGzbV1, 2, 102, 105, 300, 400, 600 and 800 with approximately 500 Ju 52/3ms, Ju 90s, Fw 200s and Me 323s. They cooperated with the Italian transport units of *SAS* (*Servizi Aerei Speciali*): *18°, 44°* and *48° Stormo* with 140 SM.75s, SM.81s, SM.82s and Fiat G.12s.[2]

As for the fighters of the *Regia Aeronautica*, still particularly engaged in North Africa during the first part of the year, their strength on Sicily on 1 January 1943 was 177 MC.202s, 64 MC.200s, 35 G.50bis' and 17 CR.42s, of which less than half were actually serviceable on this date. There were also 38 bombers (18 SM.84s, 15 Cant.Z 1007s and 5 BR.20Ms) at Palermo, Castelvetrano and Sciacca. At Sciacca, there was also the MC.202s of the *53° Stormo CT*

The railway station and the port of Messina, with a large ferry entering the latter (US Air Force)

2   Brian Cull, Nicola Malizia, Frederick Galea, *Spitfires over Sicily* (London: Grub Street, 2000), p.6.

(*Caccia Terrestre* – land-based fighters), *153° Gruppo, 372ª, 373ª* and *374ª Squadriglie*. At Trapani Chinisia (Bo Rizzo) there was the *3° Gruppo Autonomo CT* with the MC.200s of *153ª, 154ª* and *155ª Squadriglie*. Meanwhile, Castelvetrano also hosted the MC.200s of the *157° Gruppo Autonomo CT, 357ª, 379ª, 384ª Squadriglie*. To these must be added the nine BR.20M night bombers of the *202ª Squadriglia BT* (*Bombardamento Terrestre* – land-based bombers), and the CR.25s and Ca.314s of the *173ª Squadriglia RST* (*Ricognizione Strategica Terrestre* – land-based strategic reconnaissance) temporarily detached to Sciacca to assist the *10° Stormo*. Maritime reconnaissance and sea rescue was entrusted to *170ª, 186ª* and *189ª Squadriglie* of the *83° Gruppo RM* (*Ricognizione Marittima* – maritime reconnaissance) based at Augusta, and the *144ª* and *197ª Squadriglie* of the *85° Gruppo* at Marsala. Both units were equipped with CANT Z.501, CANT Z.506B and Fiat RS.14 seaplanes.

The island of Pantelleria hosted the *1° Stormo, 6° Gruppo, 79ª, 81ª* and *88ª Squadriglie*; the *17° Gruppo CT, 71ª, 72ª* and *80ª Squadriglie* (all flying the MC.202). The *151° Gruppo CT, 53° Stormo*, with *366ª, 367ª* and *368ª Squadriglie*, was equipped with the G.50bis fighter.

Detail of the ferry dock at Messina. (Antonio Bonanno)

Reconnaissance Aircraft over the Strait of Sicily

Given the intense battles in North Africa, the new year opened with the intention, especially on the American side, to cut the supplies arriving from Sicily, Sardinia and the Italian peninsula. The task of bombing ports and airfields was entrusted to heavy bombers, the Boeing B-17 Flying Fortresses of the Twelfth Air Force and the Consolidated B-24 Liberators of the Ninth Air Force, stationed at Allied air bases in North Africa.

At 10:00 a.m. on the first day of the year, No. 69 Squadron sent four PR Spitfires, flown by Sergeant Keith Durbidge, Flying Officer G.H. Maloney, Flying Officer M.G. Brown and Pilot Officer J.A. Frazer, on almost simultaneous sorties. They covered Cagliari, Palermo, Messina, and Crotone and Naples respectively. Their main purpose was to search for tankers and merchant ships. Worthy of mention is Frazer's sortie; while flying over the small port of Riposto on return from Naples, he sighted and photographed five warships sailing four miles to the south with an estimated speed of about 15 knots.

The importance of ship traffic in this first phase of the year was explained by Durbidge:

> During each pre-flight briefing we received a reminder to report immediately, by radio, if any large merchant vessels or warships were sighted at sea. Especially important in this regard were tankers, wherever they were, wherever they were heading. I noted this in my logbook for future reference. I had climbed to 25,000 ft. on my way to Taranto and Brindisi on the heel of Italy. At this operating height there was an extensive and thick layer of milky cirrus cloud ideal for hiding from the enemy. As I flew up to Cape Spartivento at the toe of Italy, I saw below me a large vessel, easily recognisable as a tanker – with pipes lying fore and aft along the deck – hugging the coast and proceeding south, just the type of sighting mentioned in the briefing. I made a radio call stating its position, speed and heading. I also took photographs to confirm my report though I thought at the time they would not be very clear because of the hazy cirrus. I then carried on with my task. The authorities in Malta acted immediately on my radio call and a couple of Fishingtons (torpedo-carrying Wellingtons) were scrambled. They found the ship and sank it, fortunately without damage to themselves.[3]

After a series of preventative recces of Palermo, carried out by pilots of 69 Squadron (Sergeant W.S. Lewis, Wing Commander Adrian Warburton and Flying Officer Brown), at 11:00 a.m., on 7 January, Frazer made a final reconnaissance of the port in anticipation of a daytime bombing raid. Anglo-American intelligence wanted nothing more than to analyse Frazer's photos so as to dispatch the bombers.[4] The Consolidated B-24 Liberators of the 376th, 98th and 93rd Bombardment Groups (BG), under the command of Major Fennell (Ninth Air Force, USAAF), and loaded with 500 and 1000lb bombs, lifted off from their sandy runways in Egypt, without fighter escort, for Palermo. A thick layer of cloud covered the port area, so much so that only 10 bombers managed to identify the target and, through a gap in the clouds, dropped their deadly loads. The surprise among the population was total thanks to the weather conditions and the unusual approach route the American planes took to reach the city; it was more typical of Axis aircraft, skirting Mount Pellegrino from the sea. The effects of the bombing were verified in the late morning the following day by Pilot Officer Laurie E. Philpotts who also flew over the Licata airstrip and Sciacca airfield complex.

---

3   Durbidge, *Memoirs of a High Flyer*, p.49.
4   Pilot Officer J.A. Frazer, an Australian and just 21 years old, disappeared into thin air during a sortie on 11 January 1943. He left Luqa at 9:25 a.m. for the airfield at Corfu-Valona airport in Spitfire BS500. Warburton and Brown took off at the same time (3:20 p.m.) to search for Frazer. Despite good weather conditions, they could not find any trace of the Australian pilot.

Very important information was obtained by Ultra on the various airfields and the movement of air units from one end of the Mediterranean to the other. On 15 January, at Biscari Santo Pietro, the presence of the Ju 88 reconnaissance aircraft of 2.(F)/122, as well as the Bf 109 fighters of II./JG 51 'Mölders' on the runway since the 6th, was ascertained. January 19 saw the arrival at Castelvetrano, from Gabès, Tunisia, of 22 Ju 52/3m transports; on the 22nd the same aircraft left between 7:00 and 7:30 a.m. to return to Tunisia with their loads of supplies, ammunition and fuel for the troops.

That same day, Keith Durbidge was sent to investigate and photograph a possible military refuge north-west of the sulphur refinery at Licata, the important Porto Empedocle power station, and the local railway station. Other Ultra decryptions revealed that, on 28 January, the airfield at Gela Ponte Olivo was operational, even at night; there were two Fw 200Ks, 29 SM.84s, three Ju 52/3ms, 14 SM.79s and four Fiat G.50s based there.

It was around noon on 29 January when the 69 Squadron Spitfire PR.IV (BR424) flown by Flight Lieutenant Raymond C. Hill (SAAF) did not return from a sortie over Taranto and Messina. It was discovered some time later, thanks to a German conversation picked up by Ultra, that the Spitfire had been intercepted by two Bf 109s of 8./JG 53 from Biscari Santo Pietro. The victory was attributed to Unteroffizier Friedrich Scheer, his first.[5] The South African pilot survived the encounter as reported in Bollettino n. 930 of 30 January:

Enemy planes yesterday made raids on some places in Sicily: one injured and minor damage. In the sky over Messina yesterday, Italian fighters intercepted a plane that crashed into the sea near S. Margherita; the South African pilot parachuted out and was captured. Another aircraft was destroyed by anti-aircraft artillery.

After receiving the information from 69 Squadron on the presence of substantial naval units, some identified as oil tankers and minesweepers, thanks to the reconnaissance carried out by Flight Lieutenant M.G. Brown on 29 January, and by Flying Officer Maloney the next day, the Vickers Wellington bombers of No. 330 Wing (Nos. 142 and 150 Squadrons) flew some night bombing raids against the ports of Palermo and Trapani. The direct offensive against Palermo was undoubtedly the heaviest. The port was bombed in three stages on the nights of 3/4, 5/6 and 8/9 February. Handley Page Halifaxes from No. 462 Squadron RAAF also contributed. At 9:17 a.m., on 5 February, Adrian Warburton took off at the controls of Spitfire BS364 to photograph the damage at Palermo before heading to the Avola power plant and the Pozzallo railway station.

On 10 February, the Palermo newspaper *L'Ora* provided a summary on the front page, covering the period from 29 October 1942 to 2 February 1943, of the losses in human lives suffered by the main Sicilian cities: Agrigento, 10 dead and 282 wounded; Caltanissetta, 1 dead and 3 wounded; Catania, 4 dead and 9 wounded; Messina, 54 dead and 125 wounded; Palermo, 153 dead and 360 wounded; Ragusa, 30 dead and 45 wounded; Syracuse, 7 dead and 36 wounded; and, finally, Trapani with 23 dead and 99 wounded.

5   Cull, Malizia, Galea, *Spitfires over Sicily*, p.20.

The port of Palermo as seen from the Spitfire PR.IV flown by Flying Officer M.G. Brown of No. 683 Squadron. (US Air Force)

The birth of No. 683 Squadron and the 3rd Photographic Group in Malta

The more than 53 pages of the 69 Squadron Operations Record Book, referring only to January 1943, summarise the 281 operational sorties carried out by the three flights of Wellingtons, Baltimores and PR Spitfires. The complicated and delicate management of the various flights led to the formation, on 8 February 1943, of No. 683 Squadron, with the motto *Nihil nos latet* (Nothing remains hidden), equipped with the Spitfire PR.IVs. Command of the new unit was assigned to the highly regarded Wing Commander Adrian Warburton DSO DFC to operate from Luqa airport with seven other pilots on strength.[6] The Wellingtons and Baltimores of 69 Squadron continued operations from the same airfield, but only flew photographic reconnaissance sorties over Sicily sporadically from then on, focusing mainly on the maritime reconnaissance of the Sicilian Strait under the leadership of Wing Commander R.C. Mackay.

The new directives imposed by the NAPRW also concerned 683 Squadron, and provided that, once the photos had been taken over Sicily, they would be sent by a courier service to England via Algiers. Given the extreme importance of the films and documents, flying over hostile territory was to be avoided. In this regard, the best route to take the films to NAPRW headquarters, and vice versa, was Algiers–Tripoli–Malta. Although this route was considered the safest, it certainly caused no shortage of problems for the pilots.

The photographic laboratory in Malta had achieved excellent results over the years but had been working for some time under great limitations of a mainly logistical nature. Despite the small workforce and dated equipment, it managed to produce a maximum of 1,500 prints in about 24 hours. The small staff of interpreters could manage the first and second stages of interpretation work. Their main interest had always been gathering Intelligence for ongoing operations on Sicily and southern Italy. On the other side of the Mediterranean, Tripoli's PRU detachment had a very small number of aircraft and pilots. The mobile laboratory there had produced around 85,000 prints since Rommel's retreat from North Africa began.[7]

On 24 February, a PR Spitfire from the new unit, with Sergeant Clayton R. Peacock at the controls, was sent on a route connecting four Sicilian municipalities–Noto, Ragusa, Comiso and Gela–flying between 22,000 feet and 26,000 feet without encountering any issues. The reason for the reconnaissance was to find the B-24D Liberator 'Blonde Bomber II' (serial 41-23659) belonging to the 343rd Bombardment Squadron, 98th BG. The Liberator, returning from a raid on the city of Naples, was hit by anti-aircraft fire and forced to make an emergency landing on the south-east coast of Sicily. Peacock found and photographed it near Pachino; in the meantime, on the nearby airfield, two small aircraft, probably fighters, were noticed.

Daily sorties continued all over the island. Over Palermo, a PR Spitfire was hit by flak without serious consequence. Over Comiso, the reconnaissance proved more fruitful: the images showed as many as 73 Ju 88s, of which a dozen were unserviceable, 20 fighters and a couple CANT Z.1007bis', a Fi 156 and two Gotha Go 242s. Once again, Catania Fontanarossa played host to a significant number of aircraft, including a Me 323 and several Heinkels used to tow Me 321 gliders which were also present on the airfield.[8]

6   The National Archives London, Royal Air Force, Operations Record Books AIR 27/2209/2.
7   AFHRA, IRISREF MAAF 257, p.1257.
8   Cull, Malizia, Galea, *Spitfires over Sicily*, p.27.

The Axis airlift was accompanied as always by a maritime one, mainly from the ports of Marsala, Trapani, Palermo and Messina, which were teeming with large vessels and warships of all kinds. This was reported in March from the results of the sorties carried out by the following 683 Squadron pilots: Sergeants R.M. Snowden and Keith Durbidge, Flight Lieutenant M.G. Brown, Sergeant C.R. Peacock,[9] Flying Officer G.H. Maloney, Flight Sergeant W.S. Lewis, Flying Officer Philpotts and Wing Commander Adrian Warburton. A great job was done over Palermo by Philpotts who later wrote about his experience:

> Jeff Geoffrey – Jeff was a gentleman with an aura of mystery about him. He spoke several languages and he seemed to know the thinking of both the military and civilian peoples in the Middle East. He was a smart guy; I knew Jeff [knew] that the cruiser had been launched and still Jeff calculated the work-hours to be done on the superstructure before a trial might be made. I kept a close watch on the action and equipment on the dock beside the cruiser. The cruiser was ready to go. Jeff advised the Navy. I sent a code as the cruiser sailed on test and the Navy was there to blow the bows off the cruiser. They got the cruiser back into dry-dock and, eventually, after another period of watching, the cruiser again went to sea and, again, after another code exchange, the Navy sunk it. The bomber boys, the torpedo boys, and the Navy boys were always champing-at-the-bit to get at the cruiser but the work-hours were of more importance to Jeff. Jeff knew something was afoot re the evacuation of the Nazis and the Fascists from North Africa when I spotted many hundreds of transport aircraft dispersed on the large, circular aerodrome where the Alpha Romeo factory was situated near Naples. The bomber boys wanted to have a picnic but Jeff knew that a raid would, in all probability, be wasted. So he wanted to find the petrol caches and facilities for the operation of these aircraft. The area was 'hot' and I was not able to hang around too long to get a visual on all of the facilities and supplies but I managed to climb back up and lure the fighters out to sea and then I came back to take aerial photography over the greater area pertinent to the aerodrome then got the hell out. I put the money-in-the-pocket. Trains were running troops and equipment, evacuated from North Africa, across Sicily to the train ferry at Messina. Although the train-busters (a Mosquito squadron on Malta) were knocking them off, Jeff thought that much energy and time were being wasted when all that was necessary would be to do away with the train ferry facilities in the Strait of Messina. At his request, I did a 'hot' low level flight to obliquely photograph the facilities so target maps could be made. He had the money-in-the-pocket. A gunboat, which was a thorn-in-the-flesh to Malta, was not to be found in the normal haunts. I found, from Jeff, as to where the gunboat had last been reported. Then, after we had discussed logistics of cover, I asked Jeff to raise a sortie for me. I finally located the gunboat behind the Island of Corfu in Greece. The damned gunboat nearly shot me from the skies. It knocked me upside-down and my muscles were strips of soreness for a number of days, but the Spit took it as the Spit could. I handed the information to my friend and he had the money-in-the-pocket.

9   Flight Sergeant Clayton Peacock RCAF (Royal Canadian Air Force) disappeared on a mission on 9 March 1943. He left Luqa at 1:00 p.m. for the ports of Taranto, Naples and Messina. Of Peacock and his Spitfire PR.IV (BS364), nothing else is known. He was just 23 years old.

Jeff had to perform, what I thought, might have been a difficult task for him. A Nazi pilot plunked his ME 109 onto Luqa. The pilot spoke the English language beautifully. It turned out that the pilot had been a friend of Jeff's in England, and of all things, Jeff was ordered to make the first interrogation. The Nazi pilot was an interesting guy and I enjoyed chatting with him in the mess. But there was another aspect here that involved me greatly. When the Nazi landed, I was out on a sortie for three hours or more, and when I got back to Luqa, the aerodrome was unusually quiet and as I was approaching turning the aeroplane to open up for a take-off when the ground crew came running out of the pen and waving like mad, but I wouldn't get out of my kite until I was perfectly satisfied re the 109. My pen happened to be the only one vacant at the time the Nazi plunked onto Luqa and they wanted to get the 109 out of the open. When studying the 109 later on, I found to my surprise, that the aircraft had Sperry instruments and Dunlop tires.[10]

The photographic laboratory of the 3rd PG on Malta. At the entrance to the tent is a sign reading '3PG MALTA'. (US Air Force photo 76059 AC)

10   Laurie E. Philpotts, *Memoirs of World War II: The True Story of a Canadian Fighter Pilot* (Lulu.com, 2013), p.149. This sortie resulted in the awarding of a DFC: 'Flying Officer Laurie Evan Philpotts (Can / J.15527), Royal Canadian Air Force, n. 683 Squadron. This officer has made many flights over Sicily and Southern Italy. Although attacked on numerous occasions by fighter aircraft he has always continued his mission. On a recent occasion, as the result of an accurate report by this officer, a submarine was enabled to damage a new Italian cruiser. Flying Officer Philpotts has displayed outstanding keenness and devotion to duty'. In *The London Gazette*, 16 April 1943.

This Potez 540 bomber, long used as a transport, was equipped as a laboratory. The aircraft and its crew were part of the first trial field unit long before basic workshops and interpretation units were established. (US Air Force)

On the reconnaissance of 8 March, three large Messerschmitt Me 323s were sighted on the Trapani Milo track. Palermo Boccadifalco accommodated 30 large transport aircraft and another 15 fighters. Many large vessels were spotted at Palermo. These were reported by Keith Durbidge who continued the sortie to the Termini Imerese landing strip and then headed towards the airfield at Licata, flying over at 11:20 a.m.

Total staff of the 3rd Photographic Reconnaissance and Mapping Group on 15 March 1943			
	Officers	**Warrant Officers**	**Enlisted Men**
Headquarters & Headquarters Sq.	25	1	34
5th Photo Recon Sq. (L)	28	2	178
12th Photo Recon Sq. (L)	29	2	185
15th Photo Recon Sq. (HV)	57	2	223
Total	139	7	620

On 14 March, Durbidge took off in Spitfire PR.IV (BP905), with two 69 Squadron Baltimores, to look for a Baltimore that did not return from a maritime reconnaissance between Sicily and Naples the previous day. A crew member was located on board his lifeboat, at the coordinates 38° 08' N, 16° 54' E, and subsequently recovered in the early hours of the following morning.[11] About another rescue Durbidge remembered:

> An amazing rescue – One of the most amazing rescues in the Med during World War II concerned a Beaufort Torpedo bomber [sic] pilot (I can't recall his name at the moment) who had to ditch his aeroplane many miles off the east coast of Sicily. He and his crew had been badly mauled. When the pilot got into his dingy [sic] he was able to, luckily, identify the corpses of his crew. Evening drew nigh. As an unidentified aircraft flew over, the pilot fired a couple of emergency flares, but these got no response from the aircraft. He fired some more when two additional aircraft flew over, but to no avail. It got dark and he was very much alone. He heard a gurgling sound not too far off and again he fired flares. A submarine surfaced, and one becomes amazed at the odds of a sub surfacing at this very spot. The pilot was taken aboard the sub and he accompanied the sub through the remainder of its patrol. When the poor pilot got back to Malta days later, he had to collect all of his personal things, which under such circumstances were usually divided up among squadron friends.[12]

On the afternoon of the same day, Flying Officer Philpotts, flying Spitfire PR.IV (AB310), miraculously managed to return to Malta after being intercepted and attacked over Trapani by four fighters, identified as Bf 109s and Re 2001s, while he was intent on taking oblique photos of the port from 1,000 feet; the clouds that in many cases prevented pilots from taking photos this time allowed him to return safely.

> Cockiness – Enemy aircraft were seen every day, when I was flying I was uneasy, as I thought that my detecting powers were not functioning to the fullest. On the other hand, one became very cocky at times. One afternoon, while I was flying from Palermo on the north coast of Sicily to Naples, the Med sun was bearing down on the hood and the cockpit, the music of the engine at 25,000 feet was soothing, and I trimmed the aeroplane for hands-off flying, and put my head back and drowsed. All of a sudden there was a terrific BANG. My waking reflexes pulled the Spit into an evasive climbing turn. I didn't see a fighter anywhere. The enemy wasn't above me, as I had positioned myself just under the condensation layer, and I didn't see a fighter in the quarters below my tail. Then I happened to look down and I noticed that the lever, which closed the vent on the glycol radiator, had jumped forward. That was the BANG; my elbow must have hit the ratchet release as I dozed. On another cocky occasion, I was carrying out aerial photography over a ME 110 (twin-engine fighter) base in Southern Italy and

---

11   The event to which Durbidge refers concerns Baltimore S' of 69 Squadron, which took off at 6:30 a.m. on 14 March 1943. The only man saved was Sergeant ME Redden. The missing, Captain Moresby Currie (102173V), Pilot Officer Peter Smailes (139925), and Flying Officer Fabian George Whelpdale (116657), are all commemorated on the Malta Memorial.

12   Philpotts, *Memoirs of World War II*, p.149.

while I was doing this, an Italian fighter (Macchi) stayed at a range behind me and kept popping away. He didn't want to close in for some reason or other and, probably, he wasn't aware that my aeroplane was not fitted with guns. Many times I tried to run enemy transport aircraft into the water and, at least, make them a splash crash (airscrews hitting the water) but I was never successful. The pilots of the transports (tri-engine Junkers and Savoia-Marchettis) either knew that the blue reco [sic] Spit was harmless or they were scared to death and just flew on. I took photographs of them, noticed the vectors, their airspeed, and datum, and then left them so they could celebrate their escape from a Spitfire when they landed.[13]

In the late morning of 14 March, Ultra caught the expected arrival in Tunisia of a large number of Ju 52/3m transports, estimated between 60 and 80, and some Me 323s from Sicily and Italy. Furthermore, a Ju 88 scout of 1.(F)/122 based at Catania was also sighted in the skies over Tunisia. The pilots of 682 Squadron, returning from their usual sorties to Sardinia, Genoa and Livorno, reported the departure from Palermo of two merchant ships (1,000 tons each), loaded with ammunition and weapons, bound for Tunisia.[14]

Lightning F-5A 42-13071 of the 3rd PG on Malta. This aircraft was lost on 11 November 1943, 100 miles north of Bizerte, resulting in the death of First Lieutenant Clifford E. Kent. (US Air Force)

13   Philpotts, *Memoirs of World War II*, p.139.
14   In March, 682 Squadron had the following aircraft: three PR Mosquitos (one posted to Malta) and 13 PR Spitfires (two posted to Malta).

A hospital ship was sighted at the entrance to the port of Taranto in the early afternoon of the 15th by Flight Sergeant W.S. Lewis. It was probably the same hospital ship spotted the previous day by Durbidge 20 miles from Capo Passero. On 23 March, Durbidge, flying over Rome and other places in southern Italy, spotted over 30 large aircraft on the airfield at Centocelle; the same situation was noted at airfields in the Naples area (Capodichino and Pomigliano d'Arco).

An F-5A of the NAPRW returning from a photographic reconnaissance mission. (US Air Force photo 25513 AC)

Malta detachment

On Sunday 21 March, the American staff of the 3rd PG, consisting of six officers and 28 men under the command of Captain Lewis H. Richardson, arrived on Malta on board four C-47 Dakota transports. Their job was to operate an American strategic reconnaissance detachment on the island. They came from Maison Blanche after making a short stop at Castel Benito. In addition to the staff there was 7,000lbs of equipment and a flying photographic laboratory in a Potez 540 aircraft. Colonel Roosevelt flew to Malta for preliminary operations but only stayed a few days before returning to North Africa. This first group of men was part of the third unit[15] of the group and had the task of mapping and pin-pointing Sicily and southern Italy. On the

15 The squadrons were not used as basic tactical organisations but contributed personnel and equipment from which four new units were formed under wing orders.

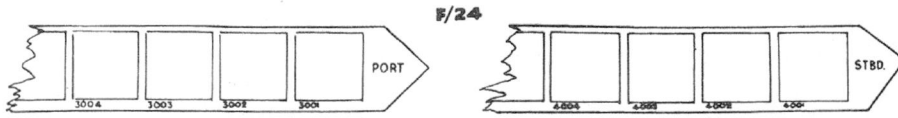

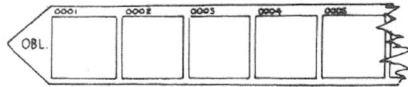

AMERICAN NIGHT MISSIONS.
NUMBERED P1,P2,ETC. FOR PORT.
- S1,S2, .. . STBD.
NUMBERING TO BE IN SAME
POSITION AS ON NORMAL K17
FILMS.

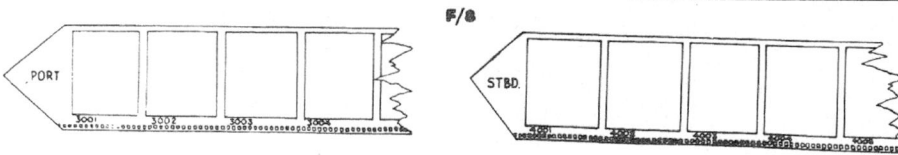

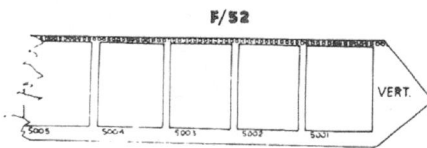

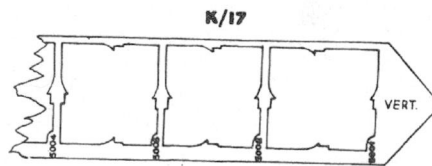

{ PORT AND STBD. ARE NUMBERED }
{ 3000 AND 4000 RESPECTIVELY. }

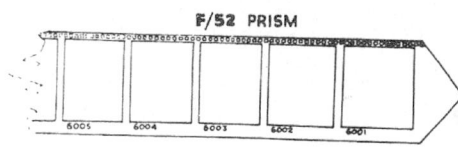

PORT · LO
STBD. · R.O.

K18 VERT: NUMBERED
7000.
OBLIQUES.
PORT OBLIQUES-
0001 - 0200
STBD: OBLIQUES -
0301 - 0500.

DIRECTION OF FLIGHT

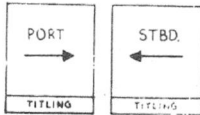

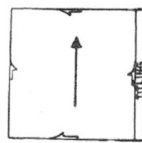

1664. 759

TITLING OF AIR NEGATIVES

SORTIE № SQUADRON DATE TIME F/L HEIGHT eg NA/I 682 P.R.Sqdn. 1.1.43 1030 F/20" 28,000'

A film titling guide taken from a 1943 RAF intelligence advisory put out by No. 682 Squadron in North Africa. (AFHRA)

23rd, the first F-5A landed on Malta; other American reconnaissance aircraft followed in rapid succession.

At the end of March, 17 officers and 34 enlisted men from NAPRW were operating on the island.[16] The unit remained there until the end of the Sicilian campaign and was subsequently absorbed by the 12th PRS, which was commanded by Major Theodore H. Erb. Since the 3rd PG's arrival in the Mediterranean, from November 1942 to March 1 1943 that is, it had operated with 36 pilots, flying 435 hours across 120 missions, carried out at an average height of 24,800 feet, reaching a maximum of 35,000 feet, and a minimum of only 500 feet (the so-called dicing missions).[17]

The photo magazine is removed from an F-5A of the NAPRW in North Africa. (US Air Force photo 66927 AC)

16   Among the pilots were Captain Lewis H. Richardson and Lieutenants Robert Spencer, George F. German, Ike B. Webb Jr., Arthur Earl Luthy, Joseph L. Sugg, Ed Berry, and John MacLaughlin.
17   AFHRA, IRISREF B0746, p.1679.

Analysis of the aerial photo of Sciacca airport shows the positions of light and heavy flak batteries. (US Air Force)

9

The Tunisian Airlift

Since the conflict began, the airfields of western Sicily offered the fastest and safest way to reach the North African coast. The so-called Gigants, Messerschmitt Me 323s, the largest transport aircraft in the *Luftwaffe*, capable of carrying up to 130 passengers, were regular visitors to the airfields at Castelvetrano, Trapani Milo, and Trapani Bo Rizzo. According to Allied estimates, eight of the big transports made a daily trip to Tunisia, transporting up to 455 tons of war material, for a weekly total of about 3,200 tons. It is estimated that, to support the Italian–German forces in Tunisia, a minimum of 40,000 tons of supplies was needed per month (in addition to the Gigants was the Ju 52/3m transport force which made dozens of daily trips between Sicily and Tunisia. Castelvetrano remained one of the primary air bases; from 26 February to 7 March, there were 54 Ju 52/3m flights from it to Tunisia, of which it has been ascertained that 23 transported fuel, with the rest carrying ammunition for the Afrika Korps.[1]

Since the end of March, the airlift had considerably increased; an average of 100 transport aircraft, including the Ju 52/3m and Me 323 fleets, regularly arriving on the island every day from Tunisia.[2] Naval traffic was also on the increase, as evidenced in the reconnaissance by No. 683 Squadron over Palermo, Marsala and Trapani: between 11:35 a.m. on 22 March and 4:20 p.m. on 23 March, 12 F-boats left Trapani. On the 23rd, at the port of Augusta, there were three U-boats and three German E-boats.

On 24 March, the American bombers of IX Bomber Command carried out a mission to Messina, between 2:00 and 5:00 p.m. Nineteen B-24D Liberators of the 98th Bombardment Group (BG), led by Captain J.R. Muehlberg, dropped 55 tons of bombs on the port; in addition to the usual strike photos of the bombed area, on the way back the bombers took some photos of Augusta where 27 vessels and three tankers were identified. The following day, another reconnaissance sortie spotted 11 F-boats that had entered the port of Trapani at 3:20 p.m.[3]

The number of transports operating between Sicily and Tunisia on 24 March was as many as 110, with 134 recorded for the 25th.[4] A radio interception picked up by the Anglo–American

---

1   The National Archives London, Royal Air Force, Sicily: reports on airfields and aircraft, AIR 40/1996.
2   Royal Air Force, Middle East Review No. 3: April-June 1943, Part 1, N.pl. H.Q. R.A.F. Middle East, p.7.
3   Photo Interpretation Report n.120 of 27.03.1943.
4   AFHRA, Intelligence Summary n. 77 of 28 March 1943.

A Messerschmitt Me 323 Gigant at Trapani Milo. (Alessandro Ragatzu)

Intelligence services revealed 'The protection escort for our navy and for air traffic has been increased in recent days.'

In the month of March alone, 683 Squadron carried out 80 photo-reconnaissance sorties; almost all concerned targets in Sicily. On 21 March, Flight Sergeant W.S. Lewis, in Spitfire PR.IV (BR665), thanks to additional fuel tanks, flew to Rome, photographing, in addition to the capital, the airfields at Furbara, Vigna di Valle and Foligno, and the localities of Viterbo, Capua and Grazzanise; the sortie lasted four and a half hours and was the squadron's third to the capital.[5]

At 1:40 p.m. on 28 March, an F-5A (42-13089) of the 5th Photographic Reconnaissance Squadron, of the 3rd Photographic Group (PG), based on Malta, was carrying out a mission over Sicily. At the controls was the detachment commander, Captain Lewis H. Richardson. At 5:40 p.m., since Richardson had not returned and could not be raised on the radio, several

---

5   The Spitfire was not armed, the wing cannons being replaced by 60-gallon tanks, one in each wing, to significantly increase the aircraft's range. The main tank, located between the cockpit and the engine, contained 87 gallons, for a total of 207 imperial gallons (not American gallons). For very long-range sorties, a detachable 90-gallon tank was sometimes carried under the fuselage. This allowed for deep penetrations of enemy territory, the pilots jettisoning the now empty tank to continue the sortie on a full internal fuel load.

Spitfires took off to look for him.[6] Flying Officer Laurie Philpotts was one of the pilots; he had just returned, 40 minutes before, from a sortie over Taranto and Messina. He related his version of the story:

> Warbie and Roosevelt became great friends and, in time, Roosevelt sent five pilots to Malta to be responsible to Warbie while they attempted to aerial photograph all of Sicily using a special type of mapping camera mounted in a P-38 (Lockheed Lightning). A captain (I can't remember the idiot's name; Richards, I think) who brought the pilots over immediately ignored Warbie. It was assumed that the captain got lost on his first

Back row, left to right: Bob Spencer, Keith Durbidge, George German, Adrian Warburton, Ike Webb and Art Luthy.
Front row, left to right: Mac Brown, Jeff Geoffrey, Laurie Philpotts, Joe Sugg, Ed Berry, John MacLaughlin and Ed Maloney. (Chris Philpotts)

6   Captain Lewis H. Richardson was the commander of the Maltese detachment and was on his first mission from Malta. The new F-5A had just been delivered to the 3rd PG on 10 March and were replacing the now obsolete F-4s and F-4As that would be relegated to courier flights. Command of the third unit of the 3rd PG in Malta was assigned to Lieutenant John P. Silliman.

Wing Commander Adrian Warburton (left, cigarette in mouth) playing poker with some No. 683 Squadron and 3rd PG pilots on Malta. (US Air Force photo 29152 AC)

flight and he plunked down, in cloudy weather, onto an aerodrome in Southeast Sicily, runabout under and in the clouds, I found the P-38 in a pen on Gerbini aerodrome. A couple of Spitfires, which were fitted with bombs, dive-bombed the P-38. Too late? We never knew. After this fiasco, the remainder of the pilots listened very closely to Warbie's experience.[7]

Operation *Flax*

On 1 April, Flight Lieutenant G.H. Maloney, on board EN331, took off from Luqa at 12:00 p.m. for Palermo, Messina and Naples. The sortie was to follow naval traffic entering the ports. The photos revealed the arrival at Palermo of a large tanker ship escorted by three other vessels

7   Philpotts, *Memoirs of World War II*, p.133.

and covered by two aircraft. The next day, Snowden, back at the controls of EN331, flew over the airfield at Boccadifalco where there were 63 aircraft, including 14 SM.79s, four Me 323s, six Ju 52/3m trimotors and two SM.81s. On Trapani Milo, the 114 aircraft photographed included two Me 323s, 11 Ju 52/3ms, one He 111, one SM.79, an Fw 58, 36 Ju 88s, a Dornier, 28 Me 110/210s, a single Ju 87 and 32 fighters (mostly Bf 109s). On Pantelleria, partial cloud cover obscured the target, but 16 aircraft were still visible, of which 12 were fighters. A U-boat was also spotted at sea; Snowden recorded its location as 38° 15' N, 14° 55' E.[8]

That same day, Captain Joe D. Scalpone arrived at the 3rd PG on Malta, assuming command of the unit from Lieutenant John P. Silliman. Scalpone recollected some anecdotes of his stay on Malta:

My eighth mission was flown from Malta. All together [sic] I flew fifteen missions there. Our hops were short. Often only an hour and a half duration. Sicily was only 65 miles away. Fighter strength there was greater than that in Tunisia, became Tunisia had fallen to us and the greater part of the German and Italian fighters had been removed to Sicily. Interceptions were not infrequent in Sicily then. But our seven pilots had "savvy". Ten or eleven interceptions in two months (about one hundred and twenty missions flown) netted the enemy no American PRU scalps. Only once or twice did they prevent the pilot from getting pictures.

I flew over Palermo two or three times and was quite impressed by their flak. Very expensive show. Catania had good flak. Real scary stuff but it only popped miles in the sky. Hang around a target a little too long and the ground gunners get madder and madder – so it seems.

But it's a rare day when high flak knocks down a PRU ship. Unexpected flak is startling. One day while covering Biscari aerodrome I had completed my single run and was well away from their field when I glanced in the rear view mirror and found the sky just behind me filled with the black stuff. I did not know that field had flak; and I jumped to see my private sky suddenly crowded with the unexpected black puffs.

On Malta our PRU boys (German, Berry, Sugg, Coughlan, Wells, Luthy and Webb) covered more and more targets each mission. We were "getting on" in our trade. From the first targets covered in Tunisia; it was now approaching the time when the PRU "veterans" were vying with each other to cover as many as twenty-five and sometimes 30 targets at one sitting. On Malta we found the British Radar particularly helpful. They warned us of enemy fighters many times, though a warning does not always mean that the enemy has a chance to contact us or is even looking for the lone, elusive PRU pilot. Anyway, it is a pleasant feeling to be kept informed of enemy activity in your area. This system is not infallible. We never depend on it even in the most effective areas that the friendly radar controls. This area ranges about one-hundred miles, according to factors that are too devious and highly technical for the casual pilot to understand, much less talk about! Radio homings saved our necks in bad weather

8   AFHRA, IRISREF A6013, p.790.

Luftwaffe personnel loading fuel drums on Ju 52/3m transports destined for the front. (ACS 18691, 18697)

when we tried to find the little island of Malta on returning from a mission. It was sweet music to hear the Malta station "bring you in" on a bearing.[9]

The following day, the cameras of the PR Spitfires of Flight Sergeant Lewis and Sergeant Pritchard captured, between 12:15 and 4:00 p.m., the airfields at Sciacca (86 aircraft), Castelvetrano (85 aircraft including nine Me 323s), Trapani Bo Rizzo (98 aircraft), Comiso (54 aircraft), Biscari Santo Pietro (22 aircraft), Catania Fontanarossa (117 aircraft), and Gela Ponte Olivo (12 aircraft). When Pritchard was five miles from Catania, however, he was warned by Maltese air traffic control that enemy planes were approaching; the pilot was advised to return to the base. In the meantime, Operation *Flax* began, a series of actions coordinated by Western Desert Air Force command and the USAAF command in northern Africa to cut the Axis air transport system supplying Italian and German forces in Tunisia.

A formation of Junkers Ju 52/3m trimotors of IV./KGzbV 1 low over the Mediterranean. (Alessandro Ragatzu)

Starting on 5 April 1943, it lasted until early May, the end of Italian–German resistance in Tunisia. On 5 April, at 11:40 a.m., Trapani Bo Rizzo was bombed by 35 B-25 Mitchells of the 310th BG escorted by 16 P-38 Lightnings of the 82nd Fighter Group (FG) from Berteaux airfield in Algeria. On the same day, Palermo was hit twice; the first incursion, by 18 B-17 Flying Fortress bombers of the 301st BG, headed for Boccadifalco; the second, made up of 23 B-24D Liberators of the 98th BG, based at Benina, Libya, hit the port. The Allies estimated

9   AFHRA, IRISREF B0747, p.400.

American B-25 Mitchells and P-38 Lightnings attack a formation of Ju 52/3m transports off the coast of Tunisia. The German aircraft were evacuating men and supplies in April 1943. (US Air Force photo 23698 AC)

they destroyed 79 aircraft on the ground at Trapani Bo Rizzo, 122 at Trapani Milo, and between 150 and 175 at Palermo Boccadifalco. On 6 April, while a heavy air raid by 18 Flying Fortresses, this time from the 97th BG, was taking place over the port of Trapani, a sortie called 'Mosaic of Catania' was entrusted to Sergeant Keith Durbidge. On board Spitfire PR.IV (BP905), he flew over the area several times, from Acireale to Paternò, and, subsequently, the area west of Augusta to Scordia. The sortie was successfully carried out, despite a small, unexpected event when an enemy fighter tried to intercept during the last pass; Durbidge managed to return to Malta unharmed at 4:00 p.m. Earlier, at 1:30 p.m., Pilot Officer N.M. Gilchrist of 683 Squadron, in Spitfire EN331, flew over the Palermo area:

> Alcamo. Photographic run 340° 4 mls. 090° Balestrate 1 ml. second run in opposite direction 7mls. Photographic runs at Lake S. of Piana dei Greci, Area Palermo aero, Capaci, Cape San Vito, Castelluzzo, Mazara del Vallo – Coast strip 180°. Visibility and weather: Good.[10]

10   The National Archives London, Royal Air Force, Operations Record Books AIR 27/2209/6.

The confluence of data from Ultra's reconnaissance and decryptions provided Intelligence with a more comprehensive picture of air traffic to and from Sicily. Transport flights servicing Tunisia, by both the *Luftwaffe* and *Regia Aeronautica*, for the first 10 days of April, numbered 378. The peak of activities was recorded in the first four days with an average of 60 daily flights. The combination of reconnaissance and Ultra intelligence even allowed an understanding of the flight routine: 30 SM.82s and an SM.75 left Castelvetrano every day, except on the 2nd, 8th and 9th, between 5:30 and 7:30 a.m.; between 12 and 15 SM.82s left Castelvetrano on the 1st, 3rd, 4th and 6th between 12:00 and 12:30 p.m.; seven SM.82s and four Fiat G.12s left Sciacca every day between 7:00 and 9:00 a.m. (except during 2–4 April). Generally, these aircraft took between an hour and one hour and 15 minutes to make it to Tunisia; another hour was consumed unloading their cargo. In most cases, 4–8 MC.202s or MC.205s escorted the transports.[11]

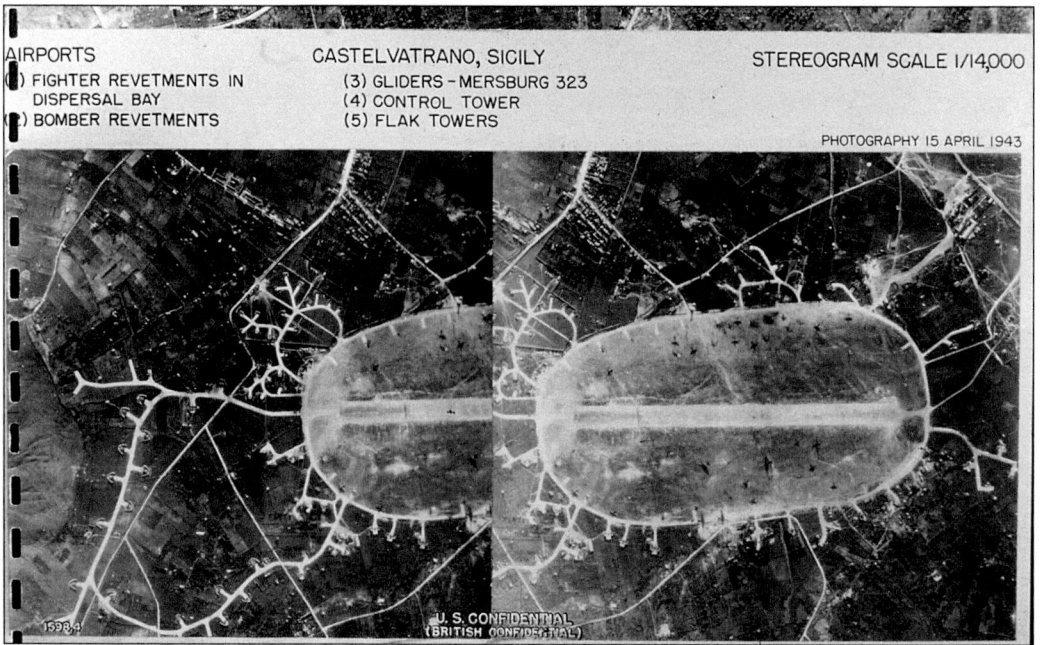

AIRPORTS	CASTELVATRANO, SICILY	STEREOGRAM SCALE 1/14,000
(1) FIGHTER REVETMENTS IN DISPERSAL BAY	(3) GLIDERS – MERSBURG 323	
(2) BOMBER REVETMENTS	(4) CONTROL TOWER	
	(5) FLAK TOWERS	PHOTOGRAPHY 15 APRIL 1943

A stereophoto of Castelvetrano airfield on 15 April 1943. (Alessandro Ragatzu)

11   AFHRA, NAAF, IRISREF A6007, Intelligence Summary n. 96, of 16 April 1943.

B-17F Flying Fortress (the F-9 photo-reconnaissance version) 41-24440 'I Got Spurs' of the 3rd PG.
The aircraft arrived in Algeria on 6 December 1942. Its last base in North Africa was La Marsa before it
moved to Grottaglie on 4 October 1943. (US Air Force photo 76200 AC)

On 13 April, Northwest African Strategic Air Force (NASAF) command sent 23 B-17 bombers of the 301st BG to Castelvetrano to drop 33 short tons of fragmentation bombs;[12] the Fortresses of the 97th BG headed to Trapani Milo, dropping more than 37 short tons of fragmentation bombs.[13] Reconnaissance was carried out immediately after the bombing; the photos, analysed by NASAF interpreters, show that, at Trapani Milo, of about 120 aircraft present, 14 were destroyed and 14 damaged. Of the 90 aircraft on the ground at Castelvetrano, three Messerschmitt Me 323s were destroyed (actually, according to German reports, five were destroyed, all belonging to II./323), and 17 other transport aircraft, and 22 unidentified machines, were hit (six were on fire). Photointerpretation could not provide the exact assessment of damage to the aircraft, given the use of fragmentation bombs and the amount of smoke

12   On the same day, there was a serious accident on the Luqa runway. At 11:40 a.m., Spitfire PR.IV (BR656) flown by the N.M. Gilchrist, landing on return from a reconnaissance mission over Naples and Capo Spartivento, collided with the No. 126 Squadron Spitfire IX (EN146/'MK-X') flown by Squadron Leader Urwin Mann, who had been authorised to take off. The Spitfires caught fire and the two pilots suffered several injuries. Gilchrist and Mann, after receiving treatment at a local hospital, were transferred to England to receive the specialist treatment.

13   One short ton corresponds to 907.18474 kilograms.

raised immediately after the bombing. In this brief period, 74,880lbs of bombs were dropped on Trapani Milo, 66,240lbs on Castelvetrano, 126,000lbs on Palermo, and 85,200 and 179,700lbs on the ports of Marsala and Trapani respectively.[14] The next day, further verification of the bombing fell on Flight Sergeant Snowden who left Luqa at 2:00 p.m. in Spitfire PR.XI (EN412). At Castelvetrano, he recorded 35–40 multi-engine aircraft, of which 15 were probably Me 323s. The sortie continued toward San Vito Lo Capo where two Siebel Ferries were sighted at sea, three miles from the coast.[15] Continuing to Naples, Snowden was intercepted by six enemy fighters. Castelvetrano was closed to aircraft; repairs were so fast, however, that 12 Me 323s left for their usual trip to Tunisia two days later. An important fact to note is the almost constant presence of Siebel Ferries in the port of Marsala; on 17 April, Snowden observed six of them leaving the port escorted by other vessels. Three days later, the scouts returned to Marsala for a further photographic sortie and found 18 moored seaplanes in plain view. Marsala, according to the Allies, was the main boarding terminal for Tunisia, the primary destination being La Goulette. The Siebel Ferries usually left Marsala between 1:00 and 4:00 p.m., arriving in Tunisia 24 hours later; the same duration was expected for the return voyage. However, incessant attacks temporarily forced the Siebel Ferries to stop near the island of Favignana.

Approximate number of coastal defence and anti-aircraft positions known in February 1943		
Location	Coastal Defence	Anti-aircraft
Trapani e Marsala	75	48
Palermo	56	80
Coast between Marsala and Porto Empedocle	7	27
Porto Empedocle	30	17
Licata		
Coast between Licata and Capo Passero	10	several
Coast between Capo Passero and Siracusa	13	
Siracusa	30	4
Augusta	69	30
Catania	35	140
Coast between Catania and Messina	12	several
Strait of Messina	175	50

14   AFHRA, NAAF, IRISREF A6007.
15   The Siebel Ferries (Siebelfähre) were armed landing craft, equipped for the transport of men and unloading vehicles on beaches through a folding bow ramp.

On 16 April, from the desert air base of Berka No. 2 in Libya, 13 B-24 Liberators of the Ninth Air Force took off at 7:15 a.m. to attack Catania, where a large tanker had been berthed for a few days; in the bombers' holds were 129 × 500lb bombs. It was the first attack of this magnitude to be carried out on the city at the foot of Mount Etna.

On 22 March 1943, the B-17F Flying Fortresses of the 301st BG carried out a heavy raid on the city of Palermo. Each bomber dropped a load of twelve 500-pound bombs. The result was devastating: the entire port area, including warehouses and ships, was destroyed. The Italian–German anti-aircraft defences hit B-17F 41-24352 'Holey Joe', commanded by Captain Jimmy Hare, causing it to explode. Five crew members were seen baling out. (US Air Force)

The formation, led by a Major Lavin was, at 11:04 a.m., placed perpendicularly over the city. Despite the radio silence imposed by the bombers, the radar stations at Portopalo and Noto detected them and sounded the alert; Catania's anti-aircraft defence then tried in vain to hit the attackers. At around 6:30 in the morning, Flight Lieutenant M.G. Brown, on an aerial survey of Catania, reported the large tanker ship had not suffered any visible damage.

It was Sergeant Durbidge who, on 24 April, flew over the Province of Enna, the seat of the Axis headquarters in Sicily, to photograph the airstrip just north of Calascibetta; on which only one aircraft, probably used by high command to move around the island, was noted.[16] The sortie continued to Augusta, where 15 seaplanes were seen tied up. The most important discovery of the mission, however, was the radar station near Noto, of which several photographs were taken. Meanwhile, six Ju 52/3m transports were seen parked at Biscari Santo Pietro airfield, as were numerous German Fw 190 fighters of III./SKG 10.

Captain Joe David Scalpone, commander of the Maltese detachment of the 3rd PG, in the cockpit of an F-5A holding the list of targets to be photographed. (US Air Force photo 76024 AC)

16   Carlo D'Este, *1943, Lo sbarco in Sicilia* [Bitter Victory: The Battle for Sicily, 1943] (Milano: Mondadori, 1990), p.366.

Some Maltese Spitfire squadrons were simultaneously engaged in armed patrols or reconnaissances over the southern coasts of Sicily. On 30 April, four Spitfires of No. 249 Squadron attacked a submarine in the Marzamemi area; Flight Sergeant Dean Kelly fired his cannons and machine guns, but the effect on the tough hull of the submarine was nil. At the same time, the radio station located on a tower about six miles south-west of Pachino, previously located by reconnaissance, was also attacked. The op, however, cost Flight Sergeant Cruse who, hit by anti-aircraft fire, was forced to make an emergency landing near Marzamemi; he was taken prisoner.

Captain Ike B. Webb Jr shortly before losing his life on a mission over France on 24 October 1943. (US Air Force photo 76022 AC)

A photo of Cagliari Elmas airfield, taken on 23 March 1943 by Flight Lieutenant McKenzie, No. 682 Squadron RAF. (US Air Force)

10

Mapping of Sicily and the PR Mosquitos of No. 60 Squadron SAAF

Mapping sorties require wide coverage of the area of interest. They are generally carried out from a high altitude, approximately 29,000 feet, in optimal weather conditions and involve numerous parallel photographic runs to create 'strips'. These predictable flight paths, however, greatly increase the aircraft's vulnerability to enemy threats. Because of these requirements, particularly the weather, terrestrial units needing these photographs had to request them well in advance.

Covering new areas of strategic interest, or mapping, required 6-inch focal-length cameras, where a single 1:50,000 scale exposure covered a seven-mile square. The 24-inch cameras, however, covered an area of three by 1.75 miles on an average scale of 1:12,500; both had a limited ability to determine the presence of minor defences. Experience showed that only 36-inch cameras captured the detail necessary to highlight coastal and anti-aircraft positions, even those of small and medium calibres. In some cases, it was also possible to identify minefields through careful analysis of disruptions to the terrain, but, obviously, everything also depended on the height from which the photos were taken. It was therefore considered unrealistic to think that 36-inch cameras could discover everything, especially in rough terrain and the adversary's application of camouflage.

Major Robert Boyle, 3rd PG officer, commented on the work of British photo-interpreters:

> Without the assistance of the British interpreters in the beginning, the photo interpretation work could not have been immediately successful. Their experience and training during nearly three years of warfare … made it possible for both American and Allied Headquarters in North Africa to receive accurate photographic interpretation, which at that time American photo units actually were not capable of producing, simply because they had no personnel training in this intricate and exacting work.[1]

The United States had previously sent Major Almond of Air Force Headquarters, and Captain Erb of the 3rd PG HQ to Malta and Tripoli, from 15 to 17 February, to discuss the use of Mosquitos from No. 1 Photographic Reconnaissance Unit (PRU), No. 540 Squadron, which

---

1   Robert Boyle, 'History of Photo Reconnaissance in North Africa Including My Experiences with the 3rd Photographic Reconnaissance Group', Ph.D. diss., University of Texas, 1948, p.3.

had arrived some time earlier from England, in important and delicate mapping sorties over Sicily. They also hoped to request the aircraft for specific, immediate, initiatives.[2]

The de Havilland Mosquito B.VII 'The Spook' (43-34926), of the 3rd PG, at La Marsa. (US Air Force)

2   Some variants, such as the Mosquito PR.IV Series II, were able to mount two vertical chambers in the bomb bay, two other vertical units further aft and one oblique on the left. The power of the two Rolls-Royce Merlin 21 engines, and the possibility of adding two additional 50-gallon tanks under the wings, made it one of the most effective, and famous, reconnaissance aircraft of the war. AFHRA, IRISREF MAAF 257, Reel 25244, p.1257.

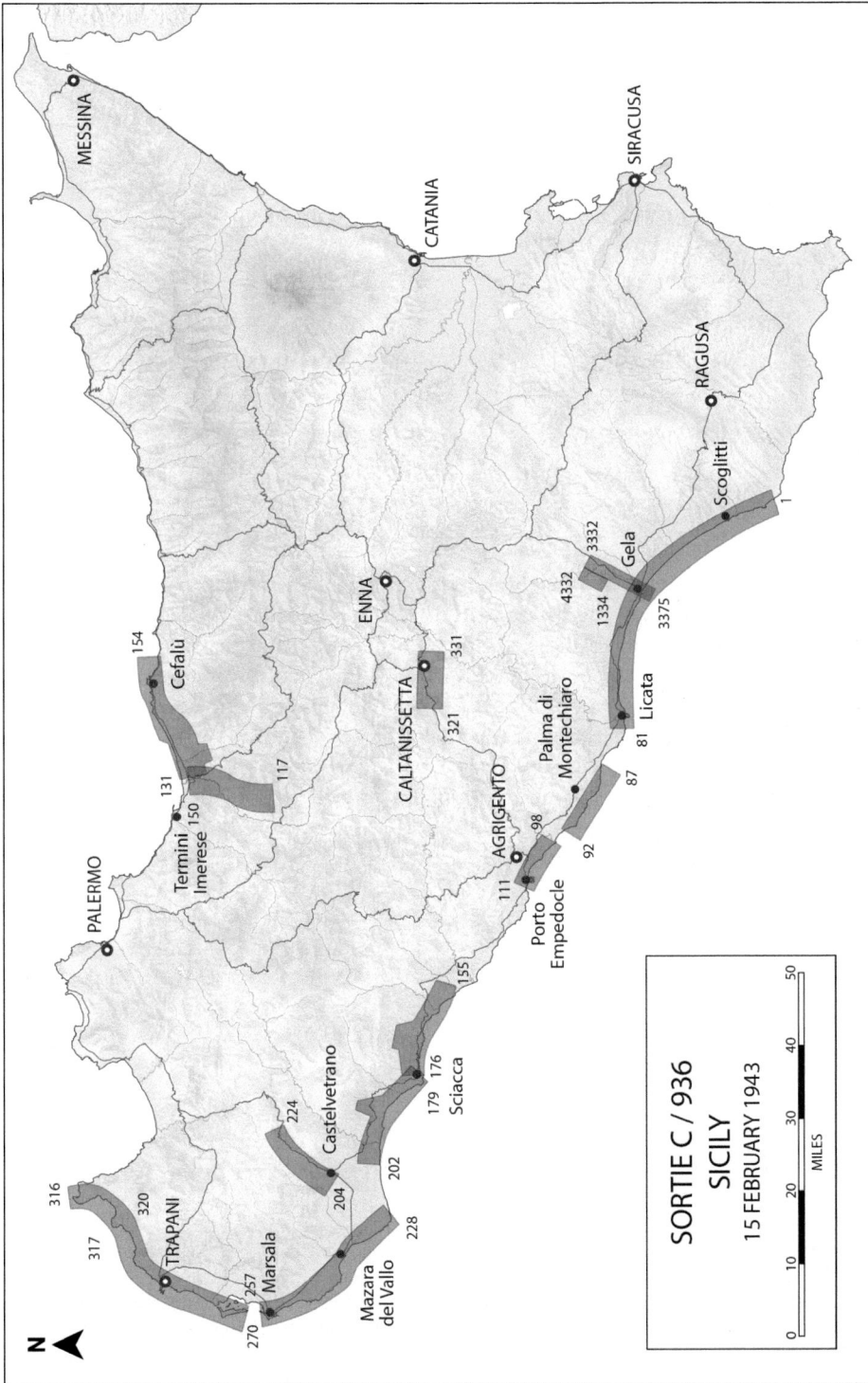

A Mosquito sortie over Sicily. (AFHRA)

Sortie	Date	Focal Length	Altitude	Target
Sorties carried out by 1 PRU in Malta from February to March 1943[3]				
C933	04/02/43	14"	27,000	M, S, SW, W SICILY, P R, S/W/NW SICILY
C934	08/02/43	14"	22,000	M P R, SE/W/SW SICILY
C935	13/02/43	14"	5,000	M & R, SE/S SICILY
C936	15/02/43	14"	25,000	Rd R, M, P A R, W/SW/S/SE SICILY
C938	15/02/43	14"	25,000	M & R, NE/S/E/SE SICILY
		36"	25,000	M & R, NW/N/NE/E/SE SICILY
C939	23/02/43	14"	25,000	P A M & R, N/NW/W/SW/S/SE
C940	27/02/43	14"	24,000	P A M & R, CE/SE/S SICILY
		36"	24,000	P A M & R, CE/SE/S SICILY
C941	17/03/43	36"	24,000	P A R & M, S/W/NW/NE SICILY

Between 17 and 26 March, three mapping sorties were successfully completed over the areas of Catania, north of Simeto, Augusta and the nearby peninsula of Magnisi, Capo Passero, Pozzallo, Scoglitti, Gela, Licata and Sciacca, with 36-inch cameras; from Cefalù to Gioiosa Marea, the photographic coverage was made with a 14-inch lens.[4] This effort was supplemented by two more Mosquitos from No. 60 Squadron SAAF, which had been operating over Sicily since 15 April. The South African unit was operating under the RAF's No. 285 Wing from Sorman, Libya, and was led by Major O.G. Davis.

May 13 marked the end of the Tunisian campaign. The crews of 60 Squadron had carried out 191 reconnaissance and mapping sorties over North Africa before the surrender of the Italian and German forces. The 154th American Tactical Reconnaissance Squadron also contributed,

3   Legend
     A: Airdromes and Landing Grou5nd
     C: Central
     D: Dicing
     E: East
     M: Mapping
     N: North
     O: High altitude oblique
     P: Ports and harbors
     R: General Reconnaissance
     S: South
     W: West
     Rd: Roads
     QR: Night and Reconnaissance
4   By 12 April, a PR Mosquito from 540 Squadron had completed 190 flying hours. This aircraft, in addition to the 36-inch camera, also carried two 14-inch lenses. It completed some sorties over Licata and Capo Scaramia and then returned to England for necessary maintenance based on the hours flown. It returned to operations a few days later, again from Malta. AFHRA, Reel 25244, p.1311.

from mid-January to mid-April, with 1,512 sorties, of which 38 were photo-reconnaissance flights.

In the early afternoon of the same day, 13 May, two members of 60 Squadron, Lieutenants Maree and Van Dijl, flew their first sortie over Sicily. They were part of the detachment based on Malta, operating under No. 683 Squadron for operational tasking and administrative purposes.[5] The survey began at 2:45 p.m., the PR Mosquito (DD744) photographing the coast from Messina to Augusta from 29,000 feet.

These sorties from Malta were not limited to objectives in the Mediterranean. Early on 19 May, 540 Squadron sent Flying Officer A. Stewart and Flight Sergeant M.W. Pike in Mosquito PR.IV (DZ352) from Benson to the Austrian capital of Vienna and Italian ports where they risked being intercepted by enemy aircraft. These evasive manoeuvres significantly increased fuel consumption, forcing the aircraft to land on Malta with 20 gallons of petrol left.

On 29 May, a Spitfire PR.XI (EN263) of 683 Squadron, flown by Sergeant Fletcher, covered Verona, Dubrovnik in Croatia, and Durres in Albania. From February to May, the Mosquitos of 60 Squadron were heavily employed, so much so they carried out 62 photographic sorties during this period alongside the unit's Baltimores and Marylands.[6] The mapping operations over Sicily, which, according to Allied plans, were already in the final phase, were clearly lagging behind, mainly due to atmospheric factors raging over the island; it was thus decided to use as many aircraft as possible to carry out these operations. To meet this need, five PR Mosquitos from No. 682 Squadron were based on Malta on 24 May,[7] and five 60 Squadron Mosquitos, and two more from an independent detachment, operated from Maison Blanche with the Western Desert Air Force.[8]

---

5   No. 60 Squadron, from 4 February, also used Mosquito PR Mk.IIs. The crew generally consisted of a pilot and an observer. The first Mosquito PRs delivered to the squadron were DD743 and DD744; they began operating on 12 February and were very active in the area of Gabes, Tunis, La Goulette (a port of call for ships from Sicily) and Tripoli, in support of the Eighth Army. From February, the unit operated from Castel Benito; in April it had 19 pilots on strength. The squadron's task in the Sicilian campaign was to map the entire area of the island under the jurisdiction of the Eighth Army, subsequently supporting it during the advance.

6   In May, 21 pilots were on the organisation chart of 60 Squadron, but only seven operational hours were carried out by the staff temporarily based on Malta, the rest of the unit remained in North Africa, performing most of the hours flown for the month on communication flights between various Allied units. Seven reconnaissance sorties were assigned to the two PR Mosquitos (HJ672 and DZ553) for the entire month of May, the aircraft mainly used in the south-east area of the island, particularly the Licata and Porto Empedocle sectors.

7   682 Squadron, under the command of Squadron Leader A.H.W. 'Freddie' Ball, joined the Northwest African Photographic Reconnaissance Wing (NAPRW) on March 1 1943 with seven PR Spitfires. By May 1943, it had 13 Spitfire PR.IVs and XIs (two of which were seconded to Malta) and three PR Mosquitos (including one on Malta). During its operational phase with NAPRW for the conquest of Sicily, the unit suffered the loss of two pilots; Flying Officer McKenzie was lost with his Spitfire PR.IV (EN347) during a sortie over Sardinia on 29 March 1943, and Flying Officer M.G. Brown, in Spitfire PR.IV AA803, was killed over Algeria on 5 May.

8   AFHRA, Reel 25244, p.1396.

60 Squadron SAAF	
Month	Hours
May	7
June	97.05 + 86.45 from Malta
July	83.10 B Flight; 21.20 A Flight within NAPRW

In the late morning of 15 June, 60 Squadron flew Mission 304 from the air base at Sorman, Libya, to Catania, flying over at noon at 27,000 feet. The Mosquito PR.II (DD744) was crewed by Lieutenants Barnes and Van Dijl. During the flight, which lasted three-and-a-quarter hours, Portopalo and Vizzini were photographed in addition to the city nestled under Mount Etna. All ended well at 2:25 p.m. without any enemy resistance being encountered. The Mosquito was equipped with a vertical Fairchild K-17 camera, with a focal length of 12 inches, a rear oblique camera of the Williamson F8 Mk.II type, with a focal length of 20 inches, and, finally, to starboard, another Williamson.[9] The following day, almost at the same time, the same aircraft, this time flown by Captain Maree and Flying Officer Murray-Prior, photographed the following locations east of Sicily during a two hour and 50 minute flight: Maddalena (on the plain of Catania) at 313° for 35 miles, Scordia, Floridia, where a strip of photos covering 35 miles at 207° was generated, and Castellana (in the Lentini territory) and Syracuse for 30 miles. The sortie produced 160 exposures.

In June, 60 Squadron provided the necessary support to complete the mapping of the entire island; it completed 87 flying hours over Sicily, across 12 sorties, using Mosquito PR.IIs DD743 and DD744. From Sorman, on the other hand, almost 100 hours were flown on photo-reconnaissance sorties, with a total of 20 men among the flying personnel (17 officers and three non-commissioned officers).[10] However, not all flights produced the desired outcome; the main cause of failure was often the presence of dense cloud cover over the target; six sorties failed because of this. The ops mainly concerned targets in the south-east of the island, including Pozzallo, Brucoli, the Gulf of Catania, Caltanissetta, Lake Lentini, Castellana, Ispica, coordinates H9760, Augusta, Punta Secca, Vizzini, H9763, H1562, Gela, Mirabella Imbaccari, Donnalucata, Satellite #7, H9768, and Licata.

9   The Williamson type cameras had a capacity of 250 exposures, while the Fairchild K-17 held 160. The sortie produced 203 exposures.
10   One of the most active pilots of 60 Squadron was undoubtedly Captain Maree, who flew more than 60 hours, of which 42 hours and 55 minutes were from Malta alongside 683 Squadron. He was followed by Van Dijl (45 hours and 5 minutes, 25 hours and 10 minutes from Malta), and Lieutenant Jefferys (34 hours and 55 minutes, 18 hours and 40 minutes from Malta). The National Archives London, Royal Air Force, Operations Record Books AIR 27/574.

Trapani Chinisia, Trapani Bo Rizzo to the Allies. The photo was taken by a No. 1 PRU Mosquito detached to Malta for mapping operations. (US Air Force)

Marsala immortalised from 24,000 feet by a No. 1 PRU Mosquito from England. The silhouettes of some Siebel Ferries are clearly visible. (US Air Force)

Comiso was bombed on 17 June at 1:22 p.m. by the Consolidated B-24 Liberators of the 515th BS, 376th BG. (US Air Force)

Hospital Ships

Hospital ships were called 'white ships' because of their white hulls on which a large red cross was painted. A long list of hospital ships is kept in the *Ufficio Storico della Marina Militare Italiana* (Historical Office of the Italian Navy). Italy went to war with seven large hospital units, to which others were soon added; they were the *Aquileia, Arno, California, Città di Trapani, Gradisca, Po, Principessa Giovanna, Ramb IV, Sicilia, Tevere, Toscana,* and *Virgilio,* all used for the transport of the sick and injured.[11] To these must be added the rescue ships, used to recover wrecked ships or aircraft, such as *Capri, Epomeo, Laurana, Meta, Giuseppe Orlando, San Giusto* and *Sorrento*. Together, they carried out 467 patient transfer voyages and 156 rescues, transporting 65,567 injured or shipwrecked personnel and 215,693 sick. The fleet, excluding *Epomeo, Gradisca* and *Sorrento*, was subjected to 39 enemy attacks. Before 8 September 1943, eight were sunk, two captured and the others damaged to varying extents; a disturbing result which was to stain the military honour of those who adhered to the international standards that established the respect and protection of health institutions. What happened to Italian hospital ships was considered so serious as to induce governments to convene a special conference in Geneva in 1949 to adapt international conventions to try to avoid the repetition of similar episodes in the future.

The reason for the attention paid to these otherwise 'off limits' vessels was because they often hid radar equipment used to detect Allied aircraft, as explained by Flying Officer Laurie Philpotts:

> Hospital ship – On the west coast of Italy, near Gaeta, I found a ship marked with hospital insignia, but it turned out that the ship had military radio equipment on it. Thusly, we found that this was the reason that allied aircraft were being detected so readily in the Med area. There was, also, reason to believe that this red-cross ship had been used elsewhere for other military purposes. Well, after I went down to closely scrutinize and take photography at full bore nosing for Malta. The temperature on the ground at Malta was over 95 degrees Fahrenheit, and when I landed after the rapid chase and taxied to my shrapnel pen, about a quarter-inch thickness of a sheet of ice fell from the underside of each mainplane. I was aghast and so were the ground crew who had guided the wing-tips while I taxied the Spit into the pen.[12]

In May 1943, another five missions covering Italian hospital ships took place off Tunisia. On 3 May, Flight Lieutenant M.G. Brown, in Spitfire PR.XI (EN331), photographed the *Principessa Giovanna* between 2:45 and 5:05 p.m. just outside the port of Trapani. The hospital ship was responsible for the rescue of 71 survivors from the *Perseo* (torpedo boat, 67) and the *Campobasso* (steamship, four), which sank 18 hours earlier (on the night of 3/4 May) following a confrontation with the British destroyers HMS *Nubian, Paladin* and *Petard*, which had radioed the position of the castaways to the *Principessa Giovanna*. The hospital ship was photographed on 5 May at 8:15 a.m. off Cape Bon, sailing at 12 knots and bearing 040°, again by Brown. Meanwhile, at Stagnone di Marsala and the airfield at Pantelleria, 15 float planes and eight medium-sized aircraft respectively were recorded.

Brown, during the same flight and 10 miles from Cape Bon, spotted the easily identifiable shapes of three Ju 52/3m transports, probably shot down by Allied fighters, floating on the sea in

---

11   The steamships were *Aquileia* (9,448 tons), *California* (13,059), *Gradisca* (13,870), *Toscana* (9,442), *Sicilia* (9,646), *Principessa Giovanna* (8,955), *Arno* (8,024), *Tevere* (8,289), and *Po* (7,289). The motorships type were *Virgilio* (11,718), *Città di Trapani* (2,467), and *Ramb IV* (3,676). Vincenzo Martines, *Le navi ospedale della Marina Militare Italiana* [*The Hospital Ships of the Italian Navy*] (Roma: Stato Maggiore Marina, 1995).

12   Philpotts, *Memoirs of World War II*, p.160.

The hospital ship *Gradisca* seen from a seaplane in the spring of 1941. It had a capacity of 760 beds and a speed of 16 knots. (ACS 16377, 04386)

flames at 37° 00' N, 11° 20 E. At 6:30 a.m. on the 9th, Philpotts photographed 25 Siebel Ferries as they arrived at the port of Marsala at the end of their voyage from Tunisia.

On 11 May, a 10,000-ton hospital ship was sighted at around 6:00 a.m., while it was four miles from the island of Favignana sailing at an estimated five knots, according to Sergeant W. Gabbott flying Spitfire PR.XI (EN263) of 683 Squadron. During the sortie, from the coasts of Algeria to Sicily, Gabbott also sighted three Siebel Ferries and two E-boats on a 180° heading eight miles off Marsala. Regarding the hospital ship, it was assumed it was the same one seen the morning before by Adrian Warburton leaving Cape Melah in Tunisia and heading north-west. Several hospital ships crossed the Mediterranean during this period; in addition to *Principessa Giovanna*, *Virgilio* was present on 7 May, taking part in the evacuation of the wounded and sick from Kélibia with the *Aquileia*. On the same day, an F-5A Lightning from the 3rd PG carried out three distinct missions. The first, covering Licata, Porto Empedocle and Sciacca, photographed the port and airfield, before continuing to Palermo. During the return trip, the pilot saw a hospital ship between Favignana and Trapani, confirming what was previously reported by Gabbott. The second sortie for the 3rd PG was carried out over the island of Lampedusa and the smaller Lampione. The third concerned the coast of North Africa, particularly the peninsula of Cape Bon.

German soldiers on a ship arriving at Catania. In front of them can be seen the unmistakable shape of the small hospital ship *Urania*. (Author's photo)

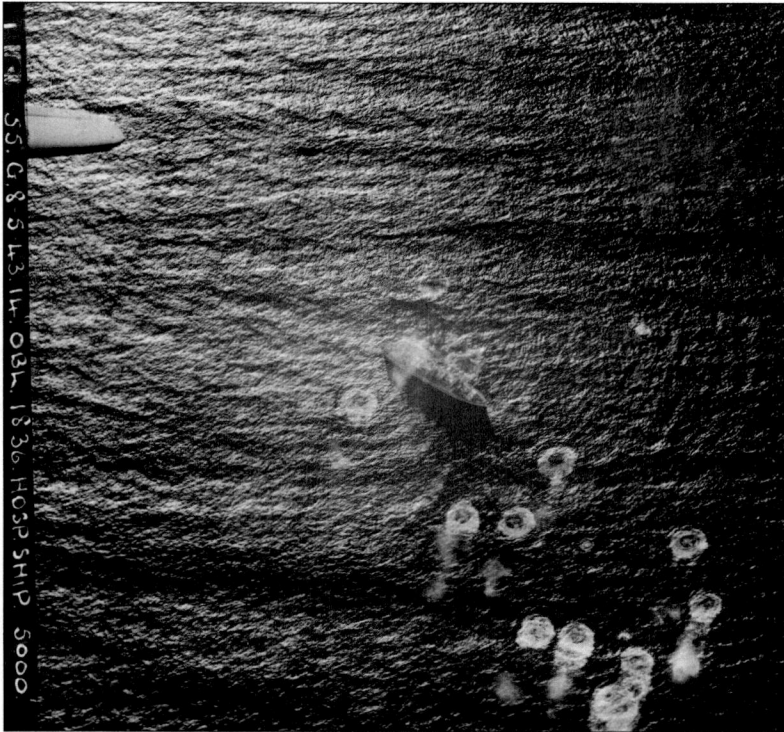

An oblique photo of the attack on a hospital ship near Cape Bon by some Baltimore IIIs of No. 55 Squadron on 8 May 1943. (Brian Spurr)

In the early hours of 15 May, the *Virgilio* entered the port of Messina. The same 683 Squadron pilot who sighted it on 12 June in Gaeta (the port of origin), Sergeant F. Simpson, recorded the event.

On the early morning of 22 June, Pilot Officer G. Craig took off from Malta to perform sortie number 992 (MA/992) for 683 Squadron in Spitfire PR.XI (EN391). Over Palermo he observed a barrage of tethered balloons; in the meantime, the *Virgilio* was preparing to leave port and a large merchant ship was alongside the pier for unloading operations. Forty-one aircraft, most of which were fighters, were seen on the perimeter track of the airfield at Boccadifalco. Compared to the surveys carried out on 14 June, there was an increase of three SM.79/84s and a decrease of about 10 fighters. At Stagnone di Marsala, five CANT Z.506Bs, and a CANT Z.501 and a Do 24, were moored to buoys; 11 military vessels of various kinds had been moored inside the port since the 15th. Twenty-four aircraft, east and west of the perimeter, were seen at Trapani Bo Rizzo (10 large aircraft were identifed as damaged). On the same day, the 15th Photographic Reconnaissance Squadron's Lieutenant Freeman also performed a sortie over Messina, Villa San Giovanni, Trapani Milo and Trapani Bo Rizzo. Dense cloud cover prevented Messina and its port from being observed and photographed. Flying towards Sant'Agata di Militello, Freeman saw some Siebel Ferries leaving the port. The *Virgilio*, photographed a few hours earlier near Palermo, was already off the coast of Milazzo and proceeding quickly in an easterly direction.

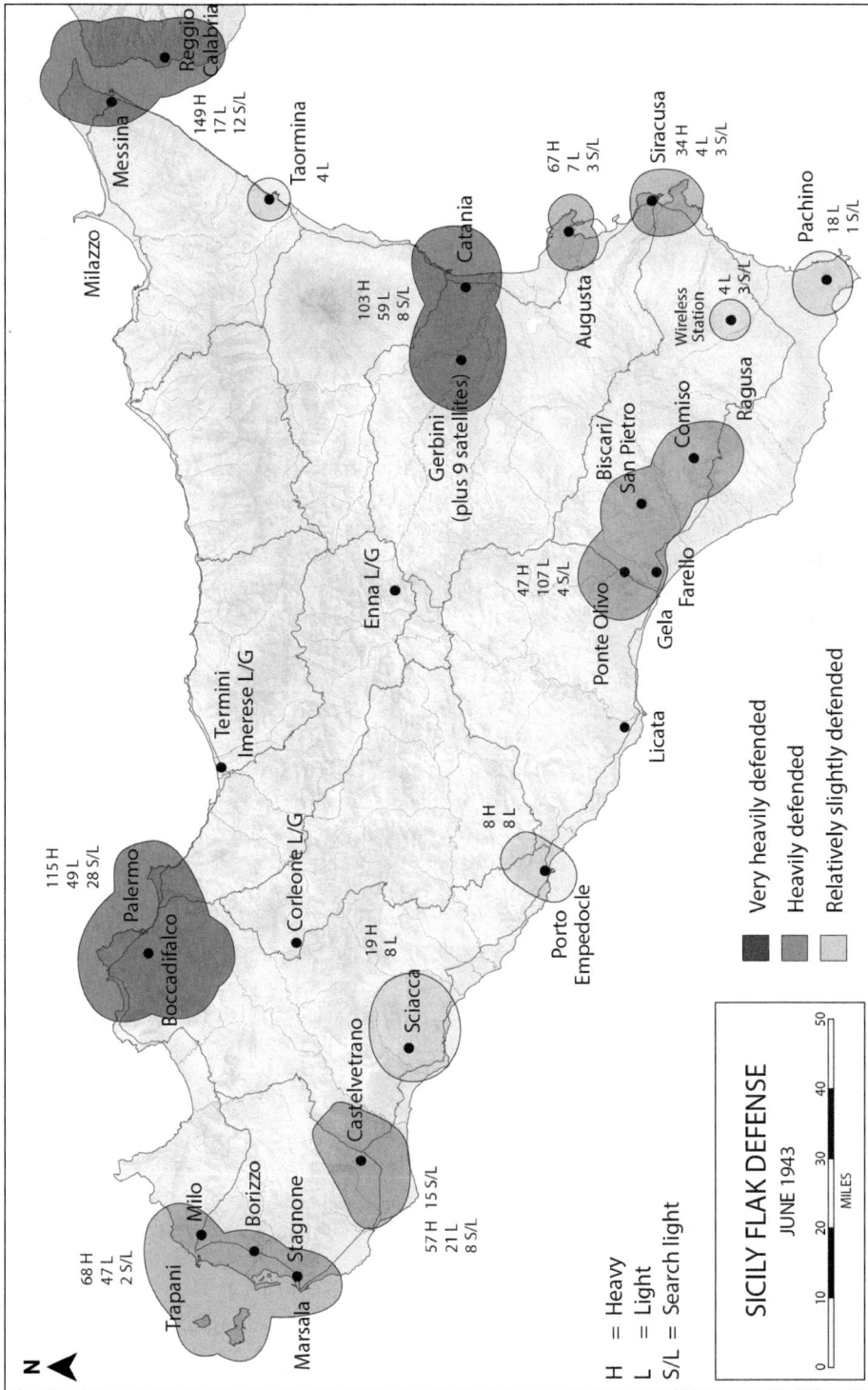

The most defended areas of Sicily. (AFHRA)

SICILY FLAK DEFENSE
JUNE 1943

H   = Heavy
L   = Light
S/L = Search light

- Very heavily defended
- Heavily defended
- Relatively slightly defended

Reggio Calabria   149 H / 17 L / 12 S/L
Messina
Milazzo
Taormina   4 L
Catania   103 H / 59 L / 8 S/L
Gerbini (plus 9 satellites)
Augusta   67 H / 7 L / 3 S/L
Siracusa   34 H / 4 L / 3 S/L
Pachino   18 L / 1 S/L
Wireless Station   4 L / 3 S/L
Biscari / San Pietro
Comiso
Ragusa
Ponte Olivo   47 H / 107 L / 4 S/L
Gela
Farello
Licata
Porto Empedocle   8 H / 8 L
Enna L/G
Termini Imerese L/G
Corleone L/G
Palermo   115 H / 49 L / 28 S/L
Boccadifalco
Sciacca   19 H / 8 L
Castelvetrano   57 H / 15 S/L / 21 L / 8 S/L
Milo
Borizzo
Stagnone
Trapani   68 H / 47 L / 2 S/L
Marsala

N

MILES
0   10   20   30   40   50

11

Target Sicily (May–June 1943)

With the remaining Axis forces in Tunisia surrendering on 13 May 1943, Allied forces prepared to attack the 'soft underbelly of Fortress Europe', to use the vivid expression from British Prime Minister Winston Churchill. All of the Allied air power in the theatre concentrated on the islands of Pantelleria and Lampedusa. Thus began the preparation for Operation *Corkscrew*, culminating in the occupation of Pantelleria. The objectives were carefully chosen according to the priorities established during the planning of Operation *Husky* (the invasion of Sicily).

As early as 9 May, General Eisenhower had decided to employ NASAF (Northwest African Strategic Air Force) heavy bombers and NATAF (Northwest African Tactical Air Force) fighters and bombers over Sicily. The 'Malta Air Force' was supposed to provide indirect support for the operation, escorting bombers to attack Sicilian air bases. The commander of the strategic air forces in the Mediterranean, General James H. Doolittle, completed his preparations by deploying most of his available assets to the areas around Constantine (Algeria), Souk-El-Arba and Djedeida (both Tunisia). The tactical air force commander, Air Vice-Marshal Arthur Coningham, had instead moved his medium and light bombers to the airfields of the Cape Bon peninsula. Overall, at the start of operations against Pantelleria, NATAF and NASAF together deployed 1,017 aircraft, supported by a reasonable number of reserve aircraft.[1] Due to the reduced range of its single-engine aircraft, XII Air Support Command (hierarchically dependent on NATAF), between 20 May and 4 June, moved its departments to the Cape Bon peninsula.[2] In addition to the aforementioned attack force, the operation was indirectly supported by other units including bombers from Middle East commands, and fighters and bombers from Malta and Coastal Command, for a total of 3,395 aircraft.[3]

For the landing operations on Pantelleria, Eisenhower chose the British 1st Infantry Division as it had received training in amphibious warfare in England but had not been selected for the invasion of Sicily. Already, a few days before the end of the battles in North Africa, attention had shifted to Pantelleria. On 10 May, reconnaissance aircraft from the 3rd Photographic Group (PG) had identified 12 aircraft (including nine fighters and a large number of destroyed machines) on the airfield at Pantelleria. On 11 May, Flight Sergeant C.A. Tardif was flying

---

1   AFHRA, 12th Air Force, Sicilian Campaign narrative, p.7.
2   AFHRA, History of the 12th Air Force, chapt. XIV p.44.
3   AFHRA, History of the 12th Air Force, p.44.

Pre-mission briefing for pilots of the 49th FS, 14th FG. Major Bernard Muldoon is synchronising his watch with his colleagues before a mission to Pantelleria. (US Air Force photo 53338 AC)

a reconnaissance over Taranto when he unexpectedly found himself witnessing one of the heaviest bombings Catania had suffered since the beginning of the war. Some large merchant ships had been identified near the port the day before by Pilot Officer Keith Durbidge. The Ninth Air Force sent 48 B-24 Liberator heavy bombers, 26 from the 98th and 22 from the 376th Bombardment Groups, based out of various Libyan airfields, escorted by 47 RAF Spitfires from Malta.[4] The bombers unloaded, in several waves from between 22,000 and 25,000 feet (depending on their relative positions inside the combat box), 230 × 500lb bombs and sixty 4lb incendiaries (113 tons). The devastating bombing of the port killed 216 people and injured 303, mostly civilians. Tardif, in his flight log, reported:

> Catania at 22000. Numerous Heavy Bombs attacking target. Heavy A.A. Intense. Burst seen in harbor. Photo Special area covered for S.A.S.O.[5]

The bombers hit and sank the motorboats MZ 717 and MZ 728 (both of 120 tons) and the 4,425-ton steamship *Partinico*. The anti-aircraft barrier was intense and accurate, so much

4   AFHRA, IRISREF B5665, p.723.
5   The National Archives London, Royal Air Force, Operations Record Books AIR 27/2209/8.

so it hit engine three (starboard inner) of Liberator B-24D (serial 41-11787), 'D', 'Shangai Lil', piloted by 1st Lieutenant Roland Ingerson of the 415th Bombardment Squadron, 98th Bombardment Group (BG). Only 1st Lieutenant Jarman G. Kennard managed to bale out; the rest of the crew fell into the sea with the bomber. Another five Liberators were damaged and three crew members wounded. The loss of Ingerson's bomber was attributed to *Flak-Abteilung 237*, a *Luftwaffe* unit, whose 88mm cannons were positioned to defend the military installations of Catania.[6]

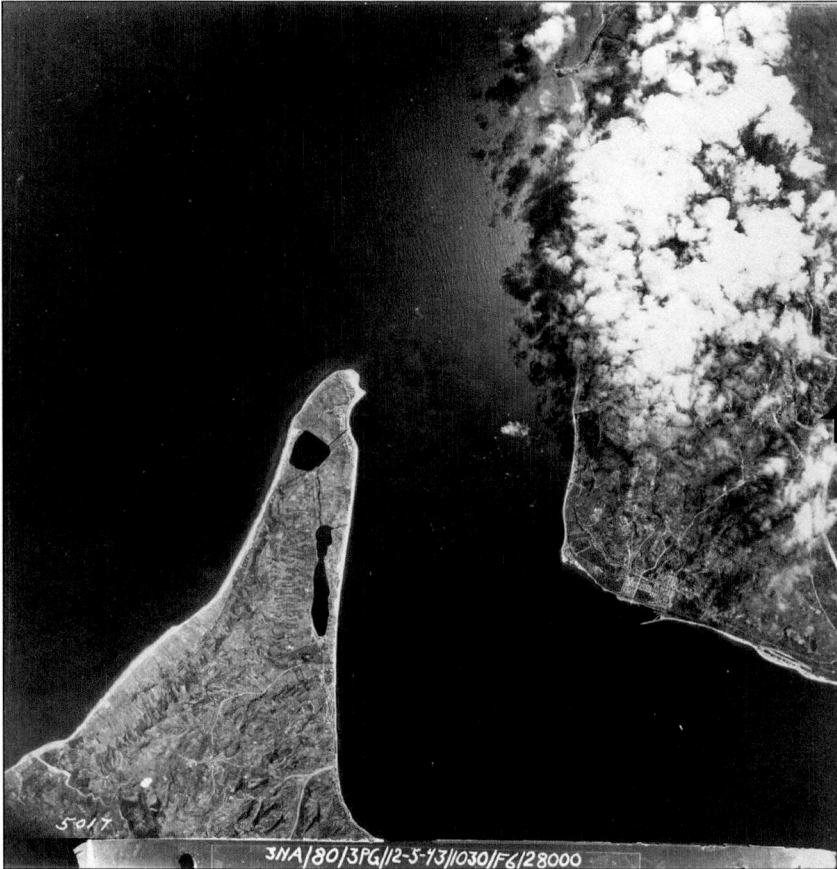

The Strait of Messina photographed at 10:30 a.m. on 12 May 1943 by an F-5A of the 3rd Photographic Group based in North Africa. (US Air Force)

6   NARA, Missing Air Crew Reports n. 15074.

That mission, which had been called a 'milk run', or a 'walk in the park', proved fatal for most of the crew of 'Shanghai Lil'. Below is the testimony of the only survivor, Jarman Kennard:

> On my sixteenth mission, May 11, 1943, my luck almost ran out. Catania, Sicily, was a milk run, lightly defended, and with five ships around one dock in the port. All was going well. We picked up our Spitfire top cover (from Malta). We were flying low element at 19.000 feet. Anti-aircraft fire was light. Bombs were away and we headed out to sea. Whack! A black puff of smoke appeared just ahead and my compartment was full of flying plexiglass and metal. The bombardier tried to cry out, fell, and did not move. I saw a hole appear in my right thumb and my right arm felt like it had been slapped. I bent over the bombardier but could get no response. I could not contact the pilots, who were in direct line of the burst. I could not see past the outlines of my compartment and realized that I was probably passing out due to lack of oxygen. There was no command to abandon ship but it felt like we were falling off to the right. So I opened the nose wheel door and jumped. The shock and pain of the chute opening brought me to but my eyes wouldn't focus so I passed out again. Of Lt. Ingerson's crew of ten, I alone survived. I came to in the water. There were two local, sail powered, fishing boats nearby and the fishermen in one pulled me into the boat. The other boat went in to report while mine waited. The fishermen stayed as far away from me as the boat would permit. One man shouted at me but the others, about three, just looked. While in the boat, I heard the rumble of the second wave hitting the target, but I couldn't see anything. When we came in the wharf was lined with people. A few spat and shook their fists, a couple threw rocks, but most were just curious. On the beach there was an ambulance, a stretcher, and a freshly starched nurse, I climbed out of the boat, lay down on the stretcher, and said "OK", and off we went. The town was still full of dust. In the administrative office of the hospital they took all my possessions including dog tags, watch and pen. "To be sent to Rome", they said. No one in the hospital spoke English, but the nurses (nuns), spoke French. [7]

On 13 May, NASAF's intelligence reports described a situation of constant evolution at the airfields of Sicily. Given the end of the war in Tunisia, most of the Axis air units had flown to the nearby island. The greatest concentration of fighters was on the airfields of western Sicily (especially at Sciacca and Trapani Milo) where 278 were spotted at 8:30 a.m. on the 13th. In eastern Sicily, about 200 were distributed almost equally across Catania, Comiso and Gerbini; 37 others were seen flying near Reggio Calabria, intent on crossing the Strait of Messina. [8]

Other important developments came from Ultra, which intercepted a message on 18 May reporting III./JG 27 was leaving Biscari Santo Pietro and would be replaced by III./SKG.10 and its Fw 190s. On the 25th, another decrypted message heralded the arrival at Castelvetrano of nine Fw 190s of 7./Sch.G.2 from Brindisi. In addition to these, Ju 88s of I./NJG 2 arrived at Castelvetrano as early as 6 May.

7   Interview with Jarman G. Kennard. The Library of Congress USA, https://memory.loc.gov/diglib/vhp-stories/loc.natlib.afc2001001.02215/pageturner?ID=pm0001001&page=10.
8   AFHRA, NASAF Intelligence Summary n. 124.

The Margana hangar in Pantelleria. Carved out of the rock, it survived the Second World War. The impressive structure was 340 metres long, 26 metres wide and 18 metres high. (US Air Force photo 24766 AC)

A dicing mission over Pantelleria carried out by Major Leon Gray, commanding officer of the 15th Photographic Reconnaissance Squadron. (US Air Force)

On 18 May, in anticipation of the invasion of Pantelleria, the PR Spitfires of 683 Squadron and the F-5As of the 3rd PG intensified their reconnaissance of the island. Wing Commander Adrian Warburton, on the sortie over Pantelleria at 3:30 p.m. that day, was escorted by three Spitfires from No. 126 Squadron.

At 1:54 p.m. on 25 May, Porto Empedocle, an important naval base of the 3rd Schnellboote Flotilla of the German Navy, suffered a heavy bombardment by 33 B-26 Marauders of the 320th BG escorted by 24 P-38 Lightnings from the 82nd Fighter Group (FG). The bombers dropped 260 × 300lb bombs from a height of 10,500 feet. An initial assessment of the post-strike photos concluded the bombing resulted in the destruction of two boats measuring 120 feet in length and four of 90 feet. Also affected was the sulphur refinery and a section of the railway. A more accurate damage assessment was carried out at 8:20 the next morning by Sergeant F. Simpson in Spitfire PR.XI (EN425) of 683 Squadron.

Objectives requiring daily reconnaissance from 29 May 1943			
Sicily	Sardinia	Southern Italy	Eastern Mediterranean
Catania	Elmas	Reggio	Heraklion
Gerbini (7 satellites)	Alghero	Bari	Kastelli
Comiso	Villacidro	Capodichino	Eleusis
Trapani Milo	Decimomannu	Taranto Group	Kalamaki
Castelvetrano	Monserrato		
Bo Rizzo	Milis		
Ponte Olivo	Oristano		
Biscari			
Boccadifalco			
Sciacca			
Pachino			
Licata			

Between 27 and 28 May, surveys highlighted a significant increase in aircraft, especially fighters, particularly at Castelvetrano where numbers increased from 16 to 48. On Comiso, 52 Bf 109s were recorded while 50 now called Biscari Santo Pietro home. Most of the Bf 109s photographed on various Sicilian airfields sported white wing tips, identifying them as German fighters from the previous campaign in Tunisia.[9]

Among the duties performed by the reconnaissance pilots was identifying whether a certain unit was present on a specific airfield. Flying Officer Laurie E. Philpotts explained the methods adopted to allow their identification:

9   AFHRA, NASAF Intelligence Summary n. 138.

Identifying fighters – Why they used to ask the reco-intelligence pilots to find whether or not a new squadron was at the enemy aerodrome, I never did understand; one would have thought that our fighters or bombers would have noticed. I had to do a low-level over Tunis aerodrome to identify the color of the airscrew spinners of the fighter aircraft and to identify other markings, if possible, as such would, in turn, designate the importance of the squadrons (staffeln) at that point in time. On another occasion, Intelligence wanted to know whether or not the FW-190 (fighter) was operating in North Africa because one of our fighters had reported that he had seen one. So I headed to Bizerta and watched two fighter rascals making dust on the aerodrome as they took off to chase me. I kept well above them in order to maintain the advantage of initial airspeed. I made positive identification then headed for Malta like a dingbat. I noticed, especially, that they did not follow me too far out over the Med. Were they short of petrol, or were they having problems of repair?[10]

On the morning of 28 May, NASAF diverted all of its offensive power to the airfields of Sciacca, Castelvetrano, Trapani Bo Rizzo and Trapani Milo. Thirty-six B-25 Mitchells of the 310th BG, escorted by 36 P-38 Lightnings from the 82nd FG, dropped 2,592 × 20lb fragmentation bombs on Sciacca airfield from 9,800 feet. Castelvetrano was subjected to two raids, one in the morning, by 29 Lightnings of the 1st FG, and one in the afternoon by 24 B-26 Marauders of the 17th BG, escorted by 50 Lightnings of the 82nd FG. The bombers of the 321st BG launched themselves for Trapani Bo Rizzo; 29 Mitchells escorted by 36 Lightnings of the 14th FG. Within the hour, Trapani Milo was hit by 22 Marauders of the 320th BG, escorted by 36 P-40 Warhawks of the 325th FG.

Surrender of Pantelleria and Lampedusa

Whilst the final attack was planned for Pantelleria, NAPRW, in June, drew up a broader photographic coverage programme for southern Europe, northern Italy, Sardinia and Corsica. Photographic surveys of the south of France and Albania also began, intially at a low priority. On 1 June, Major Leon Gray covered the area west of Pantelleria, flying over at 20,000 feet, during the bombing of the island by 19 B-17 heavy bombers of the 97th BG (escorted by 28 Lightnings from the 82nd FG). The reconnaissance lasted 25 minutes during which Gray observed the target and photographed the reaction of the coastal defence batteries, noting their exact locations. He encountered inaccurate and light flak but did not spot any enemy aircraft. The photos taken were considered excellent by the intelligence staff. The unit repeated the mission the following day, Lieutenant Marks doing the honours.

10   Philpotts, *Memoirs of World War II*, p.163.

Sorties carried out from 1 April to 31 May by NAPRW and 683 RAF Squadron[11]	
Southern France	27
Corsica	20
Sardinia	78
Sicily	185
Italy (north of latitude 42° north)	29
Italy (south of latitude 42° north)	111

Laurie Philpotts again:

> Pantelleria – On the Island of Pantelleria, which was not too far to the west of Malta, there was a military industrial complex built into the mountain of the Island. The enemy aircraft from the Island were a thorn-in-the-flesh to Malta. From the huge hangar-type doors at the entrance, the land sloped away to the town on the west shore. On the slope there was an aerodrome. It was my duty to try and get obliquely taken, aerial photography of these photographs was to be used to mock up a replica, of the approach and of the doors, on the North African desert so that Lieutenant Jimmy Freeman, flying a P-38, could practice skipping a high-explosive bomb through the doors. The sortie was a 'hot' one as I had to fly on the deck to Pantelleria, come precisely around the mountain, make a split-ass turn to fly across the slope at the face of the mountain, and fly through the many happy returns of the gun-slingers. The mock-up was made, and Jimmy, eventually, put the bomb through the doors of the real thing.[12]

The Allies were alarmed by the presence on 3 June of 525 fighters on the airfields dotted around Sicily; of these, 268 were located in the north-west. The biggest increases were recorded at Castelvetrano, with 77 aircraft present (28 more fighters than on 1 June), and Trapani Milo and Sciacca with 61. Among the main airfields in the east of the island, Biscari Santo Pietro held 59 aircraft, among which were the Fw 190s of III./SKG.10 that, coming from Gabes-West in Tunisia, had been there since March (together with the Bf 109s of JG 27). On 4 June, 84 aircraft were noted dispersed around Biscari Santo Pietro. At Catania, another 48 were recorded, Comiso, 53, and at the satellites of Gerbini, Satellite #1 and Satellite #2, 56. *Staffel 2* of (H)/14 (*Aufklärungsgruppe 14*) inhabited Gerbini's Satellite #9, called Spina Santa; this short-range reconnaissance unit had 12 Messerschmitt Bf 109s (predominantly the G-4 variant), of which only five were operational. Allied reconnaissance of this strip ascertained the presence of 14 aircraft on 4 June.

Even the port areas were not overlooked. Flight Lieutenant G.H. Maloney of 683 Squadron who, on board Spitfire PR.XI (MB744), took off at 10:00 a.m. on 3 June for a sortie to cover the ports of eastern Sicily, reported:

11   In May, 683 Squadron flew 171 sorties with 21 pilots, most of them over Sicily. By April, it had completed 108 sorties, but with only 11 pilots available.
12   Philpotts, *Memoirs of World War II*, p.141.

At 28.000 0900 Catania 10 miles. Moderate and heavy A.A. over Catania from 25/30.000 ft. Messina 1 M/V 3000 in harbour. Inbound numerous small shipping some stationary and some moving around to San Giovanni photos. Photos also of Reggio aero and town and coastline to San Giovanni. Catania 2 M/V 5000, 2 fires burning in town 2 mile from harbour 2 columns of black smoke. Photo of Augusta and Syracuse and small shipping. At 090° Cape Molino 2 mile 2 Twin A/C at 500 going N. Visibility and Weather Good.[13]

The NAPRW flew two missions against Pantelleria on 8 June. Lieutenant Barrett arrived on target in the late afternoon, precisely at 6:00 p.m., following 42 B-25 Mitchells of the 321st BG escorted by 24 Spitfires. Barrett stayed over Pantelleria for 30 minutes, taking photos of the bombing, recording the 'before and after'. Over the 24 hours of 8 June, the Anglo–American air forces carried out 502 sorties which added another 635 tons of explosives to those already dropped on the preceding days.

On 9 June, XII Air Support Command asked the Tac/R pilots of No. 225 Squadron to support the final stages of Operation *Corkscrew*. Part of the squadron (A Echelon), consisting of 12 pilots and 73 officers and military personnel (and six Spitfires and two Mustangs, half of the aircraft currently on strength with the squadron), left Ariana at 11:00 a.m. to position themselves at Korba North.

At 7:10 p.m. on the 9th, 16 Ju 52/3m transports were seen parked on the southern part of the runway of Pantelleria's airfield. The evacuation was underway, assisted by air cover from six Bf 109s and four Fw 190s. The *Luftwaffe* fighters soon clashed with a P-40 formation from the 79th FG.[14]

On 10 June, Lieutenant Jackson of the 15th Photographic Reconnaissance Squadron (PRS), flew over Pantelleria, from 8:00 to 8:45 a.m., while the Flying Fortressess and Mitchells of NASAF, escorted by the Lightnings of the 1st and 14th Fighter Groups, razed the entire island to the ground. Before he could take photos of the bombing, Jackson had to wait nine minutes for the thick cloud of smoke to clear somewhat. In the meantime, the *Luftwaffe* sent a Bf 109G-4 (WNr. 14904 'Black 14') of 2.(H)/14 to Malta. Flown by Leutnant Friedrich Zander, he was accompanied by the German ace Oberfeldwebel Rollwage and Feldwebel Reiter of 5./JG 53, based at Comiso. The unfortunate Zander was intercepted and shot down over Malta by the Spitfire flown by Flying Officer I.F. 'Hap' Kennedy of No. 185 Squadron.

At 1:55 p.m., after a short pre-mission briefing, 225 Squadron's Flying Officer Trapp (Spitfire Vc JK112) and Flying Officer Burgess (Spitfire Vc JR398), took off for Pantelleria. The purpose of the op was to look for any signs of surrender. At 2:48 p.m., Flight Lieutenant Colston (Spitfire Vc EF566) and Flying Officer Breingan, flying a Mustang II, also flew to the island in an attempt to locate the remains of a minefield; they failed to do so due to unexpected cloud cover. The day ended with a total of four sorties flown over five hours and 50 minutes.[15]

The eleventh of June was the decisive day for Pantelleria. In response to the extreme urgency and requests from the NAAF (Northwest African Air Forces), Major Leon Gray, Commanding Officer of the 15th PRS, personally took charge of a dicing mission, flying over the coast at 200

13   The National Archives London, Royal Air Force, Operations Record Books AIR 27/2209/10.
14   AFHRA, IRISREF A6332, XII ASC, p.1277.
15   The National Archives London, Royal Air Force, Operations Record Books AIR 27/1396/12.

Lampedusa photographed by a Baltimore III of No. 55 Squadron during a bombing raid on the island by 12 aircraft from the unit. (Brian Spurr)

Pantelleria received the attentions of 12 Baltimores of No. 223 Squadron and 15 from No. 55 Squadron on 8 May 1943. (Brian Spurr)

feet, to photograph the locations of coastal machine guns where the Allies planned to land from the sea. Gray spent an hour and 20minutes over the target, exposing all of the film in his cameras. Six sorties were flown over Pantelleria this day, the last just before sunset by the 15th PRS. The NAPRW had previously carried out seven photographic sorties over the island that had allowed the creation of a mosaic of the entire island in 1: 8,000 scale. In addition, 36 sorties were carried out under the order of NAAF to verify damage to the island. Confirmation of Pantelleria's surrender came from tactical reconnaissance by 225 Squadron when, at 11:10 a.m., sent two Spitfires equipped with oblique cameras to the island from Bou Ficha, Tunisia. Flying Officer Marshall (Spitfire Vc JK112) and Flying Officer Breingan (Spitfire Vc JR178), photographed a large white cross painted on the airfield's runway. The squadron repeated the recce at 12:20 p.m. with Wing Commander Millington (Spitfire Vb EF566) and Flight Lieutenant Colston (Spitfire Vc JK398) confirming the presence of the white cross. They also witnessed an attack by 12 Fw 190s on Allied convoys north-east of the island.

On 12 June, the same squadron performed 10 sorties over the island of Lampedusa. At 4:40 p.m., the final op left the Monastir runway; Flying Officer Trapp (Spitfire Vb ER852) and

A Tac/R Spitfire of No. 225 Squadron RAF. After the Sicilian Campaign, the squadron relocated to San Francesco to support the Allied advance in Italy. (US Air Force)

Flying Officer Burgess (Spitfire Vb ER121) photographed some white stripes on the airfield, a sign of surrender that was further confirmed by the presence of a white flag.

The day before, NATAF had carried out 728 sorties, across 63 missions, against Pantelleria, and 154 sorties (14 missions) against Lampedusa. In all, nearly 1,100 aircraft participated in the final assault, dropping 1,571 tons of bombs. This made a total of 4,844 tons of bombs in 3,647 sorties for the period 1–10 June.[16] From 8 May to 11 June, Pantelleria was subjected to 5,285 sorties by the NAAF, for the loss of 16 damaged aircraft, 14 lost and 6,200 tons of bombs dropped.[17]

In this phase of the war in the Mediterranean, a valuable contribution was provided by A Flight of No. 680 Squadron which performed 23 ops over Pantelleria, in some cases also covering the shores of southern Sicily.[18]

Mosaic of the Sicilian Campaign		
Area	Square miles	Scale
Sicily (complete)	4965	1:50,000
Pantelleria	45	1:10,000
Linosa	1.75	1:10,000
Sardinia airfields	101	1:15,000
Roma	45	1:15,000
Coast south-east of Sicily	67	1:5,000
Coast south of Sicily, from Licata to Pozzallo	134	1:10,000
Siracusa	53	1:20,000
Augusta	82	1:20,000
Catania	33	1:20,000
Coast from Cape Granitola to Sciacca, up to 2 miles inland	54	1:10,000
Castelvetrano in Marinella and proximal areas	54	1:10,000
Lampedusa	11	1:10,000
Capo Passero area	112	1:5,000
South-east invasion area	20	1:18,000
South-west invasion area	20	1:18,000
Sardinia	658	1:50,000

16 Wesley Craven, James Cate, *The Army Air Force in World War II vol. II* (Chicago: University of Chicago Press, 1965), p.426.
17 Craven, Cate, *The Army Air Force in World War II*, p.431.
18 The National Archives London, Royal Air Force, Operations Record Books AIR 27/2197/8.

Towards *Husky*

After the conquest of the islands of Pantelleria and Lampedusa, the campaign for the conquest of Sicily commenced. On 12 June, 2nd Lieutenant Hartle of the 3rd PG was declared missing in action during a courier flight. On the same day, the Twelfth Air Force sent its Flying Fortresses to the airfields at Palermo Boccadifalco and Castelvetrano, and B-26 Marauders to Trapani Milo. The aerial survey subsequently ascertained that, in Boccadifalco, the bombs hit the entire surface of the airfield and the nearby dispersed infrastructure. From careful analysis of the photos, it was also clear that, at the time of the attack on the Palermo runway, at least 46 of the 69 aircraft around the perimeter were affected, to varying degrees, by the bomb blasts. According to the Allies, however, the best results were achieved at Castelvetrano where, out of 86 aircraft within the airfield's boundaries, 14 were certainly destroyed, shredded by fragmentation bombs, while another eight were probably damaged by splinters. However, the expert analysts of the Twelfth Air Force would have been very surprised if they had known the actual damage caused by the bombing of Castelvetrano. According to the report of 12 June 1943 to the Italian General Staff, the total number of aircraft destroyed across the two bases was no more than half a dozen.[19] This was thanks to the newly built splinter guards which had limited damage. The large number of bombs dropped, however, prevented the immediate resumption of activity; Twelfth Air Force armourers had in fact adjusted some of the bombs to delay their detonation.

The Allied air forces employed for the Sicilian campaign numbered 3,127 aircraft, of which 461 were heavy bombers, 162 medium (night), 703 medium and light (day) bombers, 1,395 fighters and fighter-bombers, and 406 transports. In addition, there were 110 NACAF (Northwest African Coastal Air Force) Supermarine Seafires. The total strength of the Axis air forces in the Mediterranean area at the time was 1,800 aircraft.[20]

Sicily was well protected by 224 batteries, including 48 from the Army, 57 from the Navy and 119 from the Militia. To these Italian forces must be added the pieces from two German divisions and the anti-aircraft departments located on airfields used by II *Fliegerkorps*, a force of thrity-three 88mm anti-aircraft batteries (heavy flak), in addition to numerous 20mm cannons (light flak).[21] The NAPRW reconnaissance aircraft and 683 Squadron ascertained the Axis air force already had 19 important airfields on Sicily and, in the spring of 1943, at least a dozen recently built airstrips.[22]

On Sunday 13 June, Allied bombers hit the airfields in the eastern part of the island. Those of Catania and Gerbini were attacked, around lunchtime, by 24 B-24 Liberators of the 376th BG and 22 of the 98th BG, all escorted by 24 Spitfires of Nos. 229 and 249 Squadrons from Malta.

19 Minutes of the afternoon meeting of 12 June 1943, General Staff - Rome, statement by Generale Fougier, in: Stato Maggiore Esercito Ufficio Storico, *Verbali delle riunioni tenute da Capo di SM Generale* [Minutes of the meetings held by the Head of SM General], Vol. IV, p.167.
20 AFHRA, IRISREF A6020, correspondence pertaining to commander-in-chief's dispatch on Sicilian Campaign.
21 Domenico Anfora, Stefano Pepi, *Obiettivo Biscari. 9–14 luglio 1943: dal ponte Dirillo all'aeroporto 504* [Objective Biscari. 9-14 July 1943: from the Dirillo bridge to airfield 504] (Milano: Ugo Mursia Editore, 2013), p.22.
22 Ferdinando Pedriali, L'Italia nella guerra aerea - Da El Alamein alle spiagge della Sicilia [Italy in the air war – From El Alamein to the beaches of Sicily] (Roma: Aeronautica Militare, Ufficio storico, 2010), p.407.

A mosaic of Sicily hung in one of the command centres of the Allied forces. (US Air Force)

The airfield complex was seriously damaged; about 32 German aircraft were destroyed on the ground in the Gerbini area alone, while another 10 were unserviceable due to damage. The Allied crews met a tenacious resistance; 40 fighters, Bf 109s, Fw 190s, MC.202s and MC.205s, attacked the bombers in successive waves and with great determination. The RAF lost three Spitfires.[23] Among the bombers of the Ninth Air Force, two Liberators were lost. Both fell into the sea due to serious damage inflicted by anti-aircraft fire.

The bombings were even intense at night when, on 14/15 June, Vickers Wellingtons of No. 205 Group attacked the airfields at Trapani Milo, Sciacca, Castelvetrano and Boccadifalco.

The following day, Trapani Bo Rizzo and Sciacca airfields were subjected to one of the heaviest attacks ever carried out by medium bombers of the Twelfth Air Force during the preparatory phase of the invasion. Seventy-two Mitchells, escorted by about 40 Lightnings, dropped 2,382 × 20lb fragmentation bombs and 264 × 300lb bombs on Sciacca, where there were about 50 aircraft, while 36 Marauders of the 319th BG hit Trapani Bo Rizzo with 8,816 × 20lb fragmentation bombs. At the same time, Trapani Milo was also bombed by 18

An oblique photo of the coast of Falconara, headquarters of the 384th Coastal Battalion. The photo was taken at around 1:30 p.m. by Flying Officer P.J. Kelly and Leading Aircraftman R.D. Hadden flying No. 683 Squadron Mosquito HJ672. (LAC photo RG24, R112, 1984-265 NPC)

23   Wing Commander J. Ellis and Sergeant F. Davidson, both belonging to 229 Squadron, and Sergeant B.W. Sheehan RNZAF from 249 Squadron.

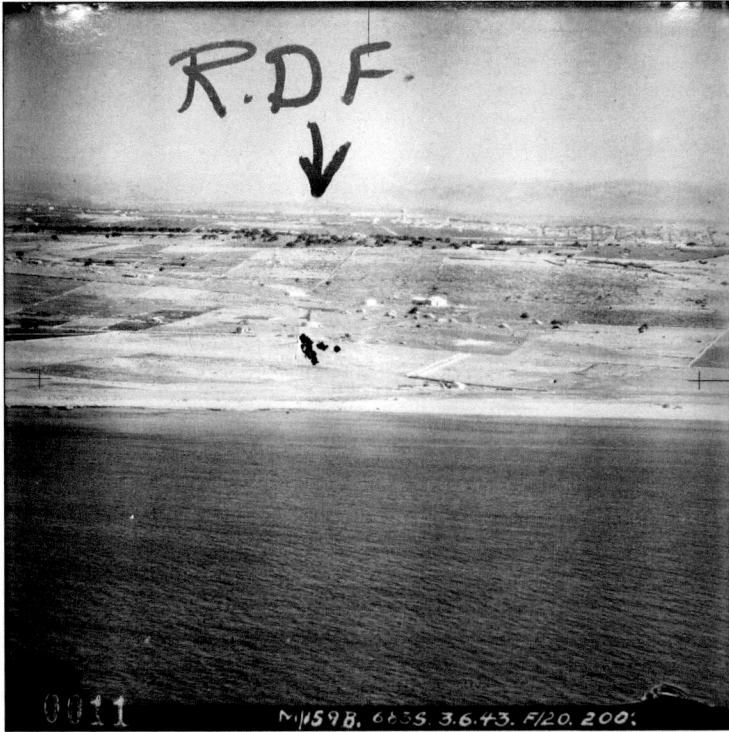

An oblique photo of one of the RDF stations along the Pachino coast, taken by Wing Commander Adrian Warburton on 3 June 1943 from a height of 200 feet. Furthermore, *Luftwaffe* radars of the Wasserman, Freya and Wurzburg types were present between Pachino and Portopalo di Capo Passero.
(LAC photo RG24, R112, 1984-265 NPC)

Marauders from the 320th BG, which dropped 242 × 300lb bombs. From 8:45 to 9:57 a.m., Palermo Boccadifalco airport was under attack by 23 B-17 Flying Fortresses of the 97th BG flying between 22,000 and 24,500 feet. They delivered 178 × 300lb bombs and 5,178 × 20lb fragmentation bombs to the target.[24]

The morning of the following day, the damage assessment was entrusted to Keith Durbidge, who performed 'Sortie X', thus named to identify a sortie that covered all of the airfields in Sicily. The 683 Squadron pilot flew over all the locations affected by the previous day's bombing and added Licata and Porto Empedocle for good measure.

On 17 June, it was the turn of Comiso when B-24 Liberators of the 376th BG dropped 68 short tons of bombs while, at the same time, Biscari Santo Pietro was attacked by B-24 Liberators of the 98th BG (113 short tons).

---

24 Message from Romulus to Superaereo (Stato Maggiore della Regia Aeronautica/Staff of *Regia Aeronautica*), operating situation on the 16th, AUSSMA SL4/41, and Jochen Prien, *Geschichte des Jagdgeschwader 77, Teil 3* [*History of Jagdeschwader 77, Part 3*] (Germany: Rogge GmbH, 1995), p.1589.

In the early afternoon of 20 June, Durbidge, in Spitfire PR.XI (EN391), flew over the airfields at Catania, Gerbini, Biscari, Comiso and Gela Ponte Olivo. There were 25 aircraft on Catania; 51 were sighted on the main runway at Gerbini, of which 26 were Ju 88s. On Gerbini's Satellite #1 there were 20fighters, while Satellite #2 housed 18, Satellite #3, 15 aircraft, and Satellites #4 and #5 shared 18 fighters between them. Satellites #6 and #9 revealed 33 and 12 fighters respectively and Satellite #8 was noted to still be under construction. Fifty-seven of the 66 aircraft at Comiso were fighters. Biscari Santo Pietro was also noted to be hosting 19 fighters and 10 airframes were dispersed around Gela Ponte Olivo.

On the 21st, Major Leon Gray flew sortie number 33 for the 15th PRS. The focus was mainly on Messina and Villa San Giovanni, in Calabria, but the long mission took him from one end of Sicily to the other. Inside the port of Messina, he noted 20pleasure boats, many of which had arrived three days earlier. There were also seven minesweepers; numbers of this type of vessel had been increasing according to the latest Allied reports. On the coast between Reggio Calabria and Villa San Giovanni, nine Siebel Ferries and 11 ferries were sighted. Reggio Calabria's airfield was also teeming with 53 aircraft, including one SM.82, five SM.79/84s, nine unidentified machines of the Caproni type, and 38 fighters. An He 111, five Ju 88s, a medium-sized aircraft and five fighters were spotted at Catania while a Ju 52/3m, five SM.79/84s, a Dornier, 19 Ju 88s, nine medium-sized aircraft, and three fighters were seen at Gerbini. Three CANT Z.501s were on the buoys at the port of Milazzo.

On 25 June, while Flying Officer E.C. Hey was busy photographing some locations in the province of Palermo, including Capaci and Partanna, at the controls of Spitfire PR.XI (EN425) of 683 Squadron, , the city of Messina suffered its seventh bombing raid of the month. It was the heaviest to date. Railway yards, warehouses, harbour piers and other districts of the city were devastated by 401 short tons of bombs (38 × 2,000lb General Purpose [GP] bombs, 38 × 1,000lb GPs, and 1,746 × 300lb GPs) unloaded from 132 Flying Fortresses from the 2nd, 97th, 99th and 301st Bomb Groups. The mission cost the B-17 (serial 42-29615) piloted by Captain Albert D. Hinsey of the 49th Bombardment Squadron (BS), 2nd BG. Lieutenant Francis R. Hiniker, the co-pilot of B-17F 42-29611, also of the 49th BS, reported what happened:

> I was flying plane No. 611 in position 6-1-1 at 24,300 feet, my bombs were away and I was turning left off the target when I saw an enemy fighter coming in from 12 O'clock slightly above, not firing, but noticed that Captain Hinsey, who was on my right, had his crew firing at the E/A. As I progressed farther into the run the E/A passed over me doing a half wheel of 90° to the left and diving at approximately 200 feet per minute and after passing my ship the E/A struck Captain Hinsey's plane just outside the No. 4 engine. There was no fire visible at the time from Captain Hinsey's ship but was turning away to the right after the impact. I watched his plane fall approximately 300 feet and then lost sight of it due to the degree of the turn of my own plane. It seemed to me that Captain Hinsey's plane was breaking up, as it fell, and enemy antiaircraft was still shooting at him as I lost sight of him. [25]

25   NARA, Missing Air Crew Report n. 46.

Despite the heavy bombardments of the previous days on Messina, on the 27th Lieutenant Barrett of the 15th PRS recorded a substantial increase in maritime activity near the strait. Some of the German Siebel Ferries were diverted to the small port of Riposto, and that of Catania, as reported by Flight Lieutenant M.G. Brown and Flying Officer H.S. Smith, both of 683 Squadron. As early as February 1943, the Germans understood they could not rely on the normal ferry service between Calabria and Sicily and had begun to use a variety of small coastal ships along three northern routes located outside the vulnerable area around Messina.

Meanwhile, Allied reconnaissance had been following a large vessel for days after it left Syracuse for Taranto on the night of 28/29 June. The merchant ship, in turn, had probably arrived from Taranto on the 22nd. The Allied intelligence services assumed the ship was capable of a load of 9,500 tons. There was also a significant increase in maritime activity at Catania during the months of May and June; a large merchant ship from Naples arrived with a heavy load between 28 and 29 June while another had already arrived between the 25th and 27th and remained anchored for a few days.

Some of the German radars operating in Sicily, here photographed by the Allies after the conquest of the island: (a) Pole Freya; (b) Wurzburg Riese; (c) Wassernmann L Girder Chimney. (US Air Force)

Reconnaissance by aircraft based on Malta from 27/28 March to 3 July 1943[26]				
Period		**Land**	**Harbour**	**Total**
27/28 March–10 April	USAAF	10	15	25
	RAF	21	46	67
10/11–24 April	USAAF	16	27	43
	RAF	26	51	77
24/25 April–8 May	USAAF	11	19	30
	RAF	21	50	71
8/9–22 May	USAAF	26	26	51
	RAF	56	68	124
22/23 May–5 June	USAAF	19	19	38
	RAF	79	88	167
5/6–19 June	USAAF	27	29	56
	RAF	61	65	126
19/20 June–3 July	USAAF	4	4	8
	RAF	64	64	128
Total	USAAF	112	139	251
	RAF	328	432	760

Meanwhile, on the small landing strip at Taormina, used by senior elements of German command, three Fieseler Fi 156 Storch liaison aircraft were seen.

After a month of incessant bombing raids over Sicily, Allied air reconnaissance revealed major changes at the end of June. The five main airfields in western Sicily showed a decrease in aircraft. Photos taken on 26 June revealed 169 aircraft, mainly concentrated at Sciacca (65) and Trapani Milo (36). Castelvetrano, one of the main bases, was unusable. No movements had been observed on it since the day before; huge craters, the result of recent bombing, were even clearly visible from high altitudes. The airfields east of Sicily, on the other hand, revealed frenetic activity; of the 236 fighters identified, 122 were located on Gerbini and its satellites, while 71 were present on Comiso.

On 30 June, the heaviest attacks of the month took place. Two hundred sorties were carried out against the airfields at Sciacca, Palermo Boccadifalco, Trapani Bo Rizzo and Trapani Milo. Between 18 and 30 June, NAAF aircraft flew 317 heavy bomber and 566 medium bomber sorties. The bombers of the Ninth Air Force also played their part, contributing 107 sorties to the supply blockade of Sicily.[27]

26   From RAF Middle East Review No.3, Headquarters Royal Air Force Middle East, p.72. In addition, there were eight USAAF and 29 RAF reconnaissance sorties flown from Malta as 'special tasks' from 4 June to 3 July.
27   Craven, Cate, *The Army Air Force in World War II*, p.435.

Operation *Husky* landing plan. (AFHRA)

Throughout June, the PR Spitfires and Mosquitos of 683 Squadron carried out several special tasks over Sicily. The last was completed on 30 June at 12.20 p.m. by Flying Officer J.B. Burnet. The reason for these special flights was to support the organisation of a very secret mission, Operation *Chestnut*, which would involve troops of the 2nd Special Air Service.

On the nights of 12, 13, 14 and 19 July, Albemarle transport aircraft of No. 296 Squadron were expected to deliver 75–100 men to north-east Sicily, specifically the areas around Randazzo (*Dandelion*), and Enna (*Columbine*). These men would sabotage the Catania–Messina telephone line, and some of the main road junctions near Enna and Randazzo, as well as attack vehicles travelling on roads SS113, SS114, SS116, SS120 and SS121.

The *Regia Aeronautica* airfield at Gela Farello as captured in an Allied strip photo. (US Air Force)

The bombing of Messina on 6 June 1943 by B-24 Liberators of the 415th BS, 98th BG. The bombs, in addition to hitting the port, also fell on some districts of the city, causing a massacre among civilians. (US Air Force)

12

Last Air Battle in Sicily and Tactical Reconnaissance

Reconnaissance activities were intense and frenetic during the first days of July. The PR Spitfires of No. 683 Squadron flew six sorties over Rome, Naples, Taranto and Sicily on the first day of the month. Those carried out over Sicily focussed their attention on the main airfields of the island and recorded the following airfield activities:

> Catania: five Ju52s, one Z1007, three SM81, three SM79, five Ju88s, two Dorniers, four Bf110s, two medium and eight small aircraft; Comiso: six Ju88s, one Ca311-type, two medium and 45 small aircraft; Gela: two Z1007s and five small aircraft; Gerbini: eleven Ju88s, six Bf110s, eleven Ca310-type, nine medium and two small aircraft; Gerbini satellite No 1: FW58, one large and 36 small aircraft; No 3: three SM82s, one SM79, three small aircraft; No 4 and No 5: one Ju 52, two medium and 40 small aircraft; satellite No 6: one Ju 52, one Bf110 and 47 small aircraft; No 8: 27 small aircraft; No 9: six medium and 19 small aircraft.[1]

A particular focus was on the area around Syracuse, preparations underway for Operation *Ladbroke*, scheduled for the late evening of 9 July, accentuating the British reconnaissance in that sector. Flying Officer J.B. Burnet, flying Spitfire PR.XI (EN425), carried out, on return from Taranto, photographic surveys of the port of Riposto, recording the presence of eight submarines. At around 2:00 p.m., he was over Augusta and Syracuse completing a special task assigned to him. His photos, and those of other pilots, allowed the Intelligence Section to identify some important enemy defensive positions.

On 3 July, a PR Spitfire of No. 682 Squadron photographed the new Carcitella airstrip, locating it at the coordinates 37° 47' 40" N, 12° 38' 07" E, adjacent to the SS188 state road that connected the towns of Salemi and Marsala; no aircraft were seen. On the same day, Lieutenant Marks of the 15th Photographic Reconnaissance Squadron (PRS) flew his unit's 51st sortie, guiding his F-5A over targets in the east of the island: Catania, Augusta, Syracuse, Comiso, Gela, Biscari Santo Pietro and Gerbini. At Catania, three ferries and two large merchant ships, one unloading, were seen; 20 aircraft (a CANT Z.1007, three SM.81s, three SM.79s, three Ju 88s, three Bf 110s, and three medium-sized and four small aircraft) were present at nearby

---

1   Cull, Malizia, Galea, *Spitfires over Sicily*, p.95.

Tac/R Spitfires of No. 40 Squadron
SAAF. (Tinus Le Roux)]

Insignia of No. 40 Squadron SAAF.
(Tinus Le Roux)

Catania Fontanarossa. The Augusta seaplane base was noted to be hosting 24 seaplanes: five CANT Z.506B,s five CANT Z.501s and 14 RS.14s. Another two Z.506Bs were on the buoys at Syracuse. Just one small aircraft was seen at Gela Farello and Gela Ponte Olivo revealed just two CANT Z.1007s and another small machine. Continuing the run of decreased sightings, 21 aircraft were identified at Comiso airport (a Ju 52/3m, an SM.79, a Ju 88, five medium-sized machines and 13 probable fighters). Only seven aircraft were visible at Biscari Santo Pietro. Importantly, at the new Satellite #10, located at 37° 22' 30" N, 14° 57' 30" E, work was underway to adapt and expand the clay runway.

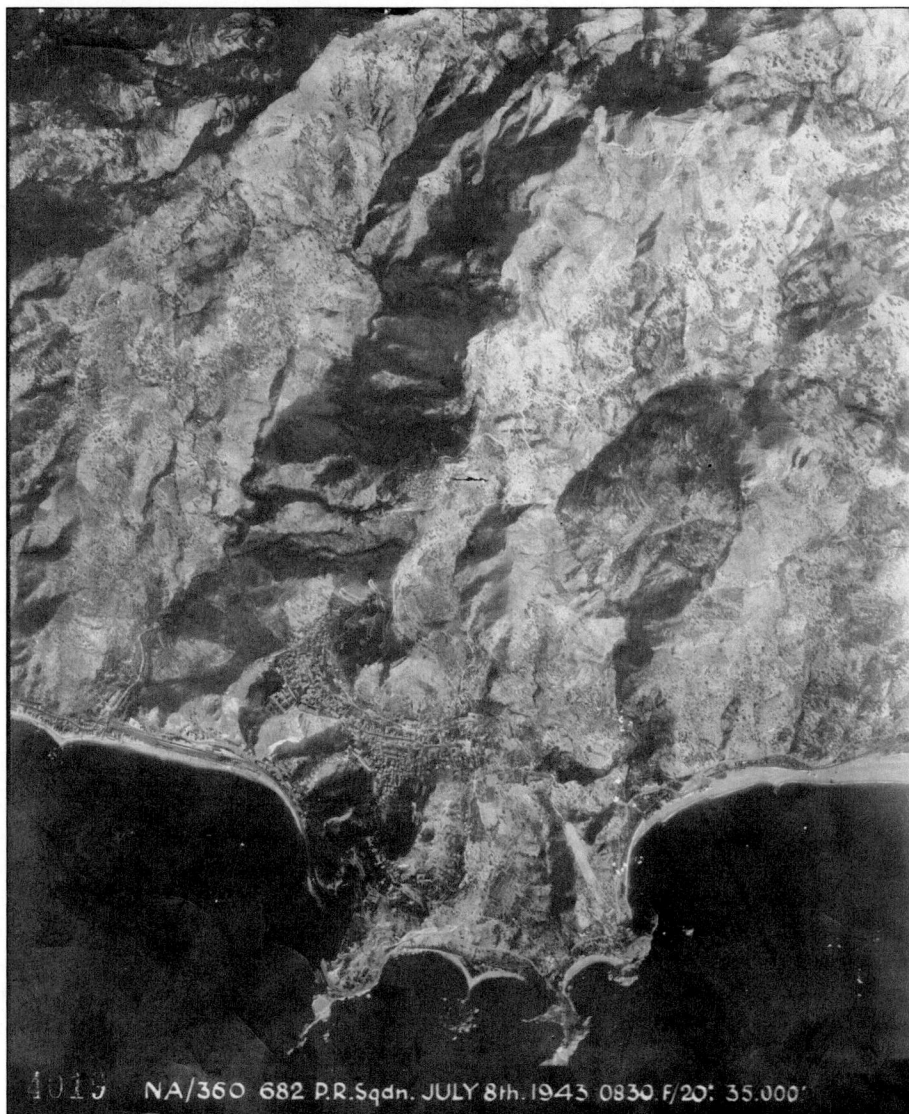

NA/360 682 P.R.Sqdn. JULY 8th. 1943 0830. F/20: 35.000'

An image of Taormina taken by No. 682 Squadron RAF before USAAF bombing. (US Air Force)

Reconnaissance by the RAF, Allied aircraft of the NAAF, Middle East Command and Malta over the central Mediterranean from 27/28 March to 3 July 1943[2]				
Period		Tac/R	Strat/R	Total
27/28 March–10 April	USAAF	9	57	66
	RAF	134	125	259
10/11–24 April	USAAF	6	79	85
	RAF	156	147	303
24/25 April–8 May	USAAF	-	76	76
	RAF	318	153	471
8/9–22 May	USAAF	8	83	91
	RAF	76	138	214
22/23 May–5 June	USAAF	38	106	81
	RAF	6	187	186
5/6–19 June	USAAF	38	106	144
	RAF	6	187	193
19/20 June–3 July	USAAF	12	62	74
	RAF	-	227	227
Total	USAAF	73	544	617
	RAF	690	1,163	1,853

During 5 July, the PR Spitfires of 683 Squadron performed seven sorties from Malta which, as well as Sicily, now concerned far more distant strategic objectives. Flying Officer E.C. Hey and the Pilot Officer K. Durbidge headed to Sicily at 8:35 a.m. Hey covered Comiso, Trapani Milo, Sciacca and Palermo. Durbidge saw two ships of 4,000 tons, one of 3,000 tons and two smaller vessels at Messina. The arrival of the small rescue ship *Meta* was recorded for Augusta while only one medium-sized aircraft was seen at Taormina. Meantime, the last of the Axis air forces were concentrating on the eastern side of the island. Major Johannes Steinhoff, commander of *Jagdgeschwader 77*, flew a Bf 109 towards Gerbini from western Sicily:

> On the night of July 5 a party of maintenance personnel from my group left by truck for the eastern portion of the island. West of Catania the plain broadened out at the foot of Etna. The fields, from which the wheat had long since been harvested, stretched away in arid desolation as far as the eye could see, dotted with parched, dusty olive trees. A narrow track led between a few wretched farms, shown on the map as Gerbini. Hence the plain, which offered some ideal stretches for take-off and landing, bore the pretentious name Gerbini Airfield. As my Messerschmitt rolled to a halt, I saw the mechanics motioning me to park beneath the olive trees. But as I was turning off the landing strip, a huge, swirling yellow-brown dust cloud enveloped the aircraft. I

2   From RAF Middle East Review No.3, Headquarters Royal Air Force Middle East, p.60. In addition, there were eight USAAF and 29 RAF reconnaissance sorties flown from Malta as 'special tasks' from 4 June to 3 July.

could see nothing at all and it was some while before the men, the trees and the hut reappeared. So thick was the dust that the color of the wings had turned dark yellow. I opened the hood and looked round. In all directions dust devils were rising up in the hot, shimmering air.[3]

Predictably, and following the same *modus operandi*, due to the concentration of German fighters at the air bases in eastern Sicily, the Northwest African Strategic Air Force (NASAF) launched a strong offensive on 5 July that led to one of the most spectacular air battles seen over the Sicilian countryside.

Steinhoff had just landed at Gerbini when, for 18 long minutes from 11:34 a.m., 52 B-17 Flying Fortresses of the 97th and 99th Bombardment Groups, from Navarin in Algeria, attacked the sprawling Gerbini complex of airstrips.[4]

Personnel install a strike camera on B-17F Flying Fortress 42-29857 of the 348th BS, 99th BG, at Navarin in Algeria. The bomber, flown by Lieutenant Flake Casto, participated in the 5 July 1943 raid on Gerbini. (US Air Force)

3   Johannes Steinhoff, *Messerschmitts over Sicily: Diary of a Luftwaffe Fighter Commander* (Mechanicsburg, Pennsylvania: Stackpole Books, 2004), p.95.
4   AFHRA, IRISREF A6012, p.990.

They were followed by another formation of 23 Flying Fortresses of the 301st Bombardment Group (BG) which focused on Satellites #4 and #5. The alarm issued by the *Luftwaffe* tracking centres allowed General Adolf Galland to organise a strong counterattack. *Jagdgeschwaders 77* and *53*, with about 100 Bf 109s, and the *4° Stormo Cavallino Rampante* of the *Regia Aeronautica*, with 27 MC.202s and MC.205s, scrambled early, managing to intercept the first wave of 27 B-17Fs of the 99th BG (escorted by 40 Spitfires of the Nos. 72 and 243 Squadrons from Malta). The clash between the opposing forces took place near Ragusa, before the Gerbini slopes. The Flying Fortresses, led by Colonel Fay R. Upthegrove, commander of the 99th BG, included elements of the 346th, 348th and 416th Bombardment Squadrons. Interception was made at about 23,000 feet. Before coming into contact with the American bombers, the leading fighters separated into four *schwarms* (formations),[5] to attack simultaneously from 3 and 9 o'clock. Three

Gerbini Main under attack on 13 June 1943. The mission was carried out by 24 B-24s of the 376th BG, which dropped nearly 55 tons of bombs on the runway. During the return journey, the formation was intercepted by Axis fighters, resulting in two casualties. (US Air Force photo 25290 AC)

---

5   During the Spanish Civil War, *Luftwaffe* aces Werner Mölders and Günther Lützow developed a new formation consisting of two *rotten* (therefore, four aircraft, a *schwarm*) arranged so as to form the image of 'four fingers'.[5] The formation guaranteed each pilot the maximum possible visibility.

Flying Fortresses at the tail end of the formation were hit. The B-17F (serial 42-29486) piloted by 1st Lieutenant Martin J. Devane exploded in midair; only five of the 10 crew members managed to escape, baling out before the Flying Fortress crashed near the new Gerbini Satellite #12, in the municipality of Ramacca at 37° 24' 06" N, 14° 44' 51" E. The second B-17F (serial 42-29492), 'Ramblin Wreck', flown by 1st Lieutenant C.M. Graham, crashed in flames just north of Palazzolo Acreide. The third bomber, 'Dee Zip Zip' (serial 42-29483), of which 1st Lieutenant Albert E. Davis was captain, fell near Scicli. Staff Sergeant Benjamin F. Warmer witnessed the loss of one of the bombers:

On July 5, 1943 I was flying as left waist gunner on aircraft 42-29857 piloted by 2nd Lt Flake Casto. Our position was right wing in the first element of the 348th Bombardment Squadron's formation. We were on the bomb run when I noticed aircraft 42-29492 on fire. The plane was flying the left wing position in the second element of the 348th Bombardment Squadron's formation. It appeared to me that number 4 engine had been hit by enemy aircraft, this causing the fire which was spreading rapidly. Even though being attacked by aircraft and enveloped in fire the pilot remained in formation for approximately 5 minutes. The plane began to lose altitude and fell out of the formation. I saw one man parachute and he was immediately pounced upon by enemy fighters. Enemy fighters made several passes at the plane and I last saw it hit the ground and explode. We returned to bomb the same target on July 6, 1943 and I observed a large

The Fairchild K-20 type camera. It was one of the lightest and most handy aerial cameras available to American airmen during the Second World War; it was particularly suitable for quickly capturing oblique images. (US Air Force photo 70268 AC)

burnt area approximately 2 miles northwest of the target, this I believe to be the spot where aircraft 42-29492 crashed and burned.[6]

A good 6,840 fragmentation bombs hit the runway and parked aircraft. In addition, 41 of the 46 aircraft on the field were destroyed along with several trucks, fuel depots and warehouses.

Coordinates of defensive posts in the Syracuse area on 1 July 1943			
Light AA	**Heavy AA**	**Coastal Defence**	**Machine Gun**
Not clearly defined	Not clearly defined	182239 (4)	183241 (2)
		162268 (6)	135305
		163279 (3)	136306
		157280 (6)	137306
		124283 (6)	180241
			181240
			183243

The Allies claimed to have shot down 45 fighters out the more than 100 that had attacked the American bombers.[7] The *Regia Aeronautica*, with the *4° Stormo* operating from Satellite #2 ('Finocchiara'), Satellite #3 (called 'Sigonella' by the Italians), and Satellite #7 ('San Salvatore'), flew 53 sorties during the day, and lost two of its aces, both flying MC.202s: Capitano Franco Lucchini, commander of the *10° Gruppo*, and Sottotenente Leonardo Ferrulli of the *91ª Squadriglia*. Johannes Steinhoff, whose aircraft was hit, was forced to make an emergency landing in a field 30 miles from Gerbini. The subsequent arrival of the 97th BG over the target at 11:52 a.m. was unmolested as the main battle had already taken place. A few moments later, 24 Flying Fortresses of the 2nd BG appeared over Satellite #6, dropping 3,168 fragmentation bombs accurately and destroying at least two aircraft on the ground in the process.

That same morning, 36 B-25 Mitchells of the 340th BG, escorted by RAF Spitfires, dropped 287 × 250lb and 120 × 300lb bombs on Comiso. In the afternoon, it was Biscari Santo Pietro's turn. Twenty-four Mitchells of the 12th BG, with the now customary aerial coverage of RAF Spitfires from Malta, dropped 250 and 300lb bombs, rendering the airfield unusable. On this day, NASAF aircraft flew 618 sorties; this includes two sorties flown by the 3rd Photographic Group (PG). They claimed the destruction of 118 enemy aircraft, 52 of which were destroyed in flight. The Allies lost 10 aircraft, including two B-26 Marauders, two Mitchells, the three Flying Fortresses mentioned above, a P-38 Lightning and, at night, two Vickers Wellington of No. 331 Wing. A Mosquito PR.II (DD744) of No. 60 Squadron SAAF, flown by Lieutenants Barnes (prisoner) and J. Van Dijl, was also lost. Van Dijl paid the ultimate price.

Damage assessment was entrusted to Lieutenant Hersey of the 15th PRS who, at 4:30 p.m. that day, flew his F-5A Lightning to Catania, Gerbini, Biscari Santo Pietro and Gela Ponte

---

6   NARA, Missing Air Crew Report n. 1132.
7   Actually, the losses of the *4° Stormo* and JG 53 and JG 77 amounted to six aircraft destroyed and eight damaged.

Olivo. At Catania, two large merchant ships, that had arrived on 3 July, were still present; the one which had come from Naples had a balloon barrage tethered to it. Another five vessels were observed as they quickly left the port. Catania Fontanarossa was teeming with aircraft of all types – He 111, Ju 88, Fi 156, SM.79, SM.81 and many fighter planes. There were 31 aircraft at Gerbini, but the runway was almost out of action due to numerous craters. Satellite #1 was badly damaged, especially in the south-east section where at least two aircraft were hit, while another 26 fighters were noted in the north-east section. Twenty fighters were spotted around the perimeter of Satellite #2; the bombing had mainly affected the area to the east where nine aircraft were damaged. West of Satellite #3 were 16 aircraft – an SM.82, one SM.79 and 14 fighters – and no evidence of bomb damage. Satellites #4 and #5 revealed 35 fighters and two Ju 52/3m transports. Satellite #6 appeared to have suffered the greatest damage: 33 fighters were scattered along the perimeter and nearby were many bomb craters. In the southern section, four aircraft were still surrounded by flames while, on the opposite side, a deposit of material seemed to be burning. Similar damage was noted at Satellite #7 where 12 fighters were parked in the western part of the field. No aircraft were visible on Satellite #8 but 21 were seen on Satellite #9.

Satellite # 10, at 37° 22' 30" N, 14° 57' 30" E, showed no change compared to the previous month but 42 fighters were calling the new Satellite #12 home. News also came from Biscari Santo Pietro that 11 aircraft were present there. Finally, the survey of Gela Ponte Olivo detected the presence of two CANT Z.1007s and a small aircraft.[8] Between 3 and 9 July, Northwest African Air Force (NAAF) bombers dropped 1,323 tons of bombs on the Gerbini complex alone, to which must be added the 197 tons contributed by the heavy bombers of the Ninth Air Force. As a result, Gerbini and seven of its 14 satellites were rendered unusable for the day of the invasion. The other airfields certainly did not fare better; Castelvetrano was abandoned while Comiso, Boccadifalco and Biscari Santo Pietro could not be used. In western Sicily, only Sciacca, Trapani Milo and Trapani Bo Rizzo remained, in part, operational.[9]

Arthur Tedder, commander-in-chief of Mediterranean Air Command, reported, regarding the bombing, that the results were good across the board, adding:

> The movement of enemy planes from one field to another, attempts to escape the attack by dispersing, the preparation of satellite tracks in clay; all of this was observed by us from above. Enemies were being attacked from one field to another. As a result, they were forced to withdraw their bombers at airports in Italy. This of course increased the range of action in which their fighters had to operate in Sicily and caused the progressive weakening of their resistance. The last serious attempt to interfere with our air operations occurred on July 5, 1943.[10]

8   AFHRA, Reel 25196, p.913.
9   Craven, Cate, *The Army Air Force in World War II*, p.439.
10   Lord Tedder, *With Prejudice* (Boston: Little, Brown and Company, 1966), p.445.

Lieutenant William K. Modrall (left) and Major James H. Deering, the latter the commander of the 111th Tactical Reconnaissance Squadron, posing in front of a Tac/R F-6 Mustang. (US Air Force)

Captain Jack W. Flowers (left) questions Major James H. Deering (centre) and Lieutenant William K. Modrall immediately upon their return from the first reconnaissance patrol covering the American landings in Sicily. (US Air Force 50439 AC)

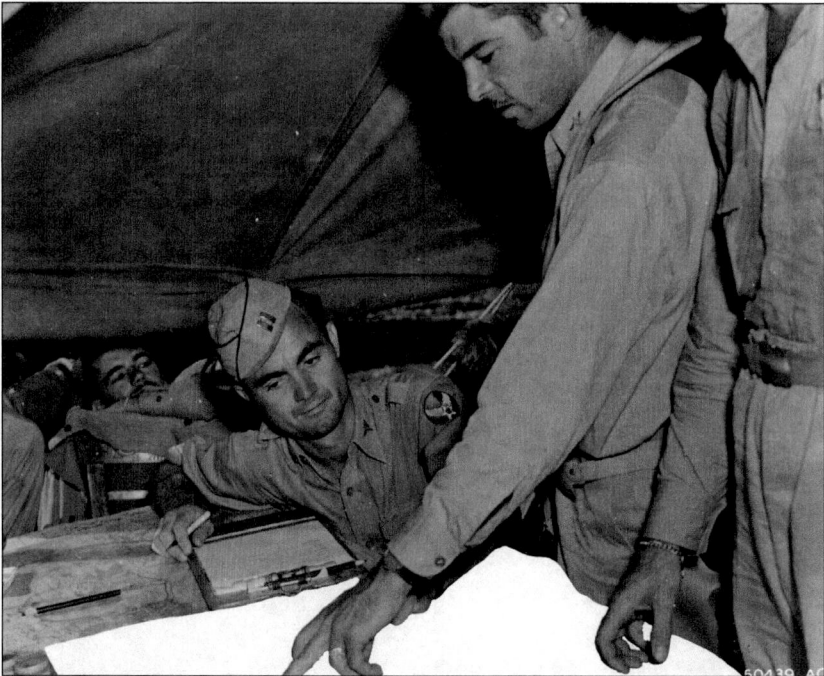

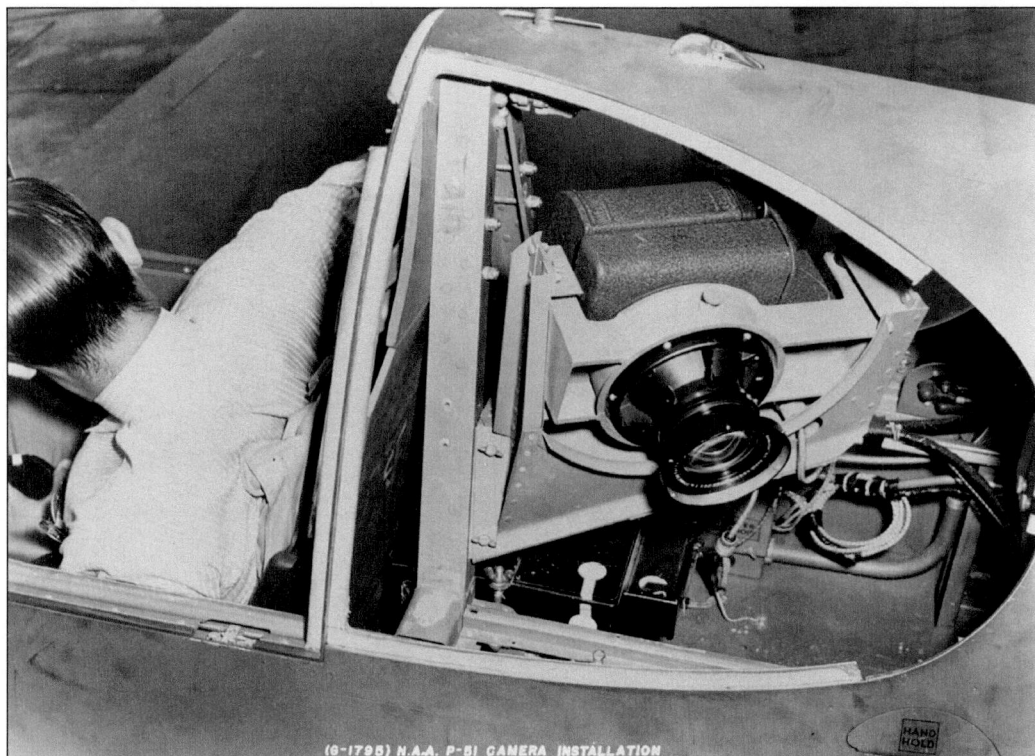

The camera installation in the F-6 Mustang. (US Air Force)

Allied tactical reconnaissance

On 6 July, at the express request of the Fifteenth Army Group, 683 Squadron Flight Sergeant W. Gabbott was engaged in a so-called finishing photo-reconnaissance sortie of the coastal area between Licata and Gela. Five other pilots of the same squadron performed sorties covering the entire island. An important development was highlighted about 3–4 miles north-east of Comiso where a new landing strip built in a simple agricultural field, 37° 02' N, 14° 40' E, was identified. At the same time, the Porto Empedocle radar station was attacked by 59 A-36A Mustangs from the 27th Fighter-Bomber Group (FBG).[11]

A German message intercepted by the American II Corps earlier in the month announced that units (most likely of the Hermann Göring Armoured Division) would carry out anti-invasion exercises in the Gela sector on 4–5 July. According to what was learned, this operation should have involved 6,000 men assisted by vehicles and tanks. Subsequent surveys ascertained these substantial units had already withdrawn from the Caltagirone area during 6 July.[12] On 6

11   AFHRA, IRISREF A6011, p.265.
12   NARA, Operational Remarks (War Diary), p.194B.

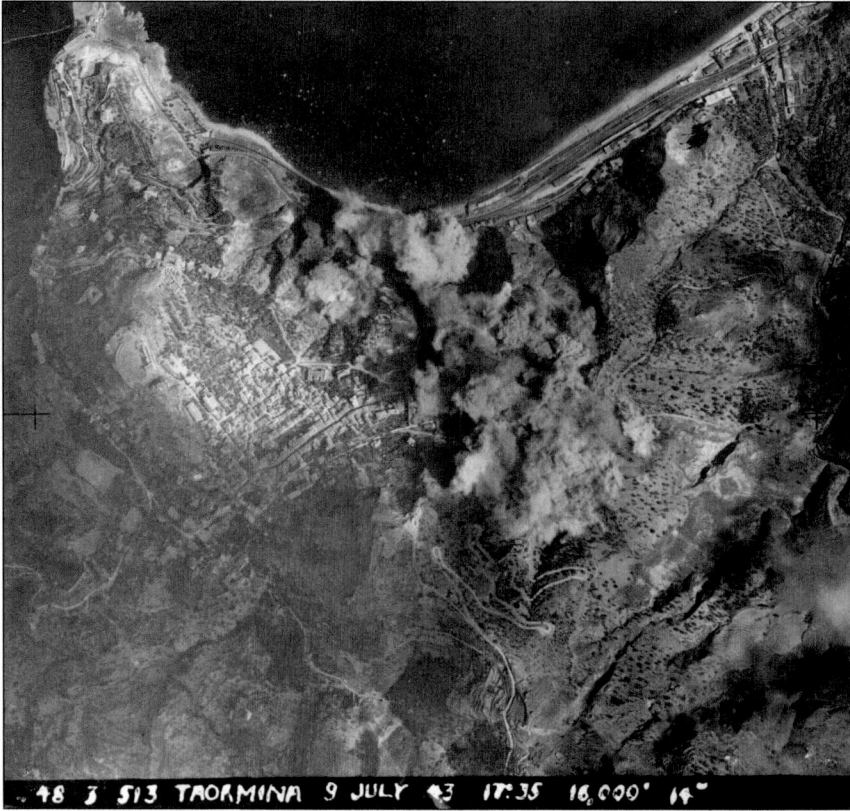

48 3 513 TAORMINA 9 JULY 43 17:35 16,000' 14"

Taormina during USAAF bombing. (Daniele Brancato)

July, taking off on a test flight from La Marsa, Wing Commander Warburton destroyed an F-4, luckily without injury to himself or others.[13]

On 7 July, two F-6 Mustangs of the 111th Tactical Reconnaissance Squadron (TRS), flown by Major Deering and Lieutenant Hicks, left Korba in Tunisia at dawn to carry out their first mission over Sicily. Unfortunately, the two pilots encountered adverse weather conditions over the target, so much so that cloud cover prevented them from taking photos.[14] The mission was repeated a few hours later by Lieutenants Rafanelli and Armstrong, this time proving more fruitful. The squadron flew eight sorties across four missions that day, covering Porto Empedocle and Marsala among others. Of the latter, several radar stations were photographed and then bombed shortly after by seven A-36A fighter-bombers of the 526th Fighter-Bomber Squadron

13   AFHRA, IRISREF C0042, p.1000.
14   Most F-6s carried two K-24 cameras. In the version of the F-6 based on the P-51B/C, an oblique camera was placed in the rear of the cockpit, with another vertical camera mounted in the fuselage behind the radiator.

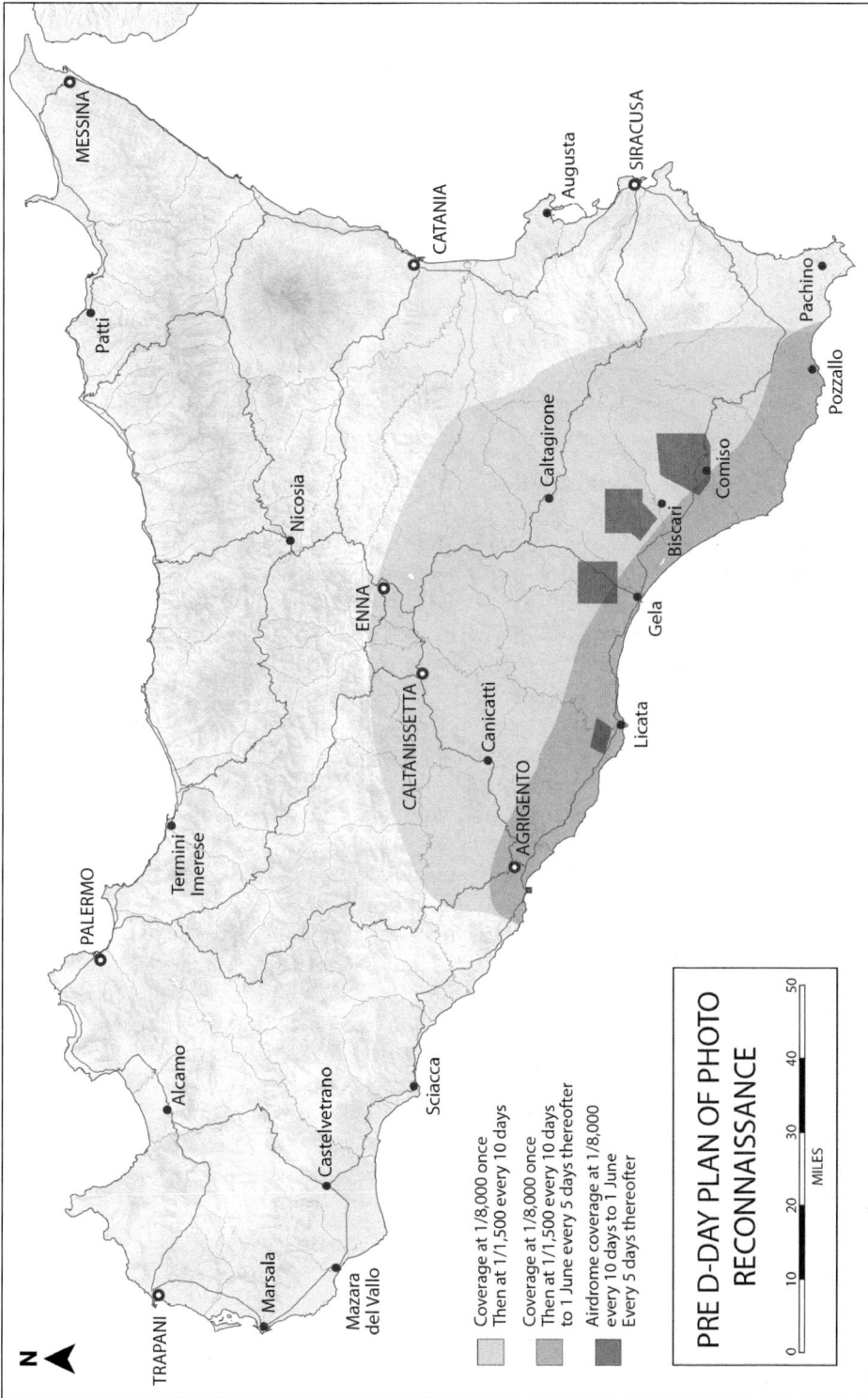

MESSINA

Augusta

SIRACUSA

CATANIA

Pachino

Patti

Pozzallo

Caltagirone

Comiso

Nicosia

Biscari

ENNA

Gela

CALTANISSETTA

Canicatti

Licata

AGRIGENTO

Termini
Imerese

PALERMO

Alcamo

Castelvetrano

Sciacca

TRAPANI

Marsala

Mazara
del Vallo

N

PRE D-DAY PLAN OF PHOTO
RECONNAISSANCE

Coverage at 1/8,000 once
Then at 1/1,500 every 10 days

Coverage at 1/8,000 once
Then at 1/1,500 every 10 days
to 1 June every 5 days thereafter

Airdrome coverage at 1/8,000
every 10 days to 1 June
Every 5 days thereafter

0   10   20   30   40   50
MILES

Routine pre D-Day photo-reconnaissance. (AFHRA)

(FBS), 86th FBG, under the command of Captains Winter and Stell. The photos taken during the attack showed a large crater; half of the Freya radar station and a Giant Würzburg were damaged. At the same time, two missions against the coastal defence positions near Porto Empedocle were entrusted to the 27th FBG.[15]

RDF stations located in June 1943			
Comiso	H524214	H540193	
Castelvetrano	H913954	H905995	
Gerbini	H736757	H790772	H769733
Catania	H956745	H947724	
Fontanarossa	H958746	H946723	

On 8 July, while 683 Squadron was engaged with photographing Monte Corvino, Foggia, Frosinone, Taranto and Naples, the 111th TRS F-6 Mustangs flew a mission over Sicily, covering some communication routes to the north-west of Gela. In the meantime, Ultra confirmed that, in addition to Bf 109s of II./JG 53 from Comiso, those of II./JG 27 from Lecce had already relocated to Satellite #12, despite the airfield still being under construction.

Another important objective was entrusted to the 12 P-38 Lightnings of the 1st FG, which, at 7:56 a.m. on the 8th, took off from Mateur in Tunisia to attack radar installations; one was previously located and photographed by Wing Commander Adrian Warburton near Capo Passero and another was just south of Catania. In the same sortie, in addition to the radar systems, a large, covered wagon 10 miles south-east of Catania, and a coastal defence post in the Capo Murro di Porco area, near Syracuse, were strafed. At 11:35 a.m., the 11 Lightnings (an aircraft had returned early due to mechanical problems) returned to the base while, almost simultaneously, another 12 from the 14th FG headed to other radar positions in the east of the island. Radar systems west of Augusta were attacked, at 37 ° 14' 20" N, 15 ° 10' 20" E, as was a mobile radar station south of the Grammichele railway station and some anti-aircraft artillery positions north-west of Militello in Val di Catania and near Scordia.[16]

Among the six sorties completed this day over Sicily by the 111th TRS, the most dangerous was undoubtedly that flown by Lieutenants Modrall and Mitchell who were detailed to follow the A-36 fighter-bombers of the 27th and 86th Fighter-Bomber Groups to photograph the results of their bombing on the Canicattì railway station and on Licata, where trains, military camps, radio stations and vehicles were impacted. During the mission, the fighter-bombers located a landing strip one mile from Canicattì. The sortie cost the A-36A (serial 42-84028) flown by Flight Officer John A. Lilly, 17th FBS, 27th FBG. He was shot down by anti-aircraft fire and crashed in the sea not far from Marina di Palma. Lilly, who escaped the crash, was captured and taken prisoner. One of the six reconnaissance sorties was flown by Lieutenant Dave C. Hearrell of the 111th TRS:

15   AFHRA, IRISREF A6011, p.266.
16   AFHRA, IRISREF A6012, p.978.

Three 1st FG pilots pictured in North Africa in front of P-38G Lightning 42-13010. Left to right: 2nd Lieutenant Howard A. Gilliam (MIA), 1st Lieutenant Leonard P. Stephan and 2nd Lieutenant Harold C. Lentz. Gilliam was shot down near Caltagirone on 10 July 1943 by a flak battery of the Hermann Göring Division. (US Air Force photo 25050 AC)

Took off at 15:10 on July 8, 1943 to join supposedly the 27th [FBG] over Korba at 15:20 but planes were already on their way so we joined them. They were flying 2 flights of 12 ships each, 3 elements of 4 in each flight. The first flight was on the left. My flight joined on their right. The second flight of 12 was on our right and behind us. We crossed the coast about 5500' climbing steadily and turning slightly about 3 mi west of Licata. A few bursts of flak to the right of the 2nd flight of 12 ships but on the right altitude. Then the flak became more intense. We proceeded on our course towards Caltanissetta, by this time the second flight was line abreast with the first flight and about 200' lower. One element of the 2nd flight was ahead of the first flight. We were climbing all the time and my wingman and myself were trying to weave but were unable to because of the crowding of the 2nd flight. The flak (all that I observed was heavy) followed us for over 10 mi., until we were about 9000'. Apparently the flak was coming from around Licata. Some of the flak burst in front of the flight but there were no hits to my knowledge. One concussion rocked my ship some. The bombers of the

Captain Dave C. Hearrell, of the 111th TRS, poses beside a Mustang bearing the unit's insignia, 'SNOOPERS', in Italy. (US Air Force photo 51715 AC)

second flight dropped off and proceeded to Enna and the first flight started their run on Caltanissetta, from 10,000'. I made a wide circle to the left and at 10,500' and came over target I observed the first 4 hits, one on the highway, one nearer town south of the highway and one directly on what appeared to be a two railroad station. I snapped 3 or 4 pictures and then split down to 15000' to join the bombers to observe the road junction north and west of Gela. One light truck was … loaded with personnel, headed west. The lake south of the junction was to be observed. It was pretty well weeded but will be visible at night. On a sandy knoll south east of the lake was a square building with rows of dark shadows in front of it. Appearing to be foxholes or supplies. I was unable to take pictures because the battery was out, the flight headed out to sea. Weaver located man on dingy [sic], weaver circled once and called on "MAYDAY" giving his call sign. Landed at 17:15. Suggest that when Recon planes are going out with bombers that they do not get between two flights or behind either flight because of flak.[17]

17   AFHRA, IRISREF A0916, p.1508.

By cross-referencing the data on the losses relating to 8 July and previous days, it is possible to identify the castaway to which Hearrell refers. He was 2nd Lieutenant Edwin G. Kocher. Earlier that day, Kocher was on board one of 73 Flying Fortresses, 17 of which were fellow aircraft of the 429th Bombardment Squadron (BS), 2nd BG, sent to bomb Satellites #1, #4, #11, and #12 of the Gerbini complex. During the outbound leg, the B-17 (serial 42-3083, 'Miss Carriage') flown by 2nd Lieutenant Roy Kline, due to some mechanical problems, had detached from the formation and tried to return to the base. Spotted by two German Bf 109s, the bomber was attacked and shot down. Of the 10 crew members, only the navigator, 2nd Lieutenant Edwin G. Kocher, survived:

> I am the Navigator of B-17F No. 42-3083 which was on a bombing mission, July 8, 1943, and our A/A was 2-2-4 in the formation. Our plane was lagging – plane couldn't put out to maintain formation position. Pilot called me and said. "If we can't catch up before hitting coast of Sicily we will turn back." We turned back approximately at the coast of Sicily at 12:10 hours at 16,000 feet altitude, on reciprocal course. All four engines were running. Nothing for a few minutes and then I saw a couple of ME 109s attack us. I started firing at one E/A off on our left wing, when a machine gun bullet must have hit ball and socket of my gun, putting it out of commission. The next thing I noticed No. 2 and 4 engines were feathered and we were losing altitude to 15,000 feet. I worked with cartridge case, smoothing ball socket of gun. During all this time I was wearing my steel helmet over head-set and did not hear the "Abandon Ship" order. I saw a small amount of blood dripping from upper turret and saw Bombardier go back. I thought he was going to take over the upper turret guns. When my gun was repaired I resumed firing at E/A. When I looked around again and noticed the escape hatch was open and the co-pilot was going out. I hooked my chute pack to harness which I was wearing and jumped through nose hatch, pulling rip-cord at once. Everything worked fine as I kicked my legs to straighten shroud lines. I could see other drifting chutes above me, with E/A fighters circling around but no firing, at chutes. I think I was the last man to leave the plane. I pulled on shrouds attempting to drift toward fellows already in water. I was approximately 200 yards from the plane which had one wing sticking out of the water. When I struck the water, I swam toward the plane. I called to the others, asking if they had a raft. Their reply was "there is no raft" upon reaching the plane I found the raft with large hole burned in one side. I opened the Carbon Dioxide bottle and it filled the good half of the raft. There were no paddles so I upon hearing Lt. Grace answer my call, tied a string around my neck and shoulders from the raft and swam to Lt. Grace. He passed out as I reached him and I pulled him aboard the raft. One half hour later a P-51 which I believed was attached to a fighter group at Telergma was circling around me. All this time Grace and several others were alive. I tried artificial resuscitation on Lt. Grace and continued to work on him, at the same time calling to the others of my crew but heard no answers. Lt. Grace did not regain consciousness. I worked on him all night and by Friday morning, July 9th, I could feel no pulse and his teeth were set. I let the air out of his vest and let him into the water. Thursday, July 8th, the first night was calm. Friday a North wind arose and sea became very rough, waves reaching a height of about 30 feet. I drifted until about 2100 hours Saturday night, July 10th, when I was picked up by a British destroyer and was told we

would reach Malta in about three or four hours, at their speed of 10 to 12 knots. In my opinion the plane crashed about 36° 42' N, 13° 32' E, coordinates.[18]

The victory was claimed by Oberfeldwebel Herbert Rollwage of 5./JG 53 'Pik As'; he claimed to have hit the B-17 at 12:28 p.m., about six miles south-west of Capo Scaramia, at an altitude of about 6,500 feet.[19]

At 4:15 p.m. on 8 July, Spitfire PR.XI (EN659) of 682 Squadron, flown by Flight Lieutenant R.E. Walker DFM, took off from La Marsa to perform a second sortie over Sicily. During the flight, however, it was intercepted and shot down near Catania. The first sortie had been completed by Sergeant Mowbray at 2:15 p.m. to check damage caused to military installations at Capo d'Orlando and Catania.

A photo of Licata's coast by Sergeant Tardif from No. 683 Squadron. (Author's photo)

18   NARA, Missing Air Crew Report n. 204.
19   *Luftwaffe* Film C.2027/1.

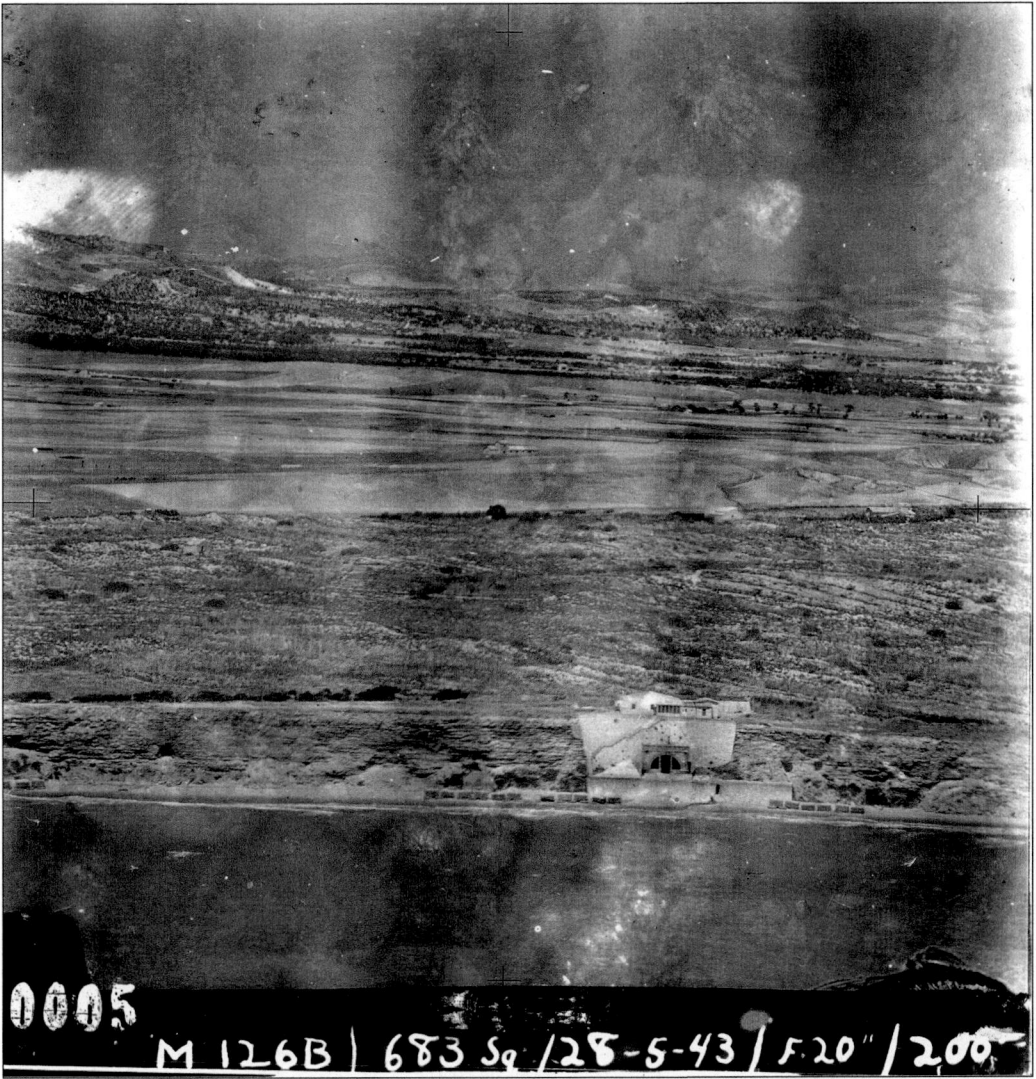

A photo of the 'Sorgente' near Licata, taken by Wing Commander Adrian Warburton flying Spitfire PR.XI EN429. This was an underground complex from which ran a tunnel, about six hundred metres long, parallel to the coast, conveying rainwater into a basin, also located underground. From here, through large pumps and a pipeline about ten kilometres long, the water reached Licata railway station.
(Author's photo)

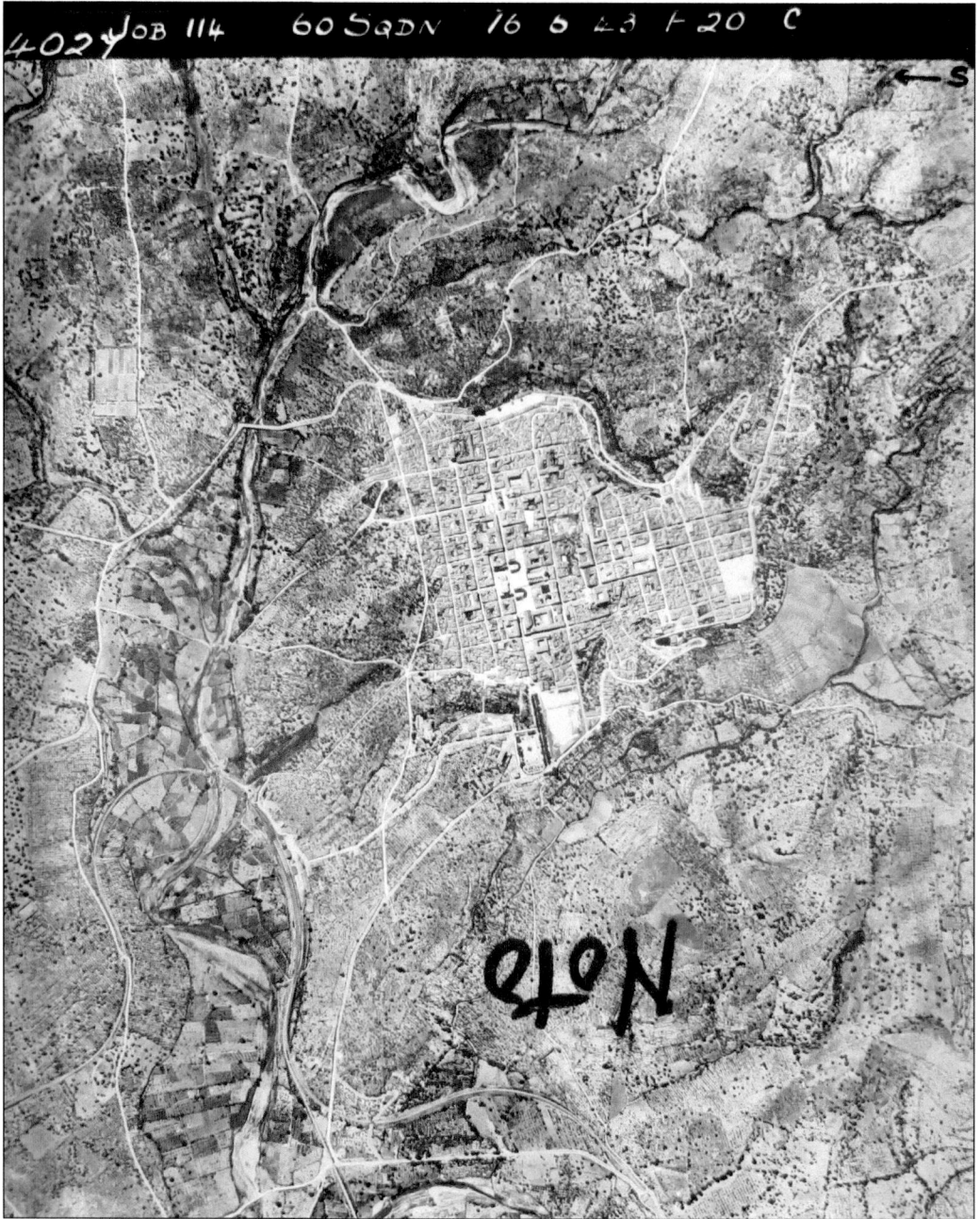

A picture of Noto taken by Mosquito II DD744, flown by Captain Maree and the Flying Officer Murray-Prior from No. 60 Squadron SAAF on 16 June 1943. For this sortie, the Mosquito had arrived in Luqa from Sorman, Libya. (LAC photo RG24, R112, 1984-265 NPC)

13

Operation *Husky*

Already, by 3:20 a.m. on 9 July 1943, a German recce aircraft had sighted about 90 ships, mostly amphibious landing craft, south-east of Pantelleria. A few hours later, at 6:35 a.m., another *Luftwaffe* aircraft spotted two large units west of Malta, but a blanket of mist prevented a more accurate search of the waters between Malta and Pantelleria. At 11:00 a.m., a new reconnaissance confirmed previous suspicions and this time identified 12 steamships and eight patrol boats off Capo Bon, and three warships of an unspecified type east of Kelibia. Finally, a Bf 109 of *II Fliegerkorps* sighted five convoys north of Gozo, totalling about 150–200 units, mostly LCTs (landing craft, tank) and escort ships. At the head of the largest convoy, moving north-west of Malta and consisting of about 80 ships, two heavy units were reported, presumably battleships. Another 69 ships, including large merchant vessels and smaller units, had been photographed in the port of Bizerte some time earlier. The Bay of Bizerte was checked again a couple of hours later by two Macchi MC.202s from Sardinia, confirming the significant presence of these ships. Even the German Ju 88 scouts, coming from Frosinone and, in some cases, Sardinia, had meticulously followed Allied naval movements in the Mediterranean for a long time, paying particular attention to the coasts north of Algeria. One of them, based in Frosinone but taking off from Crotone, came down a few miles from Malta due to a technical problem with an engine at 4:00 p.m. on the 7th; the crew was taken prisoner.[1]

After assessing the results of the reconnaissance flights, and the situation in general in the central Mediterranean, at 6:00 p.m. *Supermarina* sent the following evaluation of the situation to Supreme Command and other armed forces:

> All in all, it was quite favorable for simultaneous landing operations in both the southern and eastern coastal areas of Sicily. The remarkable consistency of transport ships and small units in Bizerte and today's sighting in the Malta area of numerous landing craft and heavy forces at sea can indicate a beginning of the landing operations at night.

Two days earlier, on 7 July, General Adolf Galland had met *Feldmarschall* Albert Kesselring and General Wolfram von Richthofen, commander of *Luftflotte 2*, at the German headquarters in

---

1   AFHRA, RAF Narrative (First Draft), *The Sicilian Campaign June–August 1943*.

Paratroopers from the 505th Parachute Infantry Regiment, 82nd Airborne Division, board Douglas C-47-DL 41-18341 'Lady from Hades' of the 61st Troop Carrier Squadron, 64th Troop Carrier Group, USAAF. The American paratroopers played an important part, first in Sicily on 10 July 1943 in Operation *Husky*, and later in southern Italy during Operation *Avalanche*. (US Air Force photo 25288 AC)

Sicily. The next day, Galland stated he was now convinced of an imminent Allied landing and that it would take place within the next 48 hours at the latest, also stating he was unable to say exactly where it would occur.

On 9 July, Major General Edwin House, head of XII Air Support Command (ASC), called all 111th Tactical Reconnaissance Squadron (TRS) pilots to a briefing; the topic was the photographic coverage plan for the Allied landings in Sicily. The RAF, for its part, scheduled the tactical reconnaissance (Tac/R) operations for the Spitfires of No. 40 Squadron SAAF,[2] which began their campaign on 9 July with three simultaneous ops over the south-east area of Sicily in

---

2   No. 40 Squadron SAAF had transferred 16 aircraft to Malta, on the morning of 23 June, from Ben Gardane airfield. Their first flight over Sicily was on 27 June 1943, when 10 Spitfires joined those of Nos. 142 and 92 Squadrons for an offensive sweep over Catania.

A wrecked Waco CG-4A glider (42-73623), in Sicily during Operation *Ladbroke* in July 1943, after crashing through two stone walls and hitting some trees. (US Air Force photo 25289 AC)

an attempt to determine movements of enemy troops along main roads. It should be noted that, after 8 July, no Italian–German movements close to the landing areas were identified.

Axis ground forces were mainly located in the central and western areas of Sicily. The sorties, carried out until late in the evening, were designed to notice small and insignificant changes. Of the two pilots of 40 Squadron who flew the last op of the day, only Lieutenant Van der Poel managed to complete the task; the other Spitfire, flown by Lieutenant Kermaek, was forced to return to Malta due to mechanical problems. Unfortunately, as a result, it was not possible to cover a very important area close to the cities of Ragusa and Giarratana. Moreover, on 9 July, of all the Allied strategic reconnaissance aircraft on hand, only No. 683 Squadron flew four sorties, covering Taranto, Naples, Messina and Milazzo.

The Northwest Strategic Air Force (NASAF), meanwhile, employed 460 bombers (this includes night bombers, of which 67 were Vickers Wellingtons of No. 205 Group RAF), to deliver the *coup de grace* to what was left of the airfield installations in the west of the island and target significant concentrations of Italian–German troops. At 8:17 a.m., 27 Flying Fortresses of the 97th Bombardment Group (BG) headed towards Sciacca hoping for a break in the cloud cover; only two of them managed to drop 186 × 20lb fragmentation bombs. At the same time, Biscari Santo Pietro was attacked by 26 Fortresses of the 2nd BG and 25 from the 301st BG; 607 × 500lb bombs were dropped, 50 percent hit the target (the rest damaged hangars and other structures east of the airfield). Piazza Armerina was hit at 10:55 a.m. by 144 × 500-pounders

Intelligence section staff catalogue photos before their distribution to various departments and units.
(US Air Force photo 76191 AC)

dropped by 24 B-26 Marauders of the 319th BG. Caltanissetta suffered the heaviest bombing, though, when, at 5:30 p.m., 42 B-25 Mitchells of the 321st BG delivered 245 × 500lb bombs and eight 300-pounders. The intense explosions and thick cloud of smoke impressed the bomber crews so much they recorded details in their war diaries. In the city, the Santa Lucia district was razed to the ground and 351 civilians were killed.

At 12:30 p.m., the tactical command of *II Fliegerkorps* in Taormina was hit with about 54 tons of explosives dropped by 18 B-24 Liberators of the 376th BG. Another 45 civilians were killed. At 7:03 p.m., it was Caltagirone's turn, targeted by 27 Marauders of the 17th BG dropping 159 × 500lb bombs. Palazzolo Acreide was also hit, bombed at 6:28 p.m. by 23 Marauders of the 320th BG carrying 132 × 500lb bombs. That night, the Wellington and Halifax bombers took over. The former flew several sorties against eastern Sicily and the airfield at Biscari Santo Pietro. The eight Halifaxes of No. 462 Squadron RAAF, each with fifteen 250lb General Purpose bombs on board, took off at 11:38 p.m. from Hosc Raui in Libya to carry out an attack along the Avola–Noto–San Paolo route.

An American serviceman of the NAPRW looking at prints coming off a Williamson Multiprinter. Note these are prints from No. 683 Squadron RAF on Malta. (US Air Force photo 76178 AC)

Luftwaffe in the Mediterranean from 14 May to 10 July 1943[3]					
Sector	14 May 1943	1 June 1943	14 June 1943	3 July 1943	10 July 1943
Sardinia	80	80	115	175	115
Siciliy	415	275	315	290	175
Central and southern Italy	200	360	290	345	460
Southern France	-	80	80	165	135
Greece and Crete	125	185	220	305	265
Total	820	980	1,020	1,280	1,150

3   AFHRA, IRISREF K1027-J.

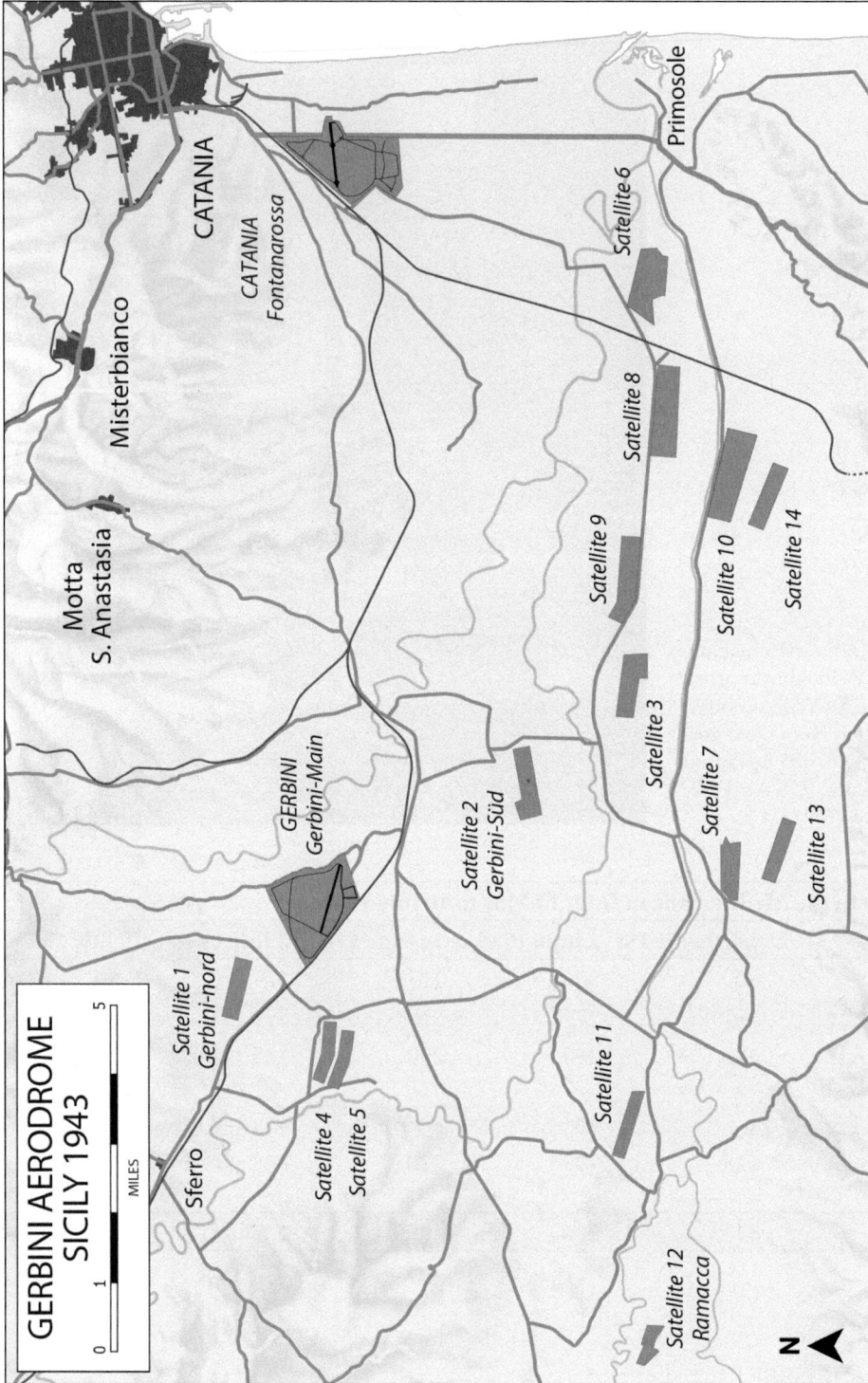

GERBINI AERODROME SICILY 1943

Gerbini airport complex during Operation *Husky*. (AFHRA)

The invasion: Planning and Photo-Reconnaissance

The attack plan had been drawn up by General Harold Alexander on 2 July during a conference called by General Eisenhower in Algiers. There would be two landing areas. The area of responsibility of the American Seventh Army, under the command of General George Patton Jr., went from Licata to Scoglitti, about 50 miles. Three divisions and other minor units would land initially, preceded by the delivery of paratroopers who were supposed to defeat and occupy some key defence positions. The British Eighth Army (four infantry divisions, two armoured brigades and other minor units), commanded by General Bernard Montgomery (the victor of El Alamein), would be responsible for an area extending from the Gulf of Noto to Punta Castelluzzo (west of Capo Passero), for over 30 miles.[4]

The operations of the Seventh Army would be supported by the Advanced Flight of the 12th Photographic Reconnaissance Squadron (PRS); in addition to its F-5As, the 15th PRS would employ some B-25 Mitchells on night photographic reconnaissance operations; a no less valuable contribution would come from B Flight of No. 682 Squadron RAF, as well as the efficient tactical reconnaissance of the 111th TRS. The mapping and study of the defences in Sicily had already been entrusted to the 5th PRS and 60 Squadron SAAF. The advance of the British Eighth Army would receive support from the veterans of 683 Squadron, tactical reconnaissance courtesy of 40 Squadron SAAF with its 16 Spitfires equipped with 14-inch F24 cameras, and the RAF's No. 1437 Strategic Reconnaissance Flight and its Tac/R Mustangs.

Focke-Wulf Fw 190A-5 (wk.nr 1339, coded 'K+I'), probably from 9./SKG 10, photographed at Gela Ponte Olivo. (Alessandro Ragatzu)

4   Anfora, Pepi, *Obiettivo Biscari*, p.16.

As early as 20 June, the Northwest African Photographic Reconnaissance Wing (NAPRW) had planned the details for the routine observation of some key areas carefully chosen by Intelligence. The photos taken during these phases had to be sent to the Photo Interpretation Section, HQ of Task Force 343, its operational headquarters in La Marsa, Tunisia, where they would then have been interpreted and finalised in a report. Of course, any news highlighted would have been transmitted quickly through encrypted radio messages to task force command.

After about two months on Malta, Captain Joe D. Scalpone was stationed at La Marsa field, outside Tunis. The Photo Wing was now centralised there. He recalled:

We now concentrated on stretching the range of the F5-G's [sic, new type of photo-recce P-38] and really getting in some picture taking. I think the fifteen or so missions I flew out of this base were the most interesting. Certainly, we pilots were more proficient at our jobs now. The F5-G's [sic] handled like a dream. We were confident in our aircraft and confident that we could go out and do whatever was asked of us, and confident that we could come home with pictures in our magazines. Rivalry was keen then to do a bangup job of reconnaissance. Our Malta experience had shown us a new and vital job for the PRU pilot to perform; shipping reconnaissance! So now we scanned the seas on our long hops and jotted down whatever we saw. It's tough, recognizing a ship for the type it is when you are sitting five miles up. Initially, we had no training in shipping reconnaissance. In that respect, so much depends on actual sightings. A pilot must see ships often from altitude before he can begin deciding that what he sees is such and such a craft … From our La Marsa base I flew the longest flights so far. It was a hard day at the tubs when your mission was, say, a "milk run" where you "stooged" all over the Italian boot picking up the "bottles" (airfields). If we were briefed for twenty airfields, we tried to pick up a few more on the way. If we had the change, we would try to get a mission that would set a new Wing record either for distance traveled or targets scored. A gratifying hop was an instance when two planned missions were joined to make a single job of it. The combined mission was an assorted lot of airfields, ports, and marshalling yards, plus some new fields not yet snapped, way up in northern Italy. Some twenty-two targets were listed, ranging up the west Italian coast, across northern Italy to the eastern ports of Venice and Trieste, thence across the Adriatic Sea and across central Italy again to make a final pass at the much photographed city of Rome. Total trip fourteen hundred and fifty miles … At the time, the mapping in the Po Valley was a specially interesting of the F5-Gs scope and also showed that the PRU pilots could handle tougher assignments … The most exciting assignment given me was a "dicing job" of Salerno Bay. I flew on the deck to the target (to help avoid detection by enemy radar), slipped into the northern end of the bay and exhausted the film of my oblique camera along the cliffs and beaches that were later to receive our invading forces. On this dicing mission the shore defenses were properly surprised and I got away clean with a magazine full of pictures. That's the best feeling a PRU pilot can have![5]

5   AFHRA, IRISREF B0747, p.406.

The photographic coverage plan had already started in recent months, with coverage of western Sicily on a scale of 1:50,000. As the date of the invasion approached, the frequency of coverage increased to identify and discern as many changes as possible and provide indications on the dispositions of German and Italian ground forces. From these photos, mosaics were made of all the beaches in the areas where the landing operations would take place. A relief model was reproduced to a 1:5,000 scale.[6] The planning also required coverage of roads and railways on a scale of 1:18,000. The American Joss Task Force[7] received only 50 mosaics, covering the area east of Licata, from Intelligence.[8] Throughout this delicate phase, a decisive role was played by the American 66th Topographic Company, assisted by artillery officers, in the identification of anti-aircraft batteries, minefields, bunkers, and everything else that could somehow counter

Lieutenant Modrall of the 111th TRS in a Tac/R F-6 before leaving for a mission to Sicily. (US Air Force photo 50435 AC)

6   David W. Dengler, Maj, *Seeing the enemy: army air force aerial reconnaissance support to U.S. Army operations in the Mediterranean in World War II*, USAF M.A., (Lincoln, Nebraska: University of Nebraska, 1998), p.91.
7   Unit of the US Seventh Army commanded by Brigadier General Lucian King Truscott.
8   Dengler, *Seeing the enemy*, p.98.

Allied operations. They worked in synergy with the 10 F-5A Lightnings of the 12th PRS. Using the technical support of some engineers, they also managed to determine whether bridges had been rigged with explosive charges and identified several minefields.

Request for photo-reconnaissance from 1942 to 1943						
Arm/Scope	Nov. 1942	Feb.	Apr.	Jun.	Aug.	Sept.
Army	10%	26%	24%	18%	23%	27%
Mapping	--	--	21%	26%	24%	19%
Naval	40%	48%	16%	13%	8%	9%
Air Force	30%	18%	21%	22%	17%	19%
General	20%	8%	18%	21%	28%	26%

The photos taken after bombing raids, and the reports on the damage inflicted, did not concern this new operational phase. Now, besides airfields, ports and railway infrastructure, the focus was also on communication routes, especially road bridges, to allow engineering units to better anticipate repairs and logistical needs following the landings.

On 5 May, in North Africa, the fourth unit of the 3rd Photographic Group (PG) was activated, consisting of five officers and 27 enlisted men of the USAAF, and six officers and 15 non-commissioned officers of the II/33 of the *Armée de l'Air Française*. From Oujida, in French Morocco, under the control of Major Glen J. McClernon, pilots and paratroopers of the Fifteenth Army Group were trained in the use of photography for combat tactics. The unit remained at Oujida for five weeks, during which it carried out 18 missions and provided the 52nd Troop Carrier Wing with 4,000 prints. The Fifteenth Army Group had already released 200 copies of the first overlapping photos on 19 May, while the Seventh Army distributed 1,900 copies. The fourth unit of the NAPRW supported, in this way, the preparatory work of the paratroopers of the 82nd Airborne Division very well; the 505th Parachute Infantry Regiment then used aerial photos and models made by Intelligence to train personnel before the start of the fighting in Sicily. The delicate work of this unit included identifying areas in North Africa similar to the coast of Sicily so exercises could be conducted. Lieutenant General Mark Clark observed:

> [NAPRW] helped to develop a method of locating drop zones for parachute troops that has proved very successful. During the combat drops, transport pilots carried photos with them given the lack of markers or pathfinder teams. This seemed satisfactory, for on a previous night reconnaissance, Colonel James Gavin found that all check points and terrain showed up clearly in the moonlight, exactly as we had memorized them from photographs.[9]

In particular, oblique photos of the beaches were requested, in order to identify defensive positions and their type of armament, quickly highlighting some important shortcomings.

9   Dengler, *Seeing the enemy*, p.96.

LST 158 was hit by Axis
aircraft off Yellow Beach,
Joss Sector. (US Air Force
photo 25192 AC)

Dummy paratroopers

On 10 July 1943, the Axis forces present on the island were under the command of VI Army, with its headquarters in Enna, under the guidance of Generale Alfredo Guzzoni, who had taken over from Mario Roatta about a month earlier. Two Army Corps, XII and XVI, were responsible for half the island each. The former, commanded by Generale Mario Arisio, based in Corleone, was entrusted with western Sicily, west of the Licata–Cefalù line, while the latter, led by Generale Carlo Rossi, based in Piazza Armerina, was in charge of the defence of eastern Sicily, from the east of Cefalù to Gela. On the eastern side, eyes were focused on the Maritime Military Square of Augusta–Syracuse, the impregnable stronghold of the *Regia Marina* well known to Allied reconnaissance. Guzzoni had more than 200,000 soldiers, including 32,000 Germans, under his command, there were many weak points, however, including the lack of mobility, unsuitable anti-aircraft and anti-tank armament or, again, the regional recruitment of personnel whose morale, particularly that of the Sicilians, was affected by suffering three long years of hunger and war.

The first stages of the American landing in the Gela area photographed by a Tac/R aircraft from the 111th TRS. (US Air Force)

In addition to the countless positions for coastal defence, located between Scoglitti and Licata, and the German Hermann Göring Division in the Caltagirone area, the Italian–German forces also had the 4th Livorno Infantry Division, located between Butera and Mazzarino, and the 54th Napoli infantry Division, with its headquarters in Vizzini.

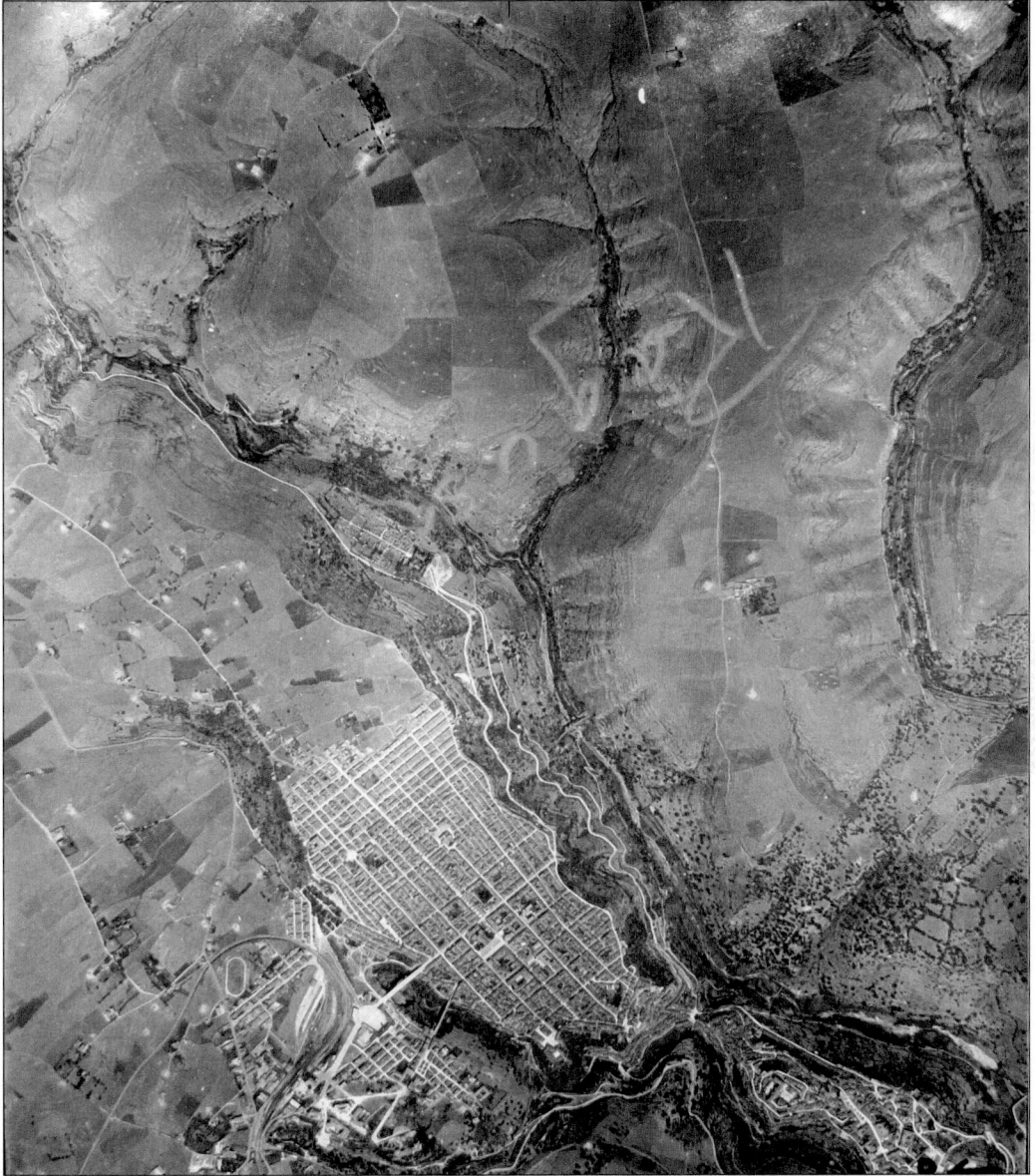

The city of Ragusa photographed on 11 July 1943 from a PR Spitfire of No. 683 Squadron. (LAC photo RG24, R112, 1984-265 NPC)

A few hours before the real launch of the paratroopers, the Allies decided to create a diversion and test the reactions of the enemy forces. Four Douglas Boston III aircraft of No. 24 Squadron SAAF took off at 9:20 p.m. local time from Benhagen, Tunisia; Lieutenant Colonel Williams, headed for Niscemi, led the formation. Visibility was average; some cloud banks partially covered the town. The South African aircraft, in addition to their bombs, carried dummies dressed as paratroopers. Before delivering the fake paratroopers, the bombers split up, probably to try to attract more attention, and dropped sixteen 250lb General Purpose (GP) bombs from 9,000–8,000 feet on some targets on the outskirts of Niscemi. As soon as they had bombed, the aircraft flew to prearranged points, coordinates H130420 and H215432, flying over at 3,500 feet to drop the dummies. The anti-aircraft response was punctual, an intense but inaccurate barrage coming from the nearby airfield at Gela Ponte Olivo. At the same time, eight Bostons

On 13 July, the Fliegerführer Sardinien reported the *Stab* of Sch.G. 2 had one Fw 190 in Sicily, I./Sch.G. 2 had 15, and II./Sch.G. 2 had six at Enna-Süd. This photo was taken by the 5th PS, 3rd PG. (US Air Force)

of No. 18 Squadron RAF, led by Lieutenant Johnson in 'Z' (Z2256), bombed the airfield at Sciacca and then flew west to Catania and Siracusa, to coordinates 822813, 870480 and 920498, dropping 72 dummies, and 20 containers of ammunition, between 9:35 and 9:58 p.m. Four more Bostons of No. 114 Squadron, after dropping some bombs on Sciacca and Palermo, let their fake paratroopers go over the latter from an altitude between 1,000 and 1,500 feet. Another South African unit, No. 12 Squadron, also took part with four Boston Mk.IIIs; Lieutenant Colonel Kotze led the formation. After dropping some 250lb GP bombs near Niscemi, Gela Ponte Olivo and San Michele di Ganzaria, the South Africans delivered some mannequins between Grammichele and Mineo, at H5948, and near Biscari Santo Pietro airfield, at H5441. All squadrons returned to their respective bases without any problems.

Launch of real paratroopers

The night before D-Day, the 52nd Troop Carrier Wing (TCW) USAAF sent 142 C-47 Dakotas of the 61st, 313th and 314th Troop Carrier Groups to North Africa to transport paratroopers from the 82nd Airborne Division to the Gela area. They were joined by another 51 C-47 transports of the 64th Troop Carrier Group (TCG), 51st TCW, and three squadrons (33 C-47s) of the 316th TCG. Combined, these units provided 226 aircraft.[10]

For the British, for Operation *Ladbroke*, 109 C-47 Dakotas of the 51st TCW, which together with RAF aircraft, 21 Albemarles and seven Halifaxes, and towed Waco and Horsa gliders, transported the paratroopers of the 1st Airborne Division to the Syracuse area; in addition to men and armaments, 98 bicycles were crammed into the gliders.[11] The first group of American paratroopers of the 505th Regimental Combat Team left Tunisia at 8:15 p.m. on board a C-47 of the 61st TCG. This first group consisted of 3,405 paratroopers, under the command of Colonel Gavin, and a 17-man general staff. However, strong wind and bad visibility forced transport pilots to change course and launch the paratroopers at random. Only 26 aircraft managed to deliver their charges on assigned targets.

About the Operation *Ladbroke* glider operation, General Eisenhower wrote:

> The record of the performance of your command on the night of 9-10 July has given us great gratification. The accomplishment of your officers and men in carrying to their destination through difficult weather, navigational obstacles and hostile fire in unarmed and unarmoured aircraft, the largest numbers of troops as yet lifted by air, is signal one. Their return to base with a loss of only two percent, and their complete readiness for operation on the following night is remarkable and shows great fortitude, superior organization and training on the part of all concerned.[12]

10 Craven, Cate, *The Army Air Force in World War II*, p.449.
11 AFHRA, Troop Carrier, General Route, p.21.
12 The National Archives London, Royal Air Force, Operations Record Books, AIR 27/1645-1, p.109.

The longest day: the landing

I was wrong. The Allied air force had definitively won the air battle, and this was evident from the first moment we landed in Sicily. The enemy air force was swept from the sky and was never allowed to disturb us ...[13]

General Bernard Law Montgomery

At 4:00 a.m. on 10 July, British, Canadian and American forces made landings across the southeast coast of Sicily, supported by Allied naval and air forces. Almost 2,800 ships of varying types participated in this large amphibious operation, several nations joining the Anglo–American landing, including India, the Netherlands, Poland and Greece. The meteorological situation caused delays in the arrival of some small boats; despite this, the landing operations were carried out according to the pre-established plans. The British Eighth Army had the capture of the landing strip at Pachino and the ports of Syracuse and Augusta as its immediate objectives. It was then to continue along the east coast towards Catania and Messina. The main objectives of the American Seventh Army were the airfields at Gela Farello, Gela Ponte Olivo, Comiso and Biscari Santo Pietro, and the ports of Licata and Gela, and then continue towards Caltanissetta and Palermo. At 1:30 p.m., Pachino was already entirely in British hands. Early in the evening, British troops crossed the bay of Syracuse and the city was conquered at 9:00 p.m.

At first light, American B-17 Flying Fortresses and B-25 Mitchells heavily bombed the airfields at Gerbini, Trapani Milo, Sciacca and Castelvetrano; the town of Palazzolo Acreide, before the arrival of the Eighth Army, was also heavily hit. In addition, the P-38 Lightnings of the 1st, 14th and 82nd Fighter Groups were sent to the west and south-east of the island on low altitude strafing missions to prevent enemy troops from flowing to the landing sectors to bolster the resistance.

The runway at Korba, in Tunisia, was still shrouded in darkness when Major James Deering, from Ventura, California, commander of the 111th TRS, climbed into his F-6 Mustang to head to the beaches of Sicily. The strip was lit for the occasion by signal flares, allowing a take-off in full darkness. Deering was the first American pilot to witness the Allied landings on European soil, but the long distance from his base in North Africa did not allow him to linger for long. Upon his return, he reported that operations were proceeding according to plan. The 111th TRS was entrusted with the delicate initial task of constantly flying over the coastline between Licata and Pozzallo, taking oblique photos at low altitude. The progressing penetration of Allied troops into Sicilian territory was the main reason for this and other missions by the squadron. The results of the reconnaissances had to be sent to Allied command every day at 10:00 a.m. and 1:00 p.m. To achieve this, the 111th TRS flew 22 sorties throughout the day. The only unexpected event of the day concerned the last sortie, during which Lieutenant Tolbert was forced to separate from his wingman, due to low fuel, and return early. The squadron believed him missing in action, but he managed to land near Cape Bon. Meanwhile, Lieutenants Modrall and Mitchell sighted enemy aircraft for the first time over Sicily. The formation of 20 aircraft forced them to withdraw via the shortest route.

---

13   Nigel Hamilton, *Monty: Master of the Battlefield, 1942-1944* (Milano: McGraw-Hill, 1984).

The Allied Task Force required both day and night reconnaissance coverage of 10 sensitive areas, including roads and other transport links between the main cities in the south of the island. Depending on the objective, operational planning required 1,000 to 1,100 reports per day. The pilots of the 111th TRS had received excellent training to assist ground forces and were able to identify enemy formations, understand their tactics, identify armoured vehicles and the road space required by these units, the formations deployed, and the capability of the German artillery.

On the day of the landings, tactical Allied air reconnaissance identified the 15th German Panzergrenadier Division moving south-west. This allowed General Truscott to move the 15th Regimental Combat Team to block the manoeuvre and preserve the beachhead.

At 2:00 p.m., the F-5As of the 3rd PG performed three sorties, flying over the same objectives from the coast of Agrigento to Aragona, and then continuing to the Pozzallo–Ragusa–Vizzini route.

The Tac/R Spitfires of 40 Squadron SAAF departed Malta for eastern Sicily. Captain Le Roux (Spitfire Vb EP690) and Lieutenant E.C. Webb (Spitfire Vb ER706) were observing the main communication routes when, two miles east of Syracuse, they were unexpectedly attacked. Before his eventual return, Webb was able to relay the bad news:

> A black day for the Squadron as Captain Clive Le Roux and Lieutenant Webb failed to return from the early morning sortie. Lieutenant Webb reported by R/T that Clive had been shot down East of Syracuse by a Spitfire and that he had not observed him baling out. Confused messages continued to come in from Lieutenant Webb culminating in the news that he was baling out. As Clive Le Roux was one of the most popular Flight Commanders time dragged on leaden feet whilst we awaited news that he had managed to get into his dinghy. No further word had been heard of Teddy Webb either and there were many sad hearts, but faces smiled again when, late that night, Webb appeared in person none the worse for his jump … Lieutenant I. N. Taylor will act as Flight Commander of "A" Flight in Clive's place.[14]

Webb flew over the crash site but did not notice a dinghy or parachute. Due to the 'excitement' well into the sortie, and the stress of losing Le Roux, he did not notice he was running low on fuel; during the return flight, just eight miles from Malta, he was forced to abandon the Spitfire and bale out into the sea. After 20 minutes in his dinghy, Webb was rescued at 10:30 a.m.. Another three Spitfires from 40 Squadron carried out a tactical reconnaissance between Syracuse and Augusta; 26 aircraft were noted at the seaplane base.[15] The South African squadron reported a consistent movement of Italian–German forces along their eastern defensive lines. Many of the squadron's pilots had only arrived the day before from the Middle East and, despite a lack of knowledge of Sicily's geography, 11 sorties were flown in short order.

---

14 Captain Clive Le Roux was 21 years old and the commander of A Flight ; Lieutenant Taylor took his place. War diary 40 Squadron SAAF. The National Archives London, Royal Air Force, Operations Record Books AIR 54/82/2.

15 This was confirmed when the port of Augusta was occupied by British forces, 20 serviceable seaplanes were still moored to their buoys.

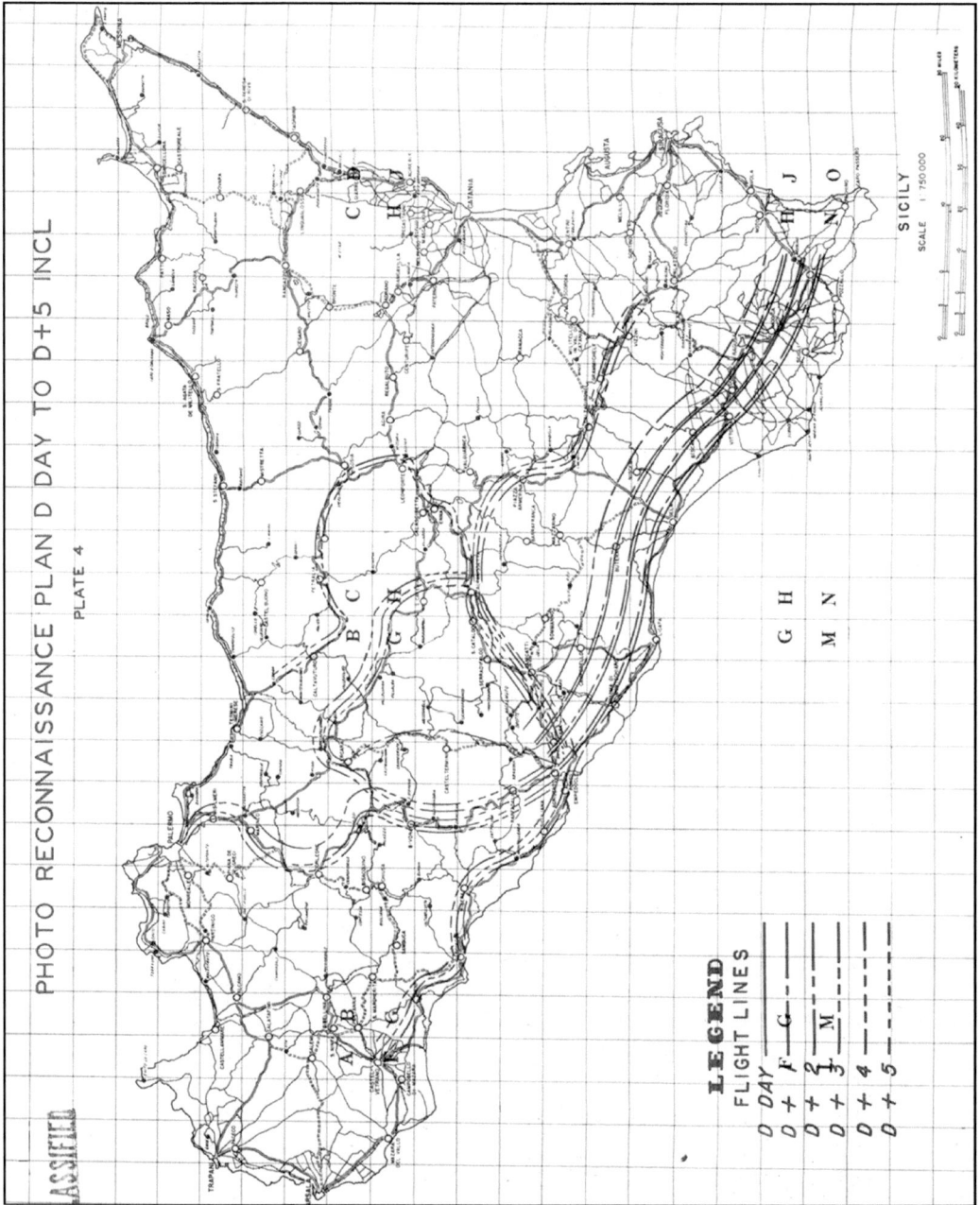

The routine
of photo-
reconnaissance
for D-Day and
D+5. (AFHRA)

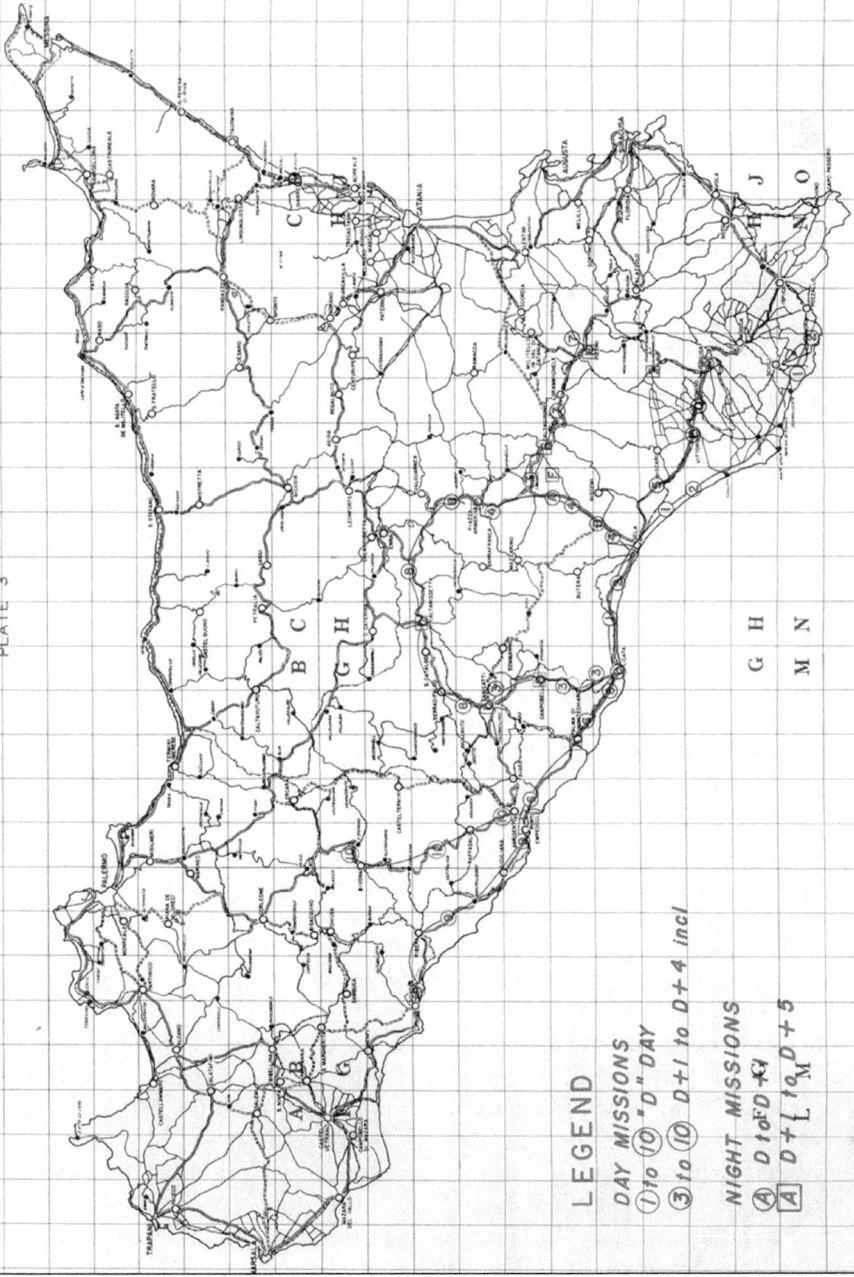

VISUAL OBSERVATION PLAN D DAY TO D+5 INCL

PLATE 3

LEGEND

DAY MISSIONS

① to ⑩ "D" DAY

③ to ⑩ D+1 to D+4 incl

NIGHT MISSIONS

Ⓐ D to F D +C

Ⓐ D+L to M D +5

SICILY

SCALE 1:750.000

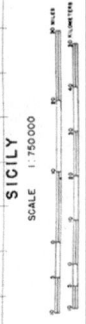

Day and
night photo-
reconnaissance
sorties for
D-Day and
D+5. (AFHRA)

Meanwhile, 683 Squadron, at 6:00 a.m., sent two of its Spitfires on sorties; Flight Sergeant C.A. Tardif (PR.XI MB780) checked out the airfields at Gerbini, Biscari Santo Pietro and Comiso, while Flight Sergeant W.S. Lewis (PR.XI EN391) covered the ports of Taranto and Brindisi. Tardif barely had time to land at Luqa, fill up with fuel, and load the new film before Pilot Officer G. Craig climbed into MB780 at 9:00 a.m. to photograph Naples and eastern Sicily. During the flight between Milazzo and Naples, Craig spotted the silhouettes of two hospital ships at sea. At Milazzo, he also noted 15 small boats while, near the Strait of Messina, various merchant ships, some Siebel Ferries and other vessels were busy shuttling from one end of Italy to the other.

At 9:45 a.m., 682 Squadron sent Sergeant Forbes on a sortie in Spitfire PR.XI (MB777); he flew over the area west of Etna and carried out photographic surveys of the railway line and the roads that crossed the municipalities of Randazzo, Bronte and Adrano. On the afternoon of 10 July, at 2:40 p.m., Wing Commander Adrian Warburton of 683 Squadron, in Spitfire PR.XI (EN429), flew at low altitude along the Licata coast, enjoying the spectacle of the Allied landing. Unexpectedly, he was targeted by US Navy gunners, earlier Italian–German attacks had led to itchy trigger fingers among the men defending their ships. Flight Lieutenant Phillip Kelley, a flight commander with 683 Squadron, remembered Warburton's flight:

> Although at times, labelled 'Mad Warby', he had a highly professional attitude to tasks which were themselves dangerous and demanding. When given the vital assignment to photograph the coastline as troops were actually going ashore, Warby, knowing all too well how trigger-happy the Americans could be, (they had even shot at him when their Liberators were bombing Tobruk) went to the trouble of sorting out the Americans most likely to be involved and telling them where he would be and what he would be doing. He even took down a photograph of his (unusually coloured) PR Spitfire, so that they would know exactly what he would look like. In spite of these sensible precautions, almost as soon as he arrived over the beachhead, US Navy gunners from ships off-shore promptly riddled his aircraft with good and accurate shooting. The Warburton luck held. The plane was severely damaged but Warby just managed to get it back to Malta. One aileron was hanging in shreds and there was a hole in one wing which has been described by Cyril Wood, as 'big enough to pass a bucket through'.[16]

For Warburton it was not enough to be able to return to Luqa miraculously unscathed; the desire to return to Sicily to see the landing was great, and although the pilots of his squadron tried in every way to persuade him, the wing commander climbed in to a Spitfire Mk.IX (EN290/'VG') loaned by No. 1435 Squadron. The 12 Spitfires of the squadron, led by Wing Commander Duncan Smith in Spitfire IX JK650 ('DS'), took off at 6:25 p.m.; shortly after they were in the Syracuse area and, at 13,500 feet, they sighted six Bf 109Gs and six Fw 190s, the latter intent on attacking British ships offshore. The Spitfires, in an advantageous position, latched on to the tails of several of the Messerschmitts. Warburton again proved his worth, probably destroying a Bf 109G and damaging another. The Spitfires returned to Malta at about 8:00 p.m., but

16 Spooner, *Warburton's War*, p.144.

two pilots were lost, shot down during the clash with the German fighters.[17] Duncan Smith recorded one of his sorties with Warburton:

> The most remarkable of the many personalities in Malta was Adrian Warburton who commanded 683 (Photo Recce) Squadron, equipped with Spitfire Mk XIs. 'Warbie' was moulded in the buccaneer style and his exploits captured the imagination. Immensely brave, he delighted in taking fearful risks, and would go out of his way to embarrass the enemy by the brazen impudence of his photographic reconnaissance missions. Apart from his normal work, which ranged over the whole Mediterranean, he had also a fine record as a fighter pilot. On the streets and in the bars he was immediately recognized and would be greeted affectionately by civilians and servicemen alike. In the next four weeks I escorted Warburton on several photo-recce missions in connection with the forthcoming invasion of Sicily. We flew together and once or twice I took a Wing pilot along as an extra pair of eyes. We usually ran into trouble. Once 'Warbie' decided to take pictures of Syracuse and without wavering I found myself following him into the harbour at zero feet to be met by the strongest ack-ack fire. We flew up, down and out with everything shooting at us and the only reason we escaped was because the enemy could not depress their medium guns sufficiently – we were so low.[18]

News of troop movements in the American sector also came from the P-38 Lightnings of the American 14th Fighter Group (FG) who, sent to guarantee air coverage in the area between Comiso and Caltagirone, spotted, at 12:15 p.m., 50 vehicles, including German tanks, well hidden in a wooded area west of, and not far from, the airfield at Comiso; another 20vehicles and tanks were located just north of the airfield. In the afternoon, the same aircraft of the 14th FG attacked 15 tanks in a wooded area on Hill 986, near Buccheri.

At 4:41 p.m., three large trucks were spotted, along the road leading to Biscari Santo Pietro airfield, by the B-26 Marauders of the 320th BG as they returned from a raid on the town of Vizzini. The information, relayed to the relevant commands, saw some Lightnings, this time of the 1st FG, assigned to the hunt; at 6:50, they found and attacked 30 trucks parked near an olive grove five miles south of Caltagirone.

On the night of 10/11 July, Air Commodore Laurence Sinclair, commander-in-chief of the tactical bomber force, ordered four Bostons from 18 Squadron, based at Grombalia, Tunisia, to head to Sicily for an armed reconnaissance along some sensitive communication routes. The first bomber, flown by Wing Commander Sandeman and his crew of three, left at 10:05 p.m. to bomb a target at 37° 28' N, 14° 21' E from 5,000 feet (near the current state road SS117bis), in the wooded area of Grottacalda; an armed reconnaissance was then conducted along the Caltanissetta–Canicattì–Licata route. At 10:19 p.m., Squadron Leader MacLaren headed to bomb the railway line, between San Cataldo and Caltanissetta. Lieutenant Johnson's Boston made its way to San Michele di Ganzaria and, at 10:40, Flying Officer Rennolds's Boston headed for the Vittoria–Gela route.

---

17   Flight Lieutenant M.R. Rowland was killed in action by a Bf 109 and Pilot Officer L.A. Stewart, who baled out into the sea, was rescued.
18   Duncan Smith, *Spitfire into Battle* (London: John Murray Ltd, 1981), p.137.

Reconnaissance operations carried out on terrestrial targets by the NAPRW from 3/4 to 17 July 1943				
Unit	Aircraft	Tac/R.	Photo/R.	Total
3rd Photo Group	Spitfire B-17 F-4 F-4A F-5A Mosquito	32	129	161
60 Squadron SAAF	Mosquito		3	3
111th TRS	P-51	132	24	156
325th Fighter Group	P-40	3		3
Total		167	156	323

Total number of casualties and the state of NAPRW aircraft during the period from 22 November 1942 to 10 July 1943	
Personnel	
Missing or killed in action	**9**
Killed on courier missions	3
Accidental deaths	1
Wounded in action	1
Emergency landings or crashed	5
Aircraft	
Operating	42
Non-operational	4
Transferred	11
Crashed or damaged (not on operations)	7
Lost due to enemy action	13

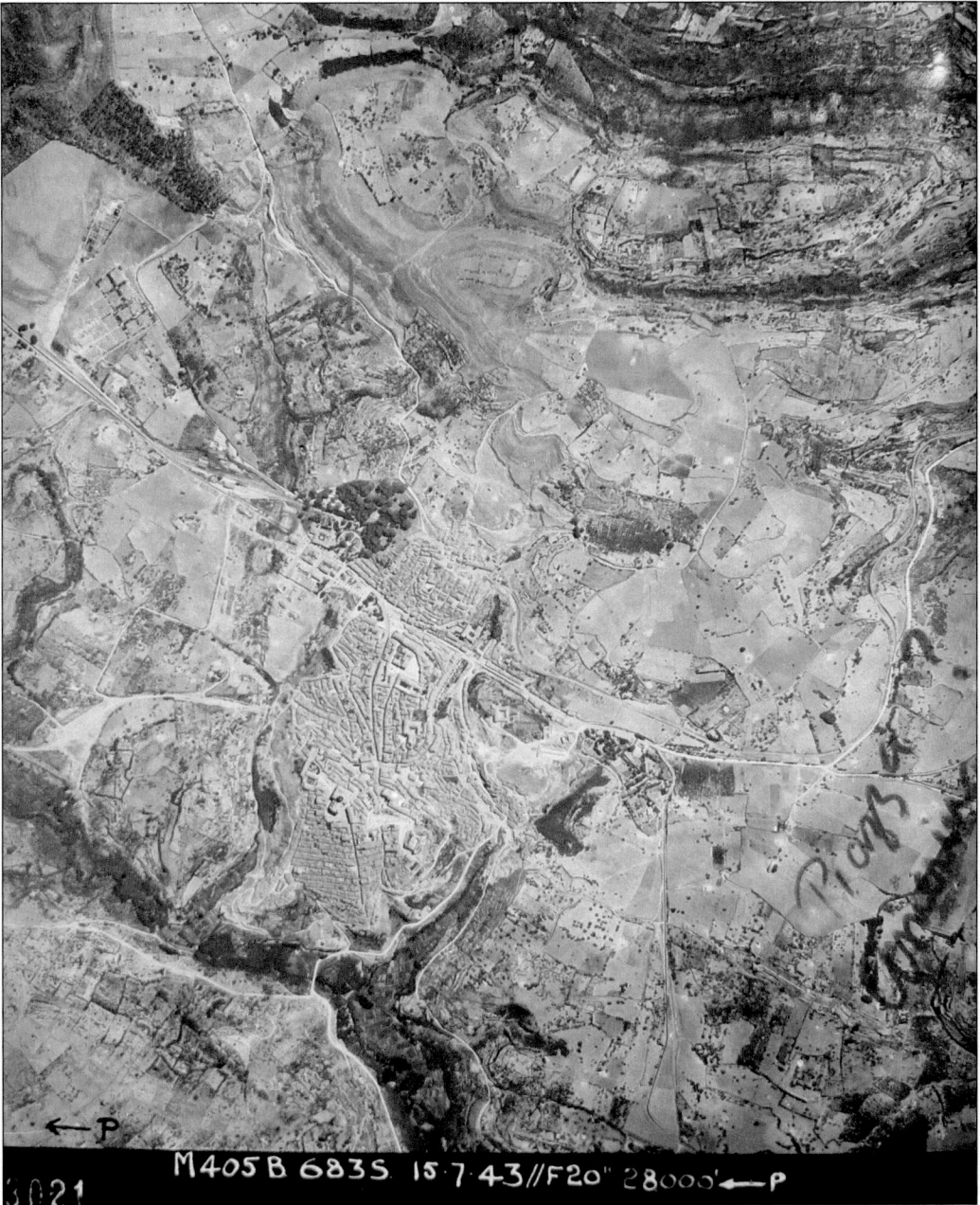

Piazza Armerina captured by the camera of the Spitfire PR.XI (MB778) flown by Pilot Officer Keith Durbidge, who flew the sortie on demand (Army Demand), at about 11:30 a.m. on 15 July 1943. (LAC photo RG24, R112, 1984-265 NPC)

Italian–German Counterattack

Given the current situation, the Italian *Superaereo*, with document no. 318 signed by the Air Force Chief of Staff, Generale Rino Corso Fougier, provided the following:

> All offensive air forces concentrated or being concentrated on the bases of the 3ª and 4ª Squadra Aerea must be engaged in possibly concomitant or repeated actions. The center of gravity of the action - unless otherwise specified later - will be the Augusta-Syracuse-Capo Passero area. Main objectives for all units of all specialties: steamers. The ammunition for the steamer attack: 100 or 160kg bombs P, for the attack on the beachheads use 100kg bombs SP. The approach route along the Sicilian east coast from the north ...[19]

At 4:24 a.m. on 10 July, a small *Luftwaffe* formation, consisting of some Fw 190s and Ju 88s, combined with some Italian bombers, began launching light rockets and attacking the American ships in the Cent area. Some bombers attacked the USS *Philadelphia* and *Jefferson*, others the 'Joss' sector. USS *Maddox* was sunk by a Ju 87 in the 'Dime' sector. The Americans immediately requested coverage from Maltese Spitfires; these scrambled at about 4:30. At 9:50, Capitano Giovanni Franchini took off in a Macchi MC.205V (351-00) of the *351ª Squadriglia* to conduct a photo-reconnaissance sortie.[20] The task entrusted to him was to fly fast and low along the Sicilian coastlines involved in the Allied landings, take photos, and return to Trapani Chinisia. Once back base, the dangerous and delicate flight having gone very well, the technicians realised someone had forgotten to load the film in the camera, much to the dismay of the pilot.[21]

Husky II

As the sun set on the first day of Operation *Husky*, from the sandy slopes of North Africa, 144 C-47 transports prepared to transport 2,300 paratroopers of the 82nd Airborne Division to Sicily; this was Operation *Husky II*. The formation was not as fortunate as that of the previous night. In fact, due to some communication problems between Allied commands, 23 C-47s were shot down by friendly fire, another 37 suffered serious damage and many paratroopers lost their lives. Captain Edwin L. Hibner, commander of one of the Dakotas, recalled:

> I last saw 506 [C-47 42-23506] piloted by Major Dekker and Captain Dobbins heading along the coast northwest from Gela, just off shore. At this time (approximately 2113 GMT) the plane flew through a barrage of anti-aircraft fire, both from the ground and from naval vessels, at which time I lost sight of it and proceeded home. The guns are believed to be friendly because they were located at points known to be in our

---

19   Francesco Mattesini, Mario Cermelli, Direttive tecnico-operative di Superaereo - Gen. 1942-Sett. 1943 [Technical-operational directives of Superaereo - Jan. 1942-Sept. 1943] (Roma: Ufficio storico dell'Aeronautica militare, 1992), p.966.

20   On board the MC.205RF was the German photo-planimetric, with electric control, Riehenbildner RB50/30-Zeiss FK 30 with Zeiss 1:5 f=50 lenses and 30x30cm film, installed behind the pilot's seat.

21   Cull, Malizia, Galea, *Spitfires over Sicily*, p.125.

possession, and also because in some cases they ceased firing when the recognition signal was flashed.[22]

At 6:40 a.m. on 11 July, the *Luftwaffe* sent a 2.(F)/122 Ju 88D-1 (WNr. 430220, 'F6+NK') reconnaissance aircraft from Frosinone to the beachheads off Gela. It was shot down by Spitfires from No. 242 Squadron and crashed four miles east of the town of Biscari. Another Ju 88D-1 of 2.(F)/122 (WNr. 430794, 'F6+GK') had been shot down just before, south-east of Sicily, killing the entire crew.

At 6:00 a.m., 682 Squadron's Flight Sergeant Samson flew Spitfire PR.XI (MB781) to Marsala to check the status of the Luftwaffe's RDF installations. The F-6s of the 111th TRS were also fully employed; during one of their sorties, they identified a new landing strip, west of Santa Ninfa, at A9509, hosting 20 Bf 109 fighters. Colonel Darcy of XII ASC and Major Deering followed the A-36A fighter-bombers of the 27th and 86th Fighter-Bomber Groups. Twelve aircraft from the 527th Fighter-Bomber Squadron (FBS), 86th Fighter-Bomber Group (FBG, led by Captain Cassidy, strafed a 100-truck column and claimed the destruction of at least 75 of them. During the same mission, the Lercara Friddi railway station was also attacked. Another sortie covered Satellite #14 on the Catania plain, at H6667, where 20 fighters were noted dispersed along the entire perimeter.

Early in the morning, three Spitfires of 40 Squadron SAAF flew a tactical reconnaissance between Canicattini and Noto, reporting no significant movement of troops. On the same day, another six Spitfires flew further ops, three to Catania, and one near Palazzolo Acreide, where a battalion of tanks on the move was spotted.

At 3:10 p.m., some P-38 Lightnings of the 1st FG were on a strafing mission east of the road that leads from Prizzi to Lercara Friddi when they intercepted 100 trucks, claiming the destruction of 40. At 17:10, it was the Lightnings of the 14th FG that, on a free hunting mission, intercepted and attacked a long column of about 35 vehicles on the road south-west of Palagonia; they claimed the destruction of eight trucks.

The 15th PRS sent an F-5A over the Strait of Messina but, due to mechanical problems, the Lightning was forced to return early. At 3:45 p.m., another F-5A from the same unit, flown by Lieutenant Clements, was sent to cover the airfields of western Sicily. Noteworthy discoveries from the overflight of the runway at Carcitella were the Fi 156 and 10 fighters, most of which were located in the northern section.

As the day closed, some No. 3 Wing SAAF bombers, belonging to the tactical bomber force, were preparing to carry out an armed reconnaissance over Sicily. At 9:14 p.m., five Bostons of 12 Squadron took off for their respective patrol areas: one headed for the Agrigento–Palermo route, while the other four tackled Agrigento–Canicattì–Enna. The latter identified and attacked more than 50 vehicles moving between Caltanissetta and San Cataldo. Due to the high number of enemy vehicles, Lieutenant Colonel Kotze, in command of the formation, decided to bomb a bridge near the Platani river to stop the convoy's progress. Another column of about 15 vehicles was strafed just north of Enna.

At first light on 12 July, a Spitfire of 40 Squadron SAAF took off to support the advance of the 231st Infantry Brigade 'Malta' which, together with some armoured vehicles of the 23rd

22   NARA, *Missing Air Crew Report* n. 768.

256 The Eyes of Malta

Armoured Brigade, advanced towards Vizzini. The pilot reported counterattack actions and consistent movements of enemy troops advancing south. A few hours later, the same area was subjected to a further survey which reported a significant concentration of various types of vehicles north of Vizzini, a situation confirmed three hours later by yet another survey.

Other South African pilots were engaged in the tactical reconnaissance of the Melilli, Carlentini, Lentini and Palazzolo Acreide area. During their sortie, Lieutenants K. Robinson and B. Clarence were intercepted, between Lentini and Pozzallo, by three Reggiane Re.2005s of the *362ª Squadriglia, 22° Gruppo CT* (*Caccia Terrestre* – land-based fighters) flown by Capitano Giulio Torresi, Tenente Enrico Salvi and Tenente Edoardo Vaghi. In the clash, Robinson was shot down; Torresi claimed the victory. The other South African pilot, Clarence, managed to return his damaged Spitfire safely to Malta.[23] Robinson was a popular officer, very scrupulous and an expert tactical reconnaissance pilot; his loss was felt by the whole squadron. Clarence recalled:

> At 1820 hours we were flying West at 3,500 ft in the area of Gerbini No.7 L.G. I saw 3 aircraft approaching above and behind us and I warned Lt. K. Robinson of their presence. These A/C which I later identified as Reggianes 2001's [sic] made two feint attacks on us breaking off well out of range each time and climbing back above and behind. I then saw one E/A make an astern attack on him and open fire. Lt. Robinson who was weaving very steeply made no attempt to avoid the attack. I had given him a warning of this attack. I next saw his A/C roll over on its back and go down. I was then attacked by two E/A and I was unable to watch Lt. Robinson any further. This pair made two concerted astern attacks on me during which time I fired two bursts without observed effect. At II8553 I saw a small fire on the ground which might have been a burning A/C.
>
> My aircraft was holed in the port wing root. Aircraft CAT.II.[24]

The day ended with another op over Comiso where reconstruction work on the runway by US engineering units was already evident.

On the same day, the 15th PRS sent two F-5As to Sicily early in the morning. The first, flown by Lieutenant Hoover, took off at 8:30 a.m., Lieutenant Jenkins following an hour and a half later. Both pilots performed the same mission which included Porto Empedocle and the airfields of Palermo and Catania. On the latter location, both reported the presence of 56 aircraft, distributed as follows: 42 fighters (25 more than the day before), five Ju 53/3m or SM.82 transports, and five medium-sized aircraft; all were in the northern corner of the base. Palermo was home to a few aircraft, four of which were Ju 87s believed to have arrived on 11 July. During this time 683 Squadron flew many reconnaissances over Taranto, to keep an eye on the Italian warships based there, and 682 Squadron covered southern France, Sardinia, the ports of Leghorn and Genova, and airfields in central Italy. The squadron even managed nine sorties in one day.

---

23 Robinson had already survived being attacked by a Bf 109 on 25 April over North Africa while on a sortie with Lieutenant Van Der Poel; that time he entered a dense bank of clouds that allowed him to escape. On 12 July, Robinson managed to bail out but was taken prisoner.
24 The National Archives London, Royal Air Force, Operations Record Books AIR 54/84_3, p.38.

The 111th TRS flew 24 sorties throughout the day. Some photos were taken of the Gela Ponte Olivo airfield, the next base from which the unit would operate. Meanwhile, attacks by the A-36A fighter-bombers of XII ASC continued against the port of Termini Imerese and central western Sicily where more than 150 vehicles were intercepted and attacked. Near Canicattì, Lieutenant Robert F. Hood, flying with the 526th FBS, 86th FBG, was hit by anti-aircraft fire and forced to bail out. A similar fate befell two other officers of the 525th FBS, Captain Paul A. Streigel and Lieutenant Greene. Greene's aircraft crashed a very short distance from Butera.

Meantime, Ultra intercepted a *Luftwaffe* radio message which confirmed the presence of Fw 190 aircraft of III./SKG 10 on the airfield at Enna-Süd, about nine miles from Enna, near Monte Gerace. The German communication also heralded the imminent arrival of some fuel-carrying Ju 52/3m transports from Vibo Valentia.

The strategic recce aircraft of 682 Squadron, flying from La Marsa in Tunisia, flew two sorties over Sicily. The first left at 7:00 a.m., Pilot Officer G. Woodhouse covering the towns of Caltanissetta and Catania; the second, departing at 3:50 p.m., Flying Officer Mellott flying Spitfire PR.XI (MB781), covered a wider area from Agrigento, Caltanissetta, Xirbi and Santo Stefano di Camastra to Calabria.

Recent photos taken by 682 Squadron of the western side of Etna served to complete the final stages of Operation *Chestnut*. At 7:30 p.m., two Albemarles of No. 296 Squadron, flown by Flight Lieutenant P.K. Smulian and Wing Commander P.R. May, took off to deliver 20men of the 2nd SAS Regiment north-west of Etna. After completing the op, during the return flight, May's aircraft disappeared for reasons still unknown.

The first Allied airfields in Sicily

By first light of 13 July, the Spitfires of 40 Squadron SAAF were already airborne, at the request of the Eighth Army, to assist the 23rd Armoured Brigade which was in serious difficulty in the area between Vizzini, Grammichele and Caltagirone; the same request was repeated at 10:30 a.m. with British troops spotted not far from Grammichele. Meanwhile, to give greater support to the advance of the British forces, the Kittyhawks of the Desert Air Force (DAF) converged on Luqa. Between 10:10 and 10:20 a.m., 12 Kittyhawks of No. 3 Squadron RAAF and 11 from No. 250 Squadron RAF left the warm Maltese airfield on an armed reconnaissance of San Michele di Ganzaria and Grammichele. After strafing some vehicles near Caltagirone at low altitude, Pilot Officer J. Hooke, just three miles north of Grammichele, found himself in front of a Bf 109 about to land on a dirt track in a field where, among other things, 10–15 various types of aircraft were seen. Hooke and Flight Lieutenant B.G. Harris were in a favourable position and fired machine gun bursts at the German aircraft but, a few moments later, were themselves under enemy fire. Six fighters identified as MC.202s forced them to abandon the attack and return home. The Australian unit, however, claimed the destruction and damage of several aircraft. Hooke was injured by a splinter in his left leg and forced to make an emergency landing near Rosolini in Kittyhawk II FS405. He returned to the squadron on the 17th.

At 2:00 p.m., 40 Squadron SAAF sent two Spitfires to the Caltagirone area where the advance of the 23rd Armoured Brigade was reported. Meanwhile, 43 men of the squadron, including 12 mechanics and armourers, on board 14 vehicles led by Lieutenant Forsyth, were ordered to proceed to the Maltese port of Valletta to await embarkation for Sicily; their task was to assist the squadron from the airfield at Pachino. The arrival of the squadron over the Sicilian coast coincided with a real fireworks display; in the early afternoon some German Fw 190s, and some SM.84s of the *242ª Squadriglia*, from Puglia, were in action over Augusta harbour, now teeming with Allied ships.[25]

At 2:10 p.m., 36 Kittyhawks from Major EC Saville's No. 260 Squadron RAF, Squadron Leader G.H. Norton's No. 112 Squadron RAF and Squadron Leader J.P. Bartle's No. 450 Squadron RAAF, flew to the Carlentini area escorted by Maltese Spitfires. Lentini railway station and several targets of opportunity near Catania were hit. The operation cost three pilots from 112 Squadron, including Norton himself, all victims of anti-aircraft fire. Flying Officer Hearn, declared missing at first, managed to make an emergency landing at Pachino.

At 3:30 p.m., two A-36As of the RAF's 1437 Strategic Reconnaissance Flight, just arrived in Malta from Sorman West, Libya, flew the first armed strategic reconnaissance mission to Sicily.[26] Australian Squadron Leader Sydney George Welshman (HK947/A) and Flying Officer J.L. Griffith (HK945/B) covered the bay of Giardini Naxos and Taormina, where they identified two pleasure craft and three Siebel ferries; the boats, in addition to being photographed, were strafed by the Mustangs.

The 15th PRS, with exceptional skill, managed to cover the entire island in just two missions. The towns of Cefalù, Mistretta, Petralia, Enna, Piazza Armerina, and Raddusa, up to Militello in Val di Catania, were consumed by the first mission. The second took in almost the entire south-western part of Sicily. Meanwhile, on the *Luftwaffe* landing strip at Ramacca, Satellite #12, 24 Bf 109s of IV./JG 3 arrived from Lecce, after a short technical stop at Vibo Valentia, to bolster the units already present; this was confirmed by Ultra.

Whilst the American Seventh Army reported it had captured 90 Axis aircraft at Comiso, including 24 Bf 109s, the news arrived that a new landing strip had just been identified by the A-36As of XII ASC; it was five miles north of Gangi and between 15 and 20 fighters were clearly visible. On the Enna-Süd landing strip, located near Monte Gerace at H2374, seven aircraft, most likely Fw 190s, were identified. The *Fliegerführer Sardinien* confirmed the presence of 22 Fw 190s of Schl.G.2. Among them was an Italian SM.81, flown by Maresciallo Pilota Guido La Corte, engaged to carry out evacuation flights to nearby Catania for a few days, often under attack from Spitfires as the pilot reported in his flight diary:

On the 13th together with Tenente Pilota Casarà, maintaining a flight altitude of 900 metres, we went to Fontanarossa in 45 minutes, during the flight the plane was attacked three times by Spitfires, 75 shots were fired by the on-board machine gun.

Throughout Sicily, only eight airfields used by Axis forces remained fully operational. Three of them were located in the west and hosted about 41 fighters: Palermo Boccadifalco had the largest number of aircraft, 17, followed by Carcitella with 16. The other five bases, located

---

25   War diary 40 Squadron SAAF. The National Archives London, Royal Air Force, Operations Record Books AIR 54/82/2.

26   The strategic reconnaissance unit had just re-equipped with six A-36As from No. 14 Squadron, which had been supplied by XII USAAF Air Support Command. The RAF assigned the serial numbers HK944, HK945, HK946, HK947, HK955 and HK957. The Flight had previously used Maryland Is (November 1941–April 1942) and Baltimore I/IIs (April 1942–July 1943). Cull, Malizia, Galea, *Spitfires over Sicily*, p.147.

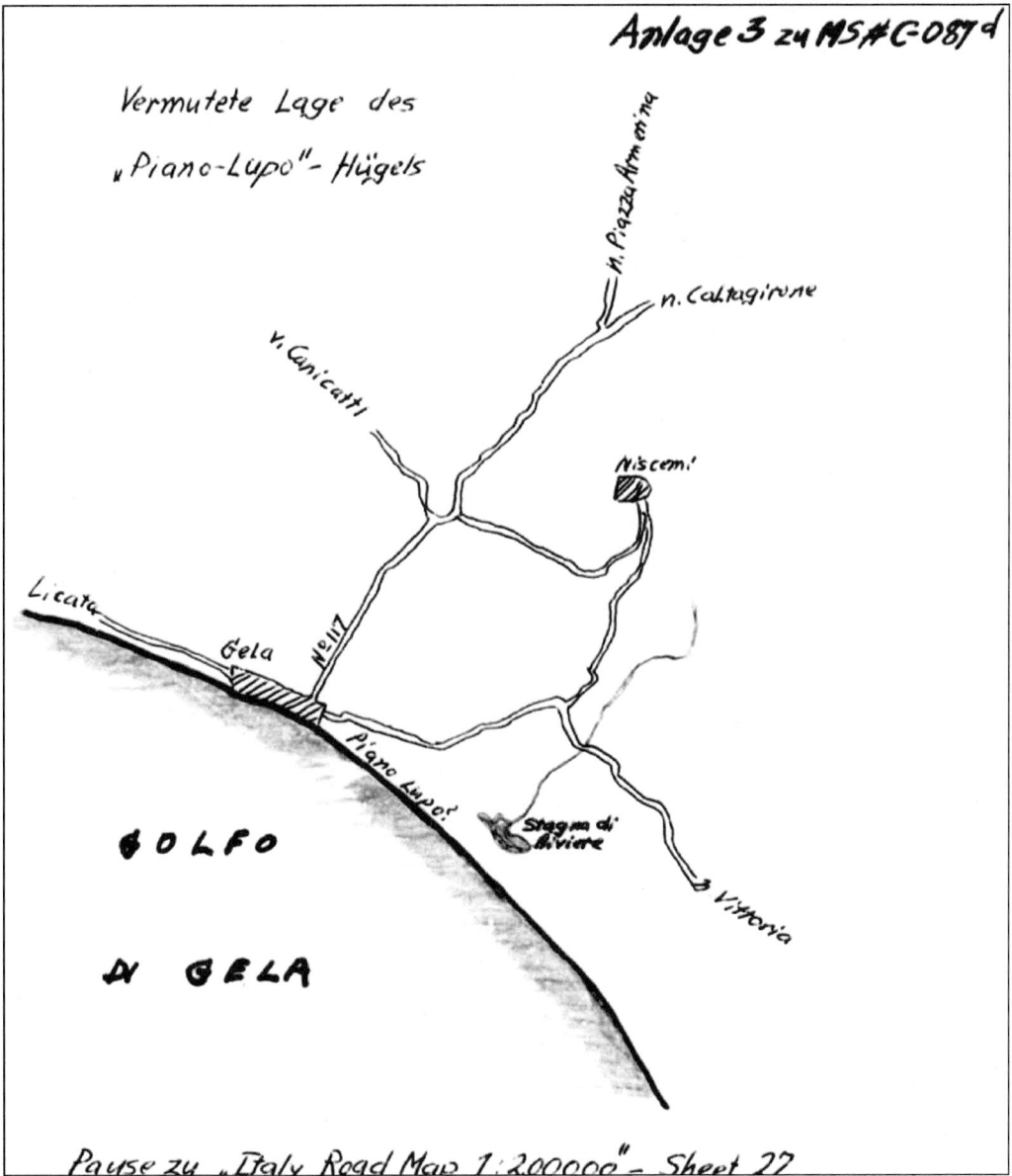

Sketch of the Gela area of the Hermann Göring Division. (NARA)

in the south-east of the island, held 83 aircraft. The main concentration was found on the slopes of the Catania plain, including Satellite #12 near Ramacca, which led the way with 36 aircraft, followed by Satellite #14 with thirty.[27] Furthermore, on the morning of 13 July, all *Luftwaffe* fighter units operating on the island received orders from *Oberbefehlshaber Süd* to transfer operational aircraft to the safest bases in southern Italy.

That evening, from Ben Hagen in Tunisia, 3 Wing SAAF sent seven Baltimores of 21 Squadron off between 21:58 and 22:50, at intervals of 5–10 minutes, arranged in two distinct formations led by Major Cormack and Lieutenant Lombaard respectively. The objectives came from recent aerial surveys and concerned the coordinates B8228, C3305 and H0677 in central Sicily. Ten troop transports were located and bombed near the city of Caltanissetta; six other trucks bound for Enna were attacked near Leonforte, and another six were located outside Leonforte at C9088. A long column of vehicles of various kinds, including trucks, cars and motorcycles, was machine-gunned in Raffadali, some of those hit quickly caught fire. The Baltimores dropped 42 × 250lb GP bombs, 150 × 4lb incendiaries and 28,000 flyers (with the inscription 'Mussolini 28 November 1940').[28]

Reconnaissance operations carried out by Malta squadrons between 9 and 17 July				
Squadron	Aircraft used	Tac/R & PR	Strategic R & PR	P/R & V/R	Total
40 SAAF	Spitfire	122			122
683	Spitfire			28 38	66
1437 Flight	Mustang	10			10
Total		132		66	198

27   AFHRA, IRISREF A6012 p.1023.
28   The National Archives London, Royal Air Force, Operations Record Books AIR 54/64.

List of places photographed

AQUINO

AUGUSTA

BAGLIO RIZZO

BARI

BARLETTA

BISCARI

BOCCA DI FALCO

BOTRICELLI

BRINDISI

CALCINETTA

CAMPO CASALE

CAPE SAN VITO

CAPODICHINO

CARCITELLA

CASTELLAMARE DI STABIA

CASTELVETRANO

CASTELBUONO

CATANIA

CENTOCELLE

CIAMPINO

CIAVOLO

CISTERNA

CIVITAVECCHIA

COMISO

CORLEONE

CROTONE

FOGGIA

FROSINONE

FURBARA

GAETA

GELA

GERBINI

GIOIA DEL COLLE

GRAZZANISE

GROTTAGLIE

GUIDONIA

LECCE

LEVERANO

LICATA

LITTORIO

MANDURIA

MANFREDONIA

MARCIGLIANA

MESSINA

MILAZZO

MILO

MONTE CORVINO

NAPLES

PACHINO

PALERMO

POMIGLIANO D'ARCO

PORTICI

POZZUOLI

PRAIA A MARE

PRATICA DI MARE

PROCIDA

RAMACCA

REGGIO DI CALABRIA

RIPOSTO

SALEMI

SALERNO

SALINA GRANDE

SAN GIOVANNI

SAN PANCRAZIO

SAN VITO DEI NORMANNI

SCIACCA

SERRA DI FALCO

STAGNONE

SYRACUSE

TAORMINA

TARANTO

TERMINI IMERESE

TORRE ANNUNZIATA

TORRE DEL GRECO

VIBO VALENTIA

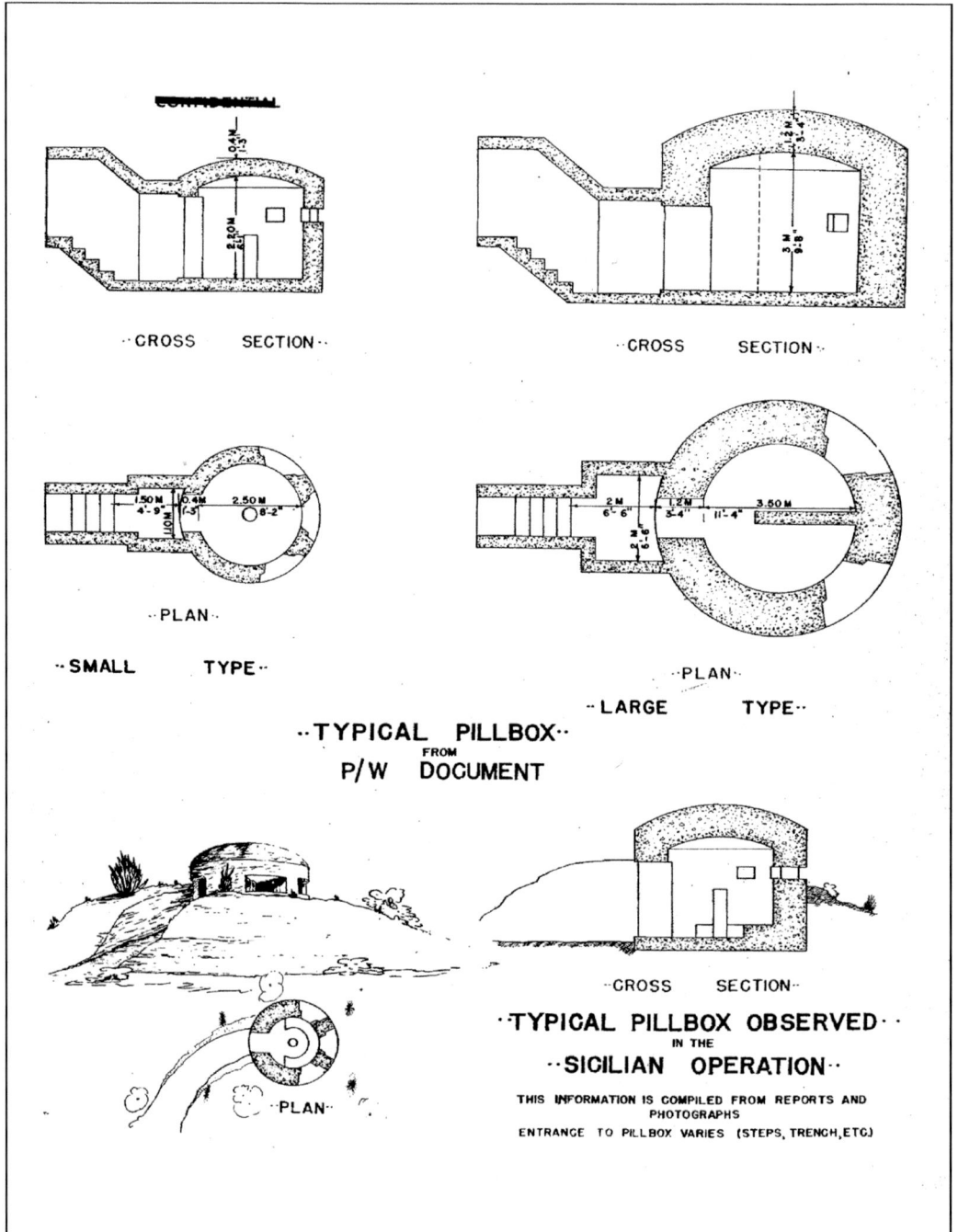

CROSS   SECTION

CROSS   SECTION

PLAN

SMALL   TYPE

PLAN

LARGE   TYPE

·TYPICAL PILLBOX·
FROM
P/W   DOCUMENT

CROSS   SECTION

·TYPICAL PILLBOX OBSERVED·
IN THE
·SICILIAN   OPERATION·

THIS INFORMATION IS COMPILED FROM REPORTS AND
PHOTOGRAPHS
ENTRANCE TO PILLBOX VARIES (STEPS, TRENCH, ETC)

PLAN

Section of a typical Italian pillbox. (NARA)

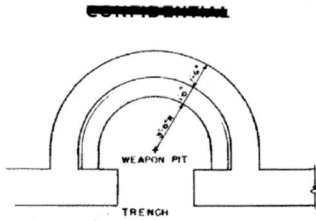

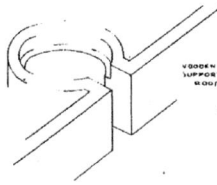

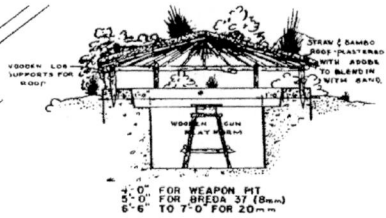

PLAN · · · OBLIQUE · CROSS · SECTION ·

··TYPICAL   DETAILS··

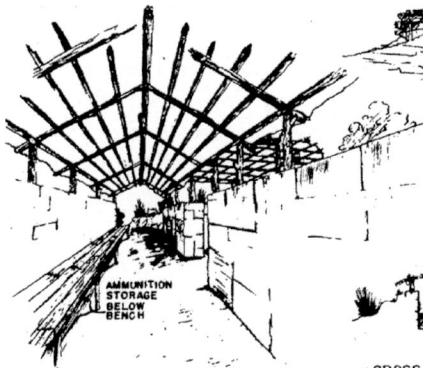

·PLAN·

··CROSS · SEC. · THRU · TRENCH · &
M.G · PIT··

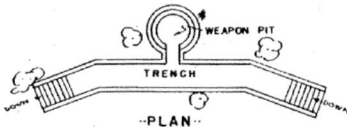

·PLAN·

· AERIAL · PERSPECTIVE··

TYPICAL POSITIONS ON HILLOCKS IN SANDY AREAS
FOR PHOTOGRAPHS SEE PAGE 18

TRENCH COMPLETELY COVERED WHEN
NOT IN USE

TYPICAL POSITIONS IN FLAT COASTAL HEADLANDS

··S I C I L I A N···
··B E A C H   D E F E N S E··

MACHINE GUN EMPLACEMENTS

Camouflage measures employed to hide trench complexes. (NARA)

Operation *Fustian*

The British 1st Airborne Division, still in reserve at its base outside Kairouan, Tunisia, was warned an airborne assault to take the Primosole bridge, just south of Catania, was scheduled for the night of 13/14 July. The 1,856 paratroopers, nicknamed 'Red Devils', of the British 1st Airborne Division were flown to Catania by 135 aircraft, including 105 C-47 Dakotas, seven Halifaxes and 23 Albemarles, 19 of which towed big Horsa gliders. Tragically, due to unexpected friendly fire, 10 Dakotas, three Albemarles and a Halifax were tragically shot down.[29]

Lieutenant Robert Cristina, an American officer who was shot down in a C-47, issued the following testimony a few months later:

> At approximately 12 miles southwest of Catania, our plane caught on fire as the result of anti-aircraft fire. I jumped from the plane but did not see any other chutes after jumping. I landed about 50 feet from the plane and hid in a hay stack and watched it burn while German soldiers patrolled the area. After about an hour, I decided it was safe [to] proceed to escape. I ran into the crew chief of my ship, S/Sgt. Robert W. Wellingham, who was crawling on the ground nearby. We did not find anyone else around the ship and the ship was in flame so we decided to get out of the area before the Germans came back.[30]

The news of the landings in Sicily had already reached Berlin. *XI Fliegerkorps*, the most powerful mobile reserve of the *Oberkommando der Wehrmacht*, consisting of 30,000 well-trained paratroopers, was alerted immediately. The Germans sent the 3rd Regiment *Fallschirmjäger*, nicknamed 'Green Devils', to the Primosole bridge area. At 6:15 p.m., the first deployment of the paratroopers took place; 1,400 FJR3 men set foot on pre-established areas in the Catania area.

On 14 July, the rapid advance of Allied ground troops allowed the occupation of six airfields which were quickly put in a position to operate. A week after the landings, 18 and a half units, seven and a half of which belonged to the USAAF, were operating from Pachino, Comiso, Biscari Santo Pietro, Gela Ponte Olivo, Gela Farello and Licata. By 18 July, another six USAAF units would take up positions on the island.

On the same day, B Company of the American 809th Engineer Aviation Battalion set to work to restore the runway at Gela Ponte Olivo so it could host the 111th TRS. Meanwhile, on the other side of the Mediterranean, Lieutenants Modrall and Bruce's F-6s took off at 6:30 a.m. from Korba, carrying out the squadron's 100th sortie with coverage of the coastal area around Licata. After the mission, they landed at Gela Ponte Olivo, waiting for the arrival of the Air Echelon, expected that day in seven C-47 Dakotas. Twenty-four sorties were completed by the end of the day. On one of them, Lieutenant Deemer reported having strafed some Italian vehicles. The unit's first night at Gela Ponte Olivo was unforgettable; the squadron had not had

29   AFHRA, Troop Carrier-General Route, p.21.
30   NARA, Missing Air Crew Report n. 1238.

the time to set up tents and the airfield was heavily bombed by the *Luftwaffe*. Luckily, the only effect was a bit of a fright.[31]

On the morning of the 14th, Eighth Army troops came into contact with some enemy rearguards in the area between Chiaramonte Gulfi and Monterosso Almo. Meanwhile, the Seventh Army had already conquered Mazzarino and Canicattì, and DAF Kittyhawks had performed armed reconnaissances over almost all of eastern Sicily. Between 11:30 and 11:45 a.m., two formations of 12 Kittyhawk IIIs each, from 3 Squadron RAAF and 250 Squadron RAF, flew an armed reconnaissance over the area between Ragusa and Caltagirone. The Kittyhawks were led by Squadron Leader Barry of 3 Squadron. They tracked along the coast near Punta Secca, then veered towards Ragusa, intercepting the first useful targets five miles south of Caltagirone. These were about 30 trucks spread out over three miles. From 10:30 a.m. to 12:05 p.m. on the same day, more than 230 bombers, including B-17 Flying Fortresses, B-25 Mitchells, B-26 Marauders and B-24 Liberators, launched one of the heaviest raids on the city of Messina.

The afternoon, 40 Squadron SAAF Spitfires performed various tactical and photographic sorties. A very delicate task involved four Tac/R aircraft with the aim of carrying out two objectives over the enemy front, the first at an altitude of 3,000 feet, and the second, more insidious, at only 800 feet. During one mission over Lentini–Scordia area, four Bf 110s attacked the aircraft flown by Lieutenants Clarence and Kruger; the 'WR' squadron codes on the fuselages of both Spitfires were literally riddled by the German gunfire. Both pilots managed to return to base. The injuries sustained by Kruger were not serious – he claimed he did not notice the Bf 110 until he was attacked; Clarence was also wounded, but to a lesser extent. At 6:50 p.m., Leutnant Gottfried Kayl of 5./ZG 1, flying a Bf 110, claimed the shooting down of a Spitfire just three miles south-east of Lentini.

Lieutenant Clarence recalled:

> At 1830 hours we were flying East in the Lentini area at 6,000 ft. I saw 4 ME.110's [sic] flying directly out of the sun at 8,000 ft into an astern attack on us. I warned Lt. Kruger and we turned about into the attack as they opened fire at about a 100 yds. range. I got in one burst but without observed result. Two of them then made single head-on attacks on us while the other pair circled above. I fired two bursts in this attack without observed effect. The E/A then broke off and returned to base.

Lieutenant Kruger also observed:

> I got in one burst during the combat described by Lieutenant Clarence but without observed effect. My aircraft was hit in the tail unit and mainplane. Aircraft CAT.I.[32]

---

31   On the night of 15/16 July, and on two other occasions between 16 and 24 July, the airfield was subjected to heavy raids. On the first occasion, the 809th Engineer Aviation Battalion lost one man killed and five seriously injured.

32   Sortie report 40 Squadron SAAF. The National Archives London, Royal Air Force, Operations Record Books AIR 54/84/3, p.51.

The Eighth Army expressed satisfaction with the work carried out by the reconnaissance pilots; in particular, one case in which a Tac/R reconnaissance officer reported, at 2:15 p.m., that he saw more than 150 vehicles of various kinds arriving, most likely German, of the *Kampfgruppe Schmalz*, from the east in the direction of Lentini. German troops had in fact received orders to fall back to Motta Sant'Anastasia. Lieutenant Colonel Blaauw, CO of 40 Squadron SAAF, commented on the incessant demands of the Eighth Army:

> The AA, MG and anti-tank stations are quite camouflaged, so as not to be easily identified by the Tac/R. Despite this, the Army persists in this type of request.[33]

XII ASC sent the A-36A fighter-bombers of the 27th and 86th Fighter-Bomber Groups to the communication lines and sensitive areas of the front line of the Seventh Army. To the north of Corleone, an ammunition depot was hit and exploded; the railway stations of Misilmeri, Vallelunga, Villarosa, Caltanissetta, Enna and Lercara Friddi were also attacked. Twenty-seven railway wagons and three locomotives were destroyed. More than 125 vehicles were intercepted at road intersections near these centres, 20destroyed and 10 damaged.

On the night of 14/15 July, the NAPRW performed the first night photographic mission over Sicily. The 15th PRS cooperated with RAF staff who had been using 6-inch cameras for some time on board night bombers. On this occasion, a B-25 Mitchell equipped with super-sensitive K-19A night cameras, and 57lb M-46 flash bombs, was used. The complex system of night aerial photographic reconnaissance involved the launch of flash bombs from a height of 12,500 feet, using an M-III device for the detonation delay of 32.9 seconds, which allows the photographic equipment to trigger at the moment of the explosion. The targets mainly consisted of roads, cities, railway stations and ports. The procedure adopted was as follows: alignment with the target began from a mile away; the bombs were then dropped at twenty-second intervals so as to explode at about 3,000 feet, illuminating the target. The crew involved consisted of a pilot, co-pilot, navigator, radio operator, photographer and two gunners. The 3rd PG did not just use the F-4 and F-5A Lightning for photo-reconnaissance; at the time it also had four Mitchells and four B-17 Flying Fortress (F-10 and F-9 photographic reconnaissance versions respectively) on hand.

Lieutenant General Carl Spaatz sent a message of praise on 15 July to the NAPRW commanding officer for the night mission just completed:

> In order to meet emergency requirements, you were directed to organize and operate night photographic facilities for the Sicilian battle. In spite of the short time available, necessary training and organization was accomplished and you are now successfully operating over hostile territory at night.
>
> I feel that this accomplishment is typical of the spirit and skill of the Northwest African Photo-Reconnaissance Wing. It adds to your fine record of achievement.

---

33   War diary 40 Squadron SAAF. The National Archives London, Royal Air Force, Operations Record Books AIR 54/82/2.

I wish to commend you and the officers of your organization on the superior performance of the difficult tasks assigned to you in connection with the operation "HUSKY".[34]

In the late evening of 14 July, from Grombalia in Tunisia, No. 326 Wing RAF sent nine Bostons of 18 Squadron and eight from 114 Squadron on an armed reconnaissance which headed to Enna, Villarosa, Adrano, Nicosia and Regalbuto. Between Villarosa and Enna, the Boston piloted by Flying Officer Edwards of 18 Squadron, attacked, at about 11:05 p.m., 200 vehicles transporting troops; once the bombs were dropped, he descended to 50 feet, firing 1,100 machine gun rounds. Another aircraft from the same unit, 'A' (Z2208) flown by Flying Officer Savage, was engaged in an armed reconnaissance between Agrigento and Alessandria della Rocca. Along the road that connects the small towns of Cianciana and San Biagio Platani, a temporary camp, within a wooded area near coordinates 37° 30' N, 13° 27' E, was identified and bombed. Five other Bostons patrolled the area between Nicosia–Adrano–Enna and then strafed and bombed the Bronte–Biancavilla railway line and another five miles south of Assoro. At the same time, Flying Officer Hanbury's 'X' (233227) of 18 Squadron, intercepted 20 vehicles two miles north-east of Nicosia, bombing them before dropping to 50 feet to machine-gun them, destroying two vehicles with 850 rounds. Other attacks on heavy vehicles were carried out near Troina and Randazzo by 114 Squadron; even a bridge, at 37° 41' N, 13° 22' E, just outside the town of Palazzo Adriano, was hit and blown up to prevent its use. That same night, seven Halifax heavy bombers from No. 462 Squadron RAAF, carrying ten 500lb GP bombs each, between 8:00 p.m. and 3:00 a.m., hit Messina's city centre, port, railway station and some peripheral wards. Halifax II W7758, piloted by the unit's CO, Wing Commander P.G.B. Warner, was seen for the last time falling into the sea about 10 miles from Capo Spartivento.

On 15 July, compared to previous days, fewer reconnaissance requests arrived from the Fifteenth Army Group. Only five 40 Squadron Spitfires carried out reconnaissance duties during the day. Among the pilots of the South African unit flying that day, Lieutenant Van Der Poel, despite his poor knowledge of Sicily, managed to identify 50 vehicles moving north-west of Ramacca, and another 75 south of Militello in Val di Catania.[35] Shortly after communicating these sightings by radio, another squadron Spitfire was sent to the same locations; other movements were observed and photographed west of the town of Valguarnera. Pilot Officer Keith Durbidge departed Luqa, flying 683 Squadron Spitfire PR.XI (MB778), for Leonforte and Piazza Armerina, flying over several times between 12,000 and 25,000 feet. Durbidge reported a vast fire clearly visible north-east of Leonforte; taking the photos, he returned to Malta at 12:40 p.m. The squadron carried out seven sorties during the day, mostly over southern Italy.

The same day, Colonel von Bonin was appointed Chief of General Staff of the XIV Panzer Corps and was interviewed by the then Chief of the Armed Forces Operations Staff, Generaloberst Jodl. The latter gave an appreciation of the situation in Italy and the following orders for General Hube, the commander of the XIV Panzer Corps:

---

34   AFHRA, IRISREF B0747, p.424.
35   Lieutenant Van Der Poel of 40 Squadron SAAF was the first of the unit's pilots to set foot in Sicily, at Pachino, on 12 July.

In view of the great numerical superiority of the Anglo-American forces, and especially in view of the great difficulties of supplying even the relatively small German Force on Sicily (chief causes of difficulty being the small capacity and the vulnerability of railroads in southern Italy, the insecurity of sea transport, and the possibility of a blockade of the Strait of Messina), it is not to be contemplated that we can continue to hold the island. It is, however, important to fight a delaying action and gain further time for stabilising the situation on the mainland. The vital factor, however, is under no circumstances to suffer the loss of our three German divisions. At the very minimum, our valuable human material must be saved.[36]

Around midday, 11 Kittyhawk IIIs of 3 Squadron RAAF, led by Squadron Leader R. Stevens, and 12 from 450 Squadron RAAF, Squadron Leader J. Bartle leading, also flew from Luqa. They patrolled between the towns of Ramacca and Piazza Armerina, where they intercepted and strafed a long column of about 200 vehicles, before flying over the airfield at Gerbini where no aircraft were seen. Near Raddusa, the Kittyhawk (FL258) flown by Flight Sergeant A.H. Collier was hit by a fighter identified as a Macchi. Collier bailed out, evaded capture and returned to the squadron a few days later.

Meanwhile, the 111th TRS Mustangs of Lieutenants Bush and Tolbert were providing air cover for some American vessels off the coast of Gela when they shot down what they identified as a Henschel Hs 129,[37] a twin-engine ground attack machine. This first victory for the squadron in the skies of Sicily was somewhat hollow, however, as the unit lost its first pilot, Lieutenant Peck, on the same day.[38] He was on a reconnaissance mission at low altitude near Agrigento, flying a Bell P-39 Airacobra, when he suddenly disappeared.[39]

While the American B-25 Mitchells of the 340th BG were busy carrying out yet another raid on the now battered city of Paternò, 95 A-36A Mustangs of the 27th and 86th Fighter-Bomber Groups flew armed reconnaissances attacking trains, railway stations, road junctions, bridges and military installations. A bridge was bombed in Alia, and at Nicosia, near Petralia, a roadblock. Near Lercara Friddi, about 20buildings, together with three rail cars, were attacked; in addition, strikes were made against seven railway wagons at Palazzo Adriano, a substantial number of vehicles near Marineo, 14 railway wagons at Santo Stefano di Camastra, an ammunition depot at coordinates B3530 west of San Giuseppe Jato, and one in Corleone, and the Termini Imerese railway station.

At 4:00 p.m., at coordinates H9467 on the Catania plain, the Eighth Army crossed the Gornalunga river and, in the meantime, on the other side of the advance, the Seventh Army had already taken 16,000 prisoners and moved forward towards Barrafranca, Pietraperzia, Racalmuto, Aragona and Raffadali.

---

36   AFHRA, Reel 23364, p.686.
37   Some of the aircraft of 8./Pz.Schl.G.2 passed through Sardinia towards the end of May. There is no other operational information regarding these aircraft in Sicily. It is very likely the American pilots mistook an Hs 129 for a Bf 110.
38   On 24 July, the squadron received a call saying Lieutenant Peck and his aircraft had been found near Raffadali. Peck was buried at the American military cemetery in Licata of the 20th of month. The previous 12 July, running out of fuel over Sicily, instead of landing at Pantelleria, he headed for Malta. The squadron, believing he was missing, was surprised to see him land at Tripoli a few days later.
39   AFHRA, IRISREF A0916, p.1493.

On the night of 15/16 July, between 10:10 p.m. and 5:04 a.m., 24 Baltimores of No. 232 Wing RAF conducted armed reconnaissances over some crucial road junctions near Alcamo, Termini Imerese and Agrigento. At the gates of Santa Ninfa, they intercepted and attacked a long column of about 200 vehicles of various kinds. Also, 3 Wing SAAF sent out 24 aircraft to patrol the roads of Termini Imerese, Enna and Caltanissetta, carrying 92 × 250lb bombs and 690 × 4lb incendiaries between them. Between Santa Caterina Villarmosa and Xirbi, they identified and attacked about 200 vehicles. From 10:50 p.m. to 4:24 a.m., 10 Bostons of No. 326 Wing RAF attacked the Nicosia–Paternò–Leonforte line. The Adrano railway station and a bridge in Randazzo were also bombed. A good target, 400 vehicles heading south, was identified between Bivona and Ribera. In the 24 hours of 15 July, more than 880 vehicles were identified and attacked by aircraft flying armed reconnaissance sorties.[40]

The same night Feldmarschall Kesselring flew to Milazzo in northern Sicily in a flying boat. He visited the front-line commander:

> [I] gave General Hube, the commander of XIV Panzer Korps, detailed instructions on the spot. His mission was to dig in on a solid line even at the cost of initially giving ground. In defiance of the axioms of the Luftwaffe hierarchy I placed the heavy flak under Hube's command. Hube could hardly count on any air support in the daytime, so to compensate I was anxious to leave no stone unturned to accelerate the arrival of the 29th Panzer Grenadiers. I also told him that I was reckoning with the evacuation of Sicily, which it was his job to postpone as long as possible. The defence preparations on both side of the Straits of Messina were proceeding apace and were now under his direction. The next day was again devoted to visiting the front and to a conference with [Generale d'Armata Alfredo] Guzzoni [commander of the Italian Sixth Army] – I left him with a feeling that our changes of holding the British Eighth Army were not entirely hopeless. On the whole I was satisfied. Hube was the right man place …[41]

Since dawn on 16 July, the island had been subjected to intense bombing raids. Forty-one Mitchells of the 12th BG and 18 of the 340th BG were sent, just before 4:00 a.m. in the morning, to bomb Randazzo and surrounding roads. The incursion cost the 340th BG the B-25 (serial 42-53376) flown by Lieutenant Bernard Corbin of the 488th BS.

At 5:35 a.m., 683 Squadron Flying Officer E.C. Hey and Spitfire PR.XI (MB785) took off for Taranto; on the return leg, Hey flew over the ports of Milazzo and Messina, photographing a hospital ship and a ship of about 4,000 tons, as well as other smaller vessels. The sortie also covered Riposto where six small vessels were stationed. At 6:20, another Spitfire (PR.XI MB778) was sent to survey the airfields at Catania Fontanarossa and Gerbini, including satellites, from an altitude of 25,000 feet. Flight Sergeant W.S. Lewis photographed and observed fires on every runway, many of which were burning aircraft. By request, of the Eighth Army, at 10:10 the squadron flew a third sortie over Sicily; Sergeant F. Simpson and PR.XI (MB772) did the honours. At 1:10 p.m., a mapping sortie was carried out around Mount Etna, a task this time entrusted to the expert Keith Durbidge.

40   AFHRA, IRISREF A6011, p.278.
41   see *The Memoirs of Field-Marshal Kesselring* in Brian Cull, Nicola Malizia, Frederick Galea, *Spitfires over Sicily*, p.164.

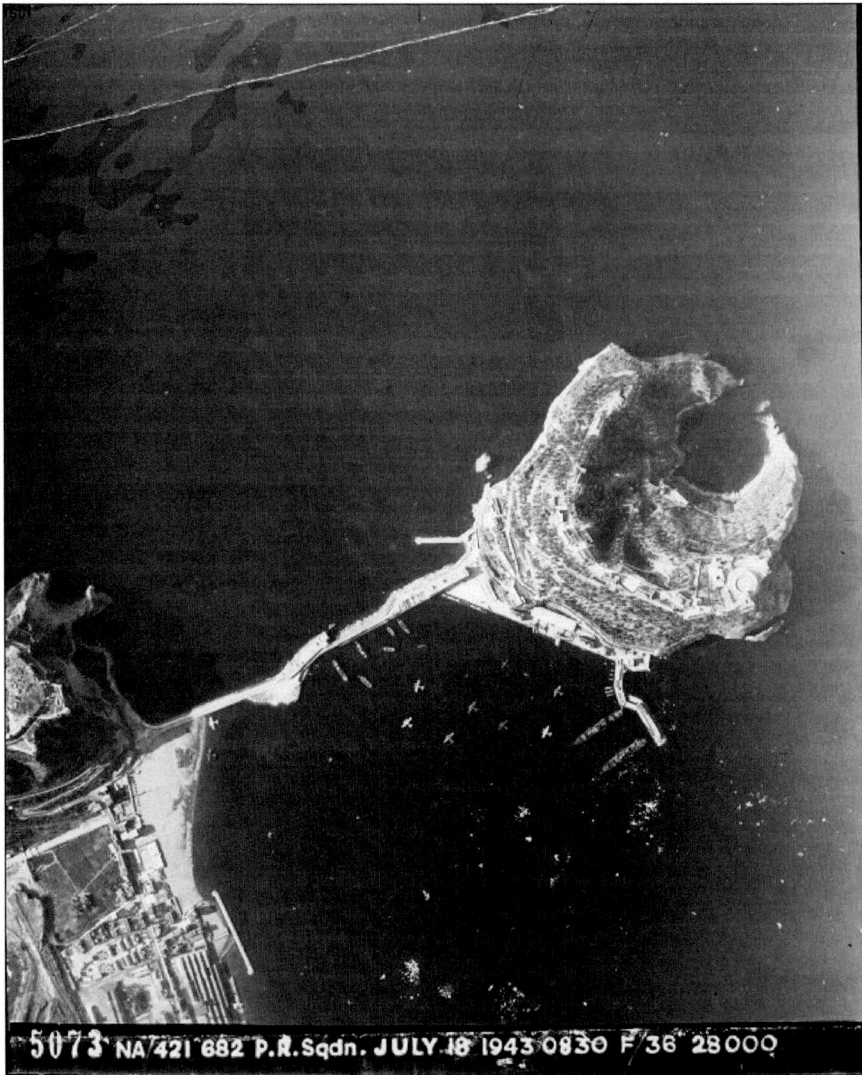

The seaplane base of Nisida in a photo taken by No. 682 Squadron RAF. (US Air Force)

At 8:45 a.m., the DAF Kittyhawks were already flying a low altitude armed reconnaissance in the area of Sferro, Catenanuova and Paternò. The Kittyhawk IIIs of 3 Squadron RAAF, and those of 260 Squadron RAF, bombed part of the railway line near the Sferro station; a little further east, 50 troop transports, heading north along the road north-west of Paternò, and well spread out with 100 metres between them, were intercepted and strafed. This supported the news that German troops of the Hermann Göring Division, and Italian troops of the Livorno Division, were retreating towards Enna. The latter division, from 15 to 19 July, set up several rearguard positions to slow the Allied advance in the vast area between the Gigliotto crossroads, Piazza Armerina, Valguarnera, Enna, Libertinia, Raddusa and Agira.

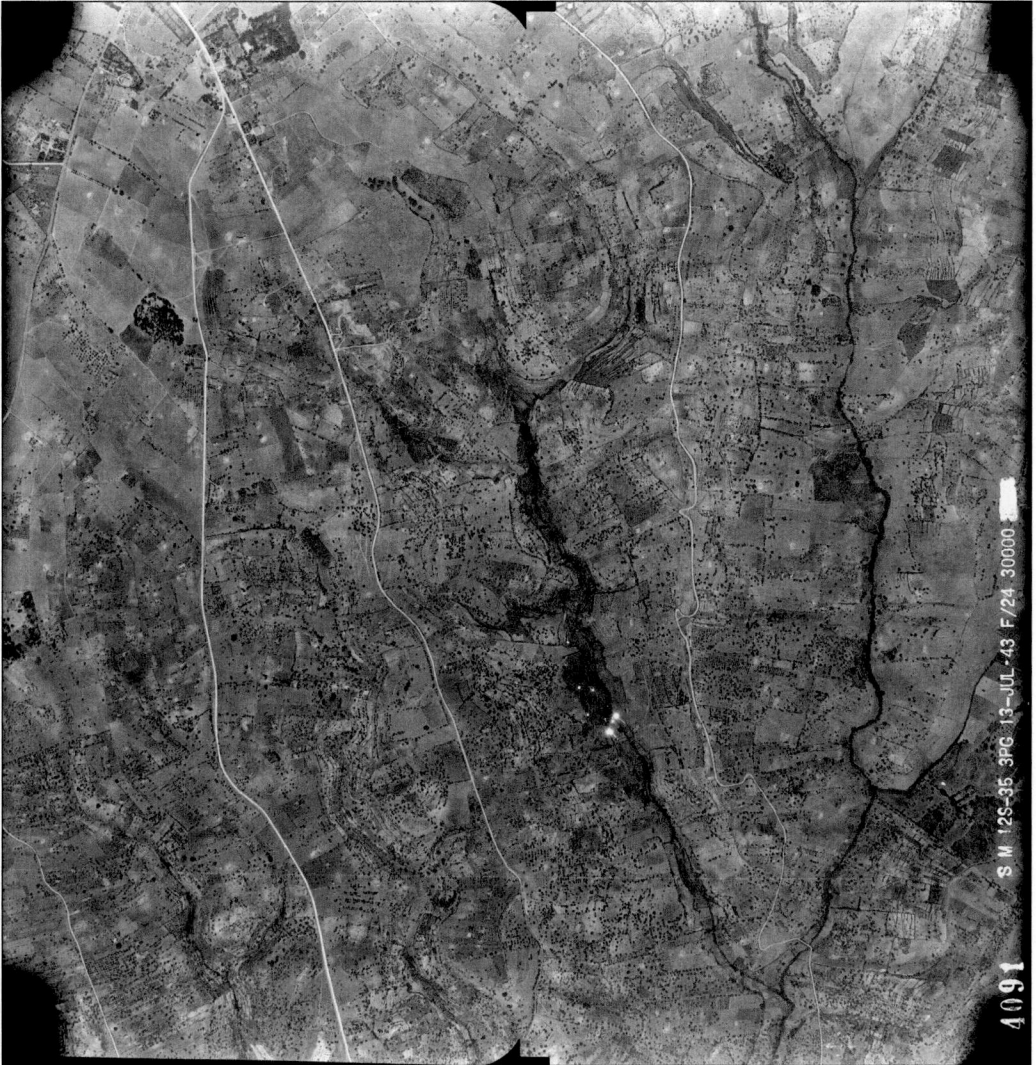

A frame taken by a 12th PRS F-5A of the area between Caltagirone and Biscari Santo Pietro on 13 July 1943. In this photo, the men of the intelligence section observed the beginning of the Axis retreat. (US Air Force)

On the British front, five Spitfires from 40 Squadron SAAF took part in the daily taskings. The area of interest remained that of Valguarnera, where, at coordinates H3478, just outside this small town in the Enna area, a high concentration of enemy troops had previously been reported. The 340th BG sent 24 Mitchells to bomb the town but, due to an unexpected worsening of the weather, only 12 found, at 12:53 p.m., a small break in the clouds which allowed them to drop their bombs. On the same mission, the nearby town of Aidone was also bombed shortly after. The entire raid was documented by 20 vertical and four oblique photos.

A photo from a sortie carried out over Agira on 19 July 1943 by Sergeant F. Simpson, No. 683 Squadron, on behalf of the Army. (LAC photo RG24, R112, 1984-265 NPC)

At the same time, the P-38 Lightnings of the 1st FG flew a strike over the central and north-eastern area of Sicily. A building was hit by a 1,000lb bomb near Bronte, and moving targets were strafed at Leonforte. At 6:00 p.m, the 111th TRS sent six F-6 Mustangs on two separate missions of three aircraft each; they performed a strategic reconnaissance of roads in, around and to Agrigento, Lercara Friddi and Corleone. On their return, the films were delivered to a Captain Zimmerman for careful analysis. Zimmerman was the liaison officer between the squadron and XII ASC; he was already in Sicily and worked closely with the men of the 111th TRS, who called him an ace of photointerpretation. During the night, personnel of the 111th TRS suffered a heavy bombing raid by the *Luftwaffe*. The German bombers damaged the Gela Ponte Olivo runway, rendering it partially unserviceable. That night, a Vickers Wellington of No. 458 Squadron RAAF, under the command of Sergeant Durmore, flew an armed reconnaissance over the Tyrrhenian Sea, attacking a radar installation on the island of Ustica with six 250 pdrs.

At dawn on the 17th, the Spitfires of 40 Squadron SAAF flew a tactical reconnaissance along the Catania–Paternò route. Near Libertinia, a small hamlet in the municipality of Ramacca, about six miles west of Catenanuova, the presence of two German Panzer III tanks was reported. That same day, Colonel von Bonin reported to General Hube at his tactical headquarters which were situated on the north slopes of Mount Etna, between Randazzo and Linguaglossa.

The Americans liberated Agrigento and Porto Empedocle; north of Barrafranca, at the same time, 16 Sherman tanks were engaged in a strong and massive counterattack, during which they lost two of their number in action. The 111th TRS, amid a thousand difficulties, managed to fly nine reconnaissance sorties. The first Mustangs, from 6:15 a.m., flew from Gela Ponte Olivo to Caltanissetta, Agira and an area 10 miles north-west of San Mauro Castelverde. At 3:35 p.m., the same F-6s were asked to observe a road intersection connecting Caltanissetta, Enna and Leonforte. Meanwhile, the Eighth Army requested the support of 683 Squadron. At 9:00 a.m., Flight Sergeant Lewis, in Spitfire PR.XI (EN420), photographed communication routes on the slopes of Etna.

The XII ASC committed A-36A fighter-bombers of the 523rd FBS, 27th FBG to an armed reconnaissance over south-western Sicily. At 5:50 p.m., the aircraft, from Korba, Tunisia, were already near Palermo when they were targeted by two enemy anti-aircraft batteries. Captain Eric J. Hollfelder, flying A-36A Apache 42-84023, lost his life. His wingman, 2nd Lieutenant John A. Wright recalled:

> I was flying number two position in Captain Eric J. Hollfelder's flight on July 17th, 1943. We were straffing [sic] on the Northern coast of Sicily between Palermo and Cape Zaffarano when we were fired upon by two batteries of guns from shore position. The Captain was hit by the first burst and began to stream glycol. He attempted to pull up and out to sea but the plane began to disintegrate and started to flame from the tail. He gained an altitude of approximately 100 feet, then pitched straight down into the water. No attempt was made to leave the plane as the canopy was not jettisoned. The remainder of the flight circled partially over the area, then left as we were still under fire.[42]

42   NARA, Missing Air Crew Report n. 419.

On 18 July, 27th and 86th FBG fighter-bombers completed 13 missions of four aircraft each. The area covered by the armed reconnaissance sorties was again between Capo Bianco and Palermo, and the road just east of Nicosia. Eighty vehicles were attacked, as were seven railway stations with trains and wagons nearby; all were successfully hit. At 3:00 in the afternoon, with information from Allied Intelligence, three flights of A-36A Mustangs (12 aircraft) of the 86th FBG took off from Biskra, Tunisia, to bomb sensitive targets located on the western slopes of Mount Etna. After delivering their 500lb bombs, and while strafing a target just 20miles west of Adrano, they were targeted by light anti-aircraft artillery. Lieutenant John P. Torland (A-36A 42-83826) was shot down; he managed to bail out but was captured by German troops. Lieutenant Michael P. Yannell witnessed Torland go down:

> After completing the above mission Red flight flew top cover and White flight was strafing [sic] the highway leading west from Adrano. Slight heavy flak was encountered at Regalbuto. At Agira there was heavy light flak and machine gun fire apparently coming from the town which is above the highway at that point. Lt. Torland was in the strafing [sic] element and was closest to the town. His ship was smoking when he bailed out. Just a second or two later it crashed and exploded against the hill, below, and on the north side of Agira. Lt. Torland came down just about halfway down the hillside. I made a circle but did not see him after he landed, through his chute was plainly visible in a small clearing. We kept our distance while making the circle and may have been too far to see him. ... No flak was fired at us as we made the circle.[43]

In the afternoon, 24 Mitchells of the 340th BG dropped 304 × 250lb GP bombs on the railway station and some streets of Paternò, but many of the bombers were hit by anti-aircraft fire. One B-25 (serial 42-32353) was seen to crash.

The advance of the Eighth Army led by Montgomery suddenly stopped near the Primosole bridge, on the Simeto river, about six miles south of Catania, which had unexpectedly become the nerve centre of the Sicilian countryside. Other than a few small exceptions, the Eighth Army, for the entire month of July, did not manage to get much closer to Catania. The battle for the Catania plain was one of the fiercest battles involving British troops during the war. A captain of the British Royal Artillery wrote sometime later:

> The fight there was the most ferocious I remember in the course of the whole war and I can still remember the stench of rotting flesh on the banks of that river.

As 1st Canadian Division conquered the streets of Piazza Armerina, on 18 July B Flight of 40 Squadron SAAF, still on Malta, moved to the new Pachino-Sud landing strip. Five Spitfires flew Tac/R sorties that day. The squadron was now completely available to the Eighth Army, which immediately began coordinating requests for coverage. The most important intelligence received was that some elements of the dreaded Hermann Göring Division had been located on Monte Judica, near the town of Castel di Judica; at the point the Germans called Punkt 764 (Point 764). Other elements of the same unit were converging on locations they identified as

---

43   NARA, Missing Air Crew Report n. 376.

Roma Termini railway station in a photo taken by the 5th PS, 3rd PG. (US Air Force)

Massa-Misterbianca/Punkt 508–609, near Misterbianco. The presence of German units was also noted a mile north of Belpasso and about two miles south of Centuripe.

At 12:05 p.m., 24 Mitchells of the 340th BG departed Hergla in Tunisia to attack various objectives of tactical importance near Randazzo. Shortly before, in fact, the Spitfires of 40 Squadron SAAF had identified some important targets, including road tunnels near Nicosia and a bridge connecting Randazzo to Floresta. During the American bombing, the absence of anti-aircraft fire was odd and recorded as such.

On the same day, Flight Sergeant C.A. Tardif failed to return from a mission over Foggia aerodrome. His friend Keith Durbidge remembers Tardif thus:

> One incident which I remember [...] concerned a good friend of mine, another P.R. Spitfire pilot named Mickey [sic] Tardif. He was detailed to fly [...] his engine coolant system developed a leak. He knew this meant trouble and he bailed out of the aircraft when the engine eventually seized-up. He evaded capture for a short time but was

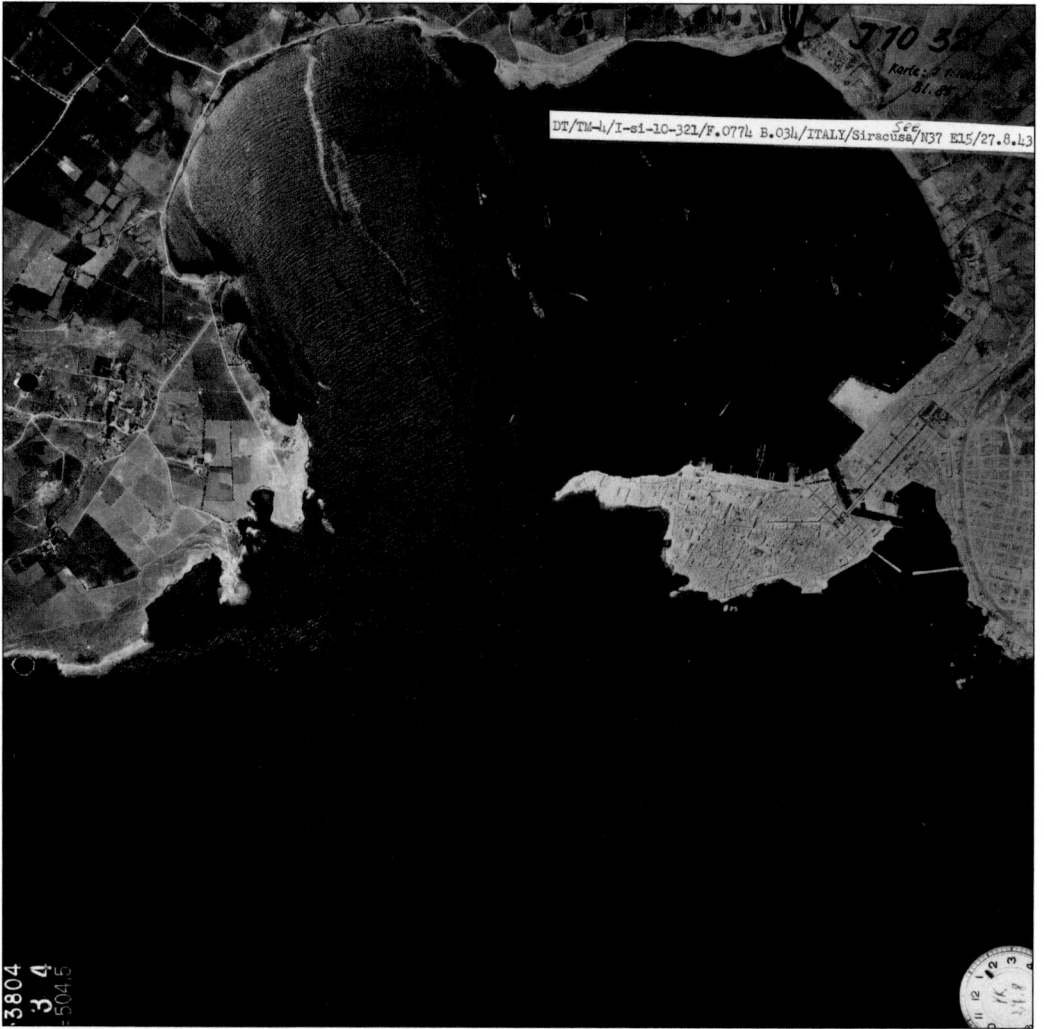

A photo taken over Syracuse by a German reconnaissance Junkers Ju 88 belonging to 1.(F)/123. The photo shows Allied ships entering the Arethusean port. (NARA)

eventually caught and was held in Taranto jail with some other prisoners of war. Sometime later they were all put on board a train for Germany. He managed to escape about half way up the western coast of Italy and spent many months with the Italian Partisans in the hills attacking enemy road convoys until the Allied forces reached his area and ferried him back to the U.K. He was awarded the M.M. (Military Medal) for his exploits, a rare decoration for a member of the Royal Air Force.[44]

44   Letter written by Keith Durbidge to Dr. Giulio Grilletta, dated 20 July 2000.

On the night of 18/19 July, Catania was bombed again, 32 tons of bombs delivered by 29 Mitchells of the 12th BG and two Bostons of 326 Wing RAF. The South Africans of 3 Wing, with four Baltimores and 20 Bostons, together with more Bostons of 326 Wing, flew armed reconnaissances over the area of Nicosia and Capo d'Orlando. During the night, five bombers reported they were intercepted and threatened by an enemy aircraft, probably German. In the meantime, Patton's army, after having entered Caltanissetta, advanced quickly to Palermo. Air coverage was ensured by the P-40 Warhawks of the 325th FG which, on 19 July, dispatched 44 aircraft, 29 armed with bombs, to the Partinico and Alcamo railway stations. During the mission, some artillery positions near Castellammare del Golfo, and the Marsala-Stagnone radar station, were strafed. Meanwhile, 24 Mitchells of the 340th BG bombed Randazzo again.

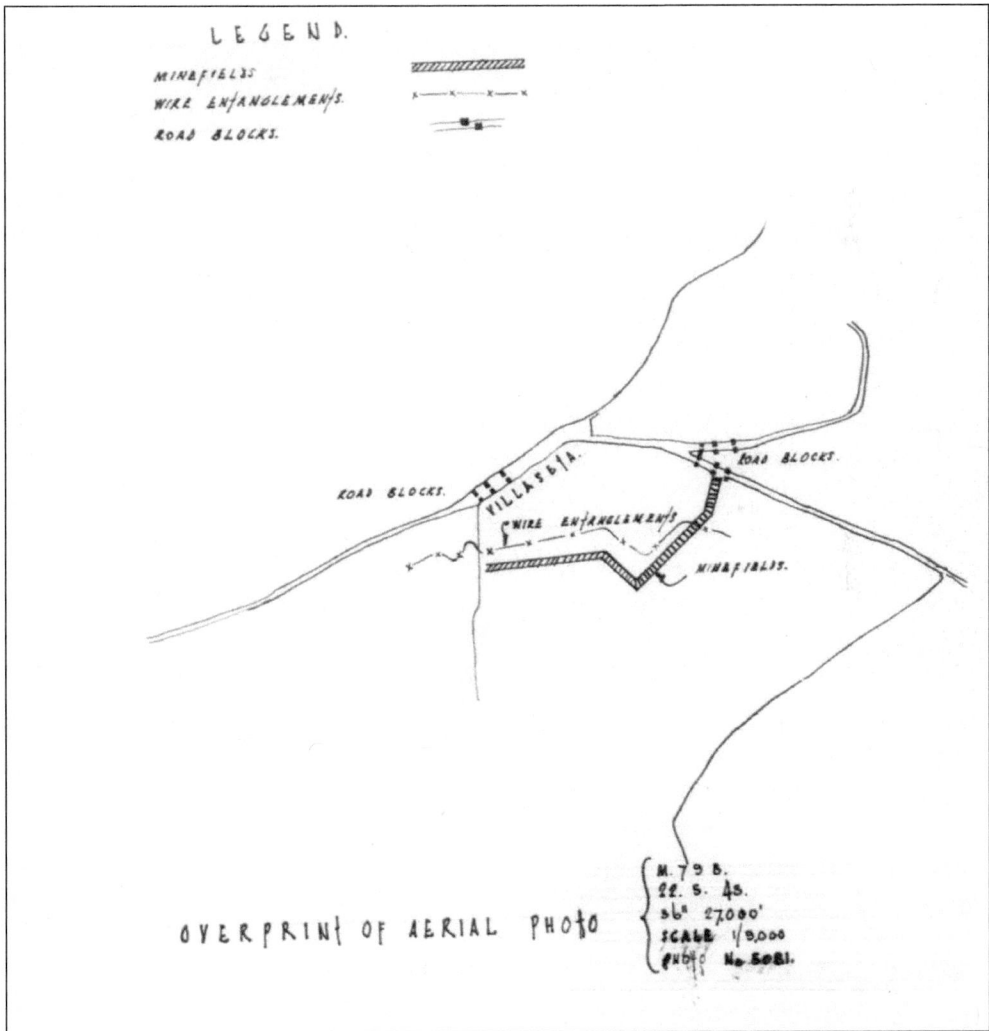

Minefield near Agrigento. (AFHRA)

At the end of the first week of the Sicily landings, Allied ground forces occupied about a third of the island and the air forces had effectively neutralised Axis air resistance. Northwest African Tactical Air Force (NATAF) aircraft had flown 7,036 fighter and fighter-bomber sorties and 768 by bombers, of which 510 were against positions of purely tactical interest. The Northwest African Strategic Air Force (NASAF) also carried out 1,720 bombing sorties, of which 1,031 were against enemy positions and communication lines. The Northwest African Coastal Air Force flew 1,562 sorties, 80 percent of which were employed escorting Allied convoys. The reconnaissance units of NATAF, PR Spitfires, NASAF, and maritime reconnaissance Wellingtons and Baltimores flew a combined 315 sorties for a total of 12,715 across all Allied aviation units. The total weight of the bombs dropped in the theatre this week reached 4,530 tons.[45]

An important target near Lercara Friddi. In this town the famous mafia boss 'Lucky' Luciano was born in 1897. (US Air Force)

45   AFHRA, Reel 23364, *The Sicilian Campaign*, p.685.

14

PR Planes Over the Island

As American positions consolidated around the Gela area, on 20 July a small, advanced unit of the 12th Photographic Reconnaissance Squadron (PRS) set foot on the island. This vanguard of specialists, led by Captain Charles Palmetier (Ground Echelon commander), arrived with two pilots, Lieutenants Robert S. Bleile and Russell B. Evans, followed by an engineering team led by Warrant Officer Micketts and 57 enlisted men. The plan had already been elaborated in detail on 21 June by Palmetier himself. The photographic laboratory that settled in Sicily would have to meet the large-scale requests from Army units spread across the entire island.

Operational requirements on Sicily included the ability to produce 2,400 aerial photos per day. During the course of the Sicilian campaign, production would extend, the photo labs reaching 3,500 daily prints, 50,500 prints across 87 sorties. From 10 to 19 July, 44 missions were carried out from Ariana airport, with an average of 255 photos printed per sortie.

The arrival in Gela of the 12th PRS detachment. (US Air Force)

With regard to the planning for the Sicilian Campaign, Captain C.H. Butler of the 13th Photo Intelligence Detachment of the NAPRW recalled:

> [For the period from 18 June to 1 July] Was transferred to G-2 Section Headquarters II Corps. Prepared report for them covering hutted camps, barracks, and dumps in invasion area, also report in form of overlay showing defences along proposed lines of advance from the coast. Answered questions coming up during briefing of various units. Also brought defence record maps up to date from reports from 7th Army Unit. Also supervised distribution of photos to 1st and 45th Divisions. Before going to II Corps I thought I would have charge of photo intelligence at that head. However, I found that Major Harper of G-2 was in charge of serial photography, and further found that Col. Carter of Coprs Engineers was furnishing the necessary enlisted men, the necessary equipment, and space on a truck for transportation of men and equipment. And also found I was supposed to move with Engineers Map Supply in Supply Echelon. ... On 16 July the Photo Intelligence Detachment landed at Gela.[1]

During the initial phase, printing operations consisted of duplicating the photos and sending the negatives the following day to Northwest African Photographic Reconnaissance Wing headquarters in North Africa. From 10 August onwards, some sorties produced three sets of prints.

The small photo lab was run by Lieutenant Wayshak. The liaison officer between the Army and the squadron was Major Harper of G-2, who, from a tent near Gela Ponte Olivo, coordinated the Intelligence Section and the requests of the Seventh Army. The men set up camp five miles from Gela Ponte Olivo airfield. On 20 July, the first F-5A Lightning, flown by Major Theodore H. Erb, arrived at Gela Ponte Olivo. Meanwhile, the rest of the squadron continued to operate from Ariana in Tunisia.[2]

At 11:00 p.m. the same day, 20 July, an urgent request from the US Army arrived. The mission was to cover all roads south and south-west of Palermo, within 25 miles, at dawn the following day. It was the first mission entirely planned by the photographic detachment near Gela Ponte Olivo. The photos obtained from this mission had to reach Allied command no later than 1:00 p.m. the following day; the tactical decisions of the American 2nd Armored Division depended on it, as expressly communicated in a note from the Army itself.

The briefing was carried out during the night so that the first F-5A was already over Sicily at 9:00 a.m. the following morning. Lieutenant Evans completed his mission at 10:15 a.m.. In just three hours and 45 minutes, the entire operating evolution was completed and the prints delivered to the 'customer'. For safety reasons, the F-5A returned to Ariana.

For this first operational phase, some of the F-5As sent to Sicily were equipped with two 24-inch cameras, from which 300–350 nine-inch square format prints were generated per sortie; the scale varying from 1:12,000 to 1:15,000. In addition, in some cases, a 36-inch lens camera was used to produce 1:9000 scale prints.

---

1   AFHRA, IRISREF C0192, p.964.
2   Among the equipment needed for a field laboratory capable of satisfying the needs of three squadrons, with an estimated production of 2.5 million prints per month, and on an average of 15 sorties per day, were the Williamson multi-printer, the Kodak continuous film processing machine and the Kodak film duplication machine.

A field photographic laboratory of the 12th PRS, likely near the airfield at Gela Ponte Olivo. (US Air Force)

76175A.C.

Photo lab (top) and photo trailer (bottom) of the NAPRW somewhere in the Mediterranean. (US Air Force)

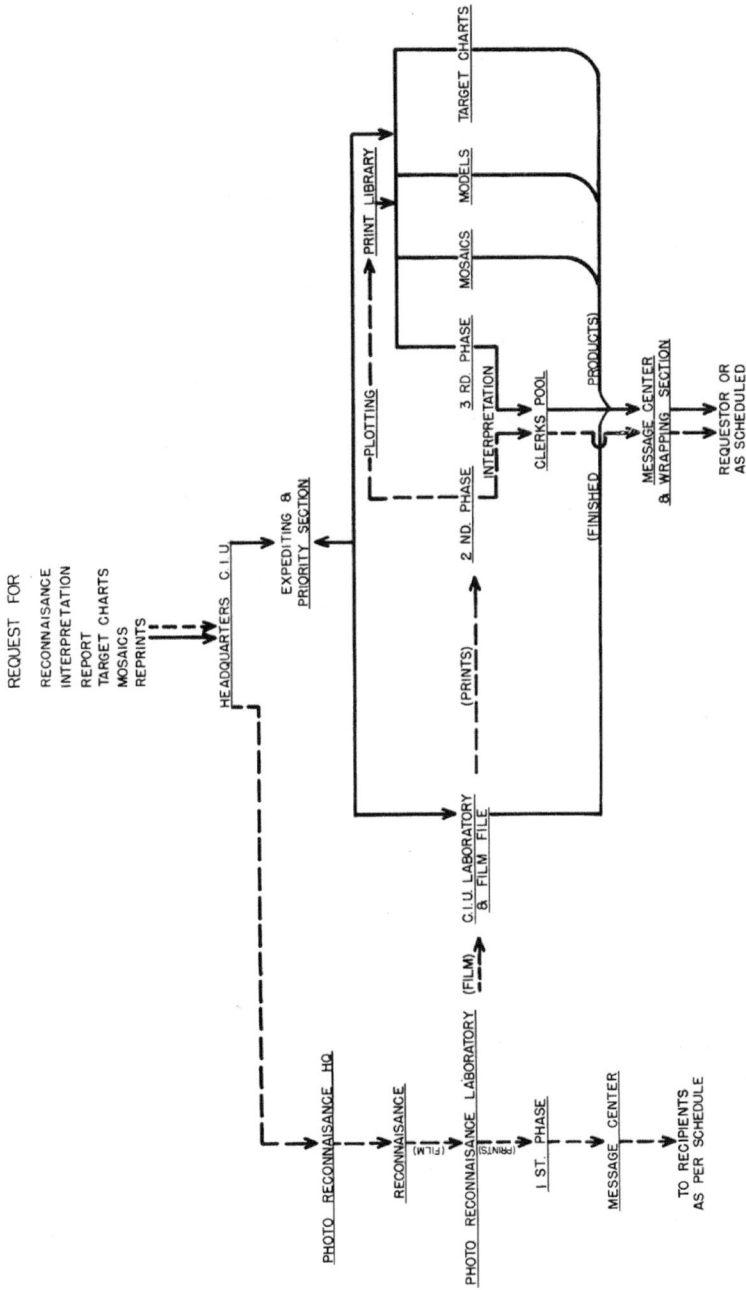

American standard application and reconnaissance process. (AFHRA)

On 27 July, after two days' sailing, a second detachment of the 12th PRS arrived at Gela; it comprised Lieutenant Byron J. Stevens and a cadre of 15 men, mostly laboratory technicians and photo-interpreters.

For the 12th PRS operating from Ariana in North Africa, this new phase consisted of miscellaneous targets which included pinpoints such as airfields, marshalling yards, rail junctions and harbours. Covering southern France, Italy (up to Milan), Albania, Greece, Sardinia and Corsica, the new operational range stretched 1,400 miles.

This allowed the unit to perform at least four of the five daily missions required by the Seventh Army to cover roads and areas of tactical interest.[3]

Missions carried out from Gela Ponte Olivo						
Period		Successful	Missed target	Weather	Mechanical	Prints
20/07/43	31/07/43	42	1			18,190
01/08/43	14/08/43	47		3	1	32,046
15/08/43	17/08/43	3				3,077
Total		92	1	3	1	53,313

Among the pilots who operated from Gela Ponte Olivo on behalf of the Seventh Army, some distinguished themselves by obtaining oblique photos at low altitude (7,000–8,000 feet) in particularly dangerous areas, using six-inch cameras:

- ✓ Major Theodore Erb: Roads and land east of the road from Santo Stefano di Camastra to Nicosia.
- ✓ Captain Sanford L. Arkin: Roads and land east of the road that leads from Sant'Agata di Militello to Cesarò and Agira.
- ✓ Captain Robert C. Spencer Jr: Roads and land east of the road from Furnari to Francavilla di Sicilia.
- ✓ Lieutenant Russell Evans: Roads and land east of the road that leads from Capo d'Orlando to Randazzo.

Ninety sorties were flown during the squadron's stay in Sicily:

- ✓ 44 sorties covered roads in Sicily with high altitude vertical photos.
- ✓ 41 sorties covered areas in Sicily with high altitude vertical photos.
- ✓ 4 sorties covered roads in Sicily with oblique photos at medium altitude, from 6,000 to 10,000 feet.
- ✓ 1 sortie through the Sicilian canal with oblique photos at low altitude.

3   AFHRA, IRISREF B0746 p.506.

Lieutenant Erb
from the 3rd PG..
(US Air Force
photo 75955 AC)

Captain Spencer
from the 3rd PG.
(US Air Force
photo 76019 AC)

Mobile Field Photographic Section

On 31 July, No. 3 MFPS (Mobile Field Photographic Section) moved to the new runway of San Francesco, at coordinates H8454 in the Lentini area, to support strategic and tactical reconnaissance provided to the advancing Eighth Army. The runway was almost two miles long and could accommodate up to 45 aircraft. Ground staff, together with photographers, and the J-type photographic semi-trailers of 3 MFPS, joined the move to Sicily. The trailers housed the equipment needed to process (automatic developer), print (universal multi-printer) and duplicate (enlarger-duplicator) films. A complete unit consisted of five trailers. The unit included a dryer and could provide contact prints, duplicates and negatives. In Lentini San Francesco, the photographic sections were based about a mile from the airfield, near a stream that provided the only water available for washing films and prints. In the beginning, however, the drying of the films presented serious problems, so much so that, not infrequently, strange scenes of groups of aviators (or photographers, electricians, mechanics and drivers) lined up in the field with long wet films in hand, shaking them gently in the breeze, could be witnessed. Despite the problem of mosquitoes, which sometimes stuck to films like flies to flypaper, good results were obtained. The J-type trailer was partially air conditioned and divided into two compartments, a small room for processing and a larger room for printing. A generator set provided an autonomous energy source in the field. The darkroom area could be increased with the addition of a steel-framed tent on the ends of which hung one or more curtains, all covered

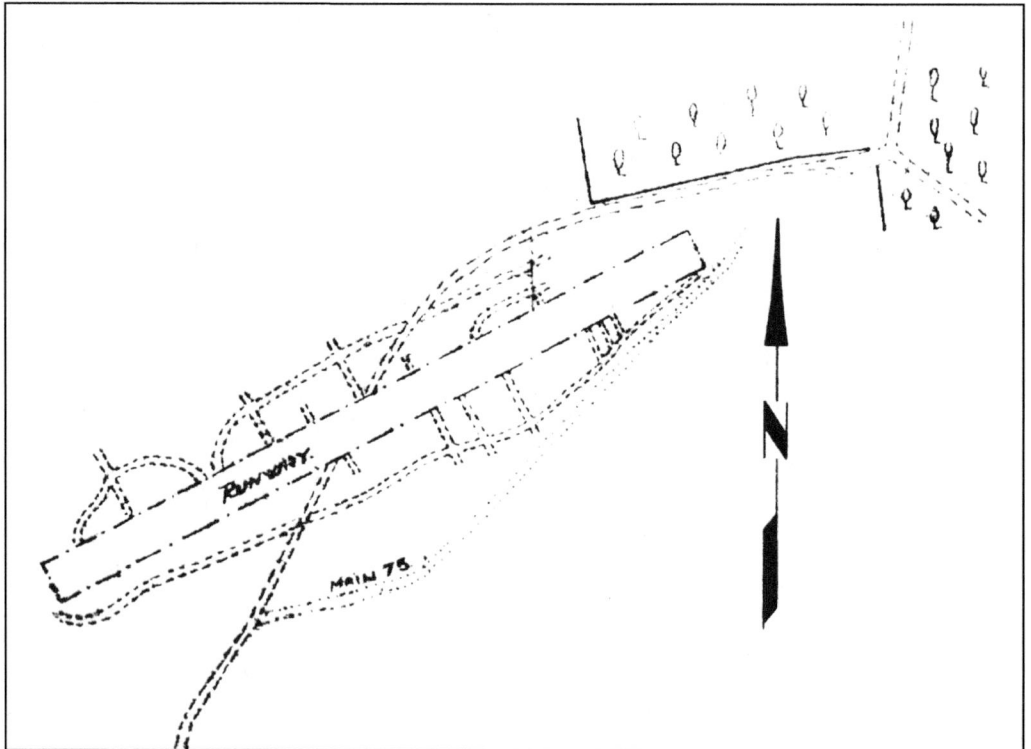

San Francesco Landing Ground. (AFHRA)

by an external waterproof canvas. This tent had a central workspace of 11 × 8 feet. In addition, a tent housed workstations for washing, drying, numbering, finishing, and sorting of films and prints. The system was not quite perfect. There were difficulties in maintaining consistent darkness when required during daylight hours and, when working at night, the detachment operated in an area subjected to enemy air raids.

Two F-5A being refuelled. From the profile of the mountains behind the aircraft, it could be a temporary stop at Gerbini airport at the end of Operation *Husky*. (US Air Force 28550 AC)

Major Leon W. Gray photographed alongside his 'No. 67' (42-13067). This aircraft was shot down and abandoned in the Adriatic on its 97th mission. Gray was saved by air–sea rescue. After completing 73 missions, he returned to the United States. In 1950, Gray became commander of the now closed Williams Air Force Base in Mesa, Arizona. He had a cameo role in the film 'Air Cadet', starring a young Rock Hudson, which tells the life of cadets who learn to become pilots. Gray died on 26 November 2007 at the age of 94 years. (US Air Force photo 75956 AC)

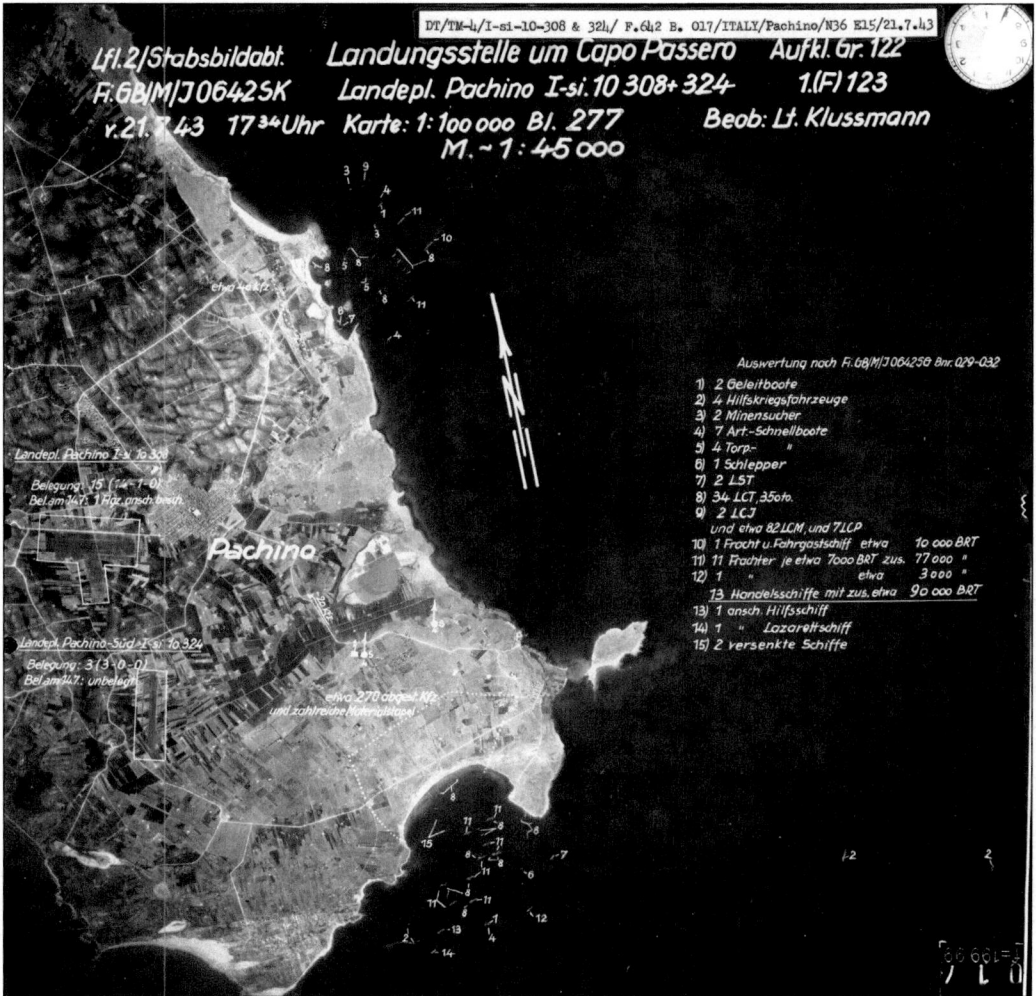

Pachino and Capo Passero photographed on 21 July 1943 by a *Luftwaffe* Ju 88 belonging to 1.(F)/123 and flown by Leutnant Klussmann. Note the new Allied track at Pachino-Sud. On the left are the details of Allied shipping noted at sea during the flight. (NARA)

15

Eagles over Etna

On 19 July 1943, the Spitfires of No. 40 Squadron SAAF flew tactical reconnaissance sorties across four separate taskings during the day. In the early morning, Lieutenants Wilson and Nicholson spotted nine boats at Riposto; moments later, they were strafed by P-38 Lightnings. One vessel was hit and sunk, and another two were damaged. One of the SAAF pilots later found his starboard wing damaged. In the American sector, Major V.J. Marshall, British Liaison Officer of the Fifteenth Army Group, ordered the 111th Tactical Reconnaissance Squadron (TRS) to move to the new airstrip at Gela West.[1] During the previous night, yet another German bombing raid on Gela Ponte Olivo damaged many aircraft, greatly reducing the operational effectiveness of the squadron, which could barely manage four sorties. Meanwhile, XII Air Support Command (ASC) commissioned the 91st Fighter-Bomber Squadron (FBS)[2], 27th Fighter-Bomber Group (FBG), now stationed on the new Gela East airfield, to carry out an armed reconnaissance over Palermo. At around 3:00 p.m., two A-36A Mustangs, flown by Captain Roger Miller and Flight Officer Leeirby Libby, approched the Sicilian capital. Reaching the target, an unexpected barrage of anti-aircraft fire hit Miller's aircraft (serial 42-53921):

> While on a reconnaissance mission along the northern shore of Sicily, Captain Roger L. Miller and I (Leeirby Libby) flew over the shore two or three miles west of Palermo in order to closely observe a large boat. Our altitude was approximately 100 ft. A gun battery of two (2) 50 Cal. machine guns opened fire. We turned out to sea, then returned to strafe the gun position. Captain Roger L. Miller was hit, pulled up to 500 ft., lost some gasoline. His plane burst into flames, he jettisoned his canopy, then

---

1   The 111th TRS was gradually moving to Sicily. A series of shifts, at the beginning of July 1943, divided the squadron into three units: Air Echelon, and the first and second Ground Echelons. On 7 July, the Air Echelon, made up of 74 other ranks, 35 officer pilots, 6 ground officers and 4 air liaison officers, began operations from Korba North, Tunisia, in conjunction with the Sicilian Campaign. The squadron had 20 P-51 Mustangs and nine P-39 Airacobras. On 14 July, the Air Echelon moved to Gela Ponte Olivo in Sicily and was followed by the first Ground Echelon of 70 other ranks and two officers. Together, they occupied the new Gela West airstrip on 19 July. The second Ground Echelon of 30 other ranks and two officers, joined them on 27 July.

2   On 23 August 1943 the 16th, 17th and 91st Bombardment Squadrons became the 522nd, 523rd and 524th Fighter-Bomber Squadrons respectively.

A Douglas A-20 Havoc of the 47th BG near Etna. In Sicily, this unit operated from the airstrips of Torrente Comunelli and Gerbini. (US Air Force)

the plane crashed into the shallow water on the shore line. Captain Roger L. Miller crashed with his plane and had no chance to survive. The time was approximately 1520 hours.

Flying Officer Leeirby Libby[3]

The city of Rome, after being observed and photographed for months by Allied aircraft, was subjected to heavy bombing. On the morning of 19 July, Northwest African Strategic Air Force (NASAF) bombers launched a devastating attack targeting San Lorenzo train station and Ciampino airport. In chronological order, the first to attack in the morning were almost 300 B-17 Flying Fortresses and Consolidated B-24 Liberators and, in the afternoon, 250 medium bombers, B-25 Mitchells and B-26 Marauders, escorted by more than 200 P-38 Lightnings; only weak resistance was encountered. The damage assessment was entrusted that afternoon to No. 682 Squadron's new CO, Squadron Leader J.T. Morgan, who covered the areas of Littorio A/D ('Army Demand', a sortie specifically requested by the Army), Centocelle A/D, Rome and Ciampino.

3   NARA, Missing Air Crew Report n. 421.

Douglas A-20 Havoc medium bombers of the 47th BG bombing the port of Milazzo on 27 July 1943.
(US Air Force)

The same day, No. 683 Squadron sent Flying Officer Smith and Sergeant Simpson over Sicily at the Army's request. The A-36A fighter-bombers of XII ASC were incredibly busy with 48 sorties, mostly directed against troop transport vehicles and railway lines, flown during the day. Two trains were attacked at Fondaco; their explosions reached 300 feet in the air.[4]

Meanwhile, the first party of No. 651 Air Observation Post (AOP) Squadron RAF, under the command of Major R.W.V. Nearthercoat with six officers and 24 other ranks, arrived at Syracuse from Sousse. A sister unit, No. 654 AOP Squadron, arrived at Pachino on the same day; Captain J.B. Brundret leading it to support the British Army. The two units flew the Taylorcraft Auster.

AOP pilots were the controlling eyes of the artillery and could direct devastating firepower onto the enemy formations over which they flew. They were expert gunners and pilots, usually from an Army background, with the unorthodox flying skills their work demanded. The Austers were ideal for the role, but were slow, unarmed and unarmoured; they often flew so low that a parachute offered no chance of escape should things go wrong. From bitter experience, the enemy soon learned to dread their presence in the skies above the battlefield. German soldiers

4   This is probably the Fondaco Motta area, near Motta Camastra.

knew that a careless movement, a puff of smoke, or a chance flash of sunlight off a truck's windscreen could bring tons of steel and high explosives raining down on them from the guns directed by the pilot, circling like a buzzard, not far above. Usually flying alone, without fighter escort or radar warnings, an unwary AOP pilot was a sitting duck for enemy fighters. Like their Royal Flying Corps and Royal Naval Air Service predecessors of the First World War, they had to be constantly alert to what was happening in the skies around them as they directed the fire of the guns onto targets. Closing at over 250mph, an attacking Messerschmitt Bf 109 or Fw 190 left little or no time for indecision. Reactions had to be instinctive and instant. Failure was fatal. Flying at low altitude also made them easy targets for an enemy keen to shoot them down before the inevitable shelling. The AOP pilots were even at risk from the guns they controlled. The intensity of artillery fire meant that, all too often, the path of the outgoing shells crossed the flight path of returning aircraft. Sometimes, a pilot's luck ran out and he was shot down by his own guns. Thanks to their unobtrusive role, with the noise of their aircraft's engine drowned by the din of the guns, they were scarcely noticed by those on their own side and, in accounts of the battles in the long hard fight for Europe's freedom, their contribution is mentioned only in passing or, more often, not mentioned at all.

Patton's Army was supported by the corps artillery officer, Colonel John M. Wilkins, who directed Captain Claude L. Shepard Jr to organise an artillery air subsection. Edgar Raines, author of *Eyes of Artillery*, observed:

> The 3rd Infantry Division was to land on the Allied left flank, and the division commander, Major General Lucian K Truscott Jr, worried about how the enemy might counterattack. Consequently, he was very receptive to a proposal by the division artillery air officer, Captain Devol, to build a runway on an LST (landing ship, tank). Two ships, LSTs 525 and 906, were converted, although only 525 actually supported the Sicily landing. A number of Field Artillery pilots assisted in the modifications. Lieutenant Strok served as a technical consultant. Each LST carried ten Piper L-4s, an equivalent aircraft to the Auster. The six aircraft stored along the sides of the flight deck had their rudders removed so those on the aft part of the deck could take off. The runways were too short to allow a landing, so Devol planned for the aircraft to land behind friendly lines; flying in relays from LST 525, they would keep the landing area under constant surveillance. The other innovation—by far the most important—owed less to planning than to an ability to adapt to changing circumstances. Maj. Gen. Omar Bradley commanded the II Corps attack through the mountainous terrain of central Sicily. Here, air observation posts proved their value by their ability to bring the far side of hill masses, hidden to ground observation posts, under observed fire. Initially, aircraft still used grasshopper tactics [making brief flights to quickly reconnoitre the area before attracting attention], but this changed as the campaign wore on. Limited resupply forced II Corps to ration artillery fire. The artillery air officer of the 45th Infantry Division, Capt. Samuel Freeman, noticed, however, that German artillery did not fire as long as one of the division's L-4s was in the air. In effect, the L-4 served as a counterbattery weapon without the Americans firing a round. The division began flying its aircraft continuously during the day, and the practice soon spread throughout the corps and then Seventh Army. Artillery[-spotting] aircraft also provided route and close reconnaissance in advance of American infantry …

Top: Lieutenant Algred W. Schultz, a pilot from Waterloo, Iowa, holds the air-ground pick-up equipment used by the Third Prov. Pack Battery while at the front. In the background is a Piper L-4B used in the pick-up system. Bottom: The pick-up system in action. (US Air Force photo 80088 AC)

The campaign in central Sicily featured rugged terrain and tenacious German resistance. Near the town of Troina, the 3d Battalion, 26th Infantry, of the 1st Infantry Division, was cut off for three days. The USAAF attempted to drop supplies but missed the dug-in-positions. Four Field Artillery officers, Lts. Donald Blair, William Cole, John Fuchs and Oscar Rich, volunteered to make resupply runs in two L-4s. They dropped sandbags filled with K-rations and water purification tablets. 'The flights,' remembered one of the participants, 'were a rather wild ride as we picked up a lot of ground fire from German rifles and machine guns both on the way in and the way out.' Although the aircraft were hit many times, none of the Americans was wounded. And they delivered the supplies. The 1st Infantry Division Artillery commander, Brig. Gen. Clift Andrus, later awarded each man a Silver Star.[5]

On 20 July, four ops were flown by the Spitfires of 40 Squadron SAAF, Lieutenant Nicholson completing his 53rd sortie. The South African Spitfires move to the new Cassibile airstrip, created in a hurry by the 904th Royal Engineers of the British Army. The South Africans left Pachino-Sud behind, but it was immediately occupied by the Kittyhawk IIIs of No. 3 Squadron RAAF from Luqa.

In the late morning, Wing Commander Adrian Warburton and Flight Lieutenant P.L. Kelley, of No. 683 Squadron, each carried out a sortie over north-eastern Sicily. Meanwhile, a formation of 18 P-40 Warhawks of the 325th Fighter Group (FG) escorted a large formation of C-47 Dakota transports carrying material and personnel to Sicily. The C-47s landed on new Allied airfields in the Gela area and on the recently occupied ones at Comiso and Gela Ponte Olivo.

Meanwhile, other P-40s from the American 325th FG were engaged in strafing operations in the Messina Strait area, where they hit and sank the *Bellini*, a 30-ton merchant vessel. Air Vice-Marshal Harry Broadhurst sent substantial Desert Air Force (DAF) P-40 fighter-bomber formations to the Messina Strait, to combat shipping, and to the coastal road linking Messina to Catania to prevent the movement of vehicles and trains.[6]

After the incessant air raids of the preceding days, American ground troops entered Enna.[7] Montgomery, meanwhile, was still in difficulty in the area south of Catania and required the swift intervention of armed reconnaissance to attack Italian–German troops at coordinates H8677, just south of Belpasso, and at points H9077 and H9379 in the Catania area. At 5:50 p.m., responsibility for the task fell to 11 Kittyhawk IIIs of 3 Squadron RAAF, escorted by 12 Kittyhawk IIIs of No. 112 Squadron RAF; they successfully attacked the reported objectives and completed the op at 6:50 p.m.

The A-36A fighter-bombers of XII ASC operated over the north-western area, between the municipalities of Messina, San Fratello, Capo d'Orlando, Randazzo and Nicosia. After moving to the new Gela West airstrip, the 111th TRS was now fully operational and flew 15 sorties,

---

5   Edgar F. Raines, *Eyes of Artillery: The Origins of Modern U.S. Army Aviation in World War II* (Washington, D.C.: Center of Military History United States Army, 2000), p.163.

6   Harry Broadhurst assumed command of DAF in January 1943, becoming the youngest air vice-marshal in the Royal Air Force at the age of 38.

7   In the period from 10 to 16 July, the city of Enna was attacked by 212 medium bombers, 30 light bombers and 107 fighter-bombers.

many of them late in the afternoon. Meantime, 654 AOP had positioned itself on the strip a mile and a half north of Lentini, a Captain Tallents performing the first Auster sortie over the enemy to locate artillery batteries.

At dawn on the 21st, four Spitfires of 40 Squadron SAAF left to meet the requests of the Army. One of these missions was carried out in the afternoon by Lieutenant-Colonel Blaauw himself who, with Lieutenant Wilson, covered the Leonforte area; they were forced to return to Cassibile early due to technical problems with their radios.[8]

At 9:55 a.m., Flying Officer E.C. Hey, of 683 Squadron, flew Spitfire PR.XI (MB774) to the Capo D'Orlando area where five vessels were sighted at sea. A consistent movement of enemy troops was reported at first light in the Petralia area by the F-6s of the 111th TRS. The information and films acquired during this mission were immediately sent to the XII ASC headquarters at Capo Bon via a P-39 Airacobra courier. Having received the information, and analysed the photos, XII ASC detailed A-36A fighter-bombers of the 27th FBG to depart Gela Farello's at 2:20 p.m. Arriving west of Petralia Soprana, the aircraft intercepted a long enemy column. During the approach, the A-36A (serial 42-84068) flown by 2nd Lieutenant William B. Korber was hit and destroyed, falling less than 300 yards from three enemy vehicles.[9]

At 1:27 p.m., 10 B-25 Mitchells of the 340th Bombardment Group (BG) attacked the city of Troina, hitting it with 48 × 300lb bombs and 88 × 250-pounders and encountering scarce and inaccurate anti-aircraft fire coming 2–3 miles west of the city.

At first light on 22 July, five 40 Squadron Spitfires flew a tactical reconnaissance over the area between Termini Imerese and Messina, where they identified some operational coastal defence positions. These artillery positions were preventing some Allied ships from approaching the coast. On the way back, Captain C.F. Geere intercepted a large column of about 300 vehicles of various kinds, many of them armed, heading towards Randazzo from Adrano and Troina. He immediately reported the information via radio; the news made its way to DAF command which, at 9:10 a.m., sent twelve 112 Squadron RAF Kittyhawk IIIs, and 12 from No. 450 Squadron RAAF, from Pachino to intercept the convoy. Wing Commander R.E. Barry, the CO of No. 239 Wing RAF, led the formation. The Kittyhawks intercepted and attacked more than 200 vehicles between Troina and Randazzo, including a tank they identified as a Panzer Tiger VI. At 12:00 p.m. on the dot, another 12 Kittyhawks, this time from 3 Squadron RAAF and led by Squadron Leader Stevens, left Pachino for Troina.

Just before 8:31 the same morning, No. 232 Wing RAF sent 24 Baltimores (12 from No. 55 Squadron and 12 from No. 223 Squadron), strongly escorted by Spitfires from Malta, to Troina. The objective of the raid was the road intersection at coordinates C5310, just north of the city, onto which 143 × 250lb bombs were dropped. At 11:30, the city of Misterbianco was also hit by 91 × 250lb bombs dropped by 24 Boston bombers of Nos. 12 and 24 Squadrons SAAF. At 2:23 p.m., it was the turn of Paternò to be bombed; 12 Baltimores of No. 21 Squadron SAAF delivering 22000lb of General Purpose (GP) bombs.

In the early afternoon, yet another tactical reconnaissance was flown by the Spitfires of 40 Squadron SAAF over the sector east of Agira, where various troop transports and tanks were identified. The 111th TRS also confirmed intense heavy vehicle movements in the north-east of

8   The National Archives London, Royal Air Force, Operations Record Books AIR 54/84.
9   NARA, Missing Air Crew Reports n. 420.

the island, and much railway traffic on the Cefalù–Termini Imerese line. A new landing ground was identified at coordinates 38° 07' 00" N, 15° 06' 25" E, 10 miles south-west of Milazzo, in a flat area located between the road and the coast; no aircraft were visible.

The 111th TRS performed 20sorties throughout the day. The unit carried out its hundredth mission during its three weeks on Sicily; Lieutenants Lincicome and Bright saw 35 boats in the stretch of sea between Santo Stefano di Camastra and Capo d'Orlando. The A-36A fighter-bombers of XII ASC, however, flew 99 sorties throughout the day, many of which engaged the intense road traffic on the Randazzo–Troina route, where about 30 vehicles were attacked (16 destroyed and many others damaged). The intense movements reported by reconnaissance was justified by the fact that the Italian command of VI Army was leaving Randazzo for new headquarters in Portella Mandrazzi, in the Peloritani mountains. In the meantime, the arrival of 11 German Gotha Go 242 gliders on the beaches of Torre Faro, in Messina, had been reported.

During the evening, the Seventh Army entered Palermo. The conquest of the Sicilian capital marked a clear turning point in the battle for Sicily. At Montgomery's invitation, Patton arrived in Syracuse by plane to discuss the common strategy to be adopted, in view of the final phase of operations in Sicily. Patton had already established that, to reach Messina, his army would

A dicing mission carried out by Major Leon Gray, 15th PRS. The image, taken on 26 July 1943 at 2:10 p.m., from a height of 350 feet with a 6-inch camera, captured this view of the small town of San Giorgio. (US Air Force)

mainly need two roads, both north of Etna: the coastal SS113 road, which goes from Palermo to Messina, and SS120, an insidious mountain road, which passes inland and crosses Sicily from Nicosia to Randazzo. Meanwhile, 1st Canadian Division troops entered Assoro.[10]

The wreck of a probable Messerschmitt Bf 110 near Rometta Marea. Photo taken by Major Leon Gray on 26 July 1943. (US Air Force)

The photos taken from high altitude at 10:30 a.m. on 23 July by the strategic reconnaissance aircraft of 683 Squadron, showed seven Go 242 gliders in flight about two miles west of Capo Peloro.

10   The fall of this small town meant the collapse of the southern end of the Italian–German defence. The capture of Assoro facilitated the fall of Leonforte, which cost 275 Canadian lives.

The RAF's 239 Wing sent twelve 3 Squadron RAAF Kittyhawk IIIs and 11 from 250 Squadron RAF on an armed reconnaissance which intercepted and attacked, at about 11:00 a.m., a long column of vehicles on SS575, in the Carcaci district, heading towards Adrano from Torina. Other German troops were deployed along the Catenanuova–Regalbuto line. At 10:00 a.m., Lieutenant Dent from 40 Squadron SAAF identified a valuable target, a merchant ship near the port area of Catania. Three hours later, under the guidance of Major S.V. Theron, 12 Kittyhawk IIIs of 450 Squadron RAAF, loaded with 250lb bombs, headed towards the Acquicella railway station in Catania; they were escorted by the Kittyhawks of 260 Squadron RAF. The same target was attacked at 3:25 p.m. by 36 Warhawks of the American 57th FG, led by Major G.D. Mobbs, from Pachino-Sud.

Meanwhile, Patton decided to launch four divisions against the German Cefalù–Petralia line and asked the 12th Photographic Reconnaissance Squadron (PRS), from Gela Ponte Olivo, for a reconnaissance of the communication routes, and a strip mission (1:25,000), of the area.

On the morning of the 24th, Lieutenant Donnelly of 40 Squadron SAAF completed a low-altitude flight over the mouth of the Simeto and surrounding areas without detecting ongoing enemy activity.

At the request of the Fifteenth Army Group, B Flight of No. 60 Squadron SAAF flew its tenth op since officially joining the Northwest African Photographic Reconnaissance Wing. The PR Mosquitos had two additional fuel tanks installed for greater range. Major Menzies of the Fifteenth Army Group took part, flying with the Mosquito pilot over the area south of Catania to Messina, and subsequently the American sector to the west; the flight lasted about three hours. After taking up a position in Lentini, 651 AOP flew its first photographic reconnaissance supporting XIII Corps on the 24th. The two AOP squadrons used the Merton method for oblique photos during their sorties.[11]

On the Eighth Army's front, cooperation with 40 Squadron was quickly established:

AIR O.P.s: The distinction between this and Arty R does not seem to be understood by all, it is one that is clearly marked. The Air O.P. is an elevated O.P. with a fully qualified Gunnery Officer, but he does not fly nearer than 1000 yds to the enemy

---

11 A series of overlapping oblique photographs taken from about 3,000 feet and on a line some distance behind the general line of forward defended localities. Any two consecutive photographs from this series cover a large area of the same ground. A target appearing in one photograph can, therefore, be identified in at least one other of the series. A grid is reproduced on the photograph during the printing process. The vertical grid lines provide a means of finding bearings on points appearing in the photograph. These lines represent the rays of a large horizontal-degree fan placed over the landscape with the apex of the fan at the plumb point; that is, the point over which the aircraft was flying at the moment the photograph was taken. The rays of the fan are at degree intervals and are numbered 0 to 36. The horizontal grid lines, in conjunction with the vertical lines, form an approximately squared grid, which has, of course, no relation to the map grid. The artillery officer is provided with the position of the plumb point, in the form of coordinates or a trace, and the bearing of the 0° grid line (the lefthand ray of the fan described above) for each photograph. This bearing is given by the coordinates of a point (orienting point) on the lefthand ray. This point is taken at a given distance from the plumb point and need not either appear on the photograph or be a map feature. The broken line joining the plumb point to the orienting point therefore represents the 0° vertical grid line. War Department, *Handbook on the British Army with supplements on the Royal Air Force and civilian defense organizations* (USA, 1942), p.231.

F.D.L's [sic, forward defended localities], therefore he is unable to fulfil demands far into enemy territory and that is the role of Arty R which normally shoots with Medium Regiments.

Targets that need great accuracy of ranging should be taken on by the Air O.P's [sic] when possible, they are observation officers who fly, while Arty R is done by flying men and artillery observation is merely one branch of their duties.

PHOTO/R: There are no vertical cameras now in the Squadron but Merton obliques and ordinary obliques, have been done frequently, the former being urgently required by the two Air P.P. Squadrons.

They have required up to a 30 miles strip and 24 copies. In a fluid battle it was impossible to fulfil all of the request as with the equipment in this Photographic Section an output of 600 prints a day is the maximum.

The full request would have taken 6 days consequently only a portion of the requirements were done, which was regretted as the Air O.Ps have found Mertons invaluable. It is hoped that 285 Wing will shortly have personnel instructed in gridding obliques so that more can be done for the Air O.P. squadrons.

MERTON OBLIQUES: Carried out with an 8" Lens and 12½° Tilt at a height of about 3800 ft.

OBLIQUES: 20" Lens Tilt 5°, 12½° or 25° Heght varying from 200 ft to 4000 ft.[12]

That same day, the 24th, the 111th TRS performed another 20sorties. Lieutenants Hicks and Sakakenny followed the 27th FBG A-36A fighter-bombers, operating from Gela East, to bomb the port of Milazzo, where a boat and two seaplanes were hit:

Took off at 18:25 on July 24, 1943 behind sixteen A-36's [sic] of the 27th Bomb Group. Twelve (12) of their ships loaded with bombs, 4 unloaded and flying top cover for the whole formation. Rendezvous over our field at 18:30. Their ships flying four formation of four line abreast. Our two Recon ships line abreast on left side of their [formation] to the north until north coast was crossed. Turned northeast still flying out into sea, then flew east passing over southern tips of Lipari Island. Turned south towards Milazzo Harbor which was the target. At this time four ME 109's [sic] passed approx. 2000' overhead from east to west. One ME 109 appeared to peel off but was turned back by our top-cover. This is first sight of enemy fighters by any of our pilots, showing small amount of Air opposition. Approach was made to the target from north to south. Target was passed over by dive-bombers which then peeled off attacking the target from south to north in contrast to their approach from the north. Began photographic run over target from west to east at same time dive-bombers began their attack. Photo run finished, turned north to sea, no friendly ships in sight. (Weaver mistook my first dive on target to be in same direction as attack by dive-bombers.) Weaver followed and we were separated. Passed within sight of target on sea side. Observed one large smoke

12   The National Archives London, South African Air Force, Operations Record Books AIR 54/84_4, p.49.

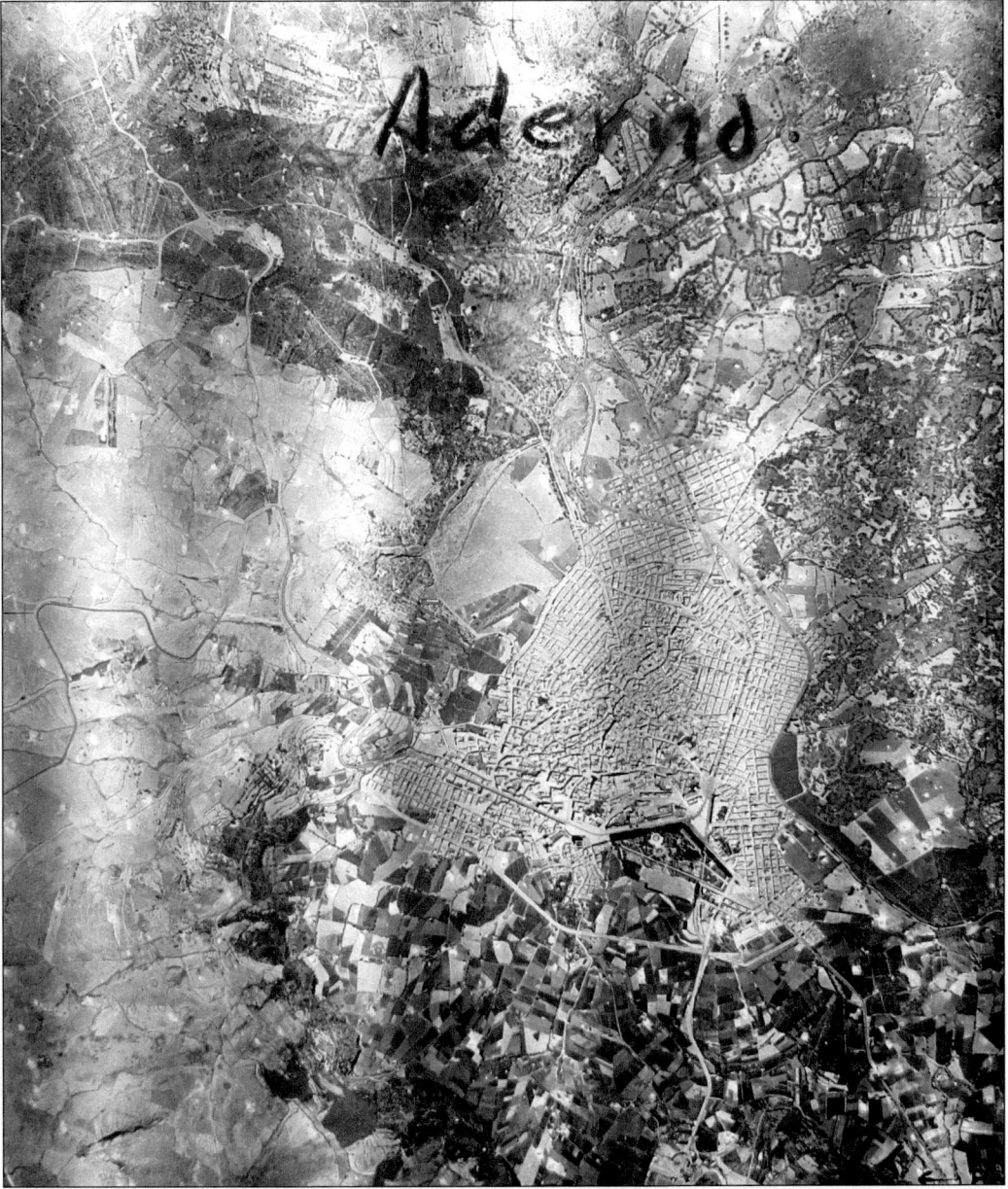

The city of Adrano photographed by No. 683 Squadron during the Axis retreat. The image was most likely taken during the morning of 27 July 1943, probably at about 11:30, by Sergeant F. Simpson and Spitfire PR.XI EN425. (LAC photo RG24, R112, 1984-265 NPC)

pall in city, bomb burst on ship and docks. Light caliber barrage type flak busting at approximately 6000'. Heavy caliber accurate flak then opened and ship was bracketed for short period even as I progressed to sea. Passed from range but was again fired on, by accurate flak as I crossed enemy coastline between Gioiosa Marea and S. Giorgia. Flew weaving course home. Encountered no more flak of any type. Landed at 19:40.

Captain Roger L. Hicks[13]

During this mission, 27th FBG lost two of its pilots, 2nd Lieutenant Charles B. Smith, 17th FBS, and James Leonard T. Sparkman, of the 16th FBS; both were captured.

2nd Lt. C. B. Smith was flying number two position of the flight in which I flew number four position. We dive-bombed the target in Milazzo Harbor and pulled out to the west. I saw Lt. Smith start his dive and that was last time I saw him. When the flight reformed after the dive he was nowhere to be seen. The flak was intense over the target.

Flight Officer Calvin D. Mosher[14]

An oblique image of Catenanuova taken on 29 July 1943, from an altitude of 1,200 feet, during a Tac/R by No. 40 Squadron SAAF. The cameras used by tactical aircraft usually had an 8-inch lens. (LAC photo RG24, R112, 1984-265 NPC)

13   AFHRA, IRISREF A0916, p.1510.
14   NARA, Missing Air Crew Report n. 358.

From 1:45 to 2:10 p.m., Messina was also targeted by 12 A-36As of the 326th FBS, 86th FBG, which took off from Gela West led by Lieutenant Harold V. Sittler. The latter claimed the sinking of the 740-ton *Cicogna*, a Gabbiano-class corvette near Ganzirri.

Meanwhile, American troops occupied Marsala and Trapani. The number of Italian–German prisoners had reached 49,200, with more than 6,900 casualties. On the central-eastern side, Canadian troops were experiencing fierce fighting and, on the Eighth Army front, resistance continued to the bitter end in the Catania area.

Armed Reconnaissance

When the American Seventh Army reached Palermo, Axis aerial activity from Sicilian bases was already almost non-existent; the Italian–German air forces had in fact already repositioned themselves to other Italian airfields. The numerical superiority of the Allies allowed their bombers to hit the lines of communication in Sicily with ease, but not targets far beyond the island. NASAF's planned air operations were expected to be sufficient. The heavy offensive put in place by Tedder neutralised Axis forces on the island while reconnaissance activities allowed the bombers to conduct missions with almost surgical precision, neutralising the airfields on Sicily. The *Luftwaffe* had lost about 740 aircraft supporting the campaign; of the 1100 aircraft abandoned or destroyed on the airfields of Sicily, between 482 and 600 were German. Allied losses amounted to approximately 375 aircraft. General Eisenhower's policy was to prioritise air operations that would, he said, directly affect the land battle; for these reasons, any available air power was used against the critical points of the enemy's communication lines.

The Twelfth Air Force, however, continued its attacks on communications targets over southern Italy. On the night of 20/21 July, a small Wellington force bombed Naples; on the 22nd, 71 Flying Fortresses of the 97th and 99th Bombardment Groups hit Foggia, 48 Mitchells bombed Battipaglia, and 52 B-26 Marauders 'christened' Salerno. The railway lines of the three cities were so badly damaged that all traffic stopped pending extensive repairs.

At 2:30 on the morning of 25 July, after 10 hours of discussion, most of the hierarchy of the Grand Council of Fascism voted to express their distrust towards 'Il Duce', Benito Mussolini. At 5:30 p.m. the same day, Mussolini was arrested by the *Carabinieri*, thus ending the fascist regime.

Later that morning, around 10:30, Colin Gray, the New Zealand wing commander of No. 322 Wing, was flying over Capo Milazzo, in Spitfire Mk.Vc ES112 ('UM-U'), with 11 other No. 152 Squadron Spitfires, all from Lentini East. The day before, Ultra had intercepted a German message that heralded the arrival at Milazzo East and West of a substantial Luftwaffe formation consisting of approximately 12 Ju 52/3m transports of I./TG 1 from the seaplane base at Vigna di Valle.[15]

The Spitfires encountered about 25 trimotors with a large escort of Bf 109s from I./JG 77 and II./JG 27, plus some Macchi MC.202s of the *161° Gruppo* of the *Regia Aeronautica*. The Kiwi ace, in his autobiography *Spitfire Patrol*, published in 1990, observed:

---

15   The National Archives London, Royal Air Force, Sicily: reports on airfields and aircraft, AIR 40/1996.

A No. 40 Squadron SAAF oblique of Regalbuto from 1,200 feet on 29 July 1943. (LAC photo RG24, R112, 1984-265 NPC)

We crossed the front-line but were past [sic] before they could fire at us, and we arrived at the Gulf of Milazzo at sea level to see a great gaggle of Ju52s circling prior to landing on the beach. A quick look around showed an escort of Messerschmitt 109s and Macchi 202s about 3,000 feet above them. There looked to be about 20 or more Ju52s and a dozen or more fighters, but there was not time to see precisely how many before we were on them. I ordered 81 Squadron with their Spitfire IXs to tackle the fighters, and the rest of us dived straight into the transports before the escort knew what was happening. I saw three Junkers in formation just ahead of me and a shot at the leader caused him to burst into flames and dive into the sea. I then turned to his number two, and the same thing happened. From the spectacular results it looked as if they must have been carrying petrol. It was all over in a few seconds, and I pulled up to see if there were any more and what had happened to the escorting fighters. It was quite a melee as there was more than 30 of us milling around. I could not see a single Junkers still in the air, and every time I saw a German fighter he had a Spitfire on his tail.[16]

16   Cull, Malizia, Galea, *Spitfires over Sicily*, p.172.

Earlier in the morning, at 9:15, No. 3 Wing SAAF sent 12 Boston III bombers of 12 Squadron, and as many from 24 Squadron, to Adrano. The Kittyhawks of 239 Wing RAF were despatched to carry out armed reconnaissances of the San Fratello line. Of particular importance was the op flown by 112 Squadron RAF which, at 2:50 p.m., sent 12 Kittyhawk IIIs, led by Squadron Leader P.F. Illingworth, to attack targets identified at coordinates C7505, near the so-called Piano dei Grilli, south of Bronte. The Kittyhawks reported they had spotted a camp, probably German, of more than 300 tents.

At first light the following morning, from Gela Ponte Olivo, the F-5A reconnaissance aircraft of the 12th PRS took off to perform photographic reconnaissance of the area between Nicosia and San Fratello. A large number of vehicles transporting troops were identified by Captain Arkin between San Fratello and Cesarò, where a tank was positioned sideways to probably hinder the possible arrival of Allied troops. Major Erb of the same unit also reported intense naval activity in the portion of the sea between Santo Stefano di Camastra, Capo d'Orlando and Milazzo. On the same day, some of 40 Squadron SAAF moved to Lentini West and flew four ops, two of which were aborted due to mechanical problems with the aircraft. The remaining ground staff left between Pachino and Cassibile soon joined the rest of the squadron at Lentini West, navigating the winding streets of Melilli, Carlentini and Lentini. The F-6s of the 111th TRS observed many armoured vehicles near Nicosia. In two of the 18 sorties, Lieutenants Bruce and Larson spotted two Fw 190s of II./SKG 10 returning from an attack on the port of Augusta.

On the other hand, 55 vehicles were sighted near Capo d'Orlando, where an intense anti-aircraft barrage was encountered, extending to include the Falcone area. Pilot Officer Keith Durbidge, the 683 Squadron veteran, covered Milazzo, between 12:15 and 1:00 p.m.; fires were clearly visible throughout the surrounding area.

Around lunchtime, a heavy bombing raid was carried out on the city of Regalbuto by the TBF (Tactical Bomber Force) Baltimore and Boston bombers. One hundred and fifteen tons of bombs were dropped on Regalbuto in a period of just 40 minutes, the bombers flying 215 sorties to do so. American P-40 Warhawk fighter-bombers and B-25 Mitchell bombers hit Milazzo, Paternò and Adrano. At 1:15 p.m., twelve 112 Squadron Kittyhawks carried out an armed reconnaissance by hitting the Catenanuova railway station and four large trucks.

At 2:10 p.m., the 3rd Photographic Group carried out one of the most dangerous missions of Operation *Husky*. A so-called dicing mission was entrusted to Major Leon Gray of the 15th PRS to cover the coast from Catania to Messina. The pilot reported being on target at an altitude of only 300 feet, continuously targeted by anti-aircraft batteries placed along the coast. Oblique images of enemy activity were taken close to the Strait of Messina, Gray even descending to 50 feet. Bullets grazed his F-5A Lightning several times but, despite this rain of fire, Gray managed to take photos of beaches, barbed wire fields and four anti-aircraft batteries.

Tactical Bomber Force	
RAF Squadron No. 225	Spitfire
RAF Squadron No. 241	Hurricane
3 Wing SAAF:	
Squadron Nos. 12, 24	Boston
Squadron Nos. 21	Baltimore
232 Wing RAF:	
Squadron Nos. 55, 223	Baltimore
326 Wing RAF:	
Squadron Nos. 18, 114	Boston
U.S. 12th, 340th Bombardment Groups – eight squadrons	Mitchell
U.S. 47th Bombardment Group – four squadron	Boston

On 12 May 1944, the now Colonel Gray delivered the following lecture on night photography and 'dicing' to a class of ground liaison officers at Will Rogers Field, Oklahoma:

Along with night flights, the one phase of photography that I got most interested in was low altitude work. My last ten or twelve missions were all "dicing" or low altitude missions. I imagine you've heard all about PR – high altitude from the other fellows, and I thought you would be interested in "dicing" missions.

"Dicing" mission are used to help the landing of the task forces. Before a task organization makes a beach landing, they have the advantage of having these low altitude flights, taken from a P-38, 60 degree angle horizontal – 400 feet – which gives the task forces the exact location of their objective. What they do with a picture like this is first check the strip to find the best place to go in. In the background of some of these pictures you might see water, which would be a bad place to have the tanks go in. So first, check the most suitable place for a landing operation.

Our organizations did the flights that supported General Patton when he leap-frogged and landed back of the enemy on the north coast of Sicily. We did the low altitude flights for the Salerno and Anzio beachhead. With all these operations, General Patton and General Clark were very well pleased. They take the pictures and make a mosaic … All these pictures were taken between 200 and 500 feet. In the North African theater, we did more in developing the range in a P-38 than in any other theater. Our range was 700 miles, we pick up between 10-30 pinpoints from the time we go out.

I was assigned to night photography July and August 1943 – in support of the Sicily invasion. Night photography has limitations. Navigation at night is the hardest part of night photography, that is to get over the right object. We were limited to 20 pictures because we carried 20 flash bombs … In night photography, we used a B-25 airplane with 20 flash bombs and two cameras – the two cameras set to give 30% side light. Taken at 12000 feet, we would cover an area two miles long and approximately 4½ miles wide, using it to discovery road communications and field communications.

… Night photo has its limitations, for instance in a B-25 we could only go a radius of 500 miles. We became very proficient in that and were getting 98% pictures and about 85-90% of the target. We had all of Italy mapped; had a mosaic of most of Italy. We picked out the target, got the terrain – landmarks, etc.[17]

At 3:25 in the afternoon, a formation of 12 Kittyhawks from 250 Squadron, led by Wing Commander Barry, took off from Pachino to bomb two targets previously reported by tactical reconnaissance at coordinates H882736 and H883735, some miles west of Catania. During the op, a small railway station in open countryside was bombed.

At 7:30 p.m., Wing Commander De Viver led 10 Kittyhawks of 3 Squadron RAAF to Catania to bomb targets in the north-west area of the city. Sergeant A. McDonald, flying Kittyhawk III FS443, experienced engine problems and was forced to bail out seven miles north of Modica at coordinates J(H)6812.[18]

Whilst Canadian troops captured Nissoria, American troops faced tough resistance along the banks of the Pollina river and between Nicosia and Geraci Siculo, particularly at coordinates C1317 just west of the latter. In order to better fulfill Eighth Army demands for photographic coverage, Montgomery needed some 683 Squadron pilots on Sicily. Flight Lieutenant P.L. Kelley, Keith Durbidge, Pilot Officer G. Craig and Flying Officer E.C. Hey were temporarily based at the new Lentini San Francesco airstrip. In the late afternoon of the same day, Kelley, in Spitfire PR.XI (MB783), and Flying Officer R.K. Davies, in Spitfire PR.XI (EN425), headed to Catania, reporting the town entirely enveloped in a thick blanket of smoke.

Durbidge, in his autobiography, *Memoirs of a High Flyer*, described Lentini San Francesco:

> Others demands on the Squadron might be made by military authorities from time to time and if it was not feasible to satisfy such a requirement within the regular scheduled tasks, additional flights would be made. One such request was given to me, I recall, just after the successful invasion of Sicily. I was to fly to Francesca in Sicily where a new airstrip had been cut out of a huge field of melons and grapes. My brief was to land there in the evening and do whatever the local Army Commanders wanted the next day. My memory of the tasks requested is quite blank but I do remember vividly my sheer delight the next morning when I stretched my arm out of the pup tent and found I had a choice of delicious melons and grapes within reach. After Malta rations, this was heaven.[19]

During the night, four Bostons of No. 326 Wing RAF, and 19 Mitchells of the 12th BG, bombed the port and the city of Milazzo, while another five Mitchells attacked Adrano and Paternò. Another eight Bostons of 326 Wing flew an armed reconnaissance over Capo d'Orlando, Nicosia and Milazzo.

On 27 July, the Axis landing strip near Falcone, still under construction and partially in use, was bombed by Allied fighter-bombers. In the meantime, 111th TRS F-6 Mustangs were seeing increasing activity on the Fiumefreddo–Randazzo–Troina–Adrano road. Near the town

---

17   AFHRA, IRISREF B0747, p.425.
18   The National Archives London, Royal Air Force, Operations Record Books AIR 27/43 p.236.
19   Durbidge, *Memoirs of a High Flyer*, p.37.

of Novara di Sicilia, more than 100 troop transports were spotted heading along the coastal road towards Messina. In two of the 14 sorties flown, Lieutenants Dickson and Sakakenny were engaged in a search for a radar station on the Aeolian islands. DAF aircraft attacked 40 troop transports along the Linguaglossa-Randazzo road; another 30–40 vehicles were identified and attacked near Francavilla di Sicilia.

Keith Durbidge took off from Lentini San Francesco at 11:00 a.m. to cover Agira; he photographed a vast fire eight miles from the town. The town had been subjected to a heavy bombing raid by 24 Bostons, of 3 Wing SAAF, escorted by six Spitfires from No. 92 Squadron RAF. Durbidge then headed to the new Falcone landing strip to assess damage from the previous air raid; only one aircraft was seen on the ground.

The A-36A fighter-bombers of XII ASC attacked a dozen moving vehicles near San Fratello and some boats and railway sections in Milazzo; several bridges were bombed to the west of Francavilla di Sicilia and north of Pancallo. The Americans captured Castelbuono and moved north of the coastal road, while British and Canadian troops advanced with difficulty between Agira and Regalbuto.

In the Etna area, it was not only Allied bombs being dropped on roads and bridges. A formation composed of Bf 109s of II./JG 53, escorted by some Fw 190s of SKG 10, reported having successfully attacked a target near Nicosia at 9:25 a.m.. A German reconnaissance Bf 109 flown by Oberleutnant Gerhard Weinert of 2 (H)/14 was shot down by Spitfires from No. 43 Squadron RAF near Reggio Calabria.

On the morning of the 28th, during a routine patrol over the coast of Syracuse, Spitfires from 92 Squadron intercepted and shot down the 1./JG77 Bf 109 ('White 5', WNr. 18119) flown by Unteroffizier Karl-Eugen Hettler. The German pilot, shot down by Flying Officer Dicks-Sherwood (JL388), managed to bail out before his Messerschmitt crashed. He was captured soon after.

The Spitfires of 40 Squadron SAAF were sent to Centuripe and Regalbuto to photograph some defensive machine gun positions.[20] Tactical reconnaissance data was quickly transmitted to the Northwest African Tactical Air Force (NATAF) which, from Hal Far on Malta, despatched 11 Baltimores of 21 Squadron SAAF at 8:33 a.m.. Headed for Regalbuto with a load of 66 × 250lb bombs, at 9:35 they were at 11,000 feet over the city of Caltagirone when they were joined by six Spitfires. Over the target at 9:41, the formation's leader, Major Cormack, initiated the attack.

The 111th TRS flew 14 sorties, reporting a significant increase in road traffic on the Troina–Cesarò–Randazzo route and intensive movement of vehicles south between Naso and Randazzo, where Lieutenants Dickson and McGowans suddenly found themselves in contact with 12 enemy aircraft, which were promptly strafed.[21]

At 10:15 a.m., XII ASC sent the A-36A fighter-bombers of the 526th FBS, 86th FBG, from Gela West to patrol the roads between Troina, Cesarò and Randazzo; more than 50 vehicles of various kinds were identified and damaged between Troina and Randazzo, while a road section

20   40 Squadron SAAF received additional reinforcements from Malta. Lieutenant Moir arrived with 59 men on transport aircraft. A Flight, including all aircraft and pilots, rejoined the squadron.
21   Meantime, Lieutenant Gentzler had returned from North Africa, bringing with him three other pilots and four Mustangs borrowed from No. 225 Squadron RAF. The Mustang IIs transferred to the 111th TRS in Sicily were serials 41-37428, 41-37361, 41-37424 and 41-37366. The National Archives London, Royal Air Force, Operations Record Books AIR 27/1396/13 p.31.

and a bridge were bombed to the east and west of Cesarò. The A-36A of Lieutenant Francis D. McCarroll was hit at the latter location. The Australians of 3 Squadron, led by Squadron Leader Stevens, headed for Cesarò and Randazzo with 12 Kittyhawks. To the north-east of Troina, they found a field hospital located at coordinates C5716. The P-40 Warhawks of the 79th FG, operating from Cassibile, flew seven missions to combat naval traffic along the Strait of Messina.

The Seventh Army captured Nicosia and, after bloody battles, the 1st Canadian Division and the 231st Infantry Brigade Malta occupied part of Agira; the rest was still occupied by Axis troops. On the 29th, Lieutenants Earl and Lamb flew the 300th sortie for the 111th TRS, which, on the same day, completed 12 flights over the Etna region. Some of the aircraft that had landed at Licata the night before moved to Gela West. The same day, the first sections of 654 AOP Squadron merged with the 1st Canadian Division, and into the British 51st and 78th Divisions, in support of the artillery, carrying out brief reconnaissance on the enemy front to support the advance on the west side of Etna. The 50th Division gunners, on the slope near Catania, were supported by 651 AOP. Twenty-three Baltimores from 232 Wing RAF, including 11 from 55 Squadron and 12 from 223 Squadron, raided the Milazzo area, but encountered many difficulties identifying the target due to bad weather. One of the bombers was hit over Bronte by anti-aircraft fire. Sergeant Vair, flying Baltimore III 'P' FA303, was left alone in the aircraft after the other three members of the crew baled out; he managed to make a miraculous landing near Lentini.[22]

Also on 29 July, from a tent near Gela Ponte Olivo, Major Harper of the American Intelligence Section planned a reconnaissance mission for the 12th PRS to identify some artillery positions north of Nicosia, and on the Axis defensive line that ran from Sant'Agata di Militello to Cesarò. The photos taken by the F-5A were sent to the 1st Infantry Division (Big Red One).. Meanwhile, at 10:23 a.m., a flight of 12 Boston IIIs from 12 Squadron SAAF, led by the veteran Lieutenant-Colonel Kotze, departed Hal Far to drop 164 × 250lb bombs on machine gun positions at coordinates H7581, to the south-west of Paternò. At 11:09, again from Hal Far, 21 Squadron SAAF, Captain Ord and Lieutenant Hodges leading 12 Baltimores, attacked gun positions at H708820, between Centuripe and Paternò. In the meantime, Italian Generale Guzzoni, commander of VI Army, ordered a withdrawal on the northern front, on the San Fratello–Monte Pelato line.

From the late morning of the 30th, until the early afternoon, 3 Wing SAAF and 232 Wing RAF carried out bombing raids on enemy positions identified at H7393, just south of Biancavilla. Meanwhile, American A-20 Havoc light bombers of the TBF, 47th BG, bombed Milazzo and Centuripe. Across five missions, the 47th deployed 60 A-20 Havoc bombers, unloading 220 × 300lb bombs and triggering a large fire. Shipping between Milazzo, Messina and Riposto was also under continuous attack from more than 100 P-40 Warhawk fighter-bombers, some from the 79th FG, operating from the new airstrip near Palagonia. Damage assessment fell to Flying Officer E.C. Hey, 683 Squadron, who, taking off from Lentini at 11:00 a.m. in Spitfire PR.XI (EN425), followed the raid from 27,000 feet. At 12:30 p.m., Allied fighter-bombers hit the Riposto pier, causing four impressive explosions. While 40 Squadron SAAF moved its Spitfires

22 The National Archives Londra AIR 27/518-12. The rest of the crew was Sergeant G. Johnstone, Sergeant W. Brokensha and Sergeant J. Stannard.

The port of Catania photographed on the morning of 31 July 1943 from 27,000 feet by Flying Officer F.R. Brocklehurst in Spitfire PR.XI (MB785) of No. 683 Squadron. (US Air Force)

to Lentini San Francesco, Lieutenant Iles flew a reconnaissance over the Paternò–Misterbianco line, and over Catania, until late that night, particularly photographing objectives at coordinates C9727 and C9724, north of Francavilla di Sicilia.

The final day of the month saw the loss of a pilot from No. 1437 Strategic Reconnaissance Flight; it was the first loss for the unit since it began operations in Sicily. Flight Sergeant Stanley, flying a tactical reconnaissance A-36A Mustang (HK945/'B'), was shot down by anti-aircraft fire in the Sant'Agata di Militello area; with him was Flying Officer Jones in HK944, 'C', who saw Stanley's Mustang plummet in flames. Even though Jones's aircraft was also hit, starting a fire on board, he managed to return to Pachino just in time.

At the request of General Terry Allen, commander of the American 1st Infantry Division, nicknamed 'Big Red One', the 12th PRS flew a mission to Troina, Cesarò and Maletto. The request from the US Army required oblique photos to be taken with a 6-inch camera from 8,000 feet in the indicated area. Despite bad weather over Sicily at the time, the bombers of the 47th BG, 3 Wing SAAF and 232 Wing RAF, all operating under the TBF, carried out 18 raids against Paternò, Santa Maria di Licodia and Centuripe. During the day, some targets were bombed six times by groups of 12 bombers; 112 tons of 250lb GP bombs were unloaded on roads and buildings to prevent the movement of enemy troops. Cesarò and Randazzo were successfully bombed by 24 B-25 Mitchells of the 340th BG and 24 from the 12th BG. American tactical reconnaissance had in fact seen, in the early hours of the morning, intensive movements of various vehicles, about 60 in all, along the Cesarò–Randazzo route. In the afternoon, the A-36A Mustangs of XII ASC attacked numerous boats in the stretch of sea between Milazzo and Capo d'Orlando and in Sant'Agata di Militello. Noteworthy is the mission carried out by the 37 B-26 Marauders of NASAF's 320th BG that, escorted by 24 P-38 Lightnings of the 1st FG, together with 18 Spitfires from Malta, headed for Adrano and Paternò. The route of the American bombers took them via Pachino, as they headed for Ramacca, turning there onto the bomb run at 12,000 feet. The bombers carried a total of 222 × 500lb bombs, an enormous load that alone would be enough to raze these two battered towns. Cloud cover prevented the first 17 bombers from identifying the target and dropping their 102 bombs. The rest of the attackers unloaded over the north-east part of Paternò up to the gates of Adrano. Anti-aircraft fire was intense, damaging two Marauders. Four batteries responded heavily from half a mile south-west of Adrano, with as many again firing from Bronte; two batteries on the hills west of Biancavilla and one just west of Nicolosi also contributed. On the same day, Cerami and Capizzi were occupied by the Seventh Army, and the 1st Canadian Division conquered Catenanuova. At 3:05 p.m. on 30 July, the *Luftwaffe* sent nine Fw 190s of II./SKG 10 from Crotone to attack Allied troops near Agira. A concentration of tanks and vehicles of various kinds was identified, hidden within a dense olive grove, and attacked by the German aircraft. They strafed and dropped eight 250kg bombs. *Luftwaffe* sorties ended in the late afternoon, with four Fw 190s of II./SKG 10 flying an armed reconnaissance over north-eastern Sicily. They reported having attacked a concentration of Allied vehicles in a valley with explosive devices. All aircraft returned at 7:45 p.m.

That night, the Northwest African Tactical Air Force's No. 205 Group RAF, which had long been committed to bombing strategic targets in the area of Naples Capodichino, Montecorvino Rovella, and Villa San Giovanni, sent 12 Vickers Wellingtons to attack Adrano, and another 10 to Randazzo. There were many recommendations made by Allied commanders to the bombers' crews; the two cities, emphasised the Allies, were located just 10 miles from the

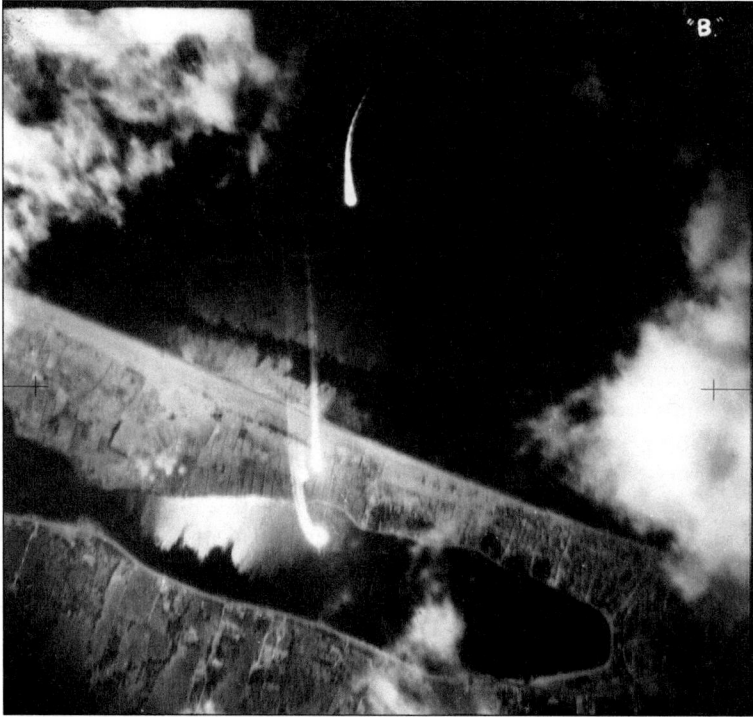

A night bombing raid over the beaches of Ganzirri in Messina by the Vickers Wellingtons of No. 70 Squadron. In the photo, flares illuminate the target. (Richard Stowers)

British–Canadian–American bomb line and it was important to identify the target precisely to avoid endangering friendly troops.

Almost all of the sorties flown during the last days of July were carried out either against terrestrial targets located by air reconnaissance or against naval traffic along the Strait of Messina and in the port of Milazzo; for the rest it was about targets of opportunity. The main targets were the cities of Troina, Santo Stefano di Camastra, Regalbuto, Randazzo and Paternò, the ports of Catania, Messina and Milazzo, and then dumps, roads, bridges, vehicles, and moving heavy vehicles and ships. During the last week of the month a big effort was directed at Milazzo which, at the time, appeared to be one of the most used Axis ports and the most active seaplane base. Between the 24th and 30th, 38 Mitchells, 196 Bostons and Baltimores, and 251 fighter-bombers made their way to this city and its port. Another main objective was Regalbuto, an important nerve centre of communication, but it was only on 26 July that 215 American, British and South African bombers attacked, seriously damaging the city and surrounding areas.

With the capture of Nicosia and Agira on the 28th, only the final assault on the Etna line remained. The terrain along this 80-mile front favoured the defenders, who positioned their artillery on the highest peaks; a relatively few men therefore managed to thwart the Allied advance. The volcano, which dominates the area, restricted the attack front; its impervious slopes provided few roads, most of which were surrounded by dense vegetation. Even when Axis troops were driven out of one location, they placed explosive charges and mined the bridges to hinder the Allied advance, allowing them time to take position on other high points. For almost the rest of the Sicilian campaign, the Allies fought against some German forces, such as the 29th German Panzer Grenadier Division, which unexpectedly arrived on the island from southern Italy. The evident intention of the enemy to resist indefinitely to cover the retreat forced the Americans of the Seventh Army and the British of the Eighth Army to fight hard along the Etna line.

Photo Reconnaissance operations carried out by the NAAF from 17/18 to 31 July 1943					
Unit	Aircraft	Ports & Bases	Airfields	Other Targets*	Total
5th PRS	F-5A	18	69	73	160
12th PRS	F-5A	-	-	140	140
15th PRS	F-5A, B-25D	84	216	105	405
682	Spitfire XI	70	208	119	397
40 SAAF	Spitfire	-	-	18	18
111th TRS	P-39, P-51	8	-	52	60
Total		180	493	507	1180

*M/Vs, roads, rivers, enemy camps, positions and towns.

Strat/R and Tac/R Reconnaissance operations carried out by the NAAF from 17/18 to 31 July 1943			
Unit	Aircraft	Strat/R	Tac/R
33rd FG	P-40	-	18
40 SAAF	Spitfire	-	143
86th FBG	A-36	-	92
417 RAF	Spitfire	-	12
111th TRS	P-39, P-51	-	105
Total		-	370

Reconnaissance operations carried out from Malta between 17/18 July and 31 July					
Squadron	Aircraft used	Tac/R & PR	Strategic R & PR	P/R & V/R	Total
1435	Spitfire	4			4
683	Spitfire			45 53	98
1437 Flight	Mustang		30		30
Total		4	30	98	132

List of places photographed

AQUINO
ARIANO IRPINO
ASCEA
BAGLIO RIZZO
BAGNOLI
BAIA
BARI
BENEVENTO
BOCCA DI FALCO
BOTRICELLE
BOVINO
BRINDISI
CAMPO CASALE
CAPE RIZZUTO
CAPE SAN VITO
CAPODICHINO
CAPRI
CAPUA
CARCITELLA
CASTELLMARE DI
STABIA
CASTELLUCCIO DI
SAURI
CASTELVETRANO
CATANIA
CENTOCELLE
CERIGNOLA
CERVETERI
CIAMPINO
CISTERNO DI ROMA
CISTERNA LITTORIA
CIVITAVECCHIA

CORLEONE
CROTONE
FALCONE
FOGGIA
FROSINONE
FURBARA
GAETA
GIOIA DEL COLLE
GRAZZANISE
GROTTAGLIE
GUIDONIA
LEVERANO
LITTORIO
LOCRI
MANURIA
MARCIGLIANA
MESSINA
MILAZZO
MILO
MONTE CORVINO
NAPLES
NICOTERA MARINA
NOCERA TERINESE
PALAZZO SAN
GERVASIO
PALERMO
PIZZO
POMIGLIANO D'ARCO
POZZUOLI
PRAIA A MARE
REGGIO DI CALABRIA
RESINA

RIPOSTO
SALEMI
SALERNO
SALINA GRANDE
SAN GIOVANNI
SAN LORENZO
SAN NICOLA
SAN PANCRAZIO
SAN VITO DEI
NORMANNI
SAPRI
SCALEA
SCIACCA
SERRA DI FALCO
SESSA AURUNCA
SEZZE ROMANO
TARANTO
TARQUINO
TERMINI IMERESE
TORRE ANNUNZIATA
TORRE DEL GRECO
VIBO VALENTIA
VILLANOVA
VITERBO

16

Recce Aircraft Over the Strait (Towards Messina)

Following Mussolini's fall on 25 July, German plans for Sicily had undergone a radical turnaround; they had moved from keeping the Sicilian bridgehead to the bitter end to the salvation of the German units engaged in battle, which at that time was equal to three divisions. Thus began the retreat towards the line at the foot of Etna they called 'Etna-Stellung'. The Germans, to allow a retreat to the Italian mainland, were in fact filling the approaches to the Strait of Messina with an imposing anti-aircraft defence system. This made it almost impossible for Allied aircraft to fly at low level in the area.

Amongst the pilots of the 3rd Photographic Group (PG) who arrived on Malta in March 1943 was Lieutenant George German, who flew 50 missions from the island. One in particular earned him the Distinguished Flying Cross. Sometime later, when promoted to captain, he recalled the flight:

> I was sent out one day to make a weather flight over Naples, Foggia, and such southern Italian points as the Messina straits. We had been having heavy weather for the past five days and meantime, the bombers had been giving those places a heavy pasting, especially in view of the fact that the Germans then were evacuating Sicily.
>
> When I reached Naples, I found a ceiling of 9,000 feet with eight-tenths cloud coverage so I had to dive down under this to take my pictures of the port and marshalling yards. Right there I ran into my first troubles. I was in the middle of my photo run when they started throwing up heavy flak and I saw fighters taking off to intercept me. After making seven runs over the city, port, marshalling yards and airdrome, I decided it was high time to run. I headed for Foggia. With the tail of the P-38 up, I soon lost the fighters and when the next bearing was picked up, I was near Pescara. From there I headed for Foggia and started shooting the marshalling yards and satellite airdromes. Flak and fighters again took a bearing on me and I spent little time there before high-tailing it out from Salerno and the rest of my mission around the "toe of the boot".
>
> The Germans must have had a good beam on me because just south of Salerno I pulled out of the clouds to find a Nazi fighter flying practically alongside. Back into the clouds I went and lost him, apparently, because nothing ever came of it. At Messina they were waiting for me. I came over the city at 8,000 feet to find a big hole in the clouds and they poured up everything they had. My ship took three flak hits and I don't deny I was scared. It was so bad, in fact, that I was flying with my head ducked down in

the cockpit and every time I looked up, there was flak bursting around my propellers. Well, I finished my run and headed for the base. Here it wasn't the Germans, but a thick cold front in which I became tangled, finally getting a heading on the fighter base and coming home safely. We were using big British 36 inch focal length cameras in split verticals at the time. The motor on one of these had burned out during the flight but the other one was all right and I brought back good pictures. These proved highly valuable and showed that the bombers had been laying their bombs on the target and heavily damaging the marshalling yards and airports in the Naples, Foggia and Messina areas.[1]

August 1 marked the entry of American troops into Santo Stefano di Camastra and Gagliano Castelferrato; British troops meanwhile captured the strategically important airfield at Gerbini.[2]

The *Luftwaffe*, after some preventative aerial reconnaissance over Sicily, sent 25 Ju 88s, of KG 26, and some Dornier Do 217s, of III./KG 100, from its airfields in southern France to bomb Palermo, now completely in American hands. The damage to the city was considerable; above all, the port area around the main pier was damaged and some fuel depots and a train

Kittyhawk III FR511, coded 'GA-F'. Australian Pilot Officer R.A. Wild of No. 112 Squadron was forced to make an emergency landing near Motta Camastra on 3 August 1943. (US Air Force photo 79531 AC)

1   AFHRA, IRISREF B0747, p.398.
2   Having conquered Gerbini and its satellites, the Allies reported on the rich booty of aircraft left behind by the Germans and Italians. There were about 1,000 aircraft, of which 234 were Bf 109s, distributed as follows: Trapani Bo Rizzo 90, Sciacca 122, Castelvetrano 121, Comiso 111, Marsala Stagnone 3, Biscari Santo Pietro 35; Gela Ponte Olivo 10, Trapani Milo 124, Palermo Boccadifalco 104, Termini Imerese 27, Gerbini 72, Satellite #6 28, Satellite #9 18, Catania Fontanarossa 105, Augusta seaplane base 29.

loaded with ammunition were destroyed. The British coastal vessel *Uskide* was sunk, while two USN minesweepers, the USS *Strive* and USS *Skill*, reported some damage. Two Dorniers were intercepted by Spitfire Mk.VIIIs of the 2nd Fighter Squadron (FS) USAAF from Palermo Boccadifalco. The first German bomber was shot down 60 miles north of the island of Salina by 2nd Lieutenant Norman E. English at around 6:00 a.m.; the other Dornier was claimed by Captain Norman L. McDonald five minutes later, 15 miles north-east of the island of Stromboli.

A Kittyhawk taxiing in typically dusty conditions. The long nose obscured much of the pilot's forward vision on the ground so the man on the wing came in handy. (Air Force Imagery Archive RAAF)

The *Luftwaffe,* in a vain attempt to stem the Allied advance, sent, at 6:35 in the morning, four Fw 190s of II./SKG (armed with ten 250kg SD and 250kg AB bombs)[3], escorted by Bf 109s of I./JG 77, on an armed reconnaissance of the Regalbuto area. They returned to Crotone at 8:12. Just two hours later, another six Fw 190 fighter-bombers from the same unit, escorted by 10 Bf 109s from I./JG 77, flew an armed reconnaissance over the Nicosia area. On the road between Nicosia and Mistretta, they successfully attacked 10 vehicles, two trucks, a tank and an Allied anti-aircraft position. However, anti-aircraft fire managed to hit the Fw 190 flown by Leutnant Wenk in a fuel tank and the fuselage. The German pilot was forced to return to base early.

---

3   German SD bombs were 'Sprengbombe Dickwandig' (anti-personnel butterfly bombs). AB bombs were 'Abwurfbehälter' (cluster bombs).

Once … I got hit in my fuel tank, I was flying in a valley after we had bombed, and saw a truck in front of a building, which I fired at and hit. But then I noticed a second truck equipped with anti-aircraft guns. I saw it much too late and flew very low above it, at about ten metres. I saw some of those flat English helmets. They shot me down, but I flew to Mount Etna, and then flew close to the lava in order to avoid being hit again. I did not know how long the engine was going to play along.[4]

The punctual and effective reaction of Allied anti-aircraft artillery succeeded in destroying two Fw 190s of the 5th *Staffel* that morning; these were flown by Feldwebel Arno Achter, who crashed in an unidentified location, and Feldwebel Rudi Riepelsiep, who was seen to come

Squadron Leader Brian Eaton (left) receives command of No. 3 Squadron RAAF from Squadron Leader R.N.B. Stevens on Agnone airstrip in Sicily. Stevens would go on to command No. 451 Squadron RAAF. (Air Force Imagery Archive RAAF)

4   Morten Jessen, Andrew Arthy, *Focke-Wulf Fw 190 in the Battle for Sicily* (Denmark: Air War Publications, 2010), p.126.

down about four miles east of Citanova, on the route to Nicosia. Leutnant Wenk, avoiding any further hits, returned to Crotone at 12:11 p.m.

With American troops just two miles north-west of Troina, the 111th Tactical Reconnaissance Squadron's (TRS) scouts were urged to carry out three recce missions, for a total of 10 sorties, all flown north of the battle in the Troina area. The fruitful sorties located eight machine gun positions near the centre of Troina and at coordinates D0405, C5867 and D6175, near Cesarò. The squadron also reported light, disorderly movement of vehicles along the roadways north of Etna.

Flying Officer Griffith and Warrant Officer Leggo flew their No. 1437 Strategic Reconnaissance Flight (SRF) Mustangs on a reconnaissance over the east coast of Sicily. Leggo intercepted a long column of vehicles, among which was a car with a senior officer on board, both Mustangs strafing at low altitude. Near Capo Spartivento in Calabria, they also located and machine-gunned a radar station. From Lentini San Francesco, Spitfire PR.XIs of No. 683 Squadron were requested by the Army to continue high-altitude reconnaissance flights over Catania. Pilot Officers Keith Durbidge and G. Craig did the honours.

From 5:50 in the morning until sunset on 1 August, large formations of No. 239 Wing RAF Kittyhawks flew a number of armed reconnaissance missions in rapid succession, attacking targets of opportunity on the flanks of Mount Etna. Of particular note was the 3:50 p.m. strike by 12 No. 3 Squadron RAAF Kittyhawk IIIs and 12 from No. 260 Squadron RAF (escorted by Spitfires). The formation was under the command of Wing Commander Barry, of 3 Squadron, who reported:

> Met with Spits at Lentini and flew N.W. across Gerbini Main, thence to Biancaville, Bronte, Adrano, back over Bronte, Randazzo Raccuira back to Randazzo, and Adrano without observing any road movement. 3 large M/T. seen heading N. at H7590 and these were bombed from 7,000' down 1,000'. The bridge was hit and a big explosion with heavy black smoke later rising to 3,000' was observed, as the result of the bombing. Turning about, A/C straffed [sic] M/T 3 miles N. of Adrano, scoring 1 flamer (F/O Matthews) and 2 damaged (F/L Susans & F/S Thomas). Continuing N. along road to Bronte, 8 M/T were seen on either side at C7404 dispersed in an orchard ...[5]

In the meantime, A-36A fighter-bombers attacked some artillery positions near the village of Naso and B-25 Mitchells of the 310th Bombardment Group (BG), from Dar el Koudia in Tunisia, hit Milazzo's port installations, warehouses and railway line again. The 340th BG continued to bomb Bronte relentlessly.

On 2 August, two Mustangs of 1437 SRF, flown by Lieutenant P.D.L. McLaren SAAF (HK946/F) and Flight Sergeant Proud (HK947/A), departed Lentini San Francesco to reconnoitre the Capo d'Orlando area and the Strait of Messina. McLaren, hit and wounded in the head by one of the many flak emplacements now protecting the strait, still managed to return to Lentini East for an emergency landing. Proud returned safely without damage. Meanwhile, the 111th TRS flew 22 sorties in support of American ground troops engaged in the Battle of Troina.

---

5   The National Archives London, Royal Air Force, Operations Record Books AIR 27/41/40, p.2.

A Macchi MC.202 captured in Catania airfield by No. 3 Squadron RAAF, to which the RAAF roundel has already been applied (the Italian unit emblem forward of the cockpit has remained). (Air Force Imagery Archive RAAF)

The Tactical Bomber Force (TBF) flew six missions with 72 Bostons, one of which (Bronte) was aborted due to not rendesvousing with the escorting Spitfires. The Mitchells of the 12th and 340th Bombardment Groups attacked Adrano and Bronte, and some gun positions south-west of Paternò. XII Air Support Command (ASC) sent A-36A Mustangs of the 27th and 86th Fighter-Bomber Groups to Barcellona Pozzo di Gotto, Capo d'Orlando, Troina, Randazzo and south of Adrano. About 35 moving vehicles were attacked and destroyed along the road west of Cesarò and on the road that leads from Naso to Capo d'Orlando.

Three tactical reconnaissance (Tac/R) sorties were flown by Spitfires from No. 40 Squadron SAAF; one discovered an enemy defensive fortification sporting a 170mm cannon. At 11:15 a.m., the Kittyhawk IIIs of 3 Squadron RAAF and the 112 Squadron RAF attacked the fortified position:

Met Spits over Pachino, and flew N.W. to Gerbini, turned N.E. towards Catania, where 112 Sqdn lead [sic] by Group Captain Darwen bombed fortifications on N. side of road at H8375. 3 Sqdn passed over Catania whilst waiting for 112 Sqdn but received only slight A/A; then bombed the same target as 112 Sqdn. Bombing was good, all landing in target area. A/C also straffed [sic] whilst going down to bomb.[6]

At 7:40 p.m., from Hosc Raui in Libya, No. 178 Squadron RAF dispatched six Halifaxes and three Liberators, followed by five Halifax IIs of No. 462 Squadron RAAF, for a raid against shipping in the Strait of Messina area.

Across the terrain approaching Etna, after days of bitter fighting, Italian–German command prepared a new retreat along a shorter defensive line, this time covering the eastern flank of Mount Etna. This new series of locations, called the 'Tortorici Line', stretched approximately from Zappulla to San Salvatore di Fitalia, Galati Mamertino, Monte Moro, Monte Colla, Randazzo, Monte Nero, Giarre and Torre Archirafi.

At 5:55 a.m. on 3 August, a flight of four Kittyhawks from 3 Squadron RAAF, led by Group Captain Darwen, carried out an armed reconnaissance along the road between Santa Teresa and Fiumefreddo, identifying and attacking more than eight means of transport. North of Fiumefreddo, four rail cars were also successfully attacked. Flying over Giardini, the flight encountered intense anti-aircraft fire; Flight Sergeant Peter Gilbert's aircraft was seriously hit, but he managed to return to base.

Early the same morning, No. 60 Squadron SAAF Mosquito LR411, a B Flight machine, was sent to Romania. From Ariana airport near Tunis, Lieutenants Miller and Allison photographed the Ploesti refineries to verify the outcome of the bombing of Operation *Tidal Wave*, the low-level attack made by American bombers flying from North Africa on 1 August. The op proved to be beyond the range of even the Mosquito and Miller and Allison were forced to land back at base with empty tanks.

The 111th TRS performed 16 sorties, two of which were flown by Lieutenants Modrall and Wickus. They reported that, during a reconnaissance between San Fratello and Cesarò, they intercepted about 50 vehicles. In the final phase of the mission, they noticed the sudden approach of four Fw 190s, which, strangely, did not attack. These were most likely the four Fw 190s of II./SKG 10 escorted by I./JG 77 that left Crotone at 6:05 a.m. for an armed reconnaissance over Sicily. *Luftwaffe* fighter-bombers reported that, at around 7:00 a.m., they had strafed and bombed (two × 250kg SD and two × 250kg AB bombs) some Allied vehicles near Nicosia, and that they sighted about 25–30 Kittyhawks; Spitfires and Mustangs attacked two Bf 109s from I./JG 77 east of Milazzo.

At 9:55 a.m., another flight of four Kittyhawks from 3 Squadron RAAF, led by Flight Lieutenant Harris, headed to Randazzo and Bronte. In an open field, near coordinates C7208, south-east of Bronte, they observed a defensive system of trenches and fortifications; just south of the same town, three large tanks were seen heading north.

The TBF carried out 19 missions, using 116 Mitchells, 94 Bostons and 36 Baltimores to drop 180 tons of bombs on the cities of Adrano and Biancavilla, and some gun positions identified by reconnaissance at coordinates H707960, H710955, H704982 and H701956, close to the Carcaci district. During one of the raids, a bridge was bombed along the road that connects Centuripe and Adrano, between H682946 and H701956 near the Simeto river. Another offensive action was also carried out near the river, with the bombing of H7097, not far from Adrano.

6   The National Archives London, Royal Air Force, Operations Record Books AIR 27/41/40, p.3.

An A-20B Havoc of the 47th BG. There is a strong probability this aircraft is 41-3449 of the 86th BS, hit in both engines during a bombing raid on Bronte, which took place in the afternoon of 6 August 1943. The pilot, Lieutenant Daniel G. Gillham, and two other crew members baled out and were captured by the Germans (MACR 705). (US Air Force)

Between 6:20 and 6:25 p.m., three flights of Kittyhawk IIIs from 260 Squadron RAF took off from the new airstrip at Agnone, near Lentini, to perform a Rhubarb over Misterbianco, Linguaglossa and Giarre.[7] The first flight was led by Major E.C. Saville who submitted the following report on his return:

> Formation headed N from base at 8000' releasing bombs while flying on a level course between Misterbianco and Biancavilla. No results were observed from the bombing. The section then flew W of Mt. Etna, turning N.E of the mountain and flying N.E to Novaro. From Novaro section flew S. to Linguaglossa and owing to very intense light A.A. here turned and flew towards Randazzo. The road between Linguaglossa and Cesaro was covered with 200 plus M.T. moving E. Straffing [sic] was carried out against this target and the following claims were made: 1 M.T. flamer, 10 M.T.

7   The National Archives London, Royal Air Force, Operations Record Books AIR 27/1537/50, p.5.

damaged and several personnel killed. 6 large gun positions were observed being dug in S of the road 4 miles E Cesaro. After straffing [sic] formation returned direct to base.

Flight Lieutenant B.H. Thomas was at the head of the second flight of four aircraft:

This section released bombs in the same area as the preceding section and turned E. N. of Etna toward Linguaglossa. This section also encountered very intense light A.A. from this area and also from Piedimonte, Nicolosi and Giarre. Straffing [sic] was carried out from Linguaglossa to Aci Catena along the secondary road and the following claims were made: 1 large bus and 3 M.T. damage and several personnel killed. After straffing [sic] formation returned direct to base.

The third flight had Flight Lieutenant L.A. Malins in the lead:

This section released bombs in the same area as the preceding section and flew E. N. of Etna, turning and straffing [sic] the Fiumefreddo/Acireale road. Light A.A. was encountered from Linguaglossa, Nicolosi and 2 Breda positions midway between these two towns. Straffing [sic] claims were as follows: 1 M.T. flamer and 11 M.T. damaged. After straffing [sic] formation returned direct to base.

Fifty-six Vickers Wellingtons from No. 205 Group unloaded 97 tons of bombs on Messina's harbour and train station overnight.

On 4 August, after a detailed briefing, the Royal Navy requested Tac/R be flown by the Spitfires of 40 Squadron SAAF. The radio systems of the Spitfires were linked via VHF radio to those of the monitor HMS *Roberts*. The ship was using its two 15-inch guns to bombard the coastal road just north of Taormina. The photographs taken by the Spitfires served to verify whether the bombardment had the desired effect; that is, to limit accessibility at three key points.

From the diary of the 40 SAAF Squadron:

It had been hoped for some time by this section that an opportunity would arise for doing Arty/R with the Navy so when the change came it was not difficult to organize the shoot. A V.H.F. set was installed on board a monitor, (next to the gunnery officer), and an A.L.O. [Air Liaison Officer] and the Squadron signal officer with one operator sailed from Augusta on 4 August with the intention of bombarding the coast road near Taormina and making it impassable for vehicles.

The aircraft established communication with the ship at the pre-arranged time of 1130 hrs and started bombarding at 1140 hrs at 19,000 yds finally closing to 15,000 yds. The shelling seemed accurate but the pilot reported no serious damage to the road after 25 rounds. The pilot had to return owing to petrol shortage but the "weaver" changed to Channel 'A' frequency, continued the shoot and reported considerable damage. Oblique photographs were taken by another reconnaissance immediately after the shoot and these showed several falls of rock, but the following morning the road was passable for one-way traffic. The shoot took an hour and 32 rounds were fired.[8]

Four Kittyhawks of 260 Squadron, in support of the Eighth Army, which was still stalled along the Misterbianco defensive line and the banks of the Simeto, near Ponte Barca a Paternò, attacked coordinates H7782 and H7777. Major E.C. Saville was leading again. The Kittyhawks flew over Catania and what remained of the railway station of a completely deserted city. Later, at 9:50 a.m., another flight of Kittyhawks, this time led by Flight Lieutenant L.A. Malins, strafed targets between the towns of Mazzarà, Novara di Sicilia and Francavilla di Sicilia, including two German Tiger tanks.

At 2:15 p.m., Saville carried out an armed reconnaissance of the Novara di Sicilia area, leading 12 aircraft from 260 Squadron. He recalled:

> Formation flew N. keeping to West of Mt. Etna and proceeding up to Novaro, turning N. of the town and bombing from N. to S. from 8000' to 4000'. Target area was woods at D9828. All bombs fell in target area but nature of target or specific results were [not] observed. No A.A was encountered from this area. About 20 M.T. were seen moving up the road towards Novaro and these were straffed [sic]. Results were 10 M.T. damaged and one set on fire; a wireless station in the vicinity was attacked. General movement N. wards of M.T. in scattered group was reported over the entire area but no suitable targets were observed. One pilot, after bombing, straffed [sic] 4 M.T. at D9024 and claimed 3 damaged and 1 flamer. 4 medium sized tanks were also seen in this area and these tanks sent up A.A. Other A.A. opposition was encountered as follows: Intense light from Piedimonte, from D9525 and Taormina; 2 shore batteries firing light A.A. from J0698. An R.T. station N. of Fiumefreddo on the coast was also straffed [sic] without observed results. A large ammo. explosion was seen in Catania town with yellowish smoke. At J0895 F/S Rattle's a/c was seen to give off black smoke. Nothing appeared wrong but F/S Rattle failed to return with the formation. He force landed in the sea, swam ashore and was taken prisoner. He remained in enemy hands for ten days but eventually made his escape and returned to his Unit on Aug. 15th.[9]

The TBF planned 14 missions for the day, but two were cancelled due to a lack of available escorts. Twenty-four Mitchells, 48 Baltimores, and 72 Bostons of the 340th BG, No. 3 Wing SAAF, No. 232 Wing RAF and the 47th BG, unloaded 97 tons of bombs on Adrano, Bronte, Riposto, Fiumefreddo and some gun positions in nearby Biancavilla. A large column of about 200 vehicles was sighted near Castroreale, close to a tree-lined area. The Desert Air Force (DAF) reported it had intercepted 430 heavy vehicles and destroyed 60, damaged another 80; among these were cars with senior officers on board. The 57th Fighter Group (FG) which, for almost the entire Sicilian campaign was engaged in anti-shipping sweeps in the area of Milazzo, Messina, Etna and Catania, flew 16 armed reconnaissance missions along the line from the new Advanced Landing Ground (ALG) at Scordia. During the eighth mission,

8   The National Archives London, South African Air Force, Operations Record Books AIR 54/84/4, p.49.
9   The National Archives London, Royal Air Force, Operations Record Books AIR 27/1537/50, p.6.

Lfl.2/Stabsbildabt.   Hafen SIRACUSA J-si 45 105   Aufkl.-Gr.122/1.(F)123
Fi.J0696 SG/060   Karte Jtalien 1:100000 Nr.274   Beobachter:
v.9.8.43 7.42 Uhr   M.~1:22 000   Lt.Ballmann

alte beschädigte Einheiten, unverändert.
Ballonsperre.

Luftwaffe aerial reconnaissance of the Syracuse roadstead. (NARA)

carried out from 11:00 a.m. to 12:05 p.m. by four Warhawks of the 65th FS over the area north of Etna, a well-defended radio antenna was identified at coordinates C9913. At 12:00 p.m., the tenth mission of the day, four Warhawks from the 66th FS identified and attacked more than 50 large vehicles (many of which were cleverly hidden behind a wooded area) along the road from coordinates D0515 to Randazzo. Among the pilots involved in a later mission was 2nd Lieutenant William George Kremer, of the 65th FS, 57th FG, who left Scordia 1:30 p.m. on an armed reconnaissance of the Etna area. Kremer was hit by anti-aircraft fire and did not return to the base. His wingman, 2nd Lieutenant James W. Hart, witnessed his loss:

On August 4, 1943 while straffing [sic] east on the east-west road north of Mt. Etna at pin point C8818, Lt. Kramer was hit light ack-ack. After calling on his radio that he had been hit, he pulled up to an altitude of 1500 feet, rolled over on his back and spun in with his engine smoking and burst into flames upon crashing. ... he was killed in the accident because from all appearances his cockpit canopy never opened or did his chute open, although I circled the immediate vicinity of the crash.[10]

XII ASC sent a large formation of A-36A fighter-bombers from the 27th and 86th Fighter-Bomber Groups over the Strait of Messina area and Troina. A radio antenna was attacked north of Messina and another near Milazzo. Some targets were hit between Gioia Tauro and Rosarno in Calabria. At the request of the American Seventh Army, in serious difficulty in the Troina area, the 86th Fighter-Bomber Group sent 36 aircraft from all three squadrons to attack specific targets near the city. Captain John Harsh led a formation of 12 aircraft of the 527th Fighter-Bomber Squadron (FBS), each armed with two bombs, which hit the target indicated by US ground troops. Captain Striegel, at the head of 12 aircraft of the 525th FBS, changed to an alternative target due to a sudden worsening of the weather over Troina; they attacked a position identified as German stronghold near Regalbuto. Unfortunately, these were civilian homes (19 civilians were killed) and the headquarters of the 1st Canadian Division.[11]

The 111th TRS flew missions until late in the evening, with Lieutenants Lincicome and Sakakenny landing at Gela West with the aid of the headlights of some jeeps illuminating the runway.

Comparison of objects with different photographic scale[12]					
Object	Real length	1:5,000	1:10,000	1:20,000	1:40,000
Foxhole	6 feet	0.0144 inches	0.0072 inches	0.0036 inches	0.0018 inches
SdKfz 124 'Wespe' (105 mm SP Artillery)	16 feet	0.0384 inches	0.0192 inches	0.0096 inches	0.0048 inches
Tiger I Tank	28 feet	0.0672 inches	0.0336 inches	0.0168 inches	0.0084 inches

On 5 August, four Spitfires from 40 Squadron SAAF flew an op over the Etna front. Captain Rogers took excellent photos of the Taormina-D2535 line from a 500-foot elevation. These photos were requested to combine both land and naval operations; Rogers's work was described by the specialists of the Officer Commanding Special Services Brigade as the best they had ever seen.

That same day, No. 60 Squadron SAAF was asked to cover Calabria. Major Brierley and Lieutenant Davies flew over the Strait of Messina and up to Siderno and Nicotera in Calabria;

10   NARA, Missing Air Crew Report n. 155.
11   Angelo Plumari, Operazione Husky. La Guerra nell'entroterra ennese [Operation Husky. The War in the Enna hinterland] (Leonforte (EN): Euno Edizioni, 2019), p.122.
12   David Doyle, Standard catalog of German military vehicles (New York: Skyhorse Pub Co Inc., 2005), pp.90, 168.

unfortunately the weather conditions were not the best and were enough to prevent the op from running smoothly.[13]

In support of Allied troops, the bombings along the Adrano line continued incessantly. The TBF put on 10 operations, employing 84 Bostons, 25 Mitchells and 12 Baltimores. Twelve Mitchells from the 12th BG bombed the centre of Troina. An important road link near Francavilla di Sicilia was bombed by another 24 Mitchells of the 12th BG, which dropped 252 × 300lb bombs. The American Warhawks of the 57th and 79th Fighter Groups confirmed the port of Milazzo was being used for the evacuation of Italian–German troops from Sicily, despite the fact it had been subjected to continuous attacks for several days.

At 7:00 a.m., from the new airfield at Palagonia, the 79th FG sent 12 Warhawks of the 86th FS to the Strait of Messina. The formation's leader Colonel Bates, reported:

> At 0740, dive bombed from 10,000' to 3,000'. Near misses on Siebel ferry going east at D3 9-59, on Siebel ferry going west D 39-58. A near miss close enough to thrown water on a regular ferry going SW at D 41-61. Obs. a medium sized ship, thought possibly a hospital ship, at D 39-62. 4 small barges seen in area, D 43-51, D 43-49. 4 plus barges stationary at D 43-42. 4 plus barges stationary at D 43-43. One of the Siebel ferries was flying a barrage balloon at approx. 2000'. There was no activity in Messina Harbor. A.A. was fired from a ferry at D 41-51, accurate. Spitfires provided good stayed well with the formation. 12 a/c landed safely.[14]

North-west of Milazzo, two merchant ships, 14 barges and two seaplanes were located. Two large vessels of about 200 feet in length, a sailing ship and a seaplane were moored at the port, along with seven other large boats. Along the Strait of Messina, small and medium-sized boats and a Siebel Ferry commuted from one end of the strait to the other. The DAF attacked 60 railway wagons at the Giardini Naxos railway station. The big news of the day, however, was announced by the BBC at 9:00 p.m.; the capture of the city of Catania was compared to the capture of Kharkov on the Eastern Front.

The Northwest African Strategic Air Force (NASAF) sent 62 Wellingtons on a night raid against ships, harbour and railway installations near the Strait of Messina; 120 tons of bombs were unloaded by the bombers of 205 Group. During the early morning hours of 6 August, the city of Troina was occupied by American troops; Eisenhower called it 'one of the most terrible battles for a small town in the entire war.' Even General Omar Bradley spared no comment and, in this regard said, 'the most fiercely fought battle in the whole campaign.'[15]

After the conquest of this small Italian–German stronghold, four Spitfires of 40 Squadron SAAF, the Tac/R specialists, were tasked with determining the direction of the enemy retreat near Centuripe. In the meantime, RAAF 'Kittybombers' attacked 30 vehicles on the Randazzo–Bronte road. Movements were also recorded on the Bronte–Linguaglossa road where an enemy anti-tank post was located close to a secondary road. Axis tanks and artillery positions were

---

13 In August, the squadron carried out only 14 hours and 10 minutes of photo-reconnaissance sorties. Two other Mosquitos arrived at the squadron; these were PR.IXs LR411 and LR437 to be used over Italy, Austria and a large part of southern Europe.
14 AFHRA, IRISREF B0165, p.190.
15 D'Este, 1943. Lo sbarco in Sicilia, p.371.

also positioned on the heights around Bronte, in the railway station area, Colla, San Marco and Monte Maletto. Their dominant position prevented Allied troops from the slightest movement forward. Another automatic weapons position was identified on the banks of a river and attacked by a 111th TRS F-6 Mustang flown by Lieutenant Schultz.

A 3rd PG pilot consults a map as he prepares for a mission over the Strait of Messina. (US Air Force photo 75960 AC)

On the American front, many difficulties were encountered with the advance. Lieutenant McNamara, an artillery counter battery officer with the Seventh Army, called up the 12th PRS at Gela Ponte Olivo at 10:30 a.m. to report visual air reconnaissance had identified artillery positions near the San Fratello Line. Further flights over the area were carried out at 24,000 feet by an F-5A of the 12th Photographic Reconnaissance Squadron (PRS) equipped with a 36-inch camera for definitive confirmation and identification.

The TBF scheduled 13 missions for its medium bombers. One hundred and forty-two B-25 Mitchells of the 12th and 340th Bombardment Groups took off from Gela Ponte Olivo and Comiso respectively, 12 Bostons of No. 326 Wing RAF from Gela following suit (No. 18 Squadron from Gela West and No. 114 Squadron from Gela proper). A further seven missions were tasked to 69 Boston and Baltimore bombers operating from Malta. Among the objectives were the road intersections east of Adrano, some roads near Biancavilla, and targets in Bronte and Randazzo. The flak over the latter was intense and accurate, so much so as to be nicknamed 'Flak Alley', and damaged five Mitchells. At 5:35 p.m., two of the 12 Bostons of No. 12 Squadron SAAF, from Hal Far and led by Major Brain, were hit at 12,700 feet over Bronte.

These aircraft were Boston III HK892,[16] piloted by Lieutenant C. Foguenne of the Belgian Air Force, and Boston III HK893,[17] Lieutenant WM Trembath at the controls. Foguenne recorded his experience of the raid:

> We turned right on to the target and made a straight run. We released our bombs. Then I saw Lt. Trembath's aircraft going down in flames. A few seconds later, we were hit ourselves in the nose. Lt. Baton, my observer, was wounded. I began to smell smoke, but the machine was completely under control. I tried to get in touch with the crew but the intercom was already gone. I followed the formation as far as I could. I was not sure what was burning. For about a minute and a half to two minutes I followed the formation making the same heading but losing height slowly. Then the nose dropped and flames began to appear. There was fire in my cockpit. I was burnt myself. When the nose dropped I again tried to tell the crew.
>
> I then released my harness, opened the top hatch, and was sucked out of the aircraft. Probably 4/5 seconds later I pulled the ripcord and the parachute opened O.K. I was about 7/8000' above the ground when the parachute opened. While descending, I saw Baton about 600' below me but I did not see the gunners. I landed on my back as I fell in a sitting position on a low stone wall. I have since had my back examined. It was bruised but not damaged. I had a second degree burn on my leg and my hair was singed.
>
> French Canadian Infantry picked me up. They belonged to the 21 or 22 Batn. They gave me tea and dressed my burns. Unfortunately they cut up my parachute. Baton landed about 200 yds. away. As soon as I could stand up I went towards him; he had already been picked up by the front line medical services. ½ hour later I saw F/Sgt. Ibbetson who had landed more towards the German lines. He was O.K. I landed about 500 yds. from the German lines. They were on the other side of hill. They did not fire on me while I was landing and as far as I know did not fire on any of the others. I was told later that F/Sgt Jonker's parachute had not opened and that he had been killed. He was the top gunner. I know that they took care of the body although they were busy with a push towards Adrano. I did not see Jonker's body myself. I heard the next day that my aircraft crashed on a Canadian artillery battery killing one and injuring 23 of whom three died the next day. I last saw Baton on the afternoon of the 8th. He had had a big toe amputated and I think he had broken a rib. Otherwise he just had scratches etc. He was being well looked after at the C.C.S. [Casualty Clearing Station] at Palagonia.[18]

DAF Warhawks and Kittyhawks meanwhile attacked shipping in the Strait of Messina. A Siebel Ferry was destroyed along with five other vehicle transport vessels and three medium-sized

---

16   The crew was Lieutenants C. Foguenne (Belgium) and A.G. Baton (Belgium), and Flight Sergeants P.H. Ibbetson and M.J. Jonker.
17   The crew was Lieutenants W.M. Trembath and LA Van Zyl, Flight Sergeant C.W. Lehman and Sergeant E. Lambert.
18   The National Archives London, South African Air Force, Operations Record Books AIR 27/179, p.116.

merchant ships. Attacks against Milazzo also continued, in addition to towns on the other side of the strait (Bagnara Calabra and Palmi). The A-36A fighter-bombers of XII ASC attacked Cesarò, Tortorici and Piraino; 43 troop transports were destroyed. The Seventh Army continued the ground offensive between Sant'Agata di Militello and San Fratello while the Eighth Army finally advanced and, after capturing Catania, entered Biancavilla, Santa Maria di Licodia, Belpasso, Paternò and Adrano.[19]

Following the seizure of Troina and Adrano, the Allies immediately launched a two-pronged offensive against Randazzo, the enemy's last stronghold at the centre of the Etna line, with the aim of dividing the Axis forces, thus forcing them to move back along the two coastal roads towards Messina.

The Seventh Army advanced along the road that crosses Cesarò; the Eighth Army pushed towards Bronte, continuing to exert pressure along the Catania–Acireale line, in order to maintain a constant presence along the entire front and prevent the enemy from moving troops to the centre.

On 7 August, the *Luftwaffe* sent a Frosinone-based Ju 88 from 1.(F)/123 to cover Sicily. At 7:50 a.m., the aircraft was at 32,000 feet, 20 miles east of Capo Passero, when it was intercepted by Spitfires of No. 185 Squadron. Pilot Officer Wyndham, flying Spitfire IX EN403, was shot down; Flight Lieutenant Chapell, meanwhile, in Spitfire IX EN533, damaged the Ju 88.[20] Wyndham was recovered from the sea at 8:40 a.m. by an air-sea rescue Supermarine Walrus. Fortunately, he was not injured. Another German aircraft was sighted over Etna; this time it was a photographic reconnaissance Bf 109 escorted by three other aircraft.

At 10:00 a.m. on 7 August, 683 Squadron's Wing Commander Adrian Warburton performed a special task, flying Spitfire PR.XI (MB773), on behalf of the Army over the north-east of Sicily and southern Italy. Less than an hour later, another pilot of the same squadron, Flight Lieutenant H.S. Smith (PR.XI EN420), flew to the more distant Corfù, Valona and Durazzo.

The photos taken by American F-5A Lightnings of the 12th PRS allowed the identification of artillery positions in a field south-east of Randazzo; some photos clearly showed armoured vehicles on the move.

19   Catania itself, from 10 July to 5 August, was attacked by 39 heavy bombers, 172 medium bombers, 10 light bombers and 309 fighter-bombers. In the capture of Troina and Adrano, both key positions on the Etna line, NATAF played a direct and important role. From 18 July to 6 August, it deployed 265 fighter-bombers, 97 light bombers and 12 medium bombers against Troina. They inflicted such serious damage that, according to an officer on the ground, it took 36 hours for the engineers to clear a path for vehicles through the city. The hardest blow, however, was inflicted on Adrano. From 10 July to 7 August, 140 fighter-bombers, 367 light bombers and 187 medium bombers hit the city, leaving it indefensible.

20   The National Archives London, Royal Air Force, Operations Record Books AIR 27/1140/39.

Gerbini, Satellite #9, known as Spinasanta to Italian and German forces. The Western Brothers, a British comic-musical duo, pose with Bf 109G-4 'Schwarze 12' of I./JG 53. (Brian Spurr)

Analysis of the data of sortie 125 on 7 August by the 12th Photographic Reconnaissance Squadron[21]	
Coordinates	Objective type highlighted
(C)571227	Only one gun remains of four seen on photo 3099, Sortie 109
(C)57202205	Possible camouflaged four-gun battery
(C)58452150	Possible camouflaged battery
(C)587212	Possible headquarters
(C)594194	Possible field battery
(C)596196	Troops bivouacked under trees

The towns of Cesarò, Bronte, Nicolosi and Acireale had been in Allied hands since 7 August. Bombing raids on Randazzo continued uninterrupted; the TBF performed 21 missions, employing 249 bombers, including 107 Mitchells, 48 Baltimores, 24 Bostons and 70 A-20 Havocs. Everything around this battered city was destroyed by the massed explosives raining down on it; 1,076 × 250lb bombs, 293 × 300 pounders and 199 × 500 pounders raised a column of smoke that reached the bombers flying at 12,000. More than 19 heavy anti-aircraft artillery batteries responded and many aircraft were hit. Even the small town of Maletto was bombed by 12 Bostons of 326 Wing RAF; some of the 48 × 250lb bombs dropped hit the city centre. The aircraft of the DAF and XII ASC attacked the Troina–Cesarò–Randazzo–Floresta line where 160 troop transport vehicles had previously been identified by tactical reconnaissance aircraft.

Most of the DAF Warhawks and Kittyhawks carried out anti-shipping sweeps, attacking vessels along the Strait of Messina and at Milazzo, identifying a large hospital ship of about 8,000 tons at sea near Ganzirri. The Australians of 3 Squadron RAAF, along with 260 Squadron RAF, continued to carry out armed reconnaissance sorties over the Randazzo area. Flight Lieutenant L.A. Malins, at the head of twelve 260 Squadron Kittyhawks that departed on a midday op, reported:

> This formation took the Western route round Mount Etna and, after a recce of the Linguaglossa main road, attacked 2 M.T. moving East (C7919) about 3 miles to the West of Randazzo. Bombing was carried out from 2000' and several near misses were seen. Formation then went down and straffed [sic] along the road; the following damage was inflicted: 1 M.T. flamer, 10 M.T. damage, 1 M/Cycle damage, 1 small car damage. Very intense and accurate 88 mm. A.A. at C8622, Randazzo, Malvagna, Lanzo and Castiglione areas. F/S Lory is missing from this operation. Just prior to bombing his a/c was hit by 88 mm. at C8622, blowing the tail off. His was seen to bail out at 8000'. His parachute opened and then caught fire.[22]

21   AFHRA, IRISREF C0192, p.966.
22   The National Archives London, Royal Air Force, Operations Record Books AIR 27/1537/50, p.9.

During the night, NASAF sent 78 Wellingtons to bomb the beaches of Messina, Scaletta and C. Barri with 150 tons of bombs.

On the American side, on the morning of 8 August, German and Italian units were deployed on the Torrenova–San Marco d'Alunzio line. To cope with this new defensive line, an amphibious operation was considered behind the Axis line to force them to withdraw.

On 8 August, 683 Squadron continued to perform special tasks at high altitude over the Etna area and the Strait of Messina up to the so-called heel of Italy. Tactical and armed reconnaissance sorties flew low over the dangerous front line.

At 6:00 in the morning, 260 Squadron sent three flights of Kittyhawks on armed reconnaissance ops over Santo Stefano di Camastra, Linguaglossa and Acireale. Of the latter location, the flight was led by Flying Officer B. Page, who reported:

> This formation headed out to sea N. of L.G. and turned N. and flew over the sea turning W. and making landfall at Giardini, than S. down the road to slightly N. of Acireale. The road appeared deserted. 1 M.T. was seen N. of Acireale and this was straffed [sic] without observed results. P/O Parlee is missing from this operation and was last seen E.N.E. Acireale heading out to sea. In all the foregoing three operations intense fairly accurate light A.A. was encountered from area roads Piedimonte/Fiumefreddo/Riposto.[23]

At 7:45 a.m., not seeing Pilot Officer William Herbert Parlee return, 260 Squadron sent Flying Officer P.S. Blomfield and Sergeant J.C. Thomson to try to find him:

> F/O Blomfield covered an area 20 miles radius Catania but failed to locate the missing pilot or any trace. A Spitfire pilot was seen to bail out at (W)H.915700. this fact was reported to the Controller.[24]

The pilot to which they refer was Lieutenant D.S. Waugh of 40 Squadron SAAF whose aircraft was hit by flak over Randazzo. Waugh managed to bail out near Gerbini.

The squadron's South African commander, Major E.C. Saville, explained the disappearance to Parlee's mother in a letter:

> Unfortunately, I cannot give you very much information on the circumstances of his non return. We had been out strafing motor transport on the coast road north east of Mount Etna where a fair amount of light anti-aircraft fire was encountered. Bill was still with us as we turned out to sea on the way home, but when we arrived back he was missing. He did not call up on the radio, and no one saw him in any difficulties at all. Aircraft were sent out afterwards to search the area where he was last seen, but the pilots returned without any information. Everyone in the squadron joins me in extending to you our deepest sympathy at this time of anguish and uncertainty.

23   The National Archives London, AIR 27/1537/50, p.9.
24   The National Archives London, Royal Air Force, Operations Record Books AIR 27/1537/50, p.10.

Bill's presence will be sorely missed in the squadron, as he was extremely popular with everyone, and also one of our most capable flyers.[25]

The RAF's 1437 SRF also risked a lot on this day; two of its pilots, Flying Officer Griffith and Warrant Officer Leggo, during a low-altitude op, were hit by intense light anti-aircraft fire. Both managed to return to Lentini San Francesco unharmed.

The laboratories of the 3rd PG at Gela Ponte Olivo analysed sortie 12S/128, which covered the north-east of Sicily:

The air offensives conducted near Etna included the systematic destruction of road bridges to prevent the enemy from retreating to the Italian peninsula. The photo shows the 'San Giuliano' bridge connecting the city of Randazzo to Santa Domenica Vittoria. (Antonio Bonanno)

25   LAC: RG 24: Vol. 28378: William Herbert Parlee's service file.

Analysis of sortie 12S/128 by the 12th Photographic Reconnaissance Squadron	
Coordinates	**Objective type highlighted**
(C)72001835	Road intersection
(C)72051830	Bridge
(C)72001830	Probable enemy headquarters
(C)72101830 to (C)72801840	Large woods in which are bivouacked troops
(C)72001810 to (C)72701710	Road intersecting Cesarò-Randazzo road, probable supply road
(C)73101720	Group of buildings, probable barracks
(C)72001720	Four guns in line
(C)789192	Probable single large gun on south side of road
(C)81302025	Probable battery of field guns

With Allied ground troops now at the gates of Randazzo, to avoid massive carpet bombing causing friendly casualties, the TBF dispatched just 14 missions, all directed towards the north-western part of the city. The A-36A Mustangs of XII ASC attacked the Giarre railway station and road links near Cesarò. A phone call was received by 111th TRS command at noon. Sadly, it was not good news; the wreckage of Captain Routh's Mustang had been found on a hill near Catania. He had mysteriously disappeared on 5 August when he was heading to Catania to meet Captain Noakes, a liaison officer with the British Army.

At 7:00 a.m., from Malta, No. 682 Squadron sent Pilot Officer O'Connell (an Australian) and Spitfire PR.XI (EN658) to cover the Falcone airstrip and the Strait of Messina. At 11:30 a.m., a German reconnaissance aircraft identified as a Ju 88 was spotted flying over Lentini at high altitude; in the late afternoon, another Ju 88 was seen, this time over Augusta.

At first light on 9 August, two Spitfires from 40 Squadron SAAF flew tactical reconnaissance sorties over the intersections of the municipalities of Taormina and Randazzo, identifying around 80 vehicles heading north-east; via radio, Kittyhawk fighter-bombers of 239 Wing were immediately requested. The task was taken on at 9:10 a.m. by the Australians of No. 450 Squadron. Flight Lieutenant G.J. Black led the 12 Kittyhawks into action.

A few hours later, another 40 Squadron Spitfire conducting a Tac/R observed that the fighter-bombers had located and attacked targets (near coordinates C7242, near Maletto), including a probable German tank, destroying 20motor transports and a car. An unfortunate accident involved Lieutenant du Plessis; his Spitfire collided with a Bristol Bombay air ambulance on Lentini San Francesco. Another two South African Spitfires returned to Lentini San Francesco with flak damage.

Despite the bad weather conditions, 48 B-25 Mitchells of the 340th and 12th Bombardment Groups continued to attack boats at Gesso and the road junctions in Messina. The DAF employed its P-40 Warhawk and Kittyhawk fighter-bombers against Randazzo and Barcellona Pozzo di Gotto.

XII ASC dispatched its A-36As to a roadblock previously identified and reported by a survey of the area between Linguaglossa and Floresta; others headed for the railway stations at Falcone, Patti and Capo d'Orlando; a vast fire was caused by bombing near Novara di Sicilia.

The heavy bombers were kept occupied too. Fifty-five B-17 Flying Fortresses, part of NASAF (26 from the 2nd BG and 29 from the 99th BG), bombed an important road bridge north of Messina.

That night, 12 Bostons of 326 Wing conducted an armed reconnaissance over the island; seven of them attacked Barcellona Pozzo di Gotto, causing a terrible explosion; another bomber headed towards the city of Linguaglossa, and another four covered the surrounding area. Four Bostons and a 3 Wing SAAF Baltimore – one Boston immediately returned due to mechanical problems – dropped 60 flares before unloading twenty 250lb bombs on roads north-east of Etna near Randazzo, Linguaglossa and Novara di Sicilia. Two South African Bostons of 12 Squadron bombed (four 250 pounders) a road junction near Castiglione di Sicilia, at coordinates C9722; other bombers delivered the same number of bombs on a target at C9837, north of Novara di Sicilia. During the op, slight anti-aircraft fire was encountered coming from the municipalities of Mistretta, Francavilla di Sicilia and Cesarò, and from some positions near Troina.

German offensive air operations, which had been on a hiatus, resumed on the night of 9/10 August. The *Luftwaffe*, which had kept busy sending recce aircraft to Sicily, had not missed the new airstrips being built, the so-called ALGs. During the night, 121 bombers attacked Augusta and Syracuse, damaging the port facilities and hitting a British anti-aircraft artillery position where four gunners perished and 15 were wounded. HMS *Tynedale*, a 1,360-ton British Hunt-class escort destroyer, and HMS *Nubian*, a 2,290-ton Tribal-class destroyer, were seriously damaged. The *Luftwaffe* lost two Ju 88s and one He 111, all shot down by No. 600 Squadron Beaufighter night fighters that scrambled from Cassibile at 10:10 p.m. At dawn on 10 August, the Seventh Army requested the 111th TRS check for an explosives and weapons dump in the Messina area. The mission was performed by Lieutenant Randerson.

The TBF coordinated 10 missions, employing 36 Bostons and 84 Mitchells contributed by the 47th, 340th and 12th Bombardment Groups, and 232 Wing RAF. The centres of Linguaglossa, Floresta and Randazzo were affected. A building was destroyed in Floresta and two large fires started. In all, 848 × 250lb bombs, 92 × 300 pounders and four 500 pounders were dropped on the various objectives. DAF aircraft carried out the now usual sorties along the strait. A 5000-ton ship was attacked at Messina; other vessels were identified just to the north-east, two of them on fire. At 10:44 a.m., eight Kittyhawk IIIs of 450 Squadron RAAF, led by Squadron Leader J.P. Bartle, flew an anti-shipping op along the Strait of Messina; after dive-bombing from 10,000 feet, four large boats and several smaller ones being the targets, the pilots spotted a motionless silhouette at sea which they identified as a hospital ship of about 6000 tons. Riposto railway station was also targeted, some trucks and rail cars there attracting attention. The A-36A fighter-bombers of XII ASC also attacked road bridges near Spadafora, Galati and Novara di Sicilia.

From 8:50 p.m. in the evening, 10 Bostons of 326 Wing, and eight Bostons and four Baltimores of 3 Wing SAAF, flew a series of armed reconnaissances between Sicily and Calabria in rapid succession. A vast fire was started near Fiumefreddo, the railway line near Giardini Naxos disrupted and a building hit in the port of Milazzo. At the same time, 18 Squadron sent Boston 'L' Z2197, flown by the crew of Squadron Leader Durmont, to the Calabrian coast to attack the coastal road between Rosarno and Gioia Tauro. Another five Bostons from the squadron set off periodically between 9:00 p.m. and 2:15 a.m. to hunt for targets on roads in and around Gesso, Novara di Sicilia, Francavilla di Sicilia, Castiglione, Fiumefreddo, Roccalumera and Santa Teresa. Noteworthy was the armed reconnaissance flown by Boston 'Q' (still carrying it US serial and referred to as '33202'); Flying Officer Hanbury strafed targets five miles east of Floresta and bombed 51 transport vehicles.

On 11 August, part of the 111th TRS (48 men, 24 of whom were officers) moved via C-47 transports to the new airfield at Termini East. Meanwhile, the American Seventh Army landed east of Capo d'Orlando, supported by A-36A fighter-bombers of XII ASC, and P-40s of the 33rd FG, which attacked concentrations of troops south of the inhabited centre, and automatic weapons and communication lines. American fighter aircraft intercepted a long column consisting of several tanks near Brolo; subsequently, they attacked a road bridge on the outskirts of Patti. In support of the Eighth Army, Northwest African Tactical Air Force (NATAF) medium bombers attacked Fiumefreddo and Randazzo. At 9:40 a.m. on the same day, at the request of the British Army, Flight Lieutenant J.R. Burnett left Lentini San Francesco to fly a strategic high-altitude reconnaissance of north-eastern Sicily in Spitfire PR.XI (MB783).

Four raids to Fiumefreddo were flown by 12 Baltimores of 232 Wing and 36 Mitchells of the 12th BG. One was directed against roads and buildings, the other three on concentrations of troops between Riposto and Fiumefreddo, at coordinates D064113. At 2:30 in the afternoon, No. 223 Squadron, of 232 Wing, flew the first operational sorties from the new Monte Lungo airstrip south of Sicily, three Baltimore bombers heading towards Randazzo. Shortly afterwards, from Comiso, 12 Mitchells of the 340th BG bombed roads and the railway line west of Randazzo.

Continuous reconnaissance by the *Luftwaffe* resulted in a heavy raid, during the night of 11/12 August, when 125 German bombers attacked Augusta and Allied airfields between Lentini and Agnone, destroying 26 aircraft, including Spitfires and Kittyhawks, and damaging many others to varying degrees; among the losses were 27 airmen and two pilots of No. 244 Wing. Two other pilots of Nos. 232 RAF and 40 SAAF Squadrons were injured, as were 31 AA gunners. The following was written in the diary of 40 Squadron SAAF:

> Great excitement prevailed from midnight on August 11/12th when 35-40 enemy bombers decided to blitz the bunch of Landing Grounds in this area. It was one of the most expansive pyrotechnic displays any of us had seen Red, White and Green flares assisted by incendiary, H.E., and anti-personnel bombs lit up the camp but we were lucky, - not a single bomb landed on our Landing Ground or in our camp although on the neighboring [sic] strips at Lentini Main and Lentini West, many were killed and wounded and a number of planes destroyed and damaged. An incendiary set alight to a nearby fuel dump and Captain Rogers called out the Squadron to assist in preventing the fire from spreading, as the M.U. personnel were sitting by watching it grow. Captain Rogers modestly insists that the chief credit for the night's successful firefighting goes to W.O.II Lyttleton-Lambert, Sgt Kennedy and A/M. Gerrard, but the burns on his own hands indicate that he personally did not lead the Squadron from the rear.[26]

26   War diary 40 Squadron SAAF. The National Archives London, Operations Record Books AIR 27/418/8, p.9.

On 12 August, the Eighth Army captured Giarre. Ten F-6 Mustangs of the 111th TRS were sent on a mission to Milazzo and Barcellona Pozzo di Gotto. The unit was fully operational at Termini East and flew nine sorties throughout the day.

At 6:20 a.m., a formation of seven Kittyhawk IIIs from 260 Squadron, led by Major E.C. Saville, headed out for an anti-shipping patrol over the Strait of Messina:

> Formation flew up West of Etna passing out to sea near Patti. A N.E. sweep was made without sighting any targets and a/c, continued S. to the Messina Strait. At D.3960 three Siebel Ferries were sighted apparently towing 4 barges in a N. direction. These were bombed from 2000' resulting in a near miss on one of the Ferries. Medium heavy and intense light A.A. was encountered from both sides of the Strait down to Roccalumera. Light A.A. was also encountered from the Siebels. Four more barges were sighted moving E. at D.3545 and a large ship was seen W. of Volcano Island. An "F" boat was also sighted moving N.W. near Cape Peloro. Visibility was fair – haze and morning mist – 6/10 to 7/10 cloud over Cape Rascolomo at 5000'. Scattered cloud further N. 4/10 cloud at 5000' N. of Etna.[27]

Although almost all of the targets attacked were covered by substantial cloud formations, 144 NATAF bombers unloaded 136 tons of bombs on Patti, Falcone, Barcellona Pozzo di Gotto, Novara di Sicilia, and Nunziata. In Barcellona Pozzo di Gotto, roads and railways were bombed, buildings and streets in Nunziata. Intense anti-aircraft fire damaged 18 bombers over Novara di Sicilia and Barcellona Pozzo di Gotto.

The A-36A Mustangs of XII ASC, and the Warhawks and Kittyhawks of the DAF, attacked artillery positions in C. Calva (east of Randazzo) and Mazzarà. Naval traffic was also repeatedly attacked near the Strait of Messina, particularly in the towns of Palmi and Gioia Tauro in Calabria. The best results against shipping were recorded by the DAF pilots who claimed to have attacked 12 landing craft and a merchant ship and sunk three. A bridge was damaged near Taormina and, along some roads between Maletto and Fiumefreddo, four troop transports were destroyed and another 11 damaged. The *Luftwaffe* sent Fw 190s and Bf 109s to attack Allied shipping; but two Fw 190s were claimed destroyed by Allied fighters and five Bf 109s were destroyed or damaged. The Fw 190s of II./SKG 10 carried out two missions during the day, for a total of 12 sorties, against targets in the port of Catania, Capo D'Orlando and Brolo.

Five PR Spitfires of 683 Squadron from Malta were assigned to cover ports and airfields in southern Italy. During the night, the TBF attacked several Calabrian towns, including Gioia Tauro, Rosarno, Pizzo, Bagnara and Palmi. Yet another heavy attack (155 tons of bombs) was carried out by 205 Group Wellingtons on the beaches of Messina.

On 13 August, with the fall of Randazzo and the convergence of the two Allied armies, Generaloberst Hans-Valentin Hube ordered a retreat on the first evacuation line via Furnari–San Marco–Francavilla–Novara di Sicilia–Castiglione di Sicilia–Linguaglossa–Fiumefreddo.

The photos taken by the recce aircraft over Messina at 9:15 a.m. on 13 August revealed a train parked near the city's railway station, while at sea on the strait were some landing craft of

27   The National Archives London, Royal Air Force, Operations Record Books AIR 27/1537/50, p.13.

about 120 feet in length, a 200-foot boat and another 150-footer. In total, 30 vessels were visible between Torre di Faro and Cannitello.

The F-6 Mustangs of the 111th TRS flew two sorties to Messina. The DAF attacked two Siebel Ferries and other small boats in the waters of the strait. Twenty-three of NATAF's Bostons, and 24 Mitchells of the 12th BG, attacked Piedimonte Etneo. Another 24 B-25s of the 340th BG attacked Falcone but, due to bad visibility, 17 bombers did not drop their bombs; some returned to Comiso without having bombed, while three jettisoned their loads into the sea south of Santa Teresa di Riva. In the late afternoon, 29 B-25 Mitchells headed to locate and attack targets in the strait; although the weather conditions had improved significantly, they were unable to identify useful targets. They then headed north of Scaletta, in Calabria, to bomb a bridge. Meanwhile, 110 sorties were carried out by NATAF bombers, with around 93 tons of bombs dropped, and 40 Squadron SAAF sent aircraft to the Francavilla di Sicilia area. Led by Lieutenant O.L. Dugmore, a pair of Spitfires took off from Lentini San Francesco. As reported in the squadron's diary, the 21-year-old South African pilot did not return:

> Lieutenant Dugmore turned back to make a further check of the area to the West and then continued back to Francaville. They encountered light ack.ack fire and the weaver saw a direct hit on the central starboard position of Lieutenant Dugmore's aircraft. They turned back and Lieutenant Dugmore called him up over R/T but did not appear to receive his reply. They flew West for 12-15 miles until over Bronte when Lieutenant Dugmore suddenly went into a steep turn at about 2000' and the aircraft spun off and crashed. He did not see him bale out and the aircraft burst into flames when it crashed. The incident, however, was observed by troops of the 6th Battalion Royal West Kents, and they have informed us that the aircraft was doing a low circuit as though to force-land when a piece broke off and the aircraft spun into the ground. The pilot baled out at a height variously estimated at 200' – 250', but the parachute failed to open completely. Lieutenant Dugmore was killed instantaneously. Although there were no signs of previous wounds on the body this is not certain. The aircraft crashed at Map Reference C.760116.[28]

On 14 August, the 111th TRS despatched 18 sorties, one of which was carried out by Lieutenant Rafannelli over the island of Lipari in search of a radar station; the other sorties, on the other hand, were destined to observe a substantial column of around 100 vehicles near Gesso. The TBF sent 35 bombers in response, but only 12 of them could identify the target, destroying 10 vehicles in the process. The rest of the aircraft dropped their bombs on the main road. Meanwhile, 24 Bostons bombed Nicola's fuel depot. An important road link was attacked north of Palmi, in Calabria, by 64 bombers, 24 of which were from 232 Wing RAF. A large fire at Taormina was reported by pilots of No. 112 Squadron RAF who were in the area on an armed reconnaissance at around 10:00 a.m.

---

28 War diary 40 Squadron SAAF. The National Archives London, Royal Air Force, Operations Record Books AIR 27/418/8, p.21.

STRAIT OF MESSINA
Defensive system and the evacuation of the Axis Armies from Sicily
3rd - 17th August 1943

Sparta
152/45

88

MS 277
90/53

Mortelle   MZ   MS 120
90/53

MS 620
90/42

Castanea   Masotto
280/9

88
Faro

Mezzacapo
120/50

Scilla

MS 434   MS 123
90/53   90/42

Ganzirri

MS 724
90/53

S. Agata   Cannatello

88

Gesso

MS 949
90/53

Pace

MS 819
90/42

MS 116
90/53

Pezzo
280/9

105

105   88

MS 477
76/40

Paradiso   MZ

170
170

MS 110
90/42

MS 253
76/40

Salvatore

FS   170
170

Villa
S. Giovanni

88

MS 905
76/40

FS

MS 475   MS 349
90/53   90/42

88

MFP - SF
ROUTE 3

MS 268
90/42

88

MS 159
90/42

76/40

MFP - SF
ROUTE 4

105   Catona   105

MS 577
76/40

88   76/40

MESSINA

88

88

76/40

MS 611
90/53

Gallico

MS 525
90/42

88   MS 320
90/53

88

ROUTE 5 (Spare)
(Not used after 8th August)

MS 250
90/53

76/40

88   Pistunina

88

Pellizzeri
280/9

MS 374
76/40

Cavalli
152/45

REGGIO
CALABRIA

88

88

90/53

88

88   MS 643
76/40

AIRFIELD

88

MS - MZ   LC - MFP-SF ROUTE 1   LC - MFP - SF ROUTE 2

ITALIAN		GERMAN	
----	Ferry routes	——	Ferry routes
FS	Ferry steamers	MFP	Naval ferry barges
MZ	Landing craft	SF	Siebel ferries
■	Coastal batteries	LC	Landing craft
▲	Batteries anti-aircraft	□	Coastal batteries
●	Batteries dual purpouse	△	Batteries anti-aircraft
90/53	Calibre in mms	○	Batteries dual purpose
		88	Calibre in mms

0   1 km   5   10

0   1 ml   5

N

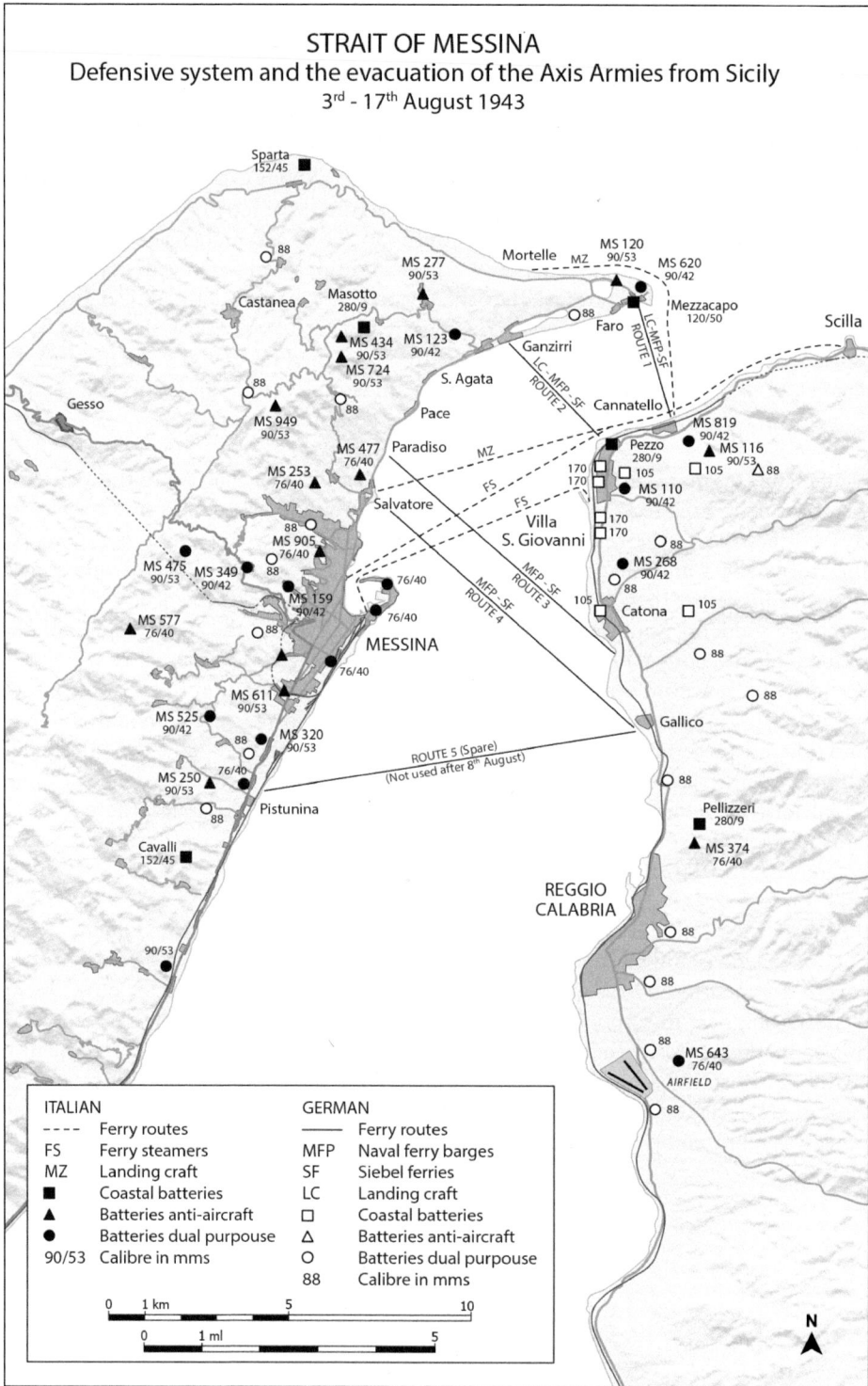

Operation *Lehrgang* evacuation routes. (NARA)

17

German Plan for Withdrawal

The number of German troops in Sicily at the time was about 50,000 and the intention was to evacuate them all to the mainland. It was realised that the Navy and Air Force could not make the crossing by day, and that the ferry service could only be maintained under the cover of darkness. With the ferry vessels at their disposal, six nights would be required to evacuate these 50,000 men with their general weapons, including machine guns, but without vehicles or heavy weapons.

The plan foresaw five defensive lines converging on Messina. The first of these lines ran from the north coast at, or just east of, Sant'Agata, over Bronte, to the south slopes of Mount Etna, to Acireale. The last line was just around Messina. In withdrawing to the first, and in each subsequent withdrawal to the second, third, fourth and fifth lines, each division was to release a fixed proportion of its manpower (from all three divisions a total of 8,000–10,000 men was to be released at each withdrawal) to be moved on foot towards Messina. On the fifth line of defence, the last remaining troops were to proceed direct to the boats during the last night before the final evacuation. Equipment was to be evacuated by the ferry service by day as opportunities arose.

Italian troops were to be moved to the mainland, without vehicles or heavy weapons, by means of their own transport which consisted principally of a large steam ferry.

The German tried to get the Italian Army Headquarters to evacuate Sicily of its own free will, and thus free themselves of a mass of Italian troops. Surprisingly enough, the Italian refused to go. It appears the Italians had had strict orders that they were not to leave the island before the Germans. All was therefore prepared for the proposed evacuation, the only question being the date on which it was to be put into operation.

After the decision had been taken, there were some anxious days at the German Headquarters, which was located initially at Barcellona and then south-west of Messina. Had the Allies realised their intentions? If not, when would they? What action would they take when the situation was clear to them? All these questions were acute and caused the German General Staff grave concern, especially as the American landings on the north coast were considered as the beginning of increased Allied activity, and a forewarning of larger scale operations. Von Bonin reported:

> Nothing of the kind occurred. The plans proceeded as laid down, and without any difficulty worthy of mention.

There was not even a notable increase in the attacks of the enemy air force against our ferry service, which continued without interruption by night, and of course now by day.

Our hope to save not only the men but also all our equipment, and thus to attain a maximum of our aim, increased from hour to hour. In order to make it possible, another night and another complete day were gained for the divisions by holding on of the intermediate defense lines longer. It would have been quite possible to win further time as the enemy followed the withdrawal of our troops only hesitantly and was moreover delayed in his advance by effective demolitions on the roads.[1]

As late as 4 August, the Allied Joint Intelligence Committee had written in a paper entitled *Estimate of enemy capabilities to evacuate Sicily* that, 'at the present time there is no sign that the enemy intends an evacuation of Sicily and there is evidence that reinforcements still continue to reach the island.'

They reported that a photographic reconnaissance on 31 July had revealed the presence of the following small craft, in the areas of the strait, which could be made available for enemy evacuation:

- Two train ferries
- 30 to 40 landing craft or Siebel ferries
- Numerous small craft

They also estimated it would be possible for the enemy to evacuate 60,000 troops every 24 hours.[2]

It was not until 10:10 p.m. on 14 August that General Alexander from the headquarters of the Fifteenth Army Group informed Air Chief Marshal Tedder as to the situation in a signal which ran as follows: 'From general information received it now appears that German evacuation has really started.'

It is now known through the medium of captured documents that the original German plan for evacuation was that the Hermann Göring Division should begin evacuation on 1 August, the 15th Panzer Grenadier Division on the 12th, and the 29th Panzer Grenadier Division on the 15th. This proposed programme was upset by Allied attacks and full scale evacuation was begun instead by the 15th Panzer Grenadier Division from Randazzo on 11 August and by the 29th Panzer Grenadier Division in the coastal sector on the night of the 12th/13th.

During 10/11 and 11/12 August, the following German personnel and equipment were ferried to the mainland:

- 615 officers, and 19,924 other ranks
- 34 tanks, 44 S.P assault guns
- 21 guns and 11 A/A guns
- 15 heavy A/T guns
- 2,185 vehicles

1   AFHRA, Reel 23364, p.707.
2   AFHRA, Reel 23364, p.707.

Captain Gustav von Liebenstein of the *Kreigsmarine* (the German Navy) commanded the 2nd Landing Craft Flotilla and submitted a report on the state of the German ferry units in the Messina Strait shortly after his unit's arrival. Von Liebenstein concluded that 'the independent operation of various units with no overall command did not prove successful.' Consequently, a new command to supervise the Strait traffic was established on 25 May with von Liebenstein at its head. At his disposal was his old command (the 2nd Landing Craft Flotilla), along with the 10th Landing Craft Flotilla (supplemented by absorbing the Siebel Ferries of the local *Luftwaffe* ferry flotilla) and Engineer Landing Battalion 771. The 4th Landing Craft Flotilla began to operate in the Strait following the Allied landings on 10 July 1943. Their respective vessel and armament totals were as follows:

Order of Battle Captain von Liebenstein's ferry service, Messina Strait[3]		
Unit	Vessels	Armament*
2nd Landing Craft Flotilla	20 ferry barges and two naval gun barges	Four 8.8cm, twelve 7.5cm, two 3.7cm, twenty-eight 2.0cm
4th Landing Craft Flotilla	24 ferry barges*	Twenty-four 7.5cm, forty-eight 2.0cm
10th Landing Craft Flotilla	Eight Siebel Ferries, 2 AA Siebel Ferries, 10 I-boats and whalers	Five 8.8cm, three 3.7cm, 11 quad 2.0cm, six 2.0cm
Engineer Landing Battalion 771	17 landing craft and four ferry barges	Eight 2.0cm
Totals	17 landing craft, eight Siebel Ferries, 2 AA Siebel Ferries, 10 I-boats and whalers, 2 naval gun barges, 48 ferry barges (87 vessels)	Nine 8.8cm, thirty-six 7.5cm, five 3.7cm, 11 quad 2.0cm, ninety 2.0cm (151 guns)

At 10:10 a.m. on 15 August, Montgomery requested No. 683 Squadron conduct a high-altitude photographic survey of the Strait of Messina. From 29,500 feet, Flying Officer F.R. Brocklehurst reported having spotted a large vessel north of the strait and other medium-sized ones near Reggio Calabria.

On the morning of the same day the 60 Squadron SAAF from Northafrica send Lieutenant Joubert aboard an F-5A over central Italy and Pratica di Mare airport.

More than 180 of NATAF's Warhawk, Kittyhawk and A-36A fighter-bombers converged on the Strait of Messina to attack 10 boats and some Siebel Ferries along the Calabrian coasts near Scilla and up to Vibo Marina and Pizzo Calabro. Even sizeable formations consisting of 24 Bostons and 36 Baltimores were sent on eight separate missions to attack a troop shipment identified south of Cape Peloro. Ninety tons of bombs were dropped on some buildings and

---

3   Aggregated from daily entries of AHB: Translations of Capture German Documents: Reference VII/156: 'War Diary of Naval Officer-in-Charge, Sea Transport, Messina Strait (1 August–17 August 1943)'. *indicates AHB: Translation Reference VII/161: 'Extracts from War Diary of Fortress Commandant, Messina Strait (14 July–25 August), p.13–14.

Operation *Lehrgang*, the evacuation of Sicily by Axis forces from 10 to 17 August 1943. A huge Allied effort tried in vain to counter the German operation with day and night bombing raids. (Antonio Bonanno)

boats; the response of the German anti-aircraft batteries was heavy and accurate, particularly that from Torre Faro, which damaged 28 aircraft. On the same day, several officers from 40 Squadron SAAF went to Bronte to pay homage to Lieutenant O.L. Dugmore, a last farewell to one of the most respected pilots of the South African unit.[4]

Number of Operations for No. 40 Squadron SAAF 9 July–16 August	
Tac/R	161
Arty/R	53
Photo/R Vertical	Nil
Photo/R Oblique	19
Average recces per day	6
Maximum	11

Throughout the day, six German reconnaissance aircraft flew over Augusta and surrounding areas, probably to assess the effectiveness of recent night raids. In the meantime, the Eighth Army occupied Taormina and Letojanni, and carried out landing operations at Alì Marina, proceeding quickly to Messina. The Seventh Army continued rapidly along the northern coast; some elements were already less than 15 miles west of Messina.

A couple of Mustangs from No. 1437 Strategic Reconnaissance Flight, over the strait early in the morning, suffered damage from anti-aircraft fire. Flying Officer Jones's Mustang (HK955/'D') returned to Lentini San Francesco with four holes in its fuselage. On 16 August, the 111th TRS pilots who flew the unit's 20sorties over the Strait of Messina that day reported the waterway was jam-packed with boats of all kinds. As a result, the Tactical Bomber Force organised eight missions (96 sorties) for the Mitchells, Baltimores and A-20 Havocs of the 12th, 47th and 340th Bombardment Groups, and 232 Wing RAF, which dropped 142 × 300lb bombs, 492 × 250 pounders, 47 × 100lb bombs, and 1095 × 20 pounders on maritime traffic and on some beaches north of Messina and Capo Peloro. Also north of Messina, two large 7,000-ton ships were sighted. A hospital ship was spotted in transit eight miles north of Scilla. Forty-four bombers reported anti-aircraft damage. The DAF concentrated its action on the Calabrian coasts; the 31st FG flew 72 sorties to guarantee air protection to the American naval fleet located between Capo d'Orlando and Capo Milazzo.

The tactical reconnaissance (Tac/R) specialists of 40 Squadron SAAF agreed to operation No. 9 with the British XXX Corps, with which it had previously worked with in conjunction with the monitor HMS *Roberts*. The squadron was requested to fly over the area from Alì Terme to Messina while remaining in constant radio contact to communicate any enemy batteries still present in the area. They were then to direct Allied naval gunfire. Another task carried out that same morning concerned the location and identification of a large ship of about 15,000 tons probably sailing from Naples and heading north of the strait. Due to poor visibility, however, the ship was not found.

---

4   War diary 40 Squadron SAAF, The National Archives London, Operations Record Books AIR 27/418/8, p.8.

Almost all tactical and armed reconnaissance operations were now directed towards targets in Calabria. While American naval units were already north of Milazzo, and British ones off the coast of Santa Teresa di Riva, the Kittyhawks of 239 Wing RAF conducted armed reconnaissance sorties along the Calabrian coast; at 11:20 a.m., 112 Squadron reported more than 100 railway wagons, including four locomotives, parked at the Reggio Calabria railway station.

Seventeenth August marked the ultimate Allied occupation of Sicily, with Patton's American troops entering Messina first. General Alexander, commader of the 15th Army Group in Sicily, wrote to Churchill that morning: 'At 10 am this morning, August 17, 1943, the last German soldier left Sicily and the whole island is therefore in our hands.'[5]

Strategic aerial reconnaissance, after years of sorties, now came to an end over Sicily. Flying Officer E.N. Huggessen, in Spitfire PR.XI (EN391), and flying from Lentini San Francesco, was the last pilot of 683 Squadron to perform a reconnaissance of the island and the heel of Italy (the first at 9:50 a.m. and the second at 1:55 p.m.) at the request of the Army.

The city of Messina. The wall of this public building reads: 'IL PARTITO È L'ARTEFICE DELLA RIVOLUZIONE, LA SPINA DORSALE DEL REGIME, IL MOTORE DELLE ATTIVITÀ NAZIONALI' ('The party is the maker of the revolution, the backbone of the regime, the engine of national activities'). This was from the speech delivered by Benito Mussolini in Genoa on 30 September 1939. (Brian Spurr)

5   D'Este, 1943. Lo sbarco in Sicilia, p.426.

Four other pilots of the unit flew high towards Taranto, Naples and Crotone, while the F-5A Lightnings of the 3rd Photographic Group crossed the borders of northern Italy to fly over Croatia and France. Tactical reconnaissance, naturally, followed 'the boot', almost tracing its shape in the sky. The construction of new airfields in the Messina area brought the units closer to their objectives. Armed reconnaissance sorties continued to attack and report on the Italo–German retreat along the Calabrian coast in dangerous low altitude operations.

Operation *Husky* was supported by devastating air strikes on the cities of Etna, small and medium-sized towns suddenly finding themselves at the centre of the conflict; all of this was summed up by the correspondent of *The Daily Telegraph*, Christopher Buckley, witness to most of these incursions, who later wrote that many Sicilian towns, among which he included Regalbuto and Randazzo, were 'canceled by aerial bombardments on an unprecedented scale in the history of war'[6] and, that, in general, the aerial bombardments were a failure from different points of view[7] (including the removal of rubble from roads slowing the advance, and, of course, the impact on the civilian population)

In a message from His Majesty the King George VI to the prime minister:

> The invasion of Sicily has proved a model of planning and execution. Its success is, of course, largely due to the gallantry and efficiency of the sailors, soldiers, and airmen engaged in the actual operation. I feel that a very special tribute should be paid to those who, with their American colleagues and comrades, were responsible for its organization. They, for months past, have laboured devotedly and with a skill, of which the fruits of their labour are the most conclusive proof, to ensure that every man, every ship, every aircraft, and every item of equipment arrived at the right place, in the right order, and at the right time.
>
> I should therefore be grateful if you, as Minister of Defence, would convey to all who were engaged, directly or indirectly both at home and overseas on this immensely important task, my hearty congratulations on the manner in which they discharged it and on the magnificent contribution that they have made toward the supreme end of winning the war.
>
> In saying this, I am, I feel sure, giving expression not only to my own gratitude but to that of all in BRITISH EMPIRE.[8]

General Alexander remarked in his memoirs:

> The capture of Sicily gave us an important strategic advantage. It opened up the Mediterranean theatre and gave us a firm base from which to conduct further operations against southern Europe. Indeed, it heralded the surrender of Italy within little more than a fortnight.[9]

---

6   Christopher Buckley, *Road to Rome* (London: Hodder and Stoughton, 1945), p.107.
7   Among the municipalities of the province of Enna, the greatest number of deaths was in: Regalbuto 133, Troina 117, Centuripe 81. See Plumari, *Operazione Husky*, p.271.
8   AFHRA, IRISREF C0192, p.874.
9   Major Peter S. Gillies, *Sicily, Analysis of a combined operations battle* (Maxwell, USA: Air Command and Staff College Air University, 1984), p.33.

Montgomery had a similar appraisal of the victory:

> The Sicilian campaign had lasted thirty-eight days and had involved fierce and continuous fighting in most difficult country at the hottest season of the year. For a second time the Germans had been pushed back into the sea and we now stood at the gates of the "Fortress of Europe".[10]

Photo Reconnaissance operations carried out by the NAAF from 31 July/1 August to 14 August 1943					
Unit	Aircraft	Ports and Bases	A/Ds	Other Targets*	Total
3rd PRG	F-5A, B-5D, Spitfire XI, P-39, P-51	367	546	387	1,300
40 SAAF	Spitfire	-	-	14	14
111th TRS	P-39, P-51	16	–	62	78
Total		383	546	463	1,392

*M/Vs, Roads, Rivers, Enemy Camps, Positions and Towns.

Strat/R and Tac/R Reconnaissance operations carried out by the NAAF from 31 July/1 August to 14 August 1943			
Unit	Aircraft	Strat/R	Tac/R
40 SAAF	Spitfire	-	136
111th TRS	P-39, P-51	-	126
Total		-	262

10   Gillies, *Sicily, Analysis of a combined operations battle*, p.33

NAAF summary operations 2 July to 17 August 1943

	Total sorties	Average daily sorties	Total tonnage bombs	Average daily bombs dropped
Fighters	34,485	733.72	-------	-------
Fighter-Bombers	9,181	195.34	3,047.99	64.85
Light-Bombers	3,097	65.89	1,891.65	40.25
Medium-Bombers	9,015	191.82	13,392.46	297.61
Heavy Bombers	2,138	45.49	5,692.40	121.11
Land Recce	4,333	92.19	-------	-------
Ground Recce & Beaufighters	3,638	77.40	44.75	0.95
Total	65,887	1,401.85	24,069.14	524.77

Reconnaissance by RAF aircraft, NAAF, Middle East Command and Malta over the central Mediterranean from 3/4 July to 28 August 1943

Period		Tac/R	Strat/R	Total
3/4–17 July	NAAF & Malta	167	264	431
	Middle East	-	47	47
17/18–31 July	NAAF & Malta	370	1,281	1,651
	Middle East	-	67	67
31 July/1 August–14 August	NAAF & Malta	262	1,488	1,750
	Middle East	-	75	75
14/15–28 August	NAAF & Malta	180	352	532
	Middle East	-	85	85
Total	NAAF & Malta	979	3,385	4,364
	Middle East	-	274	274

Reconnaissance by RAF garrison aircraft based on Malta from 3/4 July to 28 August 1943

Period	Land	Harbour	Total
3/4–17 July	49	59	108
17/18–31 July	45	56	101
31 July/1 August–14 August	43	53	96
14/15–28 August	44	42	86
Total	181	210	391

Conclusion

Sicily had been a land of experimentation and innovation in the field of aerial reconnaissance. Better performing aircraft progressively occupied the scene in those long years of war; the use of new equipment, as well as new photographic development systems, with the use of new automatic machines, greatly facilitated the work of Intelligence. Men like Adrian Warburton DSO & Bar DFC & Two Bars DFC (USA) owed their fame as aviators to Malta and Sicily. His stay on Malta made him an undisputed protagonist; several times he risked his life in dangerous sorties to Sicily, as described in this volume. He knew every corner of Sicily and the Mediterranean and was a man who made a difference in a war certainly not favourable for the island.

With the arrival of American forces in the Mediterranean, and the formation of the Northwest African Photographic Reconnaissance Wing (NAPRW) a few months later, there was a consolidation of important and strategically efficient forces.

The Intelligence Services played a significant role in planning operations and General Spaatz, head of the Northwest African Air Forces (NAAF), ensured its staff had access to all available information for detailed planning. The information gathered through Ultra, and interrogations of prisoners of war, counterintelligence, and the British Y service, provided a fairly clear picture of the Axis air forces in the Mediterranean theatre. To ensure the dissemination of intelligence reports, the NAAF's A-2 section produced the Daily and Weekly Intelligence Summaries to report and provide summaries of Axis land and airfield activities. These reports contained valuable information regarding the technical capabilities of Italian and German aircraft, and their tactical use, and greatly assisted NAAF pilots in carrying out their operations. Ultra eavesdropping proved invaluable; according to Captain RH Humphreys, NAAF's Ultra senior officer, 'we had advanced timing with regard to every intention and movement of the German aviation in Africa and Italy.'[1] All this, combined with reports from the Y service, allowed the Allies to determine the effectiveness of their attacks or if, for example, specific airfields or ports had to be attacked again.

Between the conclusion of operations in Sicily and the invasion of the Italian peninsula, the air reconnaissance units had little time to reflect. The overall situation of resources was significantly improved and the consolidation of the elements of collection, interpretation and production within the photographic centre became one of the main sources of success in Italy. The

---

1   Matthew G. St. Clair, Major, *The Twelfth US Air Force Tactical and Operational Innovations in the Mediterranean Theater of Operations, 1943–1944* (USMC School of Advanced Air and Space Studies), p.21.

addition of staff with artillery experience and engineering knowledge within the photographic centre provided an additional bonus to maximise the use and effectiveness of photo intelligence. However, while photographic reconnaissance had played an important role in most cases during pre-invasion planning, its ability to sustain ground operations later became more problematic. The integration of tactical reconnaissance partially balanced this shortcoming, becoming an important strategy for the entire Italian campaign.

In September 1943, 572 missions were carried out by all units of the NAPRW; this shows the significant increase in its activities. It is sufficient to consider, in fact, that when the American 3rd Photographic Group (PG) started operating, in November 1942, until 1 March 1943, with a staff of 36 pilots, it had only managed to perform a total of 435 hours across 120 missions. Huge developments were, therefore, brought about by the new and efficient F-5A Lightnings, capable of better performance than the old F-4s and F-4As. A total of 363 missions were carried out over Sicily before the invasion, a figure which also includes the efforts of No. 683 Squadron RAF.

During the preparation of the Sicilian campaign, the NAPRW built the first mosaic of the entire island; all of this was thanks to the pilots stationed on Malta. Statistics revealing part of the NAPRW's effort over Sicily include 383,500 prints, 15,000 printed mosaics, 3,000 enlargements, and 600 duplications of negatives. High-ranking officers from the 3rd PG reported that Operation *Husky* was the first American operation planned and executed based on information from aerial reconnaissance.

With regard to the contribution by 683 Squadron, General Alexander wrote about Operation *Husky*:

> I should like to express personally how much I appreciate the photographic work which the R.A.F. have done in preparation for operation HUSKY and I should like to pay particular tribute to W/Cdr. Warburton, who I believe, himself, took the most valuable low oblique photographs of the landing beaches.
>
> These obliques have been extremely useful both to the planning staffs and to the assaulting troops to whom they have been distributed.
>
> I fully realise the danger involved in making these sorties at very low heights and very close to any enemy coast, and they are as technically perfect and complete as if flown on a peacetime exercise.
>
> If you think fit, I would be grateful if you would convey to W/Cdr. Warburton my personal thanks.[2]

The NAPRW's activity was also closely supported by No. 682 Squadron. The total number of photographic surveys provided 1001 Intelligence reports to the various applicants in the period from 1 August to 15 September.

In preparation for future operations on the Italian peninsula, the first two tactical reconnaissance (Tac/R) Spitfires of No. 225 Squadron landed at Lentini San Francesco track at 10:40 a.m. on 19 August. Wing Commander Millington and Squadron Leader McCandlish were the pilots. Shortly thereafter, the rest of the squadron, consisting of another 14 Spitfires,

---

2   AFHRA, IRISREF C0192, p.861.

arrived at the airstrip and, subsequently, at Milazzo, to support the Allied advance on southern Italy.

Once Sicily was conquered, the Tac/R sorties of No. 40 Squadron SAAF also moved to cover the other side of the strait. During August, the squadron flew 324 hours across 305 sorties, reaching 2,257 sorties since beginning operations. On 24 August, Lieutenant General M.C. Dempsey, commander of XIII Corps, wrote to the Lieutenant-Colonel J.P. Blaauw, commander of the squadron:

> I am writing this note to you to thank you very much for the oblique photographs which you have taken for me during the last three or four days. They are quite first-class and are exactly what we wanted. I would be grateful if you would tell the pilots concerned how important these photographs are to us, and how much we appreciate their work. I would also like to take this opportunity of thanking you and the whole of 40 Squadron for the fine work you did for 13 Corps [sic] during the operations in Sicily.[3]

The 111th Tactical Reconnaissance Squadron completed 535 sorties from Sicily from 1 July to 17 August. On 28 August, the unit moved to the new San Antonio strip, six miles from Milazzo; the first to land were Captain Armstrong and Lieutenant Keizer, along with 15 men. From here they could better coordinate reconnaissance operations with Major Coykendall, the liaison officer with the 67th Armored Regiment of the Seventh Army, in anticipation of Operation *Avalanche* (the Allied landings near Salerno). On 31 August, as the transfer to San Antonio was completed, a three-engine SM.79 arrived with high-ranking Italian officers on board. Italy was already negotiating the surrender.[4]

Concerning the contribution by NAPRW, General Clark referred to Operation *Avalanche* when congratulating Colonel Elliott Roosevelt:

> I wish to congratulate you and express to you my deep and sincere appreciation for the superior work you have done for the Fifth Army recently.
>
> The fact that you overcame severe handicaps and reproduced 160,000 photographic prints available for planning and operational purpose, on scheduled time, despite necessarily very short notices, will be an outstanding contribution to the success of our operation.
>
> Special credit is due to your Mosaicing Section for their fine workmanship, as well as to Captain Scalpone, Major Gray, and Captain Barfoot for their excellent low obliques, which will be of invaluable assistance to our combat troops.
>
> I was also gratified to learn of the whole-hearted cooperation you have always shown through Air Liaison Section, which made it a pleasure to work with you.[5]

3   War diary 40 Squadron SAAF, The National Archives London, Operations Record Books AIR 27/418/8, p.3. Within a few days, Blaauw was replaced by Lieutenant Colonel W.A. Nel, who remained in the role until August 1944.
4   AFHRA, IRISREF A0916, p.1499.
5   AFHRA, IRISREF C0192, p.862.

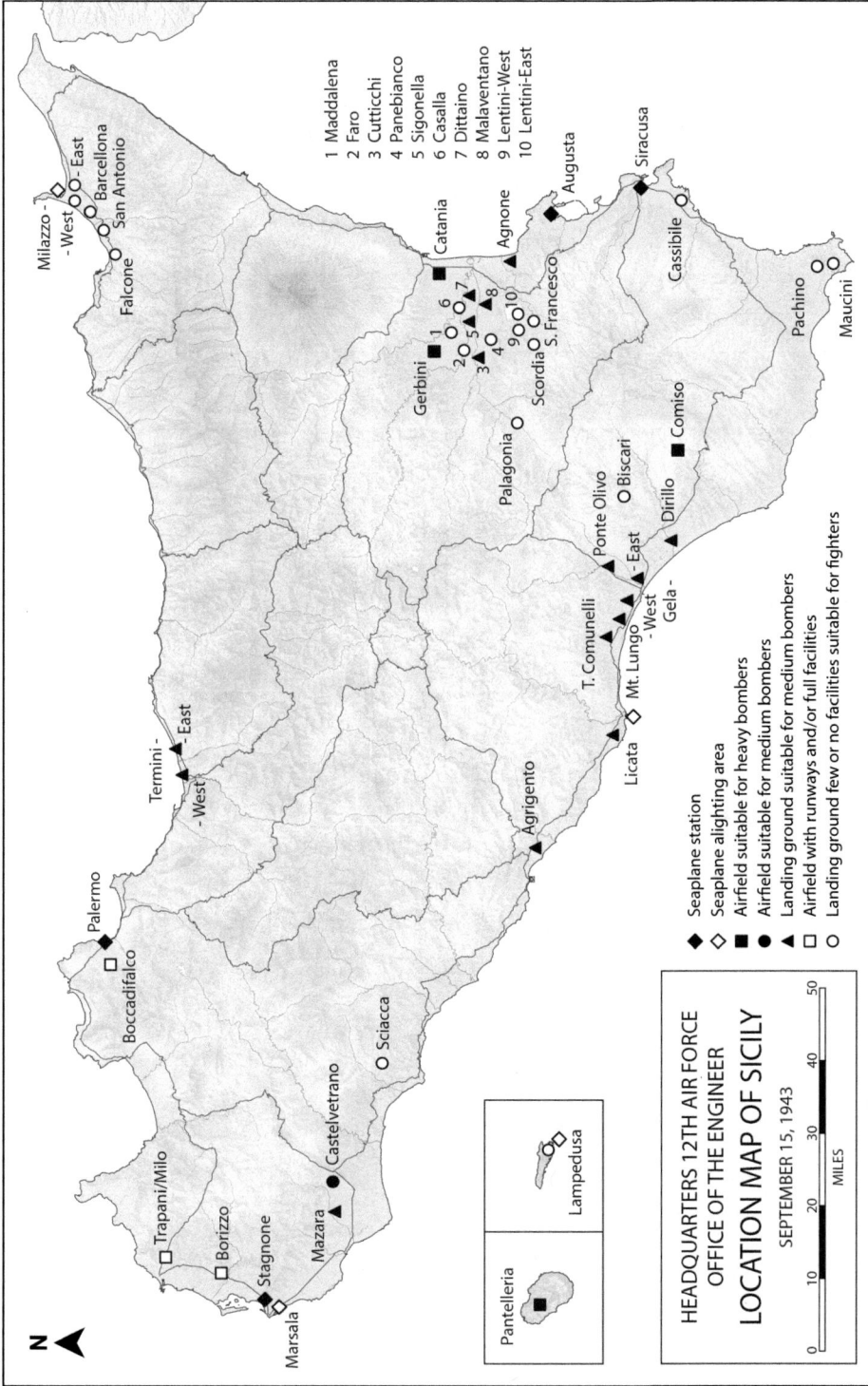

Allied airfields in Sicily after Operation *Husky*. (AFHRA)

Appendix I

3rd Photographic Group Encounters over Sicily

Unit number one			
Sortie	Date	Pilot	Note
3 PG 18	05/12/42	Eidson	Heavy intense Flak over Palermo, Boccadifalco, Bo Rizzo e Trapani
1 NA 21	20/04/43	Davis	Heavy Flak at Milo A/D
1 NA 29	12/04/43	Newman	Intercepted by 6 EA/C North of Marsala
1 NA 31	13/04/43	Nelson	Heavy Flak, accurate for height at Boccadifalco and Castelvetrano
1 NA 45	20/04/43	Davis	Heavy Flak at Boccadifalco
1 NA 46	20/04/43	De Young	Flak at Palermo and Boccadifalco
1 NA 56	27/04/43	Warburton	Heavy Flak at Palermo and Trapani
1 NA 62	29/04/43	Philpotts	Heavy inaccurate Flak at Boccadifalco
1 NA 66	02/05/43	De Young	Interception by 5 ME 109s at 36° 45' N – 10° 33' E at 20,000'
1 NA 73	06/05/43	Freeman	Intercepted by 3 EA/C near Marsala
1 NA 84	11/05/43	Vestal	Light Flak at Lampedusa
1 NA 107	25/05/43	Emswiler	Light inaccurate Flak over Pantelleria town and A/D
1 NA 112	29/05/43	Barrett	Medium Flak at Lampedusa Harbour & A/D
1 NA 139	07/06/43	Jackson	Heavy Flak over Pantelleria, after bombing raid
1 NA 140	08/06/43	Gray	Light Flak over Pantelleria directed at bombers
1 NA 142	08/06/43	Burnor	Heavy Flak and accurate over Pantelleria Island, west and during bombing raid
1 NA 143	08/06/43	Berrett	Light Flak at 5–10,000' over Pantelleria at west end

Unit number three			
Sortie	**Date**	**Pilot**	**Note**
3 NA 9	06/04/43	Sugg	Intercepted by 1 EA/C SW Sicily
3 NA 14	11/04/43	Spencer	Intercepted by 4 SE EA/C over NW Sicily
3 NA 15	11/04/43	Luthy	Encountered 'spotting Flak' over Comiso
3 NA 21	12/04/43	Berry	Warned by radio & saw 3 EA/C over Cape Pessaro
3 NA 27	14/04/43	Berry	Pilot saw red 'spotting Flak' over Biscari
3 NA 31	17/04/43	Webb	Heavy Flak over Palermo
3 NA 35	18/04/43	Scalpone	Heavy intense Flak over Palermo
3 NA 45	24/04/43	Sugg	Heavy inaccurate Flak at 27,000' over Catania A/D
3 NA 46	24/04/43	Berry	Saw 4 Ju 52s near Camporeale
3 NA 49	24/04/43	German	Light inaccurate Flak at 18,000' over Agrigento
3 NA 54	27/04/43	Sugg	Sighted 2 twin-engine A/C over Grotte
3 NA 55	28/04/43	Webb	Heavy inaccurate Flak over Licata at 23,000'
3 NA 56	28/04/43	Luthy	Warned by radio, but was intercepted by 2 SE EA/C over Catania
3 NA 61	29/04/43	Scalpone	Light inaccurate Flak over Augusta, heavy accurate Flak over Catania. 1 SE A/C escorting M/Vs
3 NA 74	09/05/43	Berry	Light inaccurate Flak over Pachino
3 NA 75	10/05/43	Colgan	Warned by radio of EA/C over Syracuse
3 NA 76	10/05/43	Spencer	Warned by radio of EA/C
3 NA 82	12/05/43	Webb	Intercepted by 2 ME 210s near Catania at 27,000'
3 NA 83	13/05/43	Spencer	Sighted 2 E/SPs escorting convoy
3 NA 86	14/05/43	Sugg	Intercepted near Gerbini by 2 EA/C at 27,000'
3 NA 91	15/05/43	Spencer	Intercepted by ME 109 at 27,000' over Trapani/Milo A/D
3 NA 98	2105/43	Webb	Saw 2 SE EA/C at 20,000' near Comiso
3 NA 99	22/05/43	Berry	Intercepted by 2 SE EA/C at 25,000' (30° 30' N – 16° 10' E)
3 NA 118	03/06/43	Sugg	Very intense accurate heavy Flak over Augusta area
3 NA 126	06/06/43	Barfoot	Sighted 6 SE EA/C 18-20,000'

Appendix II

Photo production by NAPRW[1]

Year	Prints	Negatives
1942		
December	23,294	7,991
1943		
January	46,707	11,603
February	49,914	1,703
March	102,434	3,612
April	193,396	69,506
May	320,023	79,547
June	375,042	115,658
July	666,016	73,129
August	842,227	181,504
September	782,752	220,782
Total	3,401,805	765,035

1   From December 1942 to February 1943, the data only concerns the 3rd Photographic Group USAAF.

Outcome of missions carried out by 3rd Photographic Group[2]							
Year	Month	Positive	Negative	Tot.	Training	A/C lost[3]	
						Act.	Inc.
1942	November	11	3	14	0	3	0
1942	December	69	52	121	0	3	2
1943	January	76	46	122	0	4	2
1943	February	35	16	51	0	2	1
1943	March	38	24	62	0	2	2
1943	April	241	44	285	0	2	1
1943	May	186	40	226	46	1	1
1943	June	231	31	262	22	3	2
1943	July	358	50	408	0	4	5
1943	August	484	44	528	0	4	5
1943	September	492	80	572	0	1	3
Total		2,221	430	2,651	68	29	24

Number of Interpretation Reports from NAPRW	
1942	
November	9
1943	
December	31
January	36
February	23
March	60
April	191
May	223
June	213
July	435
August	502
September	410
Total	2,133

2   From November 1943 to February 1943 by the 3rd Photographic Group USAAF and No. 682 Squadron RAF.
3   Aircraft lost in action ('Act.') and in accidents ('Inc.').

List of the abbreviations	
A/C: aircraft	A/D: aerodrome
C/R: cruiser	D/F: direction finder
D/R or D/S: destroyer	E-boat or M.A.S.: motor anti-submarine
E/V: escort vessel	E/A: enemy aircraft
F-boat or T.L.C: tank landing craft	L/G: landing ground
M/L: motor launch	M/B: motorboat
M/T: motor transport	M/V: merchant vessel
R-boat: motor anti-submarine with special motor	S/F: Siebel Ferry
S/M: submarine	S/L: searchlight
T/B: torpedo boat	S/P: seaplane
W/T: wireless or radio	TKR: tanker

Aircraft of the 3rd Photographic Group in May 1943	
No. of aircraft originally assigned	30
No. of replacements	27
No. lost enroute to theatre	4
No. lost to E/A in aerial combat	10
No. lost on ground through strafing etc.	0
No. transferred	10 (5 temporarily)
No. lost through accidents	5
No. of aircraft on hand	27

Appendix III

Sorties successfully carried out by Malta-based aircraft over Sicily from February to 9 July 1943

Month	Day	Sortie	Unit	Target
February	28	MA707	683PR	P R NW SICILY
March	1	MA709	683PR	PA R SICILY
		MA710	683PR	PA R N SICILY
	2	MA713	683PR	PR NW SICILY
	3	MA715	683PR	P R SICILY
		MA716	683PR	P R N SICILY
		MA718	683PR	P R NE SICILY
	4	MA721	683PR	P R NE SICILY
		MA722	683PR	P R W SICILY
		MA723	683PR	P R W SICILY
	5	MA724	683PR	P R W SICILY
		MA725	683PR	P R NE SICILY
		MA726	683PR	P R NE SICILY
	10	MA736	683PR	P R & O NW SICILY
	11	MA738	683PR	P R SICILY
	15	MA753	683PR	P R NE SICILY
	16	MA755	683PR	P R W SICILY
		MA756	683PR	P R W SICILY
	17	MA760	683PR	P R NW SICILY
	18	MA762	683PR	P R NE SICILY
		MA763	683PR	P R NW SICILY
	20	MA768	683PR	P R NW SICILY
		MA770	683PR	P R NE SICILY
	21	MA771	683PR	P R NW SICILY
	22	MA777	683PR	PA R SICILY
	23	MA779	683PR	PR & M NE SICILY

		MA780	683PR	P R NW SICILY
	24	MA781	683PR	P R S SICILY
		MA782	683PR	P R W, S, E SICILY
		D/79	540PR	M SE SICILY
	25	MA783	683PR	P R N SICILY
	26	MA786	683PR	P R NW SICILY
		MA787	683PR	P R NW SICILY
	27	MA789	683PR	P R NE SICILY
		MA790	683PR	P R N SICILY
	28	MA793	683PR	P R NW SICILY
	29	MA794	683PR	P R NE SICILY
		MA795	683PR	P R NW SICILY
	30	MA797	683PR	P R NE SICILY
		MA798	683PR	D & R NW SICILY
	31	MA800	683PR	PA R NW SICILY
April	1	D/80	540PR	M SE SICILIAN COAST
		MA802	683PR	PA R NW SICILY
	2	MA811	683PR	P R NW SICILY
	3	MA808	683PR	PA R NE SICILY
		MA812	683PR	R & M, S & E SICILY
	4	3NA5	3NA, 3PG	M SE SICILY
		3NA6	3NA, 3PG	M SE SICILY
		MA813	683PR	M SW SICILY
	5	MA815	683PR	P R NW SICILY
		MA816	683PR	P R NE SICILY
		MA818	683PR	M NW SICILY
	6	MA820	683PR	P R & M W SICILY
		MA822	683PR	P R NW SICILY
		3NA8	3NA, 3PG	M NW SICILY
		3NA9	3NA, 3PG	M SW SICILY
		3NA10	3NA, 3PG	M SE SICILY
		1NA16	1NA, 3PG	PA R NW SICILY
	7	3NA11	3NA, 3PG	M NW SICILY
		1NA19	1NA, 3PG	PA R S SICILY
	9	MA832	683PR	P R S SICILY

10	1NA21	1NA, 3PG	PA R SW SICILY
	MA833	683PR	PA R W SICILY
	MA834	683PR	P R NE SICILY
	MA835	683PR	P R NE SICILY
11	3NA14	3NA, 3PG	M NW SICILY
	3NA15	3NA, 3PG	M SE SICILY
	3NA16	3NA, 3PG	M NW SICILY
	3NA17	3NA, 3PG	M SE SICILY
	3NA18	3NA, 3PG	PA R W SICILY, M W SICILY
	D/81	540PR	M SE SICILY
	MA837	683PR	PA R SICILY
	MA838	683PR	PA R SICILY
	MA840	683PR	M SE SICILY
	MA839	683PR	P R NE SICILY
	MA831	683PR	P R E SICILY
12	1NA29	1NA, 3PG	PA R W SICILY
	MA843	683PR	M COAST S SICILY
	MA844	683PR	PA R SICILY
	MA845	683PR	PA R N NW W SICILY
13	1NA31	1NA, 3PG	PA R W SICILY
	MA847	683PR	PA R SICILY
14	MA852	683PR	PA R SICILY
	MA853	683PR	P R NE SICILY
	MA856	683PR	PR E SICILY
15	3NA22	3NA, 3PG	PA R SE SICILY, M SE SICILY
	3NA23	3NA, 3PG	M NW SICILY
	MA858	683PR	PA R SICILY
	MA859	683PR	PA R W & C SICILY
16	1NA34	1NA, 3PG	PA R W & N SICILY
	MA862	683PR	PA R SICILY
	MA865	683PR	PA R SICILY
	MA868	683PR	P R NE SICILY
	3NA25	3NA, 3PG	PA R SE SICILY, M SE SICILY
	3NA26	3NA, 3PG	PA R & M NW SICILY
	3NA27	3NA, 3PG	P R & M SE SICILY

	3NA28	3NA, 3PG	D R M SE SICILY
17	3NA31	3NA, 3PG	M NW SICILY
	3NA32	3NA, 3PG	M SE SICILY
	3NA33	3NA, 3PG	R & M SE SICILY
	3NA34	3NA, 3PG	M NW SICILY
	MA861	683PR	P R NE SICILY
	MA870	683PR	PA R & M SE SICILY
	MA872	683PR	PA R & M W SICILY
18	3NA35	3NA, 3PG	R NW SICILY
	3NA37	3NA, 3PG	M NW SICILY
	1NA38	1NA, 3PG	PA R W SICILY
	MA876	683PR	P R CE SICILY
	MA877	683PR	P R NW SICILY
19	MA879	683PR	PA R SICILY
	MA880	683PR	O PA R NW SICILY
20	3NA38	3NA, 3PG	M NE SICILY
	3NA39	3NA, 3PG	M C SICILY
	MA883	683PR	P R E SICILY
	MA886	683PR	P R W SICILY
	MA887	683PR	P R SICILY
21	3NA40	3NA, 3PG	M C SICILY
	3NA41	3NA, 3PG	M C SICILY
	3NA42	3NA, 3PG	M NE SICILY
	3NA43	3NA, 3PG	M C SICILY
	MA888	683PR	PA R SICILY
	MA890	683PR	PA R S SICILY
	MA891	683PR	PA R SICILY
22	3NA44	3NA, 3PG	M SE SICILY
	MA892	683PR	PA R NW SICILY
	MA894	683PR	PA R E SICILY
23	MA896	683PR	P R & O W SICILY
	MA898	683PR	P R E SICILY
	MA899	683PR	PA R & M SICILY
24	MA902	683PR	PA R SICILY
	3NA45	3NA, 3PG	R E SICILY

		3NA46	3NA, 3PG	R & M C SICILY
		3NA47	3NA, 3PG	M NC SICILY
		3NA48	3NA, 3PG	M NC SICILY
		1 NA45	3NA, 3PG	R E SICILY
		3NA46	3NA, 3PG	R & M C SICILY
		3NA47	3NA, 3PG	M NC SICILY
		3NA48	3NA, 3PG	M NC SICILY
		1NA45	1NA, 3PG	PA R W & N SICILY
	25	3NA49	3NA, 3PG	R & M C SICILY
		MA906	683PR	P R E SICILY
		MA905	683PR	P R W SICILY
	26	3NA50	3NA, 3PG	M C SICILY
		3NA51	3NA, 3PG	M NE SICILY
		3NA52	3NA, 3PG	R & M C SICILY
		MA907	683PR	PA R SICILY
		MA909	683PR	PA R SICILY
		MA911	683PR	PA R SICILY
	27	MA913	683PR	PA R E SICILY
		1NA56	1NA, 3PG	PA R N W S SICILY
		3NA53	3NA, 3PG	M NC SICILY
		3NA54	3NA, 3PG	M NC SICILY
	28	1NA62	1NA, 3PG	PA R W SICILY
		MA919	683PR	PA R NW SICILY
		3NA55	3NA, 3PG	M C SICILY
		3NA56	3NA, 3PG	M NE SICILY
		3NA57	3NA, 3PG	M SC SICILY
	29	MA924	683PR	P R SE SICILY
		1NA62	1NA, 3PG	PA R W SICILY
		3NA61	3NA, 3PG	R E SICILY
	30	MA925	683PR	PR SE SICILY
		MA926	683PR	PA R W SICILY
		MA928	683PR	P R SE SICILY
May	1	MA951	683PR	O (9000) H NW SICILY
		MA929	683PR	PA R M & NE SICILY
		MA930	683PR	PR & O NE SICILY

	MA931	683PR	M SE SICILY
2	MA934	683PR	PR NE SICILY
3	3NA64	3NA, 3PG	M BEACH S SICILY
	3NA65	3NA, 3PG	M NE SICILY
	MA935	683PR	PR NW SICILY
	MA936	683PR	PA R SICILY
	MA937	683PR	PR SICILY
	MA938	683PR	PR NE SICILY
5	MA942	683PR	PA R SICILY
	3NA68	3NA, 3PG	R E SICILY
	3NA69	3NA, 3PG	M BEACH NW SICILY
	3NA70	3NA, 3PG	R & M SE SICILY
	3NA71	3NΛ, 3PG	R & M S SICILY
	MA953	683PR	PA R SICILY
6	MA954	683PR	PA R SICILY
	MA944	683PR	PA R SICILY
7	MA949	683PR	PR NE SICILY
8	3NA73	3NA, 3PG	R SE SICILY
	MA950	683PR	PR NE SICILY
	M1B	683PR	PR W SICILY
	M3B	683PR	PR NE SICILY
9	M7B	683PR	PR SICILY
	MA956	683PR	PA R W SICILY
10	1NA81	1NA, 3PG	PA R NW SICILY
	3NA75	3NA, 3PG	R SE SICILY
	3NA76	3NA, 3PG	R & M C SICILY
11	1NA82	1NA, 3PG	PR W SICILY
	3NA77	3NA, 3PG	R & M C SICILY
	3NA79	3NA, 3PG	M NC SICILY
	M17B	683PR	PR E SICILY, M SE SICILY
	MA958	683PR	PA R SICILY
12	MA959	683PR	PA R SICILY
13	3NA84	3NA, 3PG	M SC SICILY
	M29B	683PR	PA E SICILY
	MA960	683PR	PA R SICILY

14	MA961	683PR	PA R SICILY
	3NA86	3NA, 3PG	M N SICILY
	3NA87	3NA, 3PG	R NW SICILY
	M35B	683PR	M SE SICILY
	M38B	683PR	M SE SICILY
	M39B	683PR	M SE SICILY
15	MA962	683PR	PA R W SICILY
	M43B	683PR	M SE SICILY
16	M51B	683PR	PR NE SICILY
	MA963	683PR	PA R W SICILY
17	MA964	683PR	PA R W SICILY
	M55B	683PR	PR NE SICILY
18	M57B	683PR	PR E SICILY
	M59B	683PR	PR & HIGH O, NE SICILY
	MA965	683PR	PA R W SICILY
19	1NA93	1NA, 3PG	PA R W SICILY
	MA966	683PR	PA R W SICILY
	M61B	683PR	M SE SICILY
	M65B	683PR	PA R SICILY
	3NA92	3NA, 3PG	R W SICILY
20	3NA94	3NA, 3PG	M SE SICILY
	M69B	683PR	M SE SICILY
	M70B	683PR	PA R S & W SICILY
	M71B	683PR	PA R NE SICILY
	M72B	683PR	PR E SICILY
	MA967	683PR	PA R W SICILY
21	MA968	683PR	PA R W SICILY
	3NA95	3NA, 3PG	M SE SICILY
	3NA96	3NA, 3PG	M SE SICILY
	3NA97	3NA, 3PG	M W SICILY
	3NA98	3NA, 3PG	M SE SICILY
	M74B	683PR	M SE SICILY
	M76B	683PR	M E & SE SICILY
	M77B	683PR	PA R SE SICILY
22	M79B	683PR	M SE SICILY

	M82B	683PR	PA R SICILY
	3NA100	3NA, 3PG	M W SICILY
	3NA101	3NA, 3PG	M SE SICILY
23	3NA103	3NA, 3PG	M SE SICILY
	3NA104	3NA, 3PG	M SE SICILY
	M85B	683PR	PA R SICILY
	M87B	683PR	M SE SICILY
	M89B	683PR	PR NE SICILY
	M90B	683PR	PR NW SICILY
24	M96B	683PR	M SE SICILY
	M98B	683PR	M S & SW SICILY
	MA970	683PR	PA R W SICILY
	3NA105	3NA, 3PG	M E SICILY
	3NA106	3NA, 3PG	R & M C SICILY
25	3NA108	3NA, 3PG	M C & E SICILY
	M105B	683PR	M SE SW SICILY
	M110B	683PR	M SE SW SICILY
	MA971	683PR	PA R W SICILY
26	MA972	683PR	PA R W SICILY
27	M116B	683PR	AR & M SE SICILY
	M120B	683PR	D S SICILY
	MA973	683PR	PA R W SICILY
28	MA974	683PR	PA R & M W SICILY
	M124B	683PR	M SW SICILY
	M126B	683PR	D SE SICILY
	M128B	683PR	PR NE SICILY
29	M129B	683PR	PA R E SICILY
	M130B	69PR	O (2000) SC SICILY
	M131B	683PR	M SC SICILY
	M136B	683PR	PR SICILY
	3NA111	3NA, 3PG	R NE SICILY
	3NA112	3NA, 3PG	R NE SICILY
30	M138	683PR	PR NE SICILY
	M139B	683PR	PA R S SICILY
	M140B	683PR	PR S SICILY

		M141B	683PR	PR NE SICILY
		MA976	683PR	PA R S & W SICILY
	31	MA977	683PR	PA R S & W SICILY
		3NA114	3NA, 3PG	R E SICILY
		3NA115	3NA, 3PG	R W SICILY
		M143B	683PR	PR NE SICILY
		M145	683PR	M SC SICILY
June	1	MA978	683PR	PA R W SICILY
		M150B	683PR	M S SICILY
	2	M155B	683PR	PR NW SICILY
		M156B	683PR	PR SW SICILY
		M158B	683PR	PR NE SICILY
	3	M160B	683PR	PR NE SICILY, M SE SICILY
		M162B	683PR	M EC SICILY
		M165B	683PR	PR NE SICILY
		3NA118	3NA, 3PG	M E SICILY
		MA979	683PR	PA R W & S SICILY
	4	MA980	683PR	PA R W SICILY
		MA68B	683PR	PA R SICILY, M SE SICILY
		M171B	683PR	M SE SICILY
		M172B	683PR	PR NE SICILY
	5	M173B	683PR	M SE SICILY
		M174B	683PR	PR SE SICILY
		3NA122	3NA, 3PG	M C SICILY
		M176B	683PR	PR NE SICILY
		MA981	683PR	PA R W SICILY
	6	MA982	683PR	PA R W SICILY
		M177B	683PR	M SE SICILY
		M178B	683PR	M SE SICILY
		M180B	683PR	M SE SICILY
		M181B	683PR	PR NE SICILY
	7	M184B	683PR	M SE SICILY
		M187B	683PR	M SE SICILY
		MA983	683PR	PR & PA, W SICILY
		M183B	683PR	PA R W SICILY

	3NA127	3NA, 3PG	M C SICILY
	3NA130	3NA, 3PG	R E SICILY
8	3NA131	3NA, 3PG	M & R SE SICILY
	3NA133	3NA, 3PG	M SC SICILY
	M189B	683PR	PA R W SICILY
9	M192B	683PR	M SE SICILY
	MA985	683PR	PA R W SICILY
	3NA135	3NA, 3PG	R PA, E SICILY
	3NA138	3NA, 3PG	M SE SICILY
10	3NA140	3NA, 3PG	M ROADS SE SICILY
	M195B	683PR	PA R E SICILY
	M197B	683PR	PR NW SICILY
	M198B	683PR	PA R SICILY
11	M203B	683PR	PA R SICILY
	MA986	683PR	PA R W SICILY
13	12SA1	12PS	M C SICILY
	12SA2	12PS	M ROADS SE SICILY
	12SA3	12PS	M ROADS SC SICILY
	M212B	683PR	PA R S SICILY, M SE SICILY
14	M213B	683PR	PR & M NE SICILY
	12SA5	12PS	M SE SICILY
	12SA6	12PS	M SE SICILY
	12SA7	12PS	M SE SICILY
15	12SA10	12PS	M SE SICILY
	M216B	683PR	PA R E SICILY
	M219B	683PR	M SE SICILY
16	M222B	683PR	M S SICILY
	M225B	683PR	PA R W SICILY
	12SA15	12PS	M SE SICILY
17	12SA16	12PS	M SE SICILY
	12SA17	12PS	M SE SICILY
	M229B	683PR	M SE SICILY
	M233B	683PR	A R & M C SICILY
18	MA992	683PR	PA R W SICILY
	15S29	15PS	PA R E SICILY

	12SA18	12PS	M SE SICILY
	12SA19	12PS	R SICILY ADS
19	12SA20	12PS	M SE SICILY
	12SA21	12PS	M SC SICILY
	MA993	683PR	PA R W SICILY
20	MA994	683PR	PA R W SICILY
	M241B	683PR	PA R SICILY
	M242B	683PR	M E SICILY
	M244B	683PR	M SE SICILY
	M245B	683PR	A R, E SICILY
	M247B	683PR	PR NE SICILY
21	M251B	683PR	M SE SICILY
	M253B	683PR	PR E SICILY
	15S33	15PS	PA R E & W SICILY
	MA995	683PR	PA R W SICILY
22	MA 996	683PR	PA R W SICILY
	M254B	683PR	M SE SICILY
	M255B	683PR	M SEC SICILY
	M259B	683PR	M SE SICILY
23	M281B	683PR	PA R W SICILY
	M282B	683PR	PR E SICILY
24	M286B	683PR	PR EC SICILY
	M287B	683PR	D SE SICILY
	MA997	683PR	PA R W SICILY
25	M288B	683PR	M SE, SC SICILY
	M289B	683PR	M SC SICILY
	M291B	683PR	PR E SICILY
	M293B	683PR	D SE SICILY
	M294B	683PR	AR E SICILY & M E SICILY
	15S39	15PS	P R MESSINA
	MA998	683PR	PA R W SICILY
26	MA999	683PR	PA R W SICILY
	M298B	683PR	M SE SICILY, P A R SE SW SICILY
	M300B	683PR	PA R S SICILY

	27	M297B	683PR	PR E SICILY
		15S43	15PS	PA R W & N SICILY
		M260B	683PR	PA R W SICILY
	28	M261B	683PR	PA R W & S SICILY
		M262B	683PR	PA R W SICILY
		M309B	683PR	M S & E SICILY
		M311B	683PR	M SC EC SICILY
	29	M313B	683PR	M SE SICILY
		M314B	683PR	M SE SICILY
		M315B	683PR	M C SICILY
		M316B	683PR	M C SICILY
	30	M318B	683PR	M SE SICILY
		M319B	683PR	M C SICILY
		M263B	683PR	PA R W SICILY
		15S48	15PS	PA R W SICILY
July	1	M322B	683PR	PA R SICILY, M SE SICILY
		M323B	683PR	PR E SICILY, M SE SICILY
		M324B	683PR	M SE SICILY
	2	M326B	683PR	M SE SICILY
		M327B	683PR	M SE SICILY
		M328B	683PR	M SE SICILY, PA R E SICILY
		M330B	683PR	M SE SICILY
	3	M331B	683PR	M SE SICILY
		M333B	683PR	PR EC SICILY
		M334B	683PR	M C SICILY
		M335B	683PR	M SE SICILY
		M336B	683PR	PR EC SICILY, M EC SICILY
		NA335	682PR	R SICILY
		NA336	682PR	R SICILY
		15S51	15PS	PA R E SICILY
	5	15S54	15PS	PA R E & S SICILY
		M343B	683PR	M EC SICILY
	6	M348B	683PR	PA R W SICILY, M SE SICILY
		M349B	683PR	PA R SICILY
		M350B	683PR	PA R SICILY & M SE SICILY

	M351B	683PR	M SE SICILY
7	M354B	683PR	M SE SICILY, PA R SICILY
	NA358	682PR	R S SICILY AP
8	NA360	682PR	R SICILY A
	NA365	682PR	R E SICILY & M ROADS
	M356B	683PR	M SE SICILY
	12S16	12PS	M SC SICILY
9	12S17	12PS	M SC SICILY
	12S18	12PS	M SC SICILY
	NA371	682PR	R A&P, E SICILY

Sorties successfully carried out over Sicily from all bases from 10 July to 17 August 1943			
Month	**Day**	**Sortie**	**Unit**	**Target**
July	10	NA376	682PR	A R NE SICILY
		NA378	682PR	P A R E SICILY
		12S19	12PS	R M SW SICILY
		12S20	12PS	R M S SICILY
		12S21	12PS	R M S SICILY
		12S22	12PS	R M S SICILY
		12S23	12PS	R M S SICILY
		12S24	12PS	A R SE SICILY
		12S25	12PS	R M S SICILY
		M270B	683PR	P A R SE SICILY
		M371B	683PR	P A R SE SICILY
		M368B	683PR	A R SE SICILY
		M374B	683PR	P A R E SICILY
	11	NA382	682PR	P A R NW SICILY
		5S46	5PS	P A R C SICILY
		12S26	12PS	R M SC SICILY
		12S27	12PS	R M C SICILY
		12S28	12PS	R M SC SICILY
		12S29	12PS	R M SC SICILY
		15S62	15PS	A R W SICILY
		M271B	683PR	P R M SE SICILY
		M376B	683PR	P A R E&S SICILY
		M377B	683PR	P A R N&E SICILY
		M378B	683PR	P A R S SICILY

	M380B	683PR	P NW SICILY
12	NA390	682PR	A R E SICILY
	NA392	682PR	P R N SICILY
	NA395	682PR	A R E SICILY
	12S30	12PS	R M C SICILY
	12S31	12PS	R M S SICILY
	12S32	12PS	R M S SICILY
	12S33	12PS	R M SE SICILY
	15S63	15PS	P A R N&E SICILY
	15S64	15PS	P A R S&E SICILY
	M272B	683PR	A R SE SICILY
	M384B	683PR	R E SICILY
	M385B	683PR	P R E SICILY
	M387B	683PR	P A R S&E SICILY
	M388B	683PR	P R S&E SICILY
13	NA399	682PR	A R EC SICILY
	NA400	682PR	A R W SICILY
	5S52	5PS	A R EC SICILY
	12S34	12PS	A R S&C SICILY
	12S35	12PS	A R S&C SICILY
	12S36	12PS	R S&C SICILY
	12S37	12PS	R S&C SICILY
	15SB11(N)	15PS	QR EC SICILY
	M273B	683PR	P A R W&S SICILY
	M391B	683PR	R E&S SICILY
	M392B	683PR	R P NE SICILY
14	NA403	682PR	P A R E&S SICILY
	NA404	682PR	P A R W SICILY
	12S38	12PS	R S SICILY
	12S39	12PS	R S SICILY
	12S40	12PS	R S SICILY
	12S41	12PS	R S SICILY
	15SB15(N)	15PS	QR C SICILY
	M274B	683PR	P A R S&C SICILY
	M396B	683PR	R N SICILY
	M398B	683PR	R S&C SICILY
	M400B	683PR	R C SICILY
15	NA406	682PR	P A R SE SICILY

	NA407	682PR	P R NE SICILY
	12S43	12PS	R C SICILY
	12S44	12PS	R S SICILY
	12S45	12PS	R S SICILY
	12S46	12PS	R W SICILY
	12S47	12PS	R M C SICILY
	15SB18(N)	15PS	QR C SICILY
	15SB21(N)	15PS	QR C SICILY
	M275B	683PR	P A R S&E SICILY
	M402B	683PR	R S&E SICILY
	M404B	683PR	P A R NE SICILY
	M405B	683PR	R S&E SICILY
16	NA412	682PR	P R NE SICILY
	12S48	12PS	R NC SICILY
	12S49	12PS	R M C SICILY
	12S50	12PS	R M C SICILY
	12S51	12PS	M SC SICILY
	15SB26(N)	15PS	QR C SICILY
	M276B	683PR	P A R W SICILY
	M409B	683PR	P A R E SICILY
	M410B	683PR	P R S&E SICILY
17	NA415	682PR	A R SE SICILY
	NA416	682PR	R NE SICILY
	12S52	12PS	R M S SICILY
	12S53	12PS	R C SICILY
	12S54	12PS	M C SICILY
	12S56	12PS	R M S SICILY
	15SB29(N)	15PS	QR EC SICILY
	M277B	683PR	P R W SICILY
	M416B	683PR	M SE&SC SICILY
18	12S57	12PS	R W SICILY
	12S58	12PS	R S SICILY
	15SB33	15PS	P R NE SICILY
	M278B	683PR	P A R W SICILY
	M421B	683PR	P R E SICILY
	M424B	683PR	P R E&SE SICILY
	M426B	683PR	P R E&SE SICILY
19	12S59	12PS	R Rd NW SICILY

	12S60	12PS	M SC SICILY
	12S61	12PS	R Rd SC SICILY
	12S62	12PS	R Rd NC SICILY
	M279B	683PR	P A R N SICILY
	M428B	683PR	PA R E SICILY
	M429B	683PR	R E&SE SICILY
	M430B	683PR	P R NE SICILY
	M431B	683PR	A N SICILY
	M432B	683PR	P R E&SE SICILY
20	12S63	12PS	P R NW SICILY
	12S64	12PS	R Rd SW SICILY
	12S65	12PS	R Rd C SICILY
	12S66	12PS	R Rd NC SICILY
	12S67	12PS	R Rd C SICILY
	M280B	683PR	P A R NE SICILY
	M436B	683PR	P NE SICILY
	M437B	683PR	P R E&SE SICILY
	M440B	683PR	P R E&SE SICILY
	M442B	683PR	P E SICILY
21	12S68	12PS	R Rd NW SICILY
	12S69	12PS	R Rd NW SICILY
	12S70	12PS	R Rd W SICILY
	M443B	683PR	P R E&SE SICILY
	M445B	683PR	P R E&SE SICILY
	M450B	683PR	P A R NW SICILY
22	5S83	5PS	P A R NE SICILY
	12S71	12PS	R N SICILY
	12S72	12PS	R NE SICILY
	12S73	12PS	R Rd NE SICILY
	12S74	12PS	R Rd NE SICILY
	15SB49	15PS	QR EC SICILY
	M448B	683PR	P E SICILY
	M449B	683PR	P R NE SICILY
23	12S75	12PS	R NE SICILY
	12S76	12PS	R NE SICILY
	12S77	12PS	R NE SICILY
	M475B	683PR	P R NE SICILY
	M478B	683PR	P R NE SICILY

	M480B	683PR	P R N SICILY
24	NA446	683PR	P A R NE SICILY
	5S91	5PS	P A R NE SICILY
	12S78	12PS	R Rd NE SICILY
	12S79	12PS	R Rd NE SICILY
	M481B	683PR	P A R NE SICILY
25	12S80	12PS	QR NE SICILY
	12S81	12PS	R Rd NE SICILY
	12S82	12PS	R Rd NE SICILY
	12S83	12PS	R Rd NE SICILY
	12S84	12PS	R Rd NE SICILY
	15SB63(N)	15PS	QR NE SICILY
	M486B	683PR	P R E SICILY
26	NA453	682PR	PR NE SICILY
	5S103	5PS	P R NE SICILY
	12S85	12PS	R Rd NE SICILY
	12S86	12PS	R Rd NE SICILY
	12S87	12PS	R Rd NE SICILY
	15SB65	15PS	P R NE SICILY
	M495B	683PR	P R NE SICILY
27	12S88	12PS	R Rd EC SICILY
	12S89	12PS	R Rd EC SICILY
	12S90	12PS	R Rd NC SICILY
	12S91	12PS	R Rd NC SICILY
	12S92	12PS	R Rd NE SICILY
	15SB68	15PS	P R NE SICILY
	M502B	683PR	P R NE SICILY
28	5S107	5PS	P R NE SICILY
	12S93	12PS	R Rd NE SICILY
	12S94	12PS	R Rd NE SICILY
29	12S95	12PS	R Rd NC SICILY
	12S96	12PS	R Rd NC SICILY
	M510B	683PR	P R NE SICILY
30	NA466	682PR	P R NE SICILY
	12S97	12PS	R Rd NE SICILY
	12S98	12PS	P R NE SICILY
	12S99	12PS	R Rd NE SICILY
	12S100	12PS	R Rd NE SICILY

	31	NA471	682PR	P R NE SICILY
		12S101	12PS	M NE SICILY
		12S102	12PS	R Rd NE SICILY
		12S103	12PS	R Rd NE SICILY
		12S104	12PS	R Rd NE SICILY
		M520B	683PR	P R NE SICILY
August	1	NA476	682PR	P R NE SICILY
		NA479	682PR	P R NE SICILY
		12S105	12PS	R Rd NC SICILY
		12S106	12PS	R Rd NC SICILY
		12S107	12PS	R Rd NC SICILY
		12S109	12PS	R Rd NC SICILY
		M529B	683PR	P R NE SICILY
	2	NA485	682PR	P R NE SICILY
		12S111	12PS	R Rd NE SICILY
		M530B	683PR	P R NE SICILY
	3	NA494	682PR	P R NE SICILY
		12S112	12PS	R Rd NE SICILY
		12S113	12PS	R Rd NE SICILY
		12S114	12PS	R Rd M NE SICILY
		12S115	12PS	R Rd NE SICILY
		M533B	683PR	P R NE SICILY
	4	NA496	682PR	P R NE SICILY
		12S116	12PS	R NE SICILY
		12S117	12PS	R NE SICILY
		12S118	12PS	R Rd NE SICILY
		12S119	12PS	R Rd NE SICILY
		15SB98(N)	15PS	QR NE SICILY
		M536B	683PR	P R NE SICILY
	5	12S120	12PS	D NE SICILY
		15SB101(N)	15PS	QR NE SICILY
	6	NA506	682PR	P R NE SICILY
		NA508	682PR	P R NE SICILY
		12S121	12PS	R Rd NE SICILY
		12S122	12PS	R Rd NE SICILY
		12S123	12PS	R Rd NE SICILY
		12SL1	12PS	R SC SICILY
	7	NA510	682PR	R P NE SICILY

	12S125	12PS	M NE SICILY
	12S126	12PS	R Rd NE SICILY
	12S127	12PS	R Rd NE SICILY
	M547B	683PR	P R NE SICILY
	M550B	683PR	P R NE SICILY
8	5S155	5PS	P R NE SICILY
	12S128	12PS	R Rd NE SICILY
	M554B	683PR	P R NE SICILY
9	NA521	682PR	P R NE SICILY
	12S130	12PS	R Rd NE SICILY
	12S131	12PS	R NE SICILY
	12S132	12PS	P A R NE SICILY
	M558B	683PR	P R NE SICILY
10	NA526	682PR	P R NE SICILY
	NA529	682PR	P R NE SICILY
	12S133	12PS	R NE SICILY
	12S134	12PS	R NE SICILY
	12S135	12PS	R NE SICILY
	12S136	12PS	R Rd NE SICILY
	12S137	12PS	A R NE SICILY
	M559B	683PR	P R NE SICILY
11	NA533	682PR	P R NE SICILY
	12S138	12PS	P R NE SICILY
	12S139	12PS	R Rd NE SICILY
	12S140	12PS	R Rd NE SICILY
	12S141	12PS	R Rd NE SICILY
	M566B	683PR	P R NE SICILY
12	12S142	12PS	P R NE SICILY
	12S143	12PS	R NE SICILY
	12S144	12PS	R Rd NE SICILY
	12S145	12PS	R Rd NE SICILY
	15SB120	15PS	P R NE SICILY
	M567B	683PR	P R NE SICILY
	M570B	683PR	P R NE SICILY
13	NA542	682PR	P R NE SICILY
	NA545	682PR	P R NE SICILY
	12S146	12PS	R Rd NE SICILY
	12S147	12PS	R Rd NE SICILY

	12S148	12PS	R NE SICILY
	12S149	12PS	R Rd NE SICILY
	M571B	683PR	A R NE SICILY
14	12S150	12PS	R Rd NE SICILY
	12S151	12PS	R Rd NE SICILY
	12S152	12PS	R NE SICILY
	12S153	12PS	R NE SICILY
	12S154	12PS	R NE SICILY
	15SB128	15PS	P R NE SICILY
15	NA554	682PR	P R NE SICILY
	NA555	682PR	P R NE SICILY
	12S155	12PS	R Rd NE SICILY
	M579B	683PR	P R NE SICILY
16	5S190	5PS	P R NE SICILY
	12S156	12PS	R Rd NE SICILY
	12S161	12PS	P R NE SICILY
17	NA568	682PR	P R NE SICILY

Abbreviations	
A: Airdromes and Landing Ground	**5PS:** 5th Photographic Squadron
C: Central	**12PS:** 12th Photographic Squadron
D: Dicing	**15PS:** 15th Photographic Squadron
E: East	**3PG:** 3rd Photographic Group (Recco & Mapping)
M: Mapping	**23PS:** 23rd Photographic Squadron
N: North	**33PG:** 2/33 Reconnaissance Group (French)
O: High altitude oblique	**60PR:** 60 PR Squadron RAF
P: Ports and harbors	**682PR:** 682 PR Squadron RAF
QR: Night and Reconnaissance	**683PR:** 683 PR Squadron RAF
R: General Reconnaissance	**540PR:** 540 PR Squadron RAF
Rd: Roads	**69PR:** 69 PR Squadron RAF
S: South	**1NA:** 5th Photographic Squadron
W: West	**2NA:** 12th Photographic Squadron
	3NA: 15th Photographic Squadron

Appendix IV

NAPRW: Results of operations between January–August 1943

Mese	Unit	Successful	Unsuccessful	Total
January	3rd Photo Group	40	25	65
	682 RAF	5	2	7
February	3rd Photo Group	4	3	9
	682 RAF	6	6	12
March	3rd Photo Group	0	3	3
	682 RAF	21	11	32
	Unit No.1	8	2	10
	Unit No.2	9	8	17
April	3rd Photo Group	24	3	27
	682 RAF	74	11	85
	Unit No.1	43	8	51
	Unit No.2	53	9	62
	Unit No.3	47	13	60
May	3rd Photo Group	39	12	51
	682 RAF	38	8	46
	Unit No.1	47	5	52
	Unit No.2	18	6	24
	Unit No.3	44	9	53
	Unit No.4	32	14	56 (training)
June	3rd Photo Group	7	2	
	682 RAF	60	11	
	Unit No.4	18	4	22 (training)
	5th Photo Squadron	22	5	27
	12th Photo Squadron	57	7	64
	15th Photo Squadron	84	4	88
	60 SAAF	1	2	3

July	682 RAF	130	15	145
	5th Photo Squadron	76	13	89
	12th Photo Squadron	65	11	76
	15th Photo Squadron	82	8	90
	60 SAAF	5	3	8
August	682 RAF	139	9	148
	5th Photo Squadron	101	8	109
	12th Photo Squadron	74	7	81
	15th Photo Squadron	99	8	107
	23rd Photo Squadron	53	8	61
	33rd Photo Squadron	10	0	10
	60 SAAF	8	4	12

Report issued by NACIU (Northwest African Central Interpretation Unit) on Sicily			
Section		13 May– 10 July 1943	11 July– 18 August 1943
A	Shipping Report	0	1
B	Flak Reports	0	1
B	NAPRW Detachment Seventh Army	0	29
C	Aerodromes	8	4
D	Damage Assessment	8	1
D.S.	Damage Assessment	0	2
F	Strike Attack	46	21
G	Comunications	1	0
K	Radar	14	0
Z	2nd Phase	11	51
Z	No. 1 Unit	12	2
Total		100	112

Table of photographic scales to be used in planning photo-reconnaissance			
Object	Breakdown	Minimum scale for photographic interpretation	Minimum scale for identification
Navy	Units greater than 200 feet	1/10,000	1/20,000
	Units less than 200 feet	1/5,000	1/15,000
Naval installations	Ports and landings	1/10,000	1/60,000
	Bases submarines, seaplane	1/10,000	1/20,000
	Shipyards	1/10,000	1/30,000
Aerodrome	Identification of airports	1/10,000	1/60,000
	Early stages of construction	1/10,000	1/30,000
Aircraft	Large aircraft	1/10,000	1/20,000
	Small aircraft (less than 50 feet)	1/5,000	1/15,000
Electtronics	Radar	1/5,000	1/10,000
	Communication	1/5,000	1/15,000
	Direction Finding (DF)	1/5,000 low oblique	1/15,000
Cannon	Coastal defenses	1/5,000	1/20,000
	Anti-aircraft heavy	1/5,000	1/20,000
	Anti-aircraft light (MG and auto AA)	1/5,000 low oblique	1/10,000
Minor defence	Pillbox	1/5,000	1/10,000
	Obstacles on the beach and immersed	1/2,000 low oblique	1/10,000
	Barbed wire	1/5,000 low oblique	1/10,000
	Trenches	1/10,000 low oblique	1/15,000
	Stronghold	1/5,000 low oblique	1/10,000

N.A.P.R.W.

Col. Roosevelt	Photo Wing

W/C. Fuller
Deputy

Lt. Col. Eddridge
Chief of Staff

Capt. Goodhart	Capt. Monroe	Lt. Col. Dunn	S/Ldr. Walton
A-1	A-2	A-3	A-4

Major
Briedy
60 SAAF

Lt. Col.
Dunn
3 PG
USAAF

S/Ldr.
Tilling
NACIU

23
Squadron
Photo
Recco

S/Ldr
Ball
682 RAF

W/C
Warburton
683 RAF

A-1   A-2   A-3   A-4

5 Squadron
La Marsa
F-5A

12
Squadron
La Marsa
F-5A

15 Photo
Recon
Le Khroub
F-5A

Field Units

A/C

Lab.

A/D Int. 1st Phase

Naval Int. 1st Phase

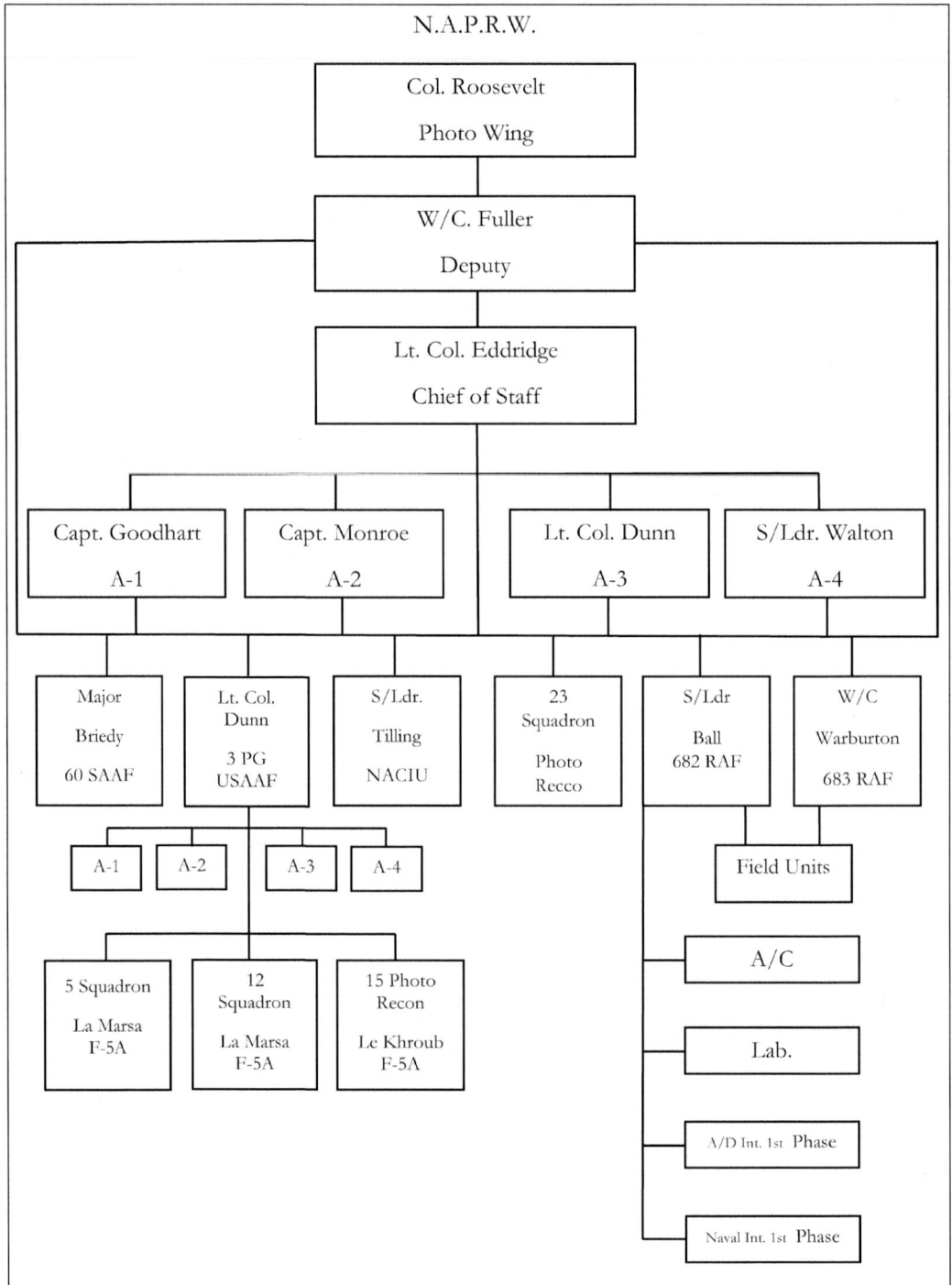

Northwest African Photographic Reconnaissance Wing in July 1943.

Appendix V

Missing in Action Correspondence

No. 683 Squadron,
R.A.F. Station,
Luqa – MALTA

17th March 1943.

Dear Mrs. Peacock,

Presumably by now, you will have been notified through official channels, of the fact that your son Clayton was reported missing on an operational flight over enemy territory on March the 9th.

I had hoped that this letter might convey news of a more pleasant nature. However, such is not the case. I might add though, that there is very probability that Clayton is a prisoner of war, but, unfortunately, some time will elapse before this news will reach you.

He joined our Unit on the 9th February, and was considered one of the finest pilots and was exceedingly popular amongst his associates.

The work he was doing was of a highly secretive nature which took him hundreds of miles inland over enemy territory and required a high degree of skill and proficiency on his part to successfully complete his mission.

May I also add here that service itself feels the loss of such a fine pilot, very keenly.

Let me repeat, that I feel quite sure that you will hear through the usual sources, that he is quite safe and well and if there is anything I can do, please do not hesitate to write to me.

Yours very sincerely,

(SGD.) M.G. Brown F/Lt

Appendix VI

Lieutenant General G.S. Patton Correspondence

HEADQUARTERS SEVENTH ARMY
Office of the Commanding General
APO 758

23 July 1943

SUBJECT: Commendation
TO: Commanding Officer, N.A.P.R.W.

1. It is desire to commend the efforts of the 12th Photographic Squadron for its high degree of efficiency, cooperation, and its ability to meet urgent demands with a keen sense of professional appreciation.

2. As an outstanding instance, an urgent request for photographic coverage was made on this unit at 2023300B July of all roads leading to PALERMO from the south and southwest, within a radius of 25 miles. It was of utmost importance that prints be delivered to the Provisional Corps by 211300B July, upon which that headquarters could base tactical decision for the employment of the 2d Armored Division.

3. The pilot was briefed during the night, and took off at 210900B July, which was the time arrival of the first aircraft in SICILY from the base in AFRICA. He took off forthwith, completing the mission at 1015B. The film was transported overland about six miles, and at 1215B the sortie was completed, printed, and awaiting air courier. The prints left at 1230B, and at 1245B, the courier arrived at his destination. The total time elapsed from take-off to delivery offprints in the hands of the tactical unit to be served was three hours and forty-five minutes.

4. This remarkable service is an absolute indication of the necessity for coordination and speed, all of which was accomplished in an exemplary manner by the unit, and every member of the detachment is entitled to due credit for this achievement.

5. Inasmuch as the direction movement of the 2d Armored Division was, to a considerable degree, dependent upon these photographs, it may well be considered that the flying of this photographic mission contributed materially to the fall of PALERMO, which occurred at 1900, 22 July.

s/G.S. Patton, Jr.

G.S. PATTON, JR.
Lieutenant General, U.S. Army
Commanding

Appendix VII

Comparative Rank Table

Regia Aeronautica	Luftwaffe	RAF	Fleet Air Arm	USAAF
Aviere	Flieger	Aircraftman	-	Air Basic
Aviere Scelto	Gefreiter	Corporal	-	Airman 3rd Class
1° Aviere	Hauptgefreiter	Leading Aircraftman	-	Airman 2nd Class
Sergente	Untederoffizier	Sergeant	Petty Officer	Sergeant
Sergente maggiore	Underfeldwell	Flight Sergeant	Chef Petty Officer	Staff Sergeant
Maresciallo 3ª Classe	Feldwebel	Warrant Officer	Warrant Officer	Technical Sergeant
Maresciallo 2ª Classe	Oberfeldwebel	Idem	Idem	Master Sergeant
Maresciallo 1ª Classe	Stabsfeldwebel	Idem	Idem	Senior Master Sergeant
Aiutante di battaglia	-	-	-	Chief Master Sergeant
S.Tenente	Leutenant	Pilot Officer	Midshipman	2nd Lieutenant
Tenente	Oberleutenant	Flying Officer	Sub Lieutenant	1st Lieutenant
Capitano	Hauptmann	Flight Lieutenant	Lieutenant	Captain
Maggiore	Major	Squadron Leader	Lieutenant Commander	Major
Tenente Colonnello	Oberstleutenant	Wing Commander	Commander	Lieutenant Colonel
Colonnello	Oberst	Group Captain	Captain	Colonel
Generale di Brigata	Geralmajor	Air Commodore	Commodore	Brigadier General
Generale di Divisione	Generalleutnant	Air ViceMarshal		Major General
Generale di Squadra Aerea	General der Flieger	Air Marshal		Lieutenant General
Capo di Stato Maggiore	Generaloberst	Air Chief Marshal	General	
Maresciallo dell'Aria	Generalfeldmarschall Reichmarschall	Marshal of the RAF		

Bibliography

Archival Sources
Air Force Historical Research Agency Maxwell (AFHRA)
AFHRA, Irisref 00895725, The Sicilian Campaign June – August 1943.
AFHRA, Irisref A0916, 111 Tactical Reconnaissance Squadron.
AFHRA, Irisref A0917, 111 Tactical Reconnaissance Squadron.
AFHRA, Irisref A5263, British Air Ministry.
AFHRA, Irisref A5363, Great Britain Naval Staff Intelligence Division.
AFHRA, Irisref A6011, Northwest African Tactical Air Force.
AFHRA, Irisref A6012, Northwest African Strategic Air Force.
AFHRA, Irisref A6013, Northwest African Strategic Air Force.
AFHRA, Irisref A6191, XII Air Force.
AFHRA, Irisref B0746, 3rd Photographic Reconnaissance Group.
AFHRA, Irisref B0747, 3rd Photographic Reconnaissance Group.
AFHRA, Irisref C0042, 90 Photographic Reconnaissance Wing.
AFHRA, Irisref C0192, Northwest African Photo Reconnaissance Wing.
AFHRA, Irisref MAAF 12, Operational plans, Mediterranean Allied Tactical Air Forces.
AFHRA, Irisref MAAF 209, Mediterranean Allied Photographic Reconnaissance Wing.
AFHRA, Irisref MAAF 257, Mediterranean Allied Air Forces.
AFHRA, Irisref MAAF 63, Mediterranean Allied Air Forces.

National Archives and Records Administration, College Park, Maryland (NARA)
Allied Airborne Operations in Sicily.
Capture German documents, Sicily.
Weekly intelligence summary.
Microfiche Publication M1035, FMS # D-089, 'Reconnaissance in the Battle of Sicily', by Max Ulich, 29 May 1947.
Microfiche Publication M1035, FMS # D-095, '29th Panzer Grenadier Division (30 July 1943)', by Max Ulich, 21 May 1947.

Service Historique de l'Armée de l'Air Paris (SHAA)
E 33 239 – E 33 258, Italie, iles et colonies (Sicile, Sardaigne, Dodécanèse, Lybie).
E 33 239 – E 33 247, Dossiers d'objectifs d'origine française. Dossiers produits avant ou au début de la seconde guerre mondiale par le Ministère de l'Air.
E 33 239 – E 33 241 Terrains d'aviation, hydrobases et hydrescales.
E 33 239 – E 33 240/1 Italie continentale.

Library and Archives Canada (LAC)
Reference: RG24, R112, 1984-265 NPC
Photographs Government Accession Canada. Dept. of National Defence collection [graphic material]. Sicily - Aerial photographs World War, 1939-1945 - Sicily - Reconnaissance operations

Aircrew Logbooks
Sergeant Frank Bastard, 431 General Reconnaissance Flight RAF, 69 Squadron RAF
Flying Officer Laurie Philpotts, 69 Squadron RAF, 683 Squadron RAF.

The National Archives (TNA), Kew
TNA, AIR 27/14: Operations Record Book of No. 1 Squadron SAAF.
TNA, AIR 27/41: Operations Record Book of No. 3 Squadron RAAF.
TNA, AIR 27/43: Operations Record Book of No. 3 Squadron RAAF.
TNA, AIR 27/179: Operations Record Book of No. 12 Squadron SAAF.
TNA, AIR 27/244: Operations Record Book of No. 18 Squadron RAF.
TNA, AIR 27/276: Operations Record Book of No. 21 Squadron SAAF.
TNA, AIR 27/275: Operations Record Book of No. 21 Squadron SAAF.
TNA, AIR 27/269: Operations Record Book of No. 21 Squadron SAAF.
TNA, AIR 27/299: Operations Record Book of No. 21 Squadron SAAF.
TNA, AIR 54/71: Operations Record Book of No. 21 Squadron SAAF.
TNA, AIR 27/278: Operations Record Book of No. 22 Squadron RAF.
TNA, AIR 27/287: Operations Record Book of No. 23 Squadron RAF.
TNA, AIR 27/304: Operations Record Book of No. 24 Squadron SAAF.
TNA, AIR 27/390: Operations Record Book of No. 37 Squadron RAF.
TNA, AIR 27/391: Operations Record Book of No. 37 Squadron RAF.
TNA, AIR 27/396: Operations Record Book of No. 37 Squadron RAF.
TNA, AIR 27/388: Operations Record Book of No. 37 Squadron RAF.
TNA, AIR 27/412: Operations Record Book of No. 40 Squadron RAF.
TNA, AIR 27/415: Operations Record Book of No. 40 Squadron RAF.
TNA, AIR 54/82: Operations Record Book of No. 40 Squadron SAAF.
TNA, AIR 54/83: Operations Record Book of No. 40 Squadron SAAF.
TNA, AIR 54/84: Operations Record Book of No. 40 Squadron SAAF.
TNA, AIR 27/444: Operations Record Book of No. 43 Squadron RAF.
TNA, AIR 27/518: Operations Record Book of No. 55 Squadron RAF.
TNA, AIR 54/90: Operations Record Book of No. 60 Squadron SAAF.
TNA, AIR 54/91: Operations Record Book of No. 60 Squadron SAAF.
TNA, AIR 54/92: Operations Record Book of No. 60 Squadron SAAF.
TNA, AIR 27/606: Operations Record Book of No. 69 Squadron RAF.
TNA, AIR 27/607: Operations Record Book of No. 69 Squadron RAF.
TNA, AIR 27/608: Operations Record Book of No. 69 Squadron RAF.
TNA, AIR 27/609: Operations Record Book of No. 69 Squadron RAF.
TNA, AIR 27/610: Operations Record Book of No. 69 Squadron RAF.
TNA, AIR 27/611: Operations Record Book of No. 69 Squadron RAF.
TNA, AIR 27/612: Operations Record Book of No. 69 Squadron RAF.

TNA, AIR 27/616: Operations Record Book of No. 70 Squadron RAF.
TNA, AIR 27/625: Operations Record Book of No. 72 Squadron RAF.
TNA, AIR 27/678: Operations Record Book of No. 81 Squadron RAF.
TNA, AIR 27/745: Operations Record Book of No. 92 Squadron RAF.
TNA, AIR 27/751: Operations Record Book of No. 93 Squadron RAF.
TNA, AIR 27/821: Operations Record Book of No. 104 Squadron RAF.
TNA, AIR 27/824: Operations Record Book of No. 104 Squadron RAF.
TNA, AIR 27/869: Operations Record Book of No. 111 Squadron RAF.
TNA, AIR 27/873: Operations Record Book of No. 112 Squadron RAF.
TNA, AIR 27/882: Operations Record Book of No. 114 Squadron RAF.
TNA, AIR 27/974: Operations Record Book of No. 142 Squadron RAF.
TNA, AIR 27/977: Operations Record Book of No. 142 Squadron RAF.
TNA, AIR 27/986: Operations Record Book of No. 145 Squadron RCAF.
TNA, AIR 27/1011: Operations Record Book of No. 150 Squadron RAF.
TNA, AIR 27/1016: Operations Record Book of No. 150 Squadron RAF.
TNA, AIR 27/1025: Operations Record Book of No. 152 Squadron RAF.
TNA, AIR 27/1034: Operations Record Book of No. 154 Squadron RAF.
TNA, AIR 27/1180: Operations Record Book of No. 202 Squadron RAF.
TNA, AIR 27/1181: Operations Record Book of No. 202 Squadron RAF.
TNA, AIR 27/1186: Operations Record Book of No. 202 Squadron RAF.
TNA, AIR 27/1187: Operations Record Book of No. 202 Squadron RAF.
TNA, AIR 27/1188: Operations Record Book of No. 202 Squadron RAF.
TNA, AIR 27/1189: Operations Record Book of No. 202 Squadron RAF.
TNA, AIR 27/21375: Operations Record Book of No. 223 Squadron RAF.
TNA, AIR 27/1396: Operations Record Book of No. 225 Squadron RAF.
TNA, AIR 27/1400: Operations Record Book of No. 225 Squadron RAF.
TNA, AIR 27/1401: Operations Record Book of No. 225 Squadron RAF.
TNA, AIR 27/1413: Operations Record Book of No. 228 Squadron RAF.
TNA, AIR 27/1417: Operations Record Book of No. 228 Squadron RAF.
TNA, AIR 27/1428: Operations Record Book of No. 232 Squadron RAF.
TNA, AIR 27/1472: Operations Record Book of No. 242 Squadron RAF.
TNA, AIR 27/1474: Operations Record Book of No. 243 Squadron RAF.
TNA, AIR 27/1501: Operations Record Book of No. 250 Squadron RAF.
TNA, AIR 27/1504: Operations Record Book of No. 250 Squadron RAF.
TNA, AIR 27/1505: Operations Record Book of No. 250 Squadron RAF.
TNA, AIR 27/1323: Operations Record Book of No. 256 Squadron RAF.
TNA, AIR 27/1325: Operations Record Book of No. 256 Squadron RAF.
TNA, AIR 27/1537: Operations Record Book of No. 260 Squadron RAF.
TNA, AIR 27/1818: Operations Record Book of No. 417 Squadron RCAF.
TNA, AIR 27/1825: Operations Record Book of No. 420 Squadron RCAF.
TNA, AIR 27/1834: Operations Record Book of No. 424 Squadron RCAF.
TNA, AIR 27/1837: Operations Record Book of No. 425 Squadron RCAF.
TNA, AIR 27/1885: Operations Record Book of No. 450 Squadron RAAF
TNA, AIR 27/1916: Operations Record Book of No. 462 Squadron RAF.
TNA, AIR 27/ 2007: Operations Record Book of No. 540 Squadron RAF.

TNA, AIR 27/2013: Operations Record Book of No. 541 Squadron RAF.
TNA, AIR 27/2017: Operations Record Book of No. 542 Squadron RAF.
TNA, AIR 27/2025: Operations Record Book of No. 543 Squadron RAF.
TNA, AIR 27/2028: Operations Record Book of No. 544 Squadron RAF.
TNA, AIR 27/2071: Operations Record Book of No. 601 Squadron RAF.
TNA, AIR 27/2167: Operations Record Book of No. 651 Squadron RAF.
TNA, AIR 27/2169: Operations Record Book of No. 651 Squadron RAF.
TNA, AIR 27/2172: Operations Record Book of No. 654 Squadron RAF.
TNA, AIR 27/2197: Operations Record Book of No. 680 Squadron RAF.
TNA, AIR 27/2203: Operations Record Book of No. 682 Squadron RAF.
TNA, AIR 27/2206: Operations Record Book of No. 682 Squadron RAF.
TNA, AIR 27/2207: Operations Record Book of No. 682 Squadron RAF.
TNA, AIR 27/2208: Operations Record Book of No. 682 Squadron RAF.
TNA, AIR 27/2209: Operations Record Book of No. 683 Squadron RAF.
TNA, AIR 40/1996: Sicily: reports on airfields and aircraft.

Published Sources

A.A.F. Historical Archives, Headquarters, Army Air Forces, *Ninth Air Force in the Western Desert Campaign to 23 January 1943*, Air Staff Intelligence Historical Division, AFHRA.

A.A.F. Historical Office, Headquarters, Army Air Forces, *A short history of the XII Tactical Air Command*, AFHRA.

A.A.F. Historical Office, Headquarters, Army Air Forces, *Air phase of Italian Campaign to 1 January 1944*, AFHRA roll K-1014.

A.A.F. Historical Office, Headquarters, Army Air Forces, *History of the XII Air Force*, AFHRA.

A.A.F. Historical Office, Headquarters, Army Air Forces, *History of the Fifteenth Air Force*, AFHRA.

A.A.F. Historical Office, Headquarters, Army Air Forces, *The Twelfth Air Force in the Sicilian Campaign*, narrative.

A.A.F. Historical Office, Headquarters, Army Air Forces, *Mediterranean Allied Photo Reconnaissance Wing: a pictorial history 1943*, AFHRA.

A.A.F. Historical Office, Headquarters, Army Air Forces, *Photo Recon for MATAF and 15th Army Group 1938-1944*, (Washington D.C.: 3rd Photo Group, 1945)

AA. VV., *The Royal Navy and the Mediterranean: Vol. II: November 1940-December 1941* (London: Routledge, 2001)

Air Historical Branch (AHB) Narrative, *Photographic Reconnaissance Vol I, 1914-April 1941*.

AHB Narrative, *Photographic Reconnaissance Vol II, May 1941 - August 1945*.

AHB Narrative, *The Middle East Campaigns*, Volume I, Appendix XXI.

AHB Narrative, *The North African Campaign, November 1942 - May 1943*.

AHB Narrative, *The Rise and Fall of the German Air Force 1933-1945*.

AHB Narrative, *The Sicilian Campaign June - August 1943*.

Air Ministry, *The air battle of Malta: The Official Account of the R.A.F. in Malta, June 1940 to November 1942*, London, 1944.

Anfora, Domenico, *La cresta a coltello. 10-15 luglio 1943: Vizzini nella bufera* (Tricase (LE): Youcanprint, 2016)

Anfora, Domenico, and Pepi, Stefano, *Obiettivo Biscari. 9-14 luglio 1943: dal ponte Dirillo all'aeroporto 504* (Milano: Ugo Mursia Editore, 2013)
Apostolo, Giorgio, *Aer. Macchi C.202* (Torino: La Bancarella Aeronautica, 1996)

Babington-Smith, Constance, *Air Spy: The story of photo intelligence in World War II* (New York: Harper & Brothers Publishers, 1957)
Babington-Smith, Constance, *Evidence in Camera: The Story of Photographic Intelligence in World War II* (Newton Abbot: David & Charles, 1974)
Bellomo, Alessandro, *1943 Il martirio di un'isola* (Genova: Associazione Culturale Italia, 2011)
Bellomo, Alessandro, *Bombe su Palermo: Cronaca degli attacchi aerei 1940-1943* (Zanica (BG): Soldiershop, 2016)
Berrett, Jim, 'Malta's Marylands', *FlyPast*, January 2003.
Bertke, Donald A., *World War II Sea War, Vol. 4: Germany Sends Russia to the Allies* (Dayton: Bertke Publications, 2012)
Blake, Steve, and Stanaway, John, *Adorimini ("up and at 'em!"): A history of the 82nd Fighter Group in World War II* (USA: 82nd Fighter Group History, Inc, 1992)
Bowman, Martin, *Mosquito Photo-Reconnaissance Units of World War 2* (Oxford: Osprey Publishing, 1999)
Boyle, Robert, *History of Photo Reconnaissance in North Africa Including My Experiences with the 3rd PRG*, Ph.D. diss. (University of Texas, 1948)
Brookes, Andrew J., *Photo Reconnaissance* (Worthing: Littlehampton Book Services Ltd, 1975)
Buckley, Christopher, *Road to Rome* (London: Hodder and Stoughton, 1945)

Caruana, Richard J., *Victory in the air* (Malta: Modelaid International Publications, 1996)
Clendenin, Ed, *376th Bomb Group Mission History Third Edition* (Lulu.com, 2010)
Clough, A. B., *Maps and survey, The Second World War, 1939-1945, Army,* (London: The War Office 1952)
Civoli, Massimo, *S.A.S. I Servizi Aerei Speciali della Regia Aeronautica 1940-1943* (Roma: IBN, 2014)
Coldbeck, Harry, *The Maltese Spitfire: One Pilot, One Plane – Find Enemy Forces on Land and Sea* (Shrewsbury: Airlife Publishing Ltd, 1997)
Conigliaro, Calogero, *I corsari del terzo Reich e i segreti di Husky. Sicilia 1940-1943* (Gorizia: Libreria Editrice Goriziana, 2017)
Craven, Wesley Frank, and Cate, James Lea, *The Army Air Force in World War II vol. II* (Chicago: University of Chicago Press, 1965)
Cull, Brian, and Galea, Frederick, *Hurricanes Over Malta June 1940-April 1942* (London: Grub Street Publishing, 2001)
Cull, Brian, with Malizia, Nicola, and Galea, Frederick, *Spitfires over Sicily* (London: Grub Street, 2000)

D'Este, Carlo, *1943. Lo sbarco in Sicilia* (Milano: Mondadori, 1990)
Delve, Ken, *Malta Strikes Back: The Role of Malta in the Mediterranean Theatre, 1940-1942* (Barnsley: Pen & Sword, 2017)
Delve, Ken, *Short Sunderland* (Ramsbury: The Crowood Press, 2000)
Delve, Ken, *The Source Book of the RAF* (Shrewsbury: Airlife Publishing Ltd, 1994)

Delve, Ken, *The Story of the Spitfire: An Operational and Combat History* (Barnsley: Greenhill Books, 2007)

Dengler, David W., Maj, *Seeing the enemy: army air force aerial reconnaissance support to U.S. Army operations in the Mediterranean in World War II*, USAF M.A. (Lincoln, Nebraska: University of Nebraska, 1998)

Doyle, David, *Standard catalog of German military vehicles* (New York: Skyhorse Pub Co Inc., 2005)

Duma, Antonio, *Quelli del Cavallino Rampante - Storia del 4° Stormo Caccia* (Roma: Aeronautica Militare, 2007)

Durbidge, Keith, *Memoirs of a High Flyer* (England: Lulu.com, 2013)

Fagone, Salvo, *Ricognitori su Husky. Il ruolo cruciale della ricognizione aerea e dell'intelligence Ultra sulla Sicilia e sul Mediterraneo. 1940-1943* (Italy: Youcanprint, 2020)

Fagone, Salvo, *Road to Rome: Shots and memories of a Rhodesian in the RAF* (Zanica (BG): Soldiershop, 2021)

Fagone, Salvo, *USAAF bombs on Italy* (Zanica (BG): Soldiershop, 2021)

Fitzgerald-Black, Alexander, *Eagles over Husky: The Allied Air Forces in the Sicilian Campaign, 14 May to 17 August 1943* (Solihull: Helion & Company, 2018)

Forty, George, *Tiger Tank Battalions in World War II* (Minneapolis, USA: Zenith Press, 2008)

Francaviglia, Fabrizio, *La breccia nella «Festung Europa». Sicilia 1943* (Parma: Albertelli Editore, 2009)

Francione, Giancarlo, *Aquile sugli Iblei. Storia dell'aeroporto di Comiso dalle origini al 10 luglio 1943* (Ragusa: Tipografia C.D.P., 2008)

Franks, Norman, *Beyond Courage: Air Sea Rescue by Walrus Squadrons in the Adriatic, Mediterranean and Tyrrhenian Seas 1942–1945* (London: Grub Street Publishing, 2003)

Freeman, Roger A., and Osborne, David, *The B-17 Flying Fortress Story* (London: Arms & Armour Press, 1998)

Gillies, Peter S., Major, *Sicily. Analysis of a combined operations battle* (Maxwell, USA: Air Command and Staff College Air University, 1984)

Goss, Chris, *Heinkel He 111: The Early Years - Fall of France, Battle of Britain and the Blitz* (Barnsley: Frontline Books, 2016)

Granfield, Alun, *Bombers over Sand and Snow: 205 Group RAF in World War II* (Barnsley: Pen & Sword, 2012)

Grilletta, Giulio, *KR 40-43. Cronache di guerra* (Crotone: Pellegrini, 2003)

Hammel, Eric, *Air War Europa: America's Air War Against Germany in Europe and North Africa 1942-1945: Chronology* (California: Pacifica Press, 1994)

Hamilton, Nigel, *Monty: Master of the Battlefield, 1942-1944* (Milano: McGraw-Hill, 1984)

Headquarters, Royal Air Force, Middle East, *R.A.F. Mediterranean review no. 1.*

Headquarters, Royal Air Force, Middle East, *R.A.F. Mediterranean review no. 2.*

Headquarters, Royal Air Force, Middle East, *R.A.F. Mediterranean review no. 3.*

Headquarters, Royal Air Force, Middle East, *R.A.F. Mediterranean review no. 4.*

Holland, James, *Sicily '43: The first assault on fortress Europe* (London: Bantam Press, 2020)

Ivie, Tom, *Patton's Eyes in the Sky: USAAF Combat Reconnaissance Missions North-West Europe 1944-1945* (Hersham: Ian Allan Publishing, 2003)

Jessen, Morten, and Arthy, Andrew, *Focke-Wulf Fw 190 in the Battle for Sicily* (Denmark: Air War Publications, 2010)

Kennedy, Irving, *Black Crosses Off My Wingtip* (Ontario: The General Store Publishing House, 1995)

Lamb, Charles, *War in a Stringbag* (London: Cassell, 1977)
Leaf, Edward, *Above All Unseen: The Royal Air Force's Photographic Reconnaissance Units 1939-1945* (Sparkford: Patrick Stephens Limited, 1997)
Luppi, Luigi, *L'arciere alato dal 1° stormo C.T. alla 1° B.A.O.S. Storia della prima unità da caccia dell'aeronautica militare italiana* (Roma: IBN, 2012)

Malizia, Nicola, *Inferno su Malta: La più lunga battaglia aeronavale nel Mediterraneo. 1940-1943* (Milano: Ugo Mursia Editore, 2015)
Malizia, Nicola, *La regia aeronautica nella Seconda guerra mondiale. Diari di guerra 1940-1942* (Roma: IBN, 2013)
Malizia, Nicola, *Uniformi degli aviatori italiani.* (Roma: IBN, 2015)
Marcon, Tullio, *Augusta 1940-1943 Cronache della piazzaforte* (Augusta (SR): Mendola, 1976)
Martines, Vincenzo, *Le navi ospedale della Marina Militare Italiana* (Roma: Stato Maggiore Marina, 1995)
Mattesini, Francesco, *L'attività aerea italo tedesca nel Mediterraneo. Il contributo del X Fliegerkorps. Gennaio-Maggio 1941* (Roma: SME Ufficio Storico, 2003)
Matusiak, Wojtek, *Classic Warbirds: Merlin Pr Spitfires*, Mushroom Model Pubns, 2007.
Millington, Air Commodore G., *The Unseen Eye* (London: Anthony Gibbs & Phillips, 1961)
Molony, C.J.C., *The Mediterranean and Middle East Volume V: The Campaign in Sicily 1943 and the campaign in Italy 3rd September 1943 to 31st March 1944* (London: HMSO, 1973)
Morgan, Eric B., *Fly High - Fly Low: Biography of Supermarine Test Pilot Les Colquhoun* (Bognor Regis: Woodfield Publishing, 2004)
Morgan Eric B., Shacklady Edward, *Spitfire: The History* (Stamford: Key Publishing Ltd., 1987)

Nesbit, Roy C., *The Armed Rovers, Beauforts and Beaufighters over Mediterranean* (Shrewsbury: Airlife Publishing Ltd, 1995)
Nesbit, Roy Conyers, *Eyes of the RAF: A History of Photo-Reconnaissance* (Godalming: Bramley Books, 1997)
Nicolosi, Salvatore, *La guerra a Catania* (Catania: Tringali editore, 1984)
Notarangelo Rolando, and Pagano, Gian Paolo, *Navi Mercantili Perdute* (Roma: Ufficio Storico della Marina Militare, 2000)

Pedriali, Ferdinando, *L'Italia nella guerra aerea - Da El Alamein alle spiagge della Sicilia* (Roma: Aeronautica Militare, Ufficio storico, 2010)
Pedriali, Ferdinando, *L'Italia nella guerra aerea – Dalla difesa della Sicilia all'8 settembre* (Roma, Aeronautica Militare, Ufficio storico, 2014)

Pesce, Giuseppe, *Giuseppe Cenni - pilota in guerra* (Roma: Aeronautica Militare, 2002)

Pesce, Giuseppe, *Guerra attraverso l'etere. Il radar durante il secondo conflitto mondiale* (Modena: Mucchi, 1978)

Philpotts, Laurie E., *Memoirs of World War II: The True Story of a Canadian Fighter Pilot* (Lulu. com, 2013)

Plumari, Angelo, *Operazione Husky. La Guerra nell'entroterra ennese* (Regalbuto (EN): Euno Edizioni, 2019)

Poolman, Kenneth, *Night Strike from Malta* (London: Jane's Publishing Company, 1980)

Prien, Jochen, *Jagdgeschwader 53: A History of the "Pik As" Geschwader, May 1942-January 1944* (Atglen, Pennsylvania: Schiffer Publishing Ltd, 2004)

RAF, *Middle East review No.1*, Headquarters Royal Air Force Middle East.

RAF, *Middle East review No.2*, Headquarters Royal Air Force Middle East.

RAF, *Middle East review No.3*, Headquarters Royal Air Force Middle East.

RAF, *Middle East review No.4*, Headquarters Royal Air Force Middle East.

Ragatzu, Alessandro, *Luftwaffe in Sardegna* (Cagliari: Alisea Edizioni, 2010)

Raines, F. Edgar, *Eyes of Artillery: The Origins of Modern U.S. Army Aviation in World War II* (Washington, D.C.: Center of Military History United States Army, 2000)

Richardson, Robert, *The Jagged Edge of Duty: A Fighter Pilot's World War II* (Mechanicsburg, Pennsylvania: Stackpole Books, 2017)

Roba, Jean-Louis, *Foreign Planes in the Service of the Luftwaffe* (Barnsley: Pen and Sword Aviation, 2010)

Santoni Alberto, *Il vero traditore. Il ruolo documentato di Ultra nella guerra del Mediterraneo* (Milano: Ugo Mursia Editore, 2005)

Santoni, Alberto, and Mattesini, Francesco, *La partecipazione tedesca alla guerra aeronavale nel Mediterraneo (1940-1945)* (Parma: Albertelli edizioni speciali, 2005)

Santoni, Alberto, *Le operazioni in Sicilia e in Calabria luglio – settembre 1943* (Roma: Stato Maggiore dell'Esercito, Ufficio Storico, 1989)

Schilirò, Gaetano, *La Guerra aerea in Sicilia e nel Mediterraneo occidentale 1940-1943* (Roma: Euravia Edizioni, 2012)

Schultz, Alfred W., *Janey: A Little Plane in a Big War* (Middletown: Southfarm Press, 1998)

Scott, Stuart R., *Battle-Axe Blenheims: No.105 Squadron RAF at War, 1940-41* (Gloucestershire: Alan Sutton Publishing Ltd, 1996)

Scutts, Jerry, *Bf 109 Aces of North Africa and the Mediterranean* (Oxford: Osprey Publishing, 1994)

Shores, Christopher, with Cull, Brian, and Malizia, Nicola, *Malta: The Spitfire Year 1942* (London: Grub Street Publishing, 1991)

Shores, Christopher, and Massimello, Giovanni, *A History of the Mediterranean Air War, 1940-1945 Volume 1: North Africa, June 1940-January 1942* (London: Grub Street Publishing, 2011)

Shores, Christopher, and Massimello, Giovanni, *A History of the Mediterranean Air War, 1940-1945 Volume 2: North African Desert, February 1942 - March 1943* (London: Grub Street Publishing, 2014)

Shores, Christopher, and Massimello, Giovanni, *A History of the Mediterranean Air War, 1940-1945 Volume 3: Tunisia and the end in Africa, November 1942-May 1943* (London: Grub Street Publishing, 2016)

Shores, Christopher, and Massimello, Giovanni, *A History of the Mediterranean Air War, 1940-1945 Volume 4: Sicily and Italy to the fall of Rome 14 May, 1943-5 June, 1944* (London: Grub Street Publishing, 2018)

Smith, Duncan, *Spitfire into Battle* (London: John Murray Ltd, 2004)

Spooner, Tony, *Warburton's War: The Life of Maverick Ace Adrian Warburton* (Manchester: Crécy Publishing, 2003)

Stanley, Roy M., *To Fool a Glass Eye: Camouflage Versus Photo-reconnaissance in World War II* (Shrewsbury: Airlife Publishing Ltd, 1998)

Stanley, Roy M., *World War II Photo Intelligence* (London: Sidgwick & Jackson, 1982)

Steinhoff, Johannes, *Messerschmitts over Sicily: Diary of a Luftwaffe Fighter Commander* (Mechanicsburg, Pennsylvania: Stackpole Books, 2004)

Stowers, Richard William, *Wellingtons over the Med: A Kiwi bomber pilot's story from the Mediterranean* (Richard Stowers, 2012)

Tedder, The Lord, *With Prejudice* (Boston: Little, Brown and Company, 1966)

Valdonio, Giuseppe Cesare, *Frecce e Saette, Folgori e Veltri – Storia critica dei caccia italiani della Seconda Guerra Mondiale* (Roma: Edizioni Rivista Aeronautica – Difesa Servizi SpA, 2019)

Weal, John, *Junkers Ju 88 Kampfgeschwader in North Africa and the Mediterranean* (Oxford: Osprey Publishing, 2009)

Wilson, Jane, *On Wing and Water: The life of Leslie R. Colquhoun, war hero, test pilot and hovercraft pioneer* (Cirencester, UK: Mereo Books, 2014)

Winterbotham, Frederick William, *Ultra Secret. La macchina che decifrava i messaggi segreti dell'Asse* (Milano: Ugo Mursia Editore, 1994)